P9-DBH-886

DVOŘÁK IN AMERICA

Antonín Dvořák. Painting by John C. Tibbetts.

DVOŘÁK IN AMERICA

1892–1895

edited by

John C. Tibbetts

AMADEUS PRESS
Reinhard G. Pauly, General Editor
Portland, Oregon

We are indebted to Rudolf and Tatiana Firkušný for providing the heirloom Czech embroideries that inspired the decorative motifs in this book.

Drawings © John C. Tibbetts

ISBN 0-931340-56-X
Designed and composed by Carol Odlum
Printed in Singapore

AMADEUS PRESS
9999 S.W. Wilshire, Suite 124
Portland, Oregon 97225

Library of Congress Cataloging-in-Publication Data

Dvořák in America. 1892-1895 / edited by John C. Tibbetts.
　　p.　　cm.
　　Includes bibliographical references and index.
　　ISBN 0-931340-56-X
　　1. Dvořák, Antonín, 1841–1904—Journeys—United States. 2. United States—Description and travel—1865-1900.　3. Composers—Czechoslovakia—Biography. I. Tibbetts, John C.
ML410.D99D9　1993
780'.92—dc20
[B]　　　　　　　　　　　　　　　　　　　　　　　　　92-19768
　　　　　　　　　　　　　　　　　　　　　　　　　　　　CIP
　　　　　　　　　　　　　　　　　　　　　　　　　　　　MN

THIS BOOK IS RESPECTFULLY DEDICATED

TO THE MEMORY OF

JOHN CLAPHAM

1908–1992

WHOSE LIFELONG DEVOTION

TO

ANTONÍN DVOŘÁK

HAS BEEN AN INSPIRATION AND EXAMPLE

FOR

FRIENDS OF CZECH MUSIC EVERYWHERE

*I*t matters little whether the inspiration for the coming folk songs of America is derived from the Negro melodies, the songs of the creoles, the red man's chant, or the plaintive ditties of the homesick German or Norwegian. Undoubtedly the germs for the best in music lie hidden among all the races that are commingled in this great country. The music of the people is like a rare and lovely flower growing amidst encroaching weeds. Thousands pass it, while others trample it underfoot, and thus the chances are that it will perish before it is seen by the one discriminating spirit who will prize it above all else."

—Antonín Dvořák

Contents

Preface

Rudolf Firkušný

Shortly before the beginning of World War II, I was in France, and among my engagements at the time was a concert in Ostende, Belgium. The originally programmed concerto was one of the usual classics, but in the last moment I was asked by the conductor Eduard van Beinum to perform Dvořák's Piano Concerto. I was happy to do it, but there was a problem: the orchestra material was in Prague. With the help of a Czech diplomat I was able to get it in time and we played it.

In Ostende I met the famous Czech soprano Jarmila Novotná with her family who strongly advised me not to return home. The war broke out several days later, and after the collapse of France it was necessary to move on. In the one suitcase containing all my possessions there was, thanks to Maestro van Beinum, the Dvořák Concerto material.

In those days Dvořák's Piano Concerto was not generally known to international conductors, the exceptions being George Szell and Sir Thomas Beecham. Sir Thomas had engaged me to play it with him in London in 1939, but owing to the German occupation of Czechoslovakia that year, I was unable to leave the country and the engagement fell through. When I finally reached the United States in 1940, I met Sir Thomas in New York and to my great joy he asked me to play the Dvořák Concerto with him at the Ravinia Festival the following summer. It was this performance that not only helped launch my career in this country but also, at long last, spurred interest in Dvořák's neglected opus.

When I settled in New York, I tried to trace Dvořák's stay in America. My most valuable source of information was Mr. Josef Kovařík, a Czech born in Spillville, Iowa, and Dvořák's faithful companion throughout his years in the New World. The American period of Dvořák's life left certain marks on his work, as he was keenly interested in Native American folklore and African American spirituals. Although his music remained always quintessentially Czech, the new material found its way into his creation, namely his *"American" Suite* in A major, the *Eight Humoresques, Biblical Songs,* the F Major Quartet, the E-flat major Quintet, and the crowning jewels among them—the "New World" Symphony and the Cello Concerto.

Dvořák's efforts to help found a national American music did not materialize, but his teaching prepared the way for later American composers. Dvořák was really the only composer of great stature active as a pedagogue in the United States. All other visiting celebrities such as Tchaikovsky, Anton Rubinstein, and later, Gustav Mahler passed through merely as visitors.

As the general orientation in American music circles of the time was predominantly towards German music, it meant that Dvořák was not as appreciated as he deserved to be. Although he remains among the most frequently performed composers in this country, he is still occasionally put into a lesser category. This is very unjust. Dvořák has his place among the truly great composers of all time, and I hope this volume will help place him where he really belongs.

—Rudolf Firkušný
New York
January 1993

PART ONE

DVOŘÁK'S NEW WORLD

AN AMERICAN SAMPLER

Antonín Dvořák. Drawing by John C. Tibbetts.

CHAPTER ONE

Introduction and Acknowledgments

John C. Tibbetts

*A*fter witnessing the Columbus Quadricentennial parades in New York City in the fall of 1892, Antonín Dvořák was inspired to write "the future American anthem," as he called it. The celebrated Bohemian composer had just arrived to take up a post as director of the newly established National Conservatory of Music of America. A few weeks later in his rooms at 327 East Seventeenth Street he dashed down a melody, scarcely more than twenty measures, dated "19 December 1892," and then, apparently forgetting about it, left it unfinished.

Or did he? Jarmil Burghauser, the eminent Dvořák authority from Prague, relates in Chapter 14 of this book that the melody subsequently reappeared in several well-known works written during the composer's three-year sojourn, including the Symphony No. 9 ("From the New World") and the E-flat String Quintet ("American"), Opus 97. Dvořák's desire to write music for and about America became an important precedent and influence on his American pupils and colleagues. Throughout the 1890s they further debated and explored just what constituted a uniquely "American" musical expression. If to this day, a hundred years later, no definitive answers have emerged, at least the debate continues. That "future American anthem," in its most general terms, remains unfinished.

Dvořák in America is not a biography of Antonín Dvořák but a portrait of a figure in a landscape. It views his New World visit through a series of interpretive lenses—the diverse perspectives of the musicologist, the cultural historian, the archivist, the educator, the musician, the psychoanalyst, the novelist, and the media reporter. A composite portrait emerges; Dvořák's notorious scowl appears and his snapping eyes glare back at us once again.

Few subjects at first seem less prepossessing. He was a stranger in a strange land. While the middle-aged composer enjoyed great prestige as an artist, he possessed neither the radical chic of Wagner nor the romantic flamboyance of Liszt. He had acquired the veneer of a cosmopolitan artist, but (as he himself always insisted) he remained at heart a simple villager. Dvořák's life was neither wracked by scandal nor terminated in ignominy, poverty, or madness. He was a good, but a reticent, man. He wrote no account of his American visit; he left behind just a few letters, interviews, and articles. Only a few eyewitness accounts of his activities survive. Moreover, the institution in New York City for which he served as director, the National Conservatory of Music of America, has long since vanished—along with most of its papers. Even the house where he lived was recently torn down. Of course, everybody remembers a few works he wrote at the time, especially the "New World" Symphony and the "American" Quartet, Opus 96, but no one can precisely define their "American" character. As for that other "classic" work from the American visit, the Cello Concerto, few associate it with America at all. Fewer still hear or perform anymore the great E-flat Quintet, Opus 97, much less the even more obscure Sonatina, Opus 100, the *Biblical Songs*, Opus 99, and the Piano Suite, Opus 98.

Yet, as this anthology demonstrates, the Dvořák visit had enormous impact on the development of American music. When we celebrate its one-hundredth anniversary in 1992–95, examining fresh historical data, reassessing the musical works, and debating the issues and controversies he engendered that continue today, we begin to understand its broader implications. Those three years marked a rare intersection of culture, personality, and history that transcended a moment and identified an age.

Many Old-World composers had come to America before Dvořák, of course. Some of them profitably exploited their celebrity status. The Russian piano virtuoso Anton Rubinstein arrived in 1872, lured by the prospect of a long tour (twenty months) and the proverbial pot of gold at the end of the rainbow. Piotr Ilyich Tchaikovsky lent his prestige to the opening festivities of Carnegie Hall in May 1891. Popular operetta composer Jacques Offenbach presented concerts of his music for two months during the American Centennial in 1876. By contrast, when Frederick Delius came to Florida for the first of his two visits in 1884, he was a complete unknown, a young man trying to "find himself." His avowed purpose was to plant oranges. He never did grow a crop, but his contacts with the spirituals of the African Americans and his fascination with the Seminoles confirmed his decision to become a professional composer. However, his America-related works, the operas *Koanga* and *The Magic Fountain*, the *Florida Suite*, and the Piano Concerto, had to wait many years to find wide audiences.

Among these composers, only Offenbach wrote an account of his experiences. *Notes d'un musicien en voyage* (1877) was a lively little book full of fascinating glimpses of life in New York and Philadelphia. Chapters were devoted to the social life of the fashionable set, the current theater season, train travel (especially in the Pullman cars), restaurant etiquette, ladies' apparel, and the Philadelphia Centennial. Although he confined himself mostly to anecdotal glimpses of American life, he did pause occasionally to ponder deeper things, such as the status of the arts. He deplored what he saw:

> [The United States] has triumphed over matter, but it has neglected all those things which charm the mind. America today is like a giant a hundred cubits tall, who has attained physical perfection, but in whom something is lacking: a soul. The soul of a people is art, the expression of thought in its most elevated aspects.[1]

Offenbach was not the first—and would not be the last—to bewail the lack of state and federal support for the arts:

> So great a people should have every greatness. It should add to its industrial power the glory which the arts alone are capable of giving a nation. . . . Since it is an announced principle in America that the State should not interfere by subventions, you must organize things yourselves. In Europe, the national government supports only some of the large theatres in the capital; it is the cities which support theatrical enterprises and museums in the small towns. . . . Imitate this example, and if the municipal councils are not willing to help you, create organizations to protect the arts, similar organizations in all the great centers. Collect funds. This will be easy for you, and let private initiative play the protective role in your country which the governments play in Europe.[2]

The establishment of schools and conservatories, he believed, would help shape a national artistic expression:

> You need especially a conservatory where you can develop excellent students if you get the right faculty; that is to say, by calling and retaining in your country artists of merit from Europe. . . . [In this way in just twenty years American culture can stand on its own feet.] Twenty years for your students to become masters, twenty years for you to become no longer mere tributaries of European art. . . .[3]

With such policies in place, he confidently predicted, America within a hundred years would "win a place among the artistic nations."[4]

Dvořák said substantially the same things during his three years in America. The difference was that he put into practice what Offenbach had only put into words. "Dvořák was really the only composer of great stature active as a pedagogue in the United States," writes pianist Rudolf Firkušný in the Preface to this book. "All other visiting celebrities such as Tchaikovsky, Anton Rubinstein, and later, Gustav Mahler passed through merely as visitors." Yet Dvořák's years at the National Conservatory have never before been properly documented and assessed. Emanuel Rubin's essay in Chapter 6 attempts to rectify this; he recounts the policies of the Conservatory (admission to students regardless of gender, race, or class), Dvořák's teaching methods, and his influence on students and colleagues. And Jean Snyder, Adrienne Fried Block, and Stuart Feder detail the careers of some of these students and colleagues—Harry T. Burleigh and Will Marion Cook (both African Americans), Rubin Goldmark, Horatio Parker—and their impact on a later generation of American composers, including Charles Ives, Duke Ellington, George Gershwin, and Aaron Copland (Chapters 9, 11, and 12).

As for Dvořák himself, it was no accident that he arrived on the eve of the Columbus Quadricentennial. He was embarking on his own "voyage of discovery"—the word is problematic, of course—traveling and absorbing what he called the "American push" of the city streets and the "sad" spaces of the great plains. In my accounts of Dvořák's life in New York and travels to Chicago, Omaha, and Spillville, Iowa (Chapters 5 and 7), I present a portrait of a man supremely sensitive to the everyday sounds of the American vernacular. Dvořák later characterized this aural tapestry as "the Negro melodies, the songs of the creoles, the red man's chant, or the plaintive ditties of the German or Norwegian . . . the melodies of whistling boys, street singers and blind organ grinders"—in short, "the music of the people."

It is clear that this kind of receptivity and sensibility to a peoples' idiomatic musical expression was Dvořák's avowed American agenda from the very beginning. Writing in the *Century Illustrated Monthly Magazine* in September 1892, critic Henry E. Krehbiel (who would become a valued friend and associate of the composer) predicted that Dvořák would bring together "popular elements and classical forms" in a new kind of music:

> The phrase that music is a cosmopolite owing allegiance to no people and no tongue is become trite. . . . [Rather,] the originality and

power in the composer rest upon the use of dialects and idioms which are national or racial in origin and structure.[5]

A few months later, in his first public declaration of his goals as the new Director of the National Conservatory, Dvořák echoed Krehbiel's statement: "I came to discover what young Americans have in them and to help them express it. . . . The new American school of music must strike its roots deeply into its own soil."

Krehbiel reminded his readers that the celebrated Bohemian composer had himself come from humble roots. Dvořák had been born the son of a butcher in Nelahozeves on 8 September 1841. With the encouragement of the village schoolmaster, he studied organ at Zlonitz and Kamnitz. Already a Czech patriot, the boy disliked having to study the German language in obedience to the law of the land. "Dvořák had inherited all the fierce hatred which the Czechs feel for the Germans," Krehbiel reported, "and even to-day necessity alone can persuade him to speak or write the German tongue."[6] Later, while studying in Prague, he kept himself alive by playing in cabaret bands and theater orchestras. He began composing in the early 1860s and a decade later wrote an opera, *King and Collier*, for the National Theater. The great Johannes Brahms used his influence to obtain some publishing contracts for Dvořák, and soon new compositions like the Slavonic Dances earned him world attention. Now a man of the world, Dvořák traveled throughout Europe and became a regular attraction at the English choral festivals. Many of his compositions, such as the Slavonic Dances and his choral works, Stabat Mater, Requiem Mass, and *The Spectre's Bride*, were being heard in New York, Boston, Chicago, and other cities. And now the Bohemian master, at the peak of his form, had come to America. He was here to establish nothing less than "the rise of a school of American composers."

Dvořák's presence and his example led to a revolution in the way we defined American culture and national identity. It was a modest revolution at first, inflected by his imperfect English and expressed in his music. But it has since grown and spread, rather like widening ripples on a pond set in motion by a small stone. Meanwhile, the issues sparked by his American visit have remained as lively, even controversial, today as they were a hundred years ago. They are the subjects of most of the articles and essays in this book—debating state support of the arts (Rubin); removing barriers to education for minority groups (Snyder); preserving, in the face of the American "melting pot," the ethnic identities of Native Americans, African Americans, and various immigrant groups (Clark, Clapham, Hamm, Block, and Beckerman:

Chapters 3, 8, 10, 11, and 15); and erasing the elitist, racist boundaries between "pop" and "classical" art (Hamm, Root, and Škvorecký: Chapters 10, 18, and 24).

The time was exactly right for some cultural house-cleaning. In the 1890s, in the last gasp of what Mark Twain called the "Gilded Age," everything seemed to be in a state of flux. America was changing from an essentially rural-agrarian federation to an industrial, urban nation-state—from an arcadian vision of paradise to an independent world power. Transcontinental rail lines and telegraph wires spanned the continent. Evolutionary science was dismantling hitherto fixed notions of religion, philosophy, and politics. America's restless population, swelled by recent waves of immigrants, was spilling into the West, the Great Plains, the Pacific slopes, subduing the remaining Indian tribes and (as a young historian named Frederick Jackson Turner pointed out at the time) closing the era of the frontier. Further expansion was halted; America henceforth would evince a different kind of growth, a compression, an *implosion* of its forces.

These developments forced a renewal of the debate on national cultural identity that had already been going on for more than fifty years. In 1837, in his essay "The American Scholar," Ralph Waldo Emerson had declared that we Americans must renounce our former dependence upon European cultural models to "walk on our own feet [and] speak our own minds." Clearly, America's ethnic and racial diversity would have to be acknowledged. According to Walt Whitman, in his late essay "November Boughs" (1885), language was the place to begin. Speech is a universal "absorber and combiner." English *as a living speech* was assimilating contributions from every ethnic group; it was becoming an amalgamation of all races, rejecting none. Slang, insisted Whitman, always renews language. Vernacular speech is the kind of process that is "not made by dictionary makers" but "by the masses, people nearest the concrete, having most to do with actual land and sea."

In the parlors of Stephen Foster's day, as Deane L. Root points out in his essay, the distinctions between American and Old-World music, popular and classical, were less rigid and important than they would later become. Operatic arias rubbed shoulders with Scots-Irish tunes and African American "plantation songs." But later in the century, notes Charles Hamm, a "sacralization of culture" took over. From certain quarters, including the New England conservatories and the hallowed pages of *Dwight's Journal of Music*,

came attacks on what John Sullivan Dwight described as the "musical bab-
ble" of eclecticism. Dwight alleged that it appealed only to "a commonplace
majority" rather than to "a higher plane of spiritual aesthetic gratification."
Hamm comments: "[This] attitude was part and parcel of the emergence of
more tightly stratified class structures in the United States." There were
political and racist agendas at work here:

> The very notion that one body of music is superior to all others and
> can be understood and "appreciated" only by a small, privileged seg-
> ment of the population is in itself elitist. . . . Less remarked was the
> fact that this cultural divide corresponded to ethnic and national
> divisions as well: most of the elite were of Anglo-Saxon descent, most
> "others" were Irish, Italian, black, German, Scandinavian, and soon
> Central European and southern Mediterranean.[6]

Dvořák observed no such biases in his own music. "It is a difficult task
at best for a foreigner to give a correct verdict of the affairs of another country," he wrote somewhat apologetically near the end of his trip. Nonetheless,
his conclusions were sound: "Undoubtedly the germs for the best in music
lie hidden among all the races that are commingled in this great country."
Dvořák himself was a foreigner in a land filled with foreigners. He didn't *discover* America so much as he *recognized* it; its divisions and contradictions
were his own. Moreover, his great lesson and example to Americans (and
how true this is today!) was that ethnic and racial diversity were not obstacles
but *opportunities* for enriched cultural growth.

Other essays in *Dvořák in America* discuss and analyze his "American" works.
John Clapham, Michael Beckerman, Alan Houtchens, and Jan Smaczny
explain Dvořák's fascination with Native American and African American
idioms in the "New World" Symphony, the F Major Quartet, and the E-flat
Major Quintet (Chapters 8 and 15–17). Charles Hamm and Dean L. Root
place Dvořák's fascination with Stephen Foster in the context of the developing tradition of the American "popular song" (Chapters 10 and 18). Jarmil
Burghauser and Nick Strimple assess the patriotic works, *The American Flag*
cantata and the recently discovered "My Country 'Tis of Thee" (Chapters 13
and 14). And Dan Jacobson and I discuss the undeservedly neglected *Biblical
Songs*, the Sonatina, and the piano works (Chapters 19–21).

Today, Dvořák continues to exert what Adrienne Fried Block calls a
"long American reach." As Hollywood gears up for a movie biography (at this
writing, actor Kevin Klein is to be featured as the composer) Dvořák has

"arrived" as a cultural icon (see my "New Soundings," Chapter 25). In his chapter, novelist Josef Škvorecký talks about his decision to use the composer as the hero of the book *Dvořák in Love* (Chapter 24). Meanwhile, Dvořák's music is finding wider audiences. David Beveridge documents the composer's renewed acceptance on the American opera stage (Chapter 23), and John Yoell provides a valuable discography of the growing number of Dvořák recordings (Appendix C). Finally, my account of the Dvořák Sesquicentennial Festival and Conference in America (New Orleans, 1991)—the first American-hosted international Dvořák event—reveals a new cross-cultural cooperation in Dvořák/Czech research (Chapter 25).

Not everything about Dvořák these days is good news. History can be fragile. The concluding essay in this book documents the poignant story of how Dvořák's house in New York City recently fell to the wrecking ball. Mark Rose and Steven Richman provide a sobering account of how the debate over its fate divided a city (Chapter 26).

This book grew out of several seemingly unrelated events. In the fall of 1990 I travelled to Spillville, Iowa on assignment from the now-defunct *Classical* magazine to retrace Dvořák's footsteps during the summer of 1893. The sight of the gentle, winding Turkey River, the music of St. Wenceslaus Church, and the gracious hospitality of the local residents suddenly brought Dvořák's music alive in a way I had not known before.

A few weeks later, while on another writing assignment, I found myself at the Stephen Foster Memorial in Pittsburgh, Pennsylvania. I was researching the materials in the archives when, unexpectedly, I saw an unpublished manuscript, Dvořák's choral arrangement of Foster's "Old Folks at Home," a work virtually unknown even to Dvořák and Foster aficionados. Later, while interviewing Ms. Jean Snyder, a musicologist working with Dr. Root on a dissertation about the eminent African American composer and performer Harry T. Burleigh, I learned Burleigh had played an important part in the genesis of Dvořák's "New World" Symphony.

Dvořák again.

Shortly thereafter I was invited to the Dvořák Sesquicentennial Festival and Conference in America, to be held in New Orleans, February 1991. There was no avoiding it anymore—

Dvořák was everywhere. He was irresistible.

I could no more have stayed away from the conference than stopped my own heartbeat. Scholars and enthusiasts from all over the world congregated in the concert halls, conference rooms, and restaurants of the Latin Quarter and the University of New Orleans. There was so much to say; and there was so much yet to learn. Before the event was two days old, I realized that a book about Dvořák in America was assuming shape in my mind.

Everything conspired to confirm my resolve. There were opportunities to interview musicians and writers. I began receiving newsletters and bulletins from Czech/Dvořák Societies in London, Prague, and St. Louis. Centennial observances of the 1892–95 period were drawing nigh. News of festivities began filtering in—proposals for a conference in New York about the "New World" Symphony, plans for a Festival in Spillville in 1993, the designation in New York of a "Dvořák Place," reissues on compact disc of the Supraphon recordings, new books about Dvořák and his associates and students, perhaps a Hollywood movie, and so on.

No, I'm not saying that this book assembled itself, although there are times when it seemed so. Without the hard work, support, enthusiasm, energy, and insight of the distinguished contributors gathered here it could not have happened.

You will meet these "good companions" in the course of your reading. They will speak in their own voices and from their own unique perspectives. If the book has a "sound" of its own, it is the sometimes motley chorus of their many accents and inflections. And yet, to paraphrase Professor Hamm, aren't we all singing the same "American song," after all?

I am grateful to all the contributors and express special thanks to the following:

Shirley Fleming of *Musical America* and Charles Passy and Lisa Marum of *Classical,* who first encouraged me to go in search of Dvořák.

The organizers of the Dvořák Sesquicentennial Conference and Festival in America (New Orleans, February 1991), particularly David Beveridge and Alan Houtchens (and his wife, Lucinda), who granted me access to the scholars and enthusiasts in attendance (many of whom contributed to this volume).

Deane L. Root, who not only shared pleasant hours with me in the Foster Memorial, but who has been a constant and invaluable source of advice and information.

Adrienne Fried Block, J. Bunker Clark, Michael Beckerman, Robert Winter, and Charles Hamm, renowned authorities on American music, who have so patiently answered my many foolish questions and unselfishly extended the fruits of their own wisdom and research.

Josef Škvorecký, who not only has been a constant correspondent and boon companion but, on occasion, has shared special enthusiasms about Kansas City jazz and detective stories.

Jack Taylor, who showed me what is left of the Dvořák neighborhood in New York and whose indefatigable efforts to preserve the heritage of the Stuyvesant district place all friends of Dvořák in his debt.

John Yoell, M.D., whose unexpected letter from Los Angeles changed the course of this book.

William Malloch, a Los Angeles radio broadcaster, whose pioneering efforts in the 1960s to locate and interview the surviving Dvořák friends and family members have benefited us all—even if they have not received the recognition and exposure they deserve.

The good citizens of Spillville, who demonstrated what real Czech-American hospitality (and cuisine) is all about—Rosalind Proshusta (Curator of the Dvořák House), Amy Balik (Coordinator of the 1993 Festival), Fritz Kala (who "talked the Czech"), Beulah Sindelar, Doris Thompson, Mr. and Mrs. Russell Loven, Mr. and Mrs. Edward Klimesh (and sons Simon and Lew), and Cyril M. Klimesh, who generously provided photographs from his Spillville archive; and special thanks to Rebecca Neuzil, who knew where Dvořák walked and who showed me the path.

Musicians Leonard Slatkin, cellist Lynn Harrell, pianist Radoslav Kvapil, and conductor Leslie Dunner, all of whom took time from busy schedules to talk about Dvořák and America.

Pianist Rudolf Firkušný, who not only wrote the Preface but, with the assistance of his wife Tatiana, furnished the Czech decorative patterns that embellish this book.

Two of the most esteemed and authoritative of Dvořák scholars: John Clapham of London, whose efforts on behalf of Dvořák scholarship have inspired us all and motivated the Dedication of this book, and Jarmil Burghauser of Prague, whose continuing research and unstinting hospitality for visiting scholars has helped form an international community of Dvořák friends.

Finally, my heartfelt thanks go to my editor, Carol Odlum, whose patience and devotion to this project cannot be overestimated.

NOTES

1. Lander MacClintock, ed. and trans., *Orpheus in America: Offenbach's Diary of His Journey to the New World* (Bloomington, IN: Indiana University Press, 1957), 69–70.

2. Lander MacClintock, ed. and trans., *Orpheus in America: Offenbach's Diary of His Journey to the New World* (Bloomington, IN: Indiana University Press, 1957), 70–71.

3. Lander MacClintock, ed. and trans., *Orpheus in America: Offenbach's Diary of His Journey to the New World* (Bloomington, IN: Indiana University Press, 1957), 72.

4. Lander MacClintock, ed. and trans., *Orpheus in America: Offenbach's Diary of His Journey to the New World* (Bloomington, IN: Indiana University Press, 1957), 73.

5. Krehbiel, Henry E., "Antonín Dvořák," *Century Illustrated Monthly Magazine*, vol. 44, no. 5 (September 1892), 657.

6. Krehbiel, Henry E., "Antonín Dvořák," *Century Illustrated Monthly Magazine*, vol. 44, no. 5 (September 1892), 658.

7. Charles Hamm, "Dvořák, Stephen Foster, and American National Song," Chapter 1 of this volume, 151.

CHAPTER TWO

A Dvořák American Chronology

1885

21 September   Mrs. Jeannette Meyer Thurber obtains a Certificate of Incorporation from the State of New York for her new National Conservatory of Music of America. The institution opens its doors a few weeks later.

1891

5 June   While at the Prague Conservatory, Dvořák is offered the Directorship of the National Conservatory of Music in America.

23 December   Dvořák signs a two-year contract with the National Conservatory.

1892

24 January   Dvořák's Requiem Mass is performed in New York City.

27 February   Dvořák's Symphony in G is performed in Boston.

25 June   Still in Prague, Dvořák composes his Te Deum, Opus 103, intended for his inaugural concert in New York.

3 August   Before leaving Prague, Dvořák begins composing his cantata *The American Flag*, Opus 102.

15 September   After entrusting four of his children to the care of his mother-in-law, Antonín Dvořák and the rest of the family depart Bohemia for America.

26 September   Dvořák, his wife, Anna, and two of their six children, Otilie and Antonín, arrive at Sandy Hook on the SS *Saale* on their way to the New Jersey port of Hoboken.

27 September   A deputation from the National Conservatory escorts the Dvořák family to the Hotel Clarendon, located at East Eighteenth Street and Fourth Avenue.

28 September	Although his duties at the Conservatory have not yet begun, Dvořák visits the offices and observes from the windows some of the Columbus Quadricentennial parades on Third Avenue. (This date is offered on the authority of J. J. Kovařík.)
September	In the first of many articles written by critic Henry Krehbiel concerning Dvořák ("Antonín Dvořák," *Century Illustrated Magazine*, September 1892), the arrival of the composer is described as heralding "the rise of a school of American composers."
1 October	Fall term of the National Conservatory begins. Dvořák is contracted to teach three composition classes and supervise orchestra rehearsals. Conservatory located three blocks away at East Seventeenth Street and Irving Place.
9 October	The Bohemian community honors Dvořák with a banquet at the Central Turnverein Halle.
12 October	The Dvořáks witness three days and nights of celebrations for the four hundredth anniversary of Columbus's arrival in the New World. The festivities transpire mostly around Union Square, an area just four blocks away.
mid-October	The Dvořák family relocates to a brick row house at 327 East Seventeenth Street, where they will remain for the rest of their visit.
21 October	The Conservatory honors Dvořák at a Music Hall concert. The Music Hall is later renamed Carnegie Hall. Anton Seidl leads the Metropolitan Orchestra and a chorus of three hundred voices. Dvořák conducts the world premiere of his Te Deum, composed for the occasion.
29–30 October	The Boston Symphony presents a public rehearsal and a performance of the Requiem Mass.
17 November	Dvořák conducts his Symphony in D for a New York Philharmonic Concert at Carnegie Hall.
29 November	Dvořák conducts his Requiem Mass in Boston with the Boston Symphony.
17 December	Dvořák conducts his Symphony in D at a Philharmonic Society concert in New York.
19 December	Inspired to create "the future American anthem," Dvořák sketches a theme he refers to as "New York Motif." The work, a vocal setting of "My Country, 'Tis of Thee," was never finished.

1893

8 January   Dvořák completes *The American Flag*. (He is destined never to hear it in public performance.)

10 January   He begins composing his Ninth Symphony. Purportedly, he derives some inspiration from black spirituals and plantation songs sung to him by a Conservatory student, Harry T. Burleigh.

30 March   In Madison Square Garden Dvořák presents the winners of the National Conservatory Composition Contest. Among his choices of award-winners are: Horatio Parker of New York (who conducted his cantata *Dream King and His Love*), Frederick Bullard of Boston (who conducted his Suite for String Orchestra), and Joshua Phippen of Boston (who played his Piano Concerto).

6 April   Dvořák conducts his Hussite Overture with the New York Symphony Society at Carnegie Hall.

8 May   At a concert of music by Dvořák's composition students, songs by Harry T. Burleigh are performed by Edward H. Kinney, the organist and choir director at St. Philip's African Episcopal Church.

21 May   Quotations from Dvořák appear in an article, "The Real Value of Negro Melodies," in the Sunday edition of the New York *Herald*. Although unsigned, Maurice Peress has speculated that it was written by critic Henry E. Krehbiel. Dvořák is acknowledged the leader of America's dramatic school of composition and urges American composers to study Negro music, such as the "plantation songs." The article is a sensation and is republished abroad.

24 May   Dvořák's Ninth Symphony is completed and contains the inscription, "Thank God . . . the children have arrived in Southampton." He has sent for his other four children to spend the upcoming summer months with him in Spillville, Iowa.

28 May   Another article quoting Dvořák, "Antonín Dvořák on Negro Melodies," appears in the Sunday New York *Herald*. He declares that the future school of American music must be based on Negro melodies. In the same paper there is reprinted an article from the International *Herald*, "Dvořák's Theory of Negro Music." Mixed reactions

from several European composers, including a positive response from Anton Rubinstein, are included.

3 June	Dvořák heads a group who entrain to Spillville, Iowa, via Chicago and Calmar. The group consists of Dvořák, his wife Anna, his six children, a housemaid, and his secretary Josef Kovařík. The journey will cover thirteen hundred miles in thirty-six hours.
5 June	The party arrives at Spillville in the morning. "It is very strange here," he later writes; "few people and a great deal of empty space."
8 June	Dvořák begins the F Major Quartet (tentatively dubbed the "Spillville" but later renamed the "American").
10 June	After completing a sketch of the F Major Quartet, he inscribes the score, "I am satisfied. It went very quickly."
23 June	Completes the F Major Quartet.
26 June–1 August	Composes the B-flat Quintet (the "American"). Sometime during this time a group of Indians, possibly of the Kickapoo and Iroquois tribes, visit the city for several days to sell "medicinal salves" and perform Indian music. There was also a traveling minstrel show with blacks in blackface playing banjos and guitars.
2 August	Dvořák arrives in Omaha, Nebraska.
12 August	Dvořák conducts his G Major Symphony and some Slavonic Dances at the World Columbian Exposition in Chicago for Bohemian Day. Present are thirty thousand Czechs and Moravians.
13 August	The Chicago *Tribune* interviews Dvořák in an article entitled "For National Music."
4–5 September	Dvořák travels to St. Paul, Minnesota, and sees the Minnehaha Falls. He scribbles down a melody on his starched cuff, and it later appears as the Larghetto of his Sonatina, Opus 100.
7 September	Dvořák returns to Spillville.
17 September	The Dvořák family packs up and departs for New York via Niagara Falls. The fall term of the Conservatory is about to begin.
28 September	Dvořák conducts his 149th Psalm and Hussite Overture at the Worchester, Massachusetts Festival.
19 November	Begins composing the Sonatina, Opus 100, for his chil-

	dren. Their subsequent performance of it in his home is called by Dvořák his "favorite premiere."
3 December	Completes the Sonatina and dedicates it to his children.
4 December	Students of the Conservatory perform a program of music under Dvořák's baton at the Scottish Rite Hall in Madison Square Garden. The black students include Will Marion Cook, Harry T. Burleigh, and Maurice Arnold.
15 December	The Ninth Symphony (now called "From the New World") is rehearsed at Carnegie Hall.
16 December	The "New World" Symphony is premiered by conductor Anton Seidl with the New York Philharmonic at Carnegie Hall.

1894

1 January	Dvořák's F Major Quartet is given its world premiere in Boston by the Kneisel Quartet.
12 January	A Carnegie Hall Recital with the Kneisel Quartet presents the world premiere of the E-flat Quintet and the New York premiere of the F Major Quartet.
23 January	At a Madison Square Garden concert, Dvořák premieres his setting of Stephen Foster's song "Old Folks at Home." Soloists are Sissieretta Jones and Harry T. Burleigh. Also on the program are composition student Maurice Arnold's *American Plantation Dances*.
19 February	Dvořák begins composing his Suite, Opus 98 ("American") for piano (work completed on March 1).
5 March	Dvořák begins composing the *Biblical Songs*, Opus 99 (work completed 26 March).
9 March	Dvořák attends the premiere of Victor Herbert's Cello Concerto. Herbert is the cello soloist with the New York Philharmonic. (This work purportedly inspires Dvořák's own subsequent Cello Concerto.)
28 March	František Dvořák (Antonín's father) dies in Bohemia.
18 April	The New York Philharmonic Society selects Dvořák as an Honorary Member.
28 April	Dvořák signs a contract to remain at his Conservatory post in New York for two more years.
19 May	Dvořák departs for Prague and arrives on 30 May.
7–21 August	The piano *Humoresques*, Opus 101, are begun.

26 October	Dvořák returns to New York with his wife and son Otakar for the fall term of the Conservatory.
? November	Dvořák is inducted as an Honorary Member of the New York Philharmonic Society.
8 November	Dvořák begins composing his Cello Concerto, Opus 104.

1895

January	"Music in America," an article by Dvořák, appears in *Harper's New Monthly Magazine.*
9 February	The Cello Concerto is completed.
26 March	Dvořák begins his A-flat Quartet, Opus 105. (It will be completed on 30 December in Bohemia.)
16 April	Dvořák and his wife and son Otakar depart America on the SS *Saale.*
Summer	The *Humoresques* for piano, Opus 101, begun in the summer of 1893 in Spillville, are completed in Vysoka, Bohemia.
17 August	Deciding to remain in Bohemia, Dvořák sends his letter of resignation to Mrs. Thurber in New York.

1941

8 September	The hundredth anniversary of Dvořák's birth is celebrated at the Dvořák House at 327 East Seventeenth Street. In attendance are New York mayor Fiorello La Guardia, the Minister of Foreign Affairs for the Czechoslovak government-in-exile, and Harry T. Burleigh. La Guardia pledges to seek "Landmark" status/protection for the structure.

1991

14–20 February	Dvořák Sesquicentennial Festival and Conference, New Orleans.
August	The Dvořák House is demolished by its owners, Beth Israel Medical Center.
28 November	New York's Mayor Dinkins signs into law the establishment of a "Dvořák Place," an area following Seventeenth Street between First and Second avenues.

CHAPTER THREE

Anthony Philip Heinrich

A Bohemian Predecessor to Dvořák
in the Wilds of America

J. Bunker Clark

*D*vořák was not the first Bohemian musician to make an impact on America, in spite of today's conventional wisdom. In the middle of the nineteenth century, American musical life was enriched by such Bohemian immigrants as violinist/impresario Max Maretzek (also spelled Mareczek, Mareček, Mraček; 1821–1897), pianist/impresario Maurice Strakosch (1825–1887), and reviewer/impresario Hans Balatka (1826–1899). These, and others, may have immigrated at least in part because of their involvement in the 1848 protests against the Austrian monarchy.[1]

This account relates the adventures of another Bohemian composer, Anthony Philip Heinrich (1781–1861), whose life and music provided some precedents for Dvořák's achievement. Heinrich traveled to what was then considered the American West, and his experience prompted him to write music with an even more fervent expression of American nationalism than can be attributed to Dvořák's "American" works. As early as 1823, Heinrich was called "the first regular or general *American* composer."[2]

Heinrich was born Anton Philipp (Antonín Filip) Heinrich in Schönbuchel (Krásný Buk), of German-Bohemian heritage, in 1781. He was adopted by his uncle, from whom he inherited the family business in linen, wines, and other goods. He first came to America in 1805 on a business trip and returned six years later to establish operations in Philadelphia. Misfortunes dogged him. Financial reverses in both Austria and Philadelphia ended his business career in 1811. He married a Boston girl whom he took back to

Bohemia in 1813, and their daughter, Antonia (Toni), was born there. The young mother became ill, and she returned with her husband to America. Shortly thereafter she died. Antonia, meanwhile, was left with relatives in Bohemia.

In 1816, having earlier held a position as musical director of the Southwark Theatre in Philadelphia, Heinrich decided on a new career as a professional musician. Being poor, he went by foot on a three-hundred-mile trek from Philadelphia to Pittsburgh with the promise of a position as a salaried musical director. Alas, the theater went bankrupt. Heinrich proceeded another four hundred miles by boat down the Ohio River, got off at Limestone (now Maysville), and walked sixty miles to Lexington. There on 12 November 1817, in an outpost of civilization, he presented a "Grand Concert of Vocal and Instrumental Music . . . assisted by the principal professors and amateurs." Astoundingly, the first number on the program was a "Sinfonia con Minuetto" by Beethoven, played by a "Full Band"—one of the first performances of a Beethoven symphony in America.[3] Heinrich's own instrument was the violin—he was the proud owner of a fine Cremona instrument—and on the program he played solos by Viotti, Fiorillo, and Giornovichi. The next spring he moved to a log cabin in Bardstown and began teaching himself composition. By January 1819 he was living at "Farmington," the estate of Judge John Speed, located between Bardstown and Louisville. (Speed's son James later became Attorney General in Lincoln's cabinet. Also living on the estate was the naturalist John James Audubon.)

In Philadelphia the following year the first fruits of Heinrich's lonely studies appeared: *The Dawning of Music in Kentucky; or, the Pleasures of Harmony in the Solitudes of Nature*, recently called "the most extraordinary Opus 1 in the history of music."[4] This was followed the same year by his Opus 2, *The Western Minstrel, a Collection of Original, Moral, Patriotic, & Sentimental Songs, for the Voice and Piano Forte, Interspersed with Airs, Waltzes, &c.* Both of these incredible works consist of a mixture of music for the pianoforte, violin, voice, and vocal ensembles, many with titles connected to Heinrich's heritage and location. According to his preface to *Dawning*, he had been "thrown, as it were, by *discordant events*, far from the emporiums of musical science, into the isolated wilds of nature, where he invoked his Muse, tutored *only* by Alma Mater" (Heinrich's emphasis). Although his stay in the west was only some three or four years, he continued to claim that his roots lay in the wilds of Kentucky.

A review in John Rowe Parker's Boston journal *The Euterpeiad, or Musical Intelligencer* on 13 April 1822 included the accolade "The Beethoven of America," and in 1823 Heinrich moved to that New England city, where he was active as a performer and continued to compose. In an effort to further his reputation abroad, he began a new collection of his works, which appeared in 1823 and 1825–26 under the title *The Sylviad; or, Minstrelsy of Nature in the Wilds of N. America,* Op. 3.[5] It was dedicated to the Royal Academy of Music, which had been recently founded in London, and it contained a similar mixture of works for piano and voice. Unfortunately, none of these had the desired effect when Heinrich traveled to London in 1826, and he was reduced to playing in pit orchestras. He was in Boston again in 1831–33. In 1835 he returned to Bohemia to see his daughter, only to find that she had already left for America to visit him! Nonetheless, he organized and participated in concerts featuring his works in various European cities, including Prague, Vienna, and Graz. Thus, he had the honor of being the first American to be included in several European encyclopedias, namely Gustav Schilling's *Encyclopädia der gesammten musikalischen Wissenschaften, oder Universal-Lexicon der Tonkunst* (1836) and François-Joseph Fétis's *Biographie universelle des musiciens* (1839).

The years 1837–57 were spent in New York and other cities, this period beginning with a long-awaited reunion with his daughter, Antonia. He was chairman of the organizational meeting of the New York Philharmonic in 1842. There were more concerts, largely devoted to his own works, among them a "Grand Musical Festival" in New York on 16 June 1842, and another on 6 May 1846.[6] He made a final European trip to Prague and other cities in 1857–60, then returned to New York where he died in poverty in 1861, his manuscripts piled high in old trunks. His large compositions were never performed in his lifetime by the more influential musical organizations in America, like the Philharmonic Society of New York and the Musical Fund Society of Philadelphia, and not one was accepted by a publisher. His extraordinary music, almost all of it programmatic, was full of chromatic passages, unexpected modulations, striking dissonances, and episodic forms. It still awaits the major revival it deserves. Undoubtedly, when Dvořák arrived in New York in 1892, he heard nothing of his fellow countryman, dead for 31 years.

Heinrich's music reveals many of the qualities that would later be generally ascribed to Dvořák. Although Dvořák has the reputation of introducing the idea to American composers of using native materials, Heinrich had advocated this practice much earlier. That American nationalism had always been a prominent feature of his music is evidenced by the titles already cited, which include individual pieces like "Yankee Doodle Waltz," "Hail Columbia! Minuet," "Kentucky March" (from *Dawning*); and "A Sylvan Scene in Kentucky; or the Barbecue Divertimento, Comprising the Ploughman's Grand March, and The Negro's Banjo Quickstep," from *Sylviad.* But any use of American musical materials or folk songs is subtle at best, even with the imitation of the Afro-American instrument in this last work, which predates Louis Moreau Gottschalk's more famous "The Banjo" by thirty years.[7]

References to birds are everywhere in Heinrich's music, anticipating Dvořák's own notorious devotion to birds, especially pigeons. *The Columbiad; or, Migration of American Wild Passenger Pigeons* (for orchestra and voices, 1858), and a symphony called *The Ornithological Combat of Kings; or, The Condor of the Andes and the Eagle of the Cordilleras* (1847), for example, doubtless are derived from his friendship with Audubon.

References to Native American musical idioms and life also predate Dvořák (and other composers like Edward MacDowell and Arthur Farwell). His symphony in one movement, *The Indian Carnival; or, the Indian's Festival of Dreams* (undated orchestral version), has descriptive titles in the piano version published in 1849.[8] The title page bears this explanation: "A Bacchanal among the North American Indians, which commonly lasts 15 days, and is celebrated about the end of Winter." The individual sections are marked "The Indian Carnival," "The Parting Adieus," "The Festival of the Dead,"[9] "The Cries of Souls." But another symphony, *Manitou Mysteries or the Voice of the Great Spirit: Gran sinfonia misteriosa indiana* (completed by 1845) has no attached program.

Some works depict historical encounters between Indians and the white man. In *The Treaty of William Penn with the Indians: Concerto Grosso, an American National Dramatic Divertissement, for a Full Orchestra, Comprising Successively Six Different Characteristic Movements United in One* (1834, revised 1847) the various sections tell the story: "The Meeting of William Penn and his associates with the Delaware Indians," "The Treaty," "Smoking of the Calumet," "The Presentation of Gifts to the Indians," "The Grand Dance of the Calumet," and "Coda Volante: The Manitou Air Dance."[10] *Pocahontas—The Royal Maid and Heroine of Virginia, the Pride of the Wilderness: Fantasia Romanza* (1837) has an unusual instrumentation that, in addition to strings, calls for triangle, cymbals, tambourine, side and bass drums, timpani, the usual winds, with piccolos and contrabassoons, and brasses comprising three trombones, ophicleide, serpent, four horns, four trumpets, and "cornetto concertante."[11] *Der Felsen von Plymouth, oder die Landung der*

Pilger Vater in Neu England, A.D. 1620 (Plymouth Rock; or, the Landing of the Pilgrim Fathers) was completed in Prague in 1858–59 and has the following movements: "*Animato: Die Einschiffung der Puritaner in Europa auf der Barke: 'Mayflower'*" (The Departure of the Puritans from Europe in the Ship "Mayflower"), "*Der Abschied (Cadenza)*" (The Farewell), "*Concertante grazioso: Eine Mondlichtscene auf dem Ocean*" (Moonlight Scene on the Ocean), "*Adagio Sublime: Gebet*" (Prayer), "*Tremolante molto agitato: Die Landung und feierliches Entgegenkommen der Indianer*" (The Landing and Celebration of the Indians), "*Baletto indico nazionale: Freudentänze der Squaws nach erhaltenen Geschenken*" (Joyful Dances of the Squaws After the Reception of Gifts), and "*Andante e Fuga: Das Calumet oder die Friedenspfeife der Indianer dem grossen Geiste* (Great spirit Manitou) *geweiht*" (The Indian Peace Pipe Dedicated to the Great Spirit Manitou). According to Wilbur Maust, the sixth section comes closest to the use of so-called primitive Native American music in the ostinato rhythms and repetitive orchestration, as well as in the use of the harmonic minor scale.[12]

Other works are devoted to the lives of great Indian chiefs. The Shawnee chief Tecumseh, who fought with the British in the War of 1812, was the subject of *The Indian War Council, Gran Concerto Bellico: A Grand Divertissement for 41 Instrumental Parts* (1834). The work falls into the category of a battle piece, with some of the movements marked "The Indian War Dance," "Advance of the Americans," and "Skirmishing." He wrote an "instrumental fantasy" called *Pushmataha, a Venerable Chief of a Western Tribe of Indians* in London in 1831. It is a programmatic work for thirty-three instruments. According to Howard Shanet, who gave the first modern performance with the Columbia University Orchestra (commemorating the centennial of Heinrich's death), it called for "a large percussion section, including timpani, bass drum, snare drum, triangle, cymbals, and tambourine [and] is obviously intended to suggest the exotic 'Indian' atmosphere in somewhat the sense in which Mozart and his contemporaries used percussion instruments for 'Turkish' music."[13] Heinrich refers to John McIntosh's book *Origin of the North American Indians* (1843) in his revised score of 1855. Another Indian leader is depicted in *Logan, the Mingo Chief: Grand Fantasia* (1834, revised 1851) and the symphony *Mastodon*. This last work consists of a first movement, "Black Thunder, the Patriarch of the Fox Tribe," a second, "The Elkhorn Pyramid; or, the Indians' Offering to the Spirit of the Prairies," and the last movement, "Shenandoah, an Oneida Chief."

Even without hearing a note of these works—to date, none of his Indian music is available on recordings—this Bohemian immigrant's interest in the Native American is obvious. Heinrich may not have been the first to write such music, but before Dvořák he was certainly the most enthusiastic.[14] No other composer of his time could rival that. His disadvantage was that he had little or no direct contact with Indians or their music; he seemed to rely mainly on books for his descriptive programs and themes. The first important study of Native American music, Theodore Baker's German dissertation *Über die Musik der nordamerikanischen Wilden* (1882) did not appear until after Heinrich's death. It would be the source of some themes in MacDowell's Second ("Indian") Suite, written in 1891–92. Dvořák's advocacy of native American resources for musical inspiration in the 1890s was not new, but it bore fruit because of his fame and the growing availability of actual indigenous musical materials.

NOTES

1. See Jaroslav Mraček, "Czech and Slovak Musicians in the United States, 1848–1938," in *Grossbritannien, die USA, und die böhmischen Länder 1848–1938* (Great Britain, the United States, and the Bohemian Lands 1848–1938), ed. Eva Schmidt-Hartmann and Stanley B. Winters, Vorträge der Tagung des Collegium Carolinum in Bad Wiessee vom 2. bis 6. November 1988 (Munich: R. Oldenbourg, 1991), 47–57.

2. Boston *Daily Advertiser*, 29 May 1823, quoted from William Treat Upton, *Anthony Philip Heinrich: A Nineteenth-Century Composer in America* (New York: Columbia University Press, 1939; reprint, New York: AMS Press, 1967), 70. This is the basic biography of Heinrich and the source of most of the biographical information here. See also the article, with list of works and bibliography, by David Barron in *The New Grove Dictionary of American Music* (1986).

3. The program is in Upton, 29.

4. H. Wiley Hitchcock, foreword to the reprint edition, Earlier American Music series, 10 (New York: Da Capo, 1972), which includes *The Western Minstrel*, Op. 2. Heinrich's piano music composed prior to 1830 is also the subject of the last chapter in my book (whose title shadows that of Heinrich's Op. 1), *The Dawning of American Keyboard Music* (Westport, Conn.: Greenwood Press, 1988).

5. A reprint, collected with a foreword by this author, is anticipated in the Earlier American Music series, 28 (New York: Da Capo).

6. For an account of these concerts, see Vera Brodsky Lawrence, *Strong on Music: The New York Music Scene in the Days of George Templeton Strong, 1836–1875*, vol. 1: *Resonances, 1836–1850* (New York: Oxford University Press, 1988), 168–170 and 407–409.

7. Gottschalk (1829–69), of course, also preceded Dvořák in using American themes in his music. Some examples for piano are "*Bamboula: Danse de nègres,*" Op. 2, "*La Savane (ballade créole),*" Op. 3, and "*Le Bananier (chanson nègre),*" Op. 5. These works date from 1845–46, when he was in Paris, and all are based on Louisiana Creole melodies. He was well regarded in Europe as a virtuoso pianist and as an exotic composer (New Orleans was regarded this way in Paris). He also used materials from the Caribbean. Concerning his "*O! ma charmante, épargnez moi*" (O my charmer, spare me), the 1862 publication includes this note: "The author in this morceau has endeavored to convey an idea of the singular rhythm and charming character of the music which exists among the Creoles of the Spanish Antilles. Chopin it is well known transferred the national traits of Poland to his Mazurkas and Polonaises, and Mr. Gottschalk has endeavored to reproduce in works of an appropriate character, the characteristic traits of the dances of the West Indies." Gottschalk, however, was regarded as a musical charlatan by the Boston musical establishment, especially by John Sullivan Dwight in his *Dwight's Journal of Music* (published 1852–81), whose musical taste followed that of classical German music.

8. Facsimile reprint in J. Bunker Clark, ed., *American Keyboard Music through 1865,* Three Centuries of American Music, vol. 3 (Boston: G. K. Hall, 1990), 266–277.

9. "The most singular religious Ceremony of the Savages, which is renewed every eight Years among some Indian Nations, and every ten Years among the Hurons and Irequois [*sic*]."

10. See Wilbur R. Maust, "The American Indian in the Orchestral Music of Anthony Philip Heinrich," *Music East and West: Essays in Honor of Walter Kaufmann,* ed. Thomas Noblitt (New York: Pendragon Press, 1981), 314. The information on Heinrich's orchestral music is derived from this article.

11. Maust, "American Indian," 313.

12. Maust, "American Indian," 315.

13. Program notes for the 6 December 1961 performance, quoted in Maust, "The Symphonies of Anthony Philip Heinrich Based on American Themes (Ph.D. diss., Indiana University, 1973), 86.

14. John Bray's "operatic melo-drama" *The Indian Princess; or, La Belle Sauvage,* for example, was performed and published in Philadelphia in 1808 (reprint, New York: Da Capo, 1972).

CHAPTER FOUR

From London to New York
Dvořák's Introduction to America

Graham Melville-Mason

*T*he many studies of the life and work
of Antonín Dvořák carried out during the Prague-organized five-year
research program that led up to the world-wide conferences and celebrations
in 1991 marking the 150th anniversary of Dvořák's birth (see John C. Tib-
bett's essay, Chapter 25), has led to a reassessment of many of the long-held,
but often erroneous views of his career. There is now a new appreciation, for
example, of the central significance of England in Dvořák's achieving international recognition as a major composer, as well as providing him with the
impetus for a trip to America.

The more traditional and popular view has credited Brahms and the
Vienna jury, in addition to the introduction to a Berlin publisher, with
Dvořák's wider fame. Certainly, in the simplest and most immediate terms,
this is true. Had Dvořák not applied for and then received his first Austro-
Hungarian State Scholarship from Vienna in 1875, thereby bringing his talent to the attention of men like Hanslick and, in the following year, Brahms,
he would not have been introduced to so powerful a European music publisher as Fritz Simrock in Berlin. This, in turn, had attracted the attention of
other influential musicians like Joseph Joachim, Hans Richter, and August
Manns.

However, the real international breakthrough came first in London.
This not only brought Dvořák a much needed recognition outside Bohemia,
but it restored his self-confidence and sense of purpose at a time when he was
racked by self-doubts. Should he remain in Bohemia, where his heart lay, or

venture abroad where other musicians were tempting him with richer rewards?

Richter and Manns had introduced Dvořák's music to England in their London and provincial concert series from the 1870s. Soon the great British choral societies were to learn that Dvořák had written a particularly fine work that would fit the tradition of their repertoire—the Stabat Mater, Opus 58 (1876–77). The London performance under Joseph Barnby in the Royal Albert Hall on 10 March 1883, as the distinguished British Dvořák scholar John Clapham says, "sparked off a whole series of performances in England and the United States. American choral societies were a year ahead of similar organizations in Germany and Austria."[1] The Philharmonic Society (now the Royal Philharmonic Society), which had commissioned Beethoven's Ninth Symphony in 1822, was quick to recognize Dvořák's growing international potential. As Clapham continues: "Barnby's successful concert was also influential in helping to bring about another important development, one that marks the beginning of a new stage in Dvořák's career as a composer."[2] On 3 August 1883, the Secretary of the Philharmonic Society, Mr. Henry Hersee, sent Dvořák an invitation to come to London in the following season, commissioning a work from him (which was to be the Seventh Symphony, Opus 70) and inviting him to conduct. After further correspondence between Dvořák, August Manns, and Francesco Berger (now Secretary of the Philharmonic Society), the first of Dvořák's nine memorable visits commenced on 8 March 1884. He conducted his Stabat Mater in the Royal Albert Hall on 13 March.

These nine visits, between 1884 and 1896, occasioned some of his most important works and captured the attention of the Americans. In addition to the Seventh Symphony, he received immediate commissions for major choral works from the Festivals of Birmingham and Leeds. These would include *The Spectre's Bride*, Opus 69, in late 1884, and *St. Ludmila* a year later. The Requiem was written for Birmingham in 1890. Alas, a projected choral work for the Cardiff Festival, a cantata to be called *Zahor's Couch*, never materialized. Other works closely associated with Britain included an overture, *In Nature's Realm*, Opus 91, which he dedicated to Cambridge University on the occasion of his being made an honorary Doctor of Music, and the Eighth Symphony, Opus 88. The Symphony, although not specifically written for England, received its second performance under Dvořák at a London Philharmonic Society concert on 24 April 1890. To this day the work is subtitled *"Anglicka"* (English) in Czechoslovakia, even though that appellation would be more appropriate to the Seventh Sym-

phony.[3] Finally, the Cello Concerto No. 2, Opus 104, although written in America in 1895, received its first performance in Queen's Hall, London, with Dvořák conducting and Leo Stern as the soloist (see Robert Battey's essay, Chapter 21).

There were close musical connections between America and Britain at the time, and Dvořák profited from them. John Clapham writes:

> It is interesting, and certainly significant, that in these two countries a great deal of this support for Dvořák emanated from the sponsorship of leading musicians with either German or Austrian ancestry, who were temporarily or permanently domiciled there. In England Manchester had its Charles Hallé, Willy Hess, Carl Fuchs and Bauerkeller, and London benefitted from the presence of August Manns, George Henschel, Richard Gomperts, Edward Dannreuther, and by no means least, Joseph Joachim, an Austro-Hungarian. In Boston we encounter Emil Pauer, Bernhard Listemann, George Henschel, Wilhelm Gericke, Carl Zerrahn and the Austro-Hungarian Arthur Nikisch—a formidable group. The three Damrosches were in New York, together with Frank Van der Stucken, who moved later to Cincinnati, Gustav Dannreuther, Theodore Thomas from Esens, who spent some time in Cincinnati and Chicago, Emil Pauer once again, and Anton Seidl. Dvořák benefitted greatly from the efforts of all these men.[4]

Performances in America of Dvořák's works often followed hard on the heels of their British presentations. To cite just a few:

The Slavonic Dances, perhaps understandably, seem to be the first works to be heard in both countries. By 2 August 1878, Dvořák had orchestrated Nos. 1, 3, and 4 of the first set, Opus 46, and in February 1879, Manns performed them at the Crystal Palace in London. In America No. 4 was subsequently performed by Thomas in New York on 6 October 1879 and Nos. 5 and 6 by Listemann in Boston on 7 November that same year.

The Third Slavonic Rhapsody, Opus 45, was performed in London by Richter on 27 May 1879 and in Cincinnati by Thomas on 4 February 1880. Stabat Mater, having been given in London by Barnby on 10 March 1883, was heard in a truncated version (Nos. 3–7) in Boston, conducted by Benjamin J. Lang, on 24 January 1884 and in complete form, by Thomas, in New York on 3 April 1884.

The world premiere of the Seventh Symphony was given by Dvořák in London on 22 April 1885, and the first American performance by Thomas in New York on 9 January 1886.

Less than two and a half months after the Birmingham performance of *The Spectre's Bride* under Dvořák on 27 August 1885, it was heard in Providence, Rhode Island, on 18 November, conducted by Jules Jordan.

Inevitably, American interest in meeting the composer was growing. Before Mrs. Jeannette M. Thurber's invitation to come to New York in 1892, there were several indications that Dvořák might visit America. A report in the *Neue Zeitschrift für Musik* on 18 July 1884, for example, gave the first public notice about a possible American tour. A few months later, in September 1884, Dvořák made his second London visit and was the guest of music publisher Henry Littleton at his home in Westwood House, Sydenham. The firm, one of the most important in England, published Dvořák's Stabat Mater in 1883. The American composer, Dudley Buck, who became assistant conductor of the Theodore Thomas orchestra in 1875, had been visiting Littleton in connection with the forthcoming premiere of his *Light of Asia* in the Novello Oratorio Concerts in London in 1885. Hearing that Dvořák was soon to arrive, he delayed his departure in order to meet him. It seems that he discussed the possibility of Dvořák visiting America. The Czech critic, V. J. Novotný, who accompanied Dvořák on this visit, recorded that the composer was coming round to the idea, provided the terms were acceptable.

Henry Littleton was Dvořák's friend and publisher in England. Drawing by John C. Tibbetts.

After that encounter nothing more was heard of an American visit until the issue of the directorship of the National Conservatory of Music of America, formed in 1885, arose. Mrs. Thurber was seeking a successor to the first director, Jacques Bouhy (the first Escamillo in Bizet's *Carmen*), who had resigned in 1889. Some biographers state that it was on the advice of her friend and colleague, Adele Margulies, that Mrs. Thurber considered two options—the young Finnish composer Jan Sibelius, and Dvořák.[5]

From the surviving notes and correspondence, it is clear that Henry Littleton's son, Alfred, played a crucial role in both the choice of Dvořák and in Dvořák's own decision to accept the post. After the death of his father, Alfred had taken over the operations of Novello & Co.; and it was he who supported Thurber's ultimate choice of Dvořák and who acted as intermediary and negotiator for her. Pertinent correspondence survives, including many of Dvořák's letters on the matter to Mrs. Thurber and Littleton, as well as letters to his close friends in Bohemia, like Alois Göbl (secretary and tutor to Prince Kamil of Rohan at Sychrov, where Dvořák frequently visited), August Bohdanecký (son-in-law of his old friend Judge Antonín Rus of Písek), and to Rus himself.[6]

Mrs. Jeannette Meyer Thurber was Dvořák's sponsor at the National Conservatory of Music of America, which she founded. Drawing by John C. Tibbetts.

Dvořák was excited by the offer but worried over details of his salary, the New York climate, and the important matter of the care and education of his six children during his absence. He also stipulated that he would first have to obtain a leave of absence from the Prague Conservatory.

Littleton reported these concerns to Thurber on 25 June 1891. Two weeks later she agreed to his request to deposit $7,500 in Prague, half of his agreed-upon annual salary. Littleton then prepared a draft contract specifying that the composer would be obliged to teach three hours a week and conduct concerts of his students' compositions as well as his own. Dvořák, in turn, suggested terms for the payment of the second half of his salary, proposed he teach composition to only the most promising students, and decided to bring his wife and one or two of the children. More negotiations followed until Littleton mailed Dvořák a final version of the contract on 21 December. It was returned, signed, just before Christmas.[7]

In a letter to Mrs. Thurber on 21 December, Dvořák was characteristically, modest about his capabilities in his new post:

> Mrs. Dvořák and my eldest daughter Otilka are very anxious to see Amerika [*sic*], but I am a little afraid that I shall not be able to please you in everything in my new position. As a teacher and instructor and conductor I feel myself quite sure, but there [are] many other trifles which will make me much sorrow and grieve—but I rely on your kindness and indulgence and be sure I shall do all to please you.[8]

After entrusting four of his children to the care of his mother-in-law, Dvořák left Bohemia on 15 September 1892 with his wife, Anna, fourteen-year-old Otilka, nine-year-old Antonín, and his secretary, Josef Jan Kovařík, a young Czech who had grown up in America.

NOTES

1. John Clapham, *Dvořák* (London and New York: W. W. Norton & Co., Inc., 1979), 60.

2. John Clapham, *Dvořák*, 61.

3. The reason lies in the fact that it was published by Novello, Ewer & Co. in London in 1892, at a time when Dvořák had fallen out with his German publisher, Simrock.

4. John Clapham, "Dvořák on the American Scene," *Nineteenth Century Music*, vol. 5, no. 1 (Summer 1981), 17.

5. See Alec Robertson, *Dvořák* (London: J. M. Dent and Sons, Ltd., 1947), 60; and Paul Stefan-Gruenfeldt, *Antonín Dvořák* (New York: The Greystone Press, 1941), 186.

6. See Milan Kuna, Ed., Antonín *Dvořák: korespondence a dokumenty*, vol. 3, 1890—1895 (Prague: Supraphon, 1989).

7. Although the letters from Dvořák to Littleton are mostly in private hands, the Dvořák Museum in Prague holds several of the letters sent from Littleton to Dvořák in 1891 regarding the American contract (Nos. 1138, 1139, 1141).

8. Quoted in John Clapham, *Dvořák*, 109.

CHAPTER FIVE

Dvořák's New York

An American Street Scene

John C. Tibbetts

On a late Monday afternoon, 26 September 1892, Antonín Dvořák's steamship, the SS *Saale*, sailed past the lighthouse at Sandy Hook and came through the Narrows on the way toward the New Jersey port of Hoboken. With his wife, Anna, and two of his children, Otilka and Antonín, he gaped in astonishment at the busy harbor. The ship's master, Captain Rinck, came over and pointed out the sights: There on the right was Brooklyn, on the left was Staten Island. And dead ahead was a sight Dvořák would never forget—soaring 151 feet into the air, high atop its new base on Bedloe's Island, proudly stood the Statue of Liberty. After a long look, the composer marvelled: "In the head alone there is room for sixty persons!"[1]

Waves of excitement and nervous apprehension churned through him. He felt diminished and strange. He was only one of millions of Europeans who had come to this port since 1881. Yet he knew his lot was better than that of most of these "aliens." After all, he was not officially classified as an immigrant. He had not had to spend the nine-day voyage below decks in steerage, and he would not have to be "processed" at nearby Ellis Island. He was a man of some means, and a good job was awaiting him at Mrs. Thurber's National Conservatory of Music. He was a guest of this new land and, in some quarters at least, was already well known to many of the citizens. New Yorkers had already heard some of his music, such as the Slavonic Dances and Piano Trios. Only last February his Requiem Mass had been performed here.[2]

"The Americans expect great things of me," Dvořák mused to himself; "and the main thing is, so they say, to show them to the promised land and kingdom of a new and independent art, in short, to create a national music. If the small Czech nation can have such musicians, they say, why could not they, too, when their country and people are so immense."[3] He scowled amiably. The irony amused him: Four hundred years after Columbus, and America is still trying to discover itself!

A day later a deputation from the National Conservatory, led by Mrs. Thurber's secretary, Mr. Stanton, and a group of Czech citizens greeted the Dvořáks in Hoboken. A carriage took them to the Hotel Clarendon on the corner of East Eighteenth and Fourth Avenue, near Union Square. Flowers were arranged everywhere in their reserved room, and there in the parlor was a lovely new Steinway concert grand. He had never seen such luxury. But he quickly learned it came at an exorbitant price—$55 a week. Further, the noise was excessive, and two weeks after complaining to his secretary, J. J. Kovařík, who was staying with them, they moved into a nearby modest brick row house at 327 East Seventeenth, located on the north side of the street between First and Second avenues. They occupied the basement story, which was a few steps below grade, and the parlor story, which was slightly above grade at the top of the stoop. There were five rooms—a parlor sitting-room with a piano (again provided by William Steinway), a small furnished room, and three other rooms. The rent was only $80 a month—"a lot for us but the normal price here," he said—and the view through the windows of a sector of Stuyvesant Square Park was charming.[4] He was pleased to discover he had famous neighbors. Just a short walk away, at 241 East Seventeenth Street between Second and Third avenue, lived William Dean Howells, America's leading "realist" writer and current editor of the prestigious *Harper's Weekly* and *Harper's Monthly* magazines (which would soon publish some of Dvořák's articles). Edwin Booth, the eminent tragedian, was spending his last days at 16 Gramercy Park South, the home he had converted into the Players Club. And novelist Herman Melville lived just minutes away at 104 East Twenty-sixth.[5]

It was a modestly fashionable area, and in those first few weeks, when he could get away from his duties at the Conservatory, Dvořák cut quite an arresting figure as he escorted his family on their daily walks. Passers-by cast curious backward glances at his wild whiskers, swarthy complexion, wide nose, and deep-set, snapping eyes. He was obviously proud of his ostentatious emerald-green necktie, silk vest, ulster coat, and homburg hat, which he wore at a rakish angle. Reports of his rather striking appearance had already reached the newspapers, and he must have winced at the description: "He is not an awesome personality at all," wrote a reporter. "He is not beautiful in the forms of face . . . but there is so much emotional life in the fiery eyes and lined face, that when he lightens up in conversation, his face is not easily forgotten. . . . He is much taller than his pictures would imply . . . about 5-foot-10 or 5-11, of great natural dignity, a man of character."[6]

Looking about Stuyvesant Square, his first reactions were enthusiastic: "The city itself is magnificent, lovely buildings and beautiful streets and, everywhere, the greatest cleanliness."[7] He proudly showed Anna and the children the nearby areas around Fourteenth Street and Union Square, the center of the city's cultural life. The National Conservatory was just four minutes away at East Seventeenth Street and Irving Place. On the north side of East Fourteenth Street was the Academy of Music, and between Union Square and Irving Place stood Steinway Hall and the Steinway Piano Company showrooms. There was proud old St. George's Episcopal Church on East Sixteenth Street (which claimed millionaire J. P. Morgan as a parishioner and would soon echo to the singing of Dvořák's friend, Harry T. Burleigh); and nearby was Gramercy Park.

The population of this part of the city had been dominated early in the century by Dutch descendants. More recently there had been an influx of Germans, Irish, Russian Jews, and Slavs. Some of the streets were already laid out in the new asphalt, which was beginning to replace the old rough granite blocks. Street fashions were strictly observed. Some well-dressed men about town wore derbies, spats, and covert coats (a fawn-colored box cloth, cut to expose the tails of the cutaway). Others preferred plug hats with reefers and straw hats with swallowtails. The collars were celluloid and the neckties were made-up. A new style in shirtwaists encouraged the use of belts rather than suspenders. A few daring souls experimented with those curious new fasteners called "zippers." Although the ladies still wore bustles and trailing skirts, the style would soon disappear in favor of skirt lengths above the ankles. A few society belles in skirts glided about on bicycles, enjoying the resurgence of a craze that had last surfaced back in the fifties.

Dvořák's New York was a city of quick and ready contrasts. On the one hand it retained vestiges of the inherited wealth and gentility of the Gilded Age. As yet there were no automobiles or subway system. Only a few of the new skyscrapers, like Joseph Pulitzer's sixteen-story New York World Building, had appeared. The disastrous Panic of 1893 was a year away. On the other hand, a deadly cholera epidemic had recently ravaged the city. Disappointed city officials bemoaned the loss of the 1893 World's Fair to Chicago. The population growth was out of control. Since the Civil War, New York had become a whirlpool that sucked in the wealth and wreckage of the rest of the country and other countries abroad. One-third of its almost one and a half million inhabitants were foreign-born. Moreover, Manhattan was straining at the leash to consolidate with Brooklyn, the Bronx, Queens, and Staten Island to become the nation's most important metropolis. (The merger would take place just five years later.) As a character in one of William Dean Howells's new novels declared, "[The city] shrieks and yells with ugliness here and there, but it never loses its spirits."[8]

Sometimes the Dvořák family ventured over to the "Ladies Mile" shopping district on the West Side around Fifth and Sixth avenues between Fourteenth and Twenty-third streets. Here were the first great department stores with famous names, like W&J Sloane, Arnold Constable, and Lord & Taylor. On special occasions they would dine at the fabulous Delmonicos, at Twenty-sixth Street between Broadway and Fifth Avenue, near Madison Square. Farther uptown, past Twenty-eighth Street, were the city's poshest residential areas, resplendent with the chateaux of the Vanderbilts, the Astors, the Huntingtons, the Depews, and Andrew Carnegie. These pseudo-palazzos, these symphonies in terra-cotta, marble, and bronze, were enclosed by wrought-iron fences, safe from the prying eyes of tourists and other rabble.

While preparing for his first concert in New York on 21 October, the premiere of his Te Deum, Dvořák spent a lot of time at the new Music Hall (which six years later would be officially renamed for its chief benefactor, Andrew Carnegie) at the corner of Fifty-seventh and Seventh Avenue. One of the city's first all-fireproof buildings, its eclectic blend of German, Greco-Roman, and Renaissance Italian architecture had been designed by Richard Morris Hunt, the same man who had designed the pedestal for the Statue of Liberty. The Music Hall had been dedicated just last May in several concerts by Dvořák's friend, Tchaikovsky. Since then such artists as pianists Leopold Godowsky and Ignace Paderewski and opera stars Emma Eames and Lillian Nordica had given recitals there, and the New York Philharmonic, under the baton of Anton Seidl, was preparing to move in.

The fashionable lifestyle uptown—view of the new Dakota House from Central Park, ca. 1890.

Dvořák had looked forward to attending the Metropolitan Opera, but unfortunately a few months before, disaster had struck their new building on Broadway between Thirty-ninth and Fortieth streets. A fire had started in the paint room, and the house, which had already seen the likes of singers Eduard and Jean de Reszke and Lili Lehmann in cycles of operas by Meyerbeer and Wagner, would be closed for the entire 1892–93 season. Dvořák realized, of course, that anything performed here would be sung in its original language. That was unfortunate—no wonder such a small percentage of people here went to the opera! He remembered Mrs. Thurber's ill-fated efforts to present opera in English; and he wondered how long it would be before the idea would catch on. . . .

But there were many other entertainments to savor as he walked home every day from the Conservatory. Dvořák loved the Cafe Boulevard on Second Avenue, where he could puff furiously away at his long, thin cigars, drink great quantities of coffee, and read the New York *Herald* as well as the latest newspapers from Prague. He also spent many evenings at the Cafe Fleischman at Broadway and Tenth Street, Healy's Tavern (later known at Pete's Tavern) on Eighteenth and Irving Place, and the fabulous Luchow's, home for many local artists and personalities including his new friend Victor Herbert. At Central Park he discovered a small zoological garden and hundreds of pigeons—although they couldn't compare with his "pouters" and "fantails" back home in Vysoka.

"Winter—Fifth Avenue" by photographer Alfred Stieglitz. New York streets in 1893. (Courtesy Photography Collection, Spencer Museum, University of Kansas.)

By contrast he was taken aback by his first stroll through the theater district, which began at Tony Pastor's on East Fourteenth Street between Third Avenue and Fourth avenues and Broadway and extended uptown to the new Berkeley Lyceum Theater at Forty-fourth and Fifth Avenue. Variety shows were all the rage, and some of the vaudeville bills ran from noon until midnight. Bessie Bonehill, a male impersonator from England, was the hottest act in town; Frank Bush, one of the first Jewish comedians, specialized in dialect stories and songs; and there was the usual assortment of rope dancers, jugglers, declaimers, and knife-throwers. Although the legendary Edwin Booth had just retired, Dvořák had the opportunity to catch many other prestigious "legitimate" stars of the day—Henry Irving and Ellen Terry in *Becket* at the Abbey Theatre, Lillian Russell in *Princess Nicotine*, and Eleonora Duse's first New York appearances. Playwright David Belasco was featuring Mrs. Leslie Carter in *Miss Helyett* and *The Girl I Left Behind Me* (a frontier melodrama). Ned Harrigan (late of the celebrated team of Harrigan and Hart, whose musical plays for the last fifteen years had presented outrageous escapades among the German, Irish, and blacks) had just returned to Broadway with a new smash hit, *Reilly and the Four Hundred.* Charles Hoyt's *A Trip to Chinatown*, with its popular tune, "After the Ball," was in the middle of its spectacular run at the Madison Square Theater—on the way to becoming the longest running play of the decade. And Reginald De Koven's

new musical show, *Robin Hood*, was mixing the forms of the European operetta with the American revue.

At night the electric trolleys, brightly illuminated from one end to the
other with multi-colored lights, gave the area a festive carnival atmosphere.
What sights there were in these magical streets!

> Fire signs announcing the night's amusements blazed on every hand.
> Cabs and carriages, their lamps gleaming like yellow eyes, pattered
> by. . . . Across the way the great hotels showed a hundred gleaming
> windows, their cafes and billiard-rooms filled with a comfortable,
> well-dressed and pleasure-loving throng. All about was the night, pul-
> sating with the thoughts of pleasure and exhilaration—the curious
> enthusiasm of a great city bent upon finding joy in a thousand differ-
> ent ways.[9]

Never had Dvořák seen anything like New York's elevated trains!
Since the mid-1870s they had been winding their aerial skyways along Second, Third, Sixth, and Ninth Avenues. The clattering, shrieking cars were
powered by cables hooked to stationary steam engines. Cinders, soot, and
hot ashes soiled the passengers' faces and clothes and showered down onto
the streets below. When Dvořák first took "the El" at Third Avenue to
Chatham Square or up to Grand Central, he looked around the crowded car
in some astonishment. There were relatively few Irish, supposedly the dominant element in this part of town. Far outnumbering the Celts were the Jews
from the Lower East Side, the Italians working on the constructions far up
the line, and others of Germanic, Slavonic, Pelasgic, Scandinavian, and
Mongolian stock.

A "frantic panorama" of city life rushed by outside—Corinthian theater fronts and saloons, livery stables, horsecars and vendors, bowler-hatted
youths, and prostitutes. The tenements were so close you could lean out and
almost touch them, their windows framing fleeting glimpses of domestic life.
It was better than going to the theater . . .

> to see those people through the windows: a family party of work-folk
> at a late tea, some of the men in their shirt sleeves; a woman sewing
> by a lamp; a mother laying her child in its cradle; a man with his head
> fallen on his hands upon a table; a girl and her lover leaning over the
> windowsill together.[10]

In a few of the rooms you could catch a glimpse of the tin bathing
tubs (and a few new porcelain ones, too). Parlor coal stoves were in the main
rooms, since the buildings had no central heating. Gaslights lit the interiors.
Although Thomas Edison had been generating electricity from his plant on

Pearl Street for several years already, electrical room lighting was still a costly luxury.

Uptown at Forty-second Street, as night descended on the city, Dvořák paused on the bridge that crossed the track to the branch road for the Central Depot and gazed up and down, north and south along the elevated lines, marveling in amazement. He had never seen freight yards like this:

> The sheen of the electrics mixing with the reddish points and blots of gas far and near . . . the coming and going of the trains marking the stations with vivider or fainter plumes of flame-shot steam . . . the great night trains lying on the tracks dim under the rain of gas-lights that starred without dispersing the vast darkness of the place.[11]

Impatient to get closer to the great locomotives he loved so much, Dvořák and his secretary, Kovařík, took the El on the hour's trip all the way north to 155th Street. They waited on the bank overlooking the comings and goings of the Chicago and Boston expresses. Unfortunately, to Dvořák's bitter disappointment, they could get no closer.

There were other days when Dvořák—with companions like James Huneker—felt especially adventurous. In their rambles south, down toward the Lower East Side, they felt an edgy excitement. Here was an area densely populated by Eastern European and Russian Jews. For more than a decade they had been thronging to the area bounded by East Houston on the north, Broadway to the west, and Worth and Catherine streets on the south. By 1892, fully seventy-five percent of the Eastern European Jews who had come to America were settled here. The population density was over seven hundred inhabitants per acre—more crowded than Bombay. One block contained thirty-nine tenement buildings, 2,781 people, and only 264 toilets. The streets were crammed with horsecars, kids, shoppers, and peddlers with their pushcarts. Peddling was a major industry along Hester, Ludlow, and Orchard streets. The "sweatshops" were everywhere, where immigrants earned four dollars for a six-day work week.

Innumerable cafes and restaurants greeted him with their bold signs proclaiming every variety of culinary fare: "REGULAR DINNER TWENTY CENTS" competed with advertisements for the new "Spaghetti Joints," whose machines, imported from Staten Island, threatened to replace the tradition of handmade spaghetti. And there was the new rage, the hot dog. Other current novelties delighted him—coin-operated phonograph parlors with the

The Lower East Side, ca. 1892, had some of the city's most crowded tenement districts; it was the target of exposés in the 1890s by Parkhurst, Riis, and Roosevelt.

newest cylinders (flat discs were still five years away), viewing machines for that new wonder of the age, "moving pictures," and the telephone pay stations located inside every tobacconist's shop. The newsboys were everywhere, too, hawking editions of the *New York Times,* Joseph Pulitzer's anti-Tammany *World,* and Charles A. Dana's pro-Tammany *Sun.* The bookstalls were crowded with photogravure magazines such as *Harper's Weekly, Century,* and *Scribner's,* with the new "half-tone" methods of reproducing photographs, and the ever-popular dime novels about "Buffalo Bill," "Young Wild West," and modern-day detective Nick Carter. Of particular interest was a book of stories about the sensational new detective Sherlock Holmes.

The air rang with the *clap* of the iron-shod horses' hooves, the clattering wheels of the horsecars that moved crosstown, the jingling bells of the new electrically powered streetcars, and the street cries of the merchants and beggars. The slang was singular: "Aw, gee, missed it!" "Wotcher lose?" "Gimme a swipe!" He heard Yiddish, of course, and Italian around Mulberry Street, Ukrainian near St. Mark's Place east of Greenwich Village, the black vernacular just beyond the Tenderloin between Broadway and Seventh Avenue from Twenty-third Street to Forty-second, Chinese in the Chatham Square area below Canal Street, and German east of the Bowery and Third Avenue.

Suddenly, a horse-drawn fire patrol wagon appeared, all red trim and polished brass. Men in rubber coats and helmets clung to the rear. Instantly, the crowd scattered and converged again as the wagon sharply careened around a corner and disappeared.

There were more than eighty saloons and barrooms in the fourteen-block stretch along Bowery Street, beginning below Canal Street and ending at Sixth. The Bock Beer signs were plastered all over establishments with colorful names, like "Sammy's Bowery Follies," McGurk's "Suicide Hall," and Harry Johnson's "Little Jumbo." As much as he enjoyed the beer, Dvořák was even more fascinated by the exotic, unfamiliar music, a veritable collage of diverse ethnic traditions. Typically, an orchestra of women dressed in yellow silk played from a little stage in the center of the main room. Customers pounded their glasses on the tables in rhythm to the new song hit, "The Bowery"—

> I was out to enjoy the sights,
> There was the Bow'ry ablaze with lights;
> I had one of the devill's own nights!
> I'll never go there anymore!

—and then a woman in short pink skirts arrived on stage and sang a Negro melody. This was followed by a sorrowful lay of motherly love. Then a tune about Ireland bursting her bonds. The finale, "The Star-Spangled Banner," drew enthusiastic applause, particularly from the foreign-born laborers.

Strolling by outside were a group of young Irish toughs, the fabled Bowery B'hoys. They sported dyed moustaches and close-cropped hair (except for the temple locks, which grew long and were carefully oiled); they wore tight trousers, polished boots, silk hats, and black silk scarves. They had a language and poetry all their own. One fellow might look skyward, past the snarl of telegraph and telephone wires, and exclaim to his Bowery Girl in rapture, "Deh moon looks like hell, don't it?" Doubtless these rascals appreciatively eyed Dvořák's homburg, noted his sturdy figure, and offered him a personal tour of the area for a dollar.

Over on the West Side the streets really came to life in the evenings. Between Seventh and Fifth avenues, from Twenty-fourth Street almost to Forty-second, lay one of New York's most notorious sectors, the Tenderloin. Dubbed "Satan's Circus," it was a vivid and noisy confusion of flashy dance halls, theaters, and cafes. Some of the "amusements" included "waiter girls" in the so-called concert saloons who wore nothing but makeup and who would perform private auditions for their gentlemen of something euphemistically called a French Circus. Anyone frequenting the brothels was in danger of losing his wallet and his life and having his body stuffed in a furnace somewhere. But for twenty-five cents Dvořák could find the best dance music in town at halls like the Haymarket, the Sans Souci, and the Egyptian.

Of particular interest was an area along West Twenty-eighth Street that in a few years would be dubbed "Tin Pan Alley." America was hungry for music. Pianos, pump organs, pianolas, guitars, mandolins, and banjos were being mass produced and becoming a fixture in every middle-class home. The big publishers like Harms and Witmark were springing up and cranking out thousands of new songs; and everywhere along these streets Dvořák could hear song-pluggers hawking the new tunes. There was no rag-time yet, and jazz was several decades away, but he was moved by the Stephen Foster songs and the sentimental ballads like "Always Take a Moth-er's Advice" by the redoubtable Willis Woodward; and he was especially intrigued and delighted at the lively syncopations of the new musical craze, the "coon" songs. When he heard unauthorized versions of Gilbert and Sulli-van music, he understood why the rights of foreign composers and their publishers had to be protected. Just a year before his arrival, the work of composers outside America could be published here royalty-free. The Inter-national Copyright Law of 1891 was beginning to change all that, and in a couple of decades the newly formed Manuscript Society, under the guidance of his friend Victor Herbert, would become the powerful American Society of Composers, Authors, and Publishers (ASCAP).[12]

No matter where he went Dvořák felt an irrepressible energy, a brashness—that "American push," as he described it. "The enthusiasm of most Americans for all things new is apparently without limit. . . . Nothing better pleases the average American, especially the American youth, than to be able to say that this or that building, this or that new patent appliance, is the finest or the grandest in the world. . . . They are unwilling to stop at any-thing."[13]

Beneath the brittle gaiety and frenzied vitality of the New York streets, how-ever, lurked a different reality—a sordid, troubling underside. When Dvořák first walked north along Mulberry Street, site of the city's worst crime rate, the four-story tenement houses with their dull-paned, sightless windows crowded together, closing like grim lips against the light. This was a notori-ous area known as Five Points—so called because it marked the intersection of five streets at Chatham Square. Here, in conditions that Charles Dickens years before had described as "all that is loathsome, drooping, and decayed," lived Protestant Irish, Italians, and blacks. Yellow dust arose from the cob-bles. Long streamers of garments fluttered from the fire escapes. Buckets, brooms, rags, and bottles were scattered everywhere. Unkempt old women gossiped from the railings and stoops and dully watched the visitors who came to the abortionists' rooms back in the narrow alleys. Gangs roamed here—the Dead Rabbits and the Plug Uglies. They were vicious and boldly flaunted their contempt of the police. Garbage collectors, called ash men, trundled their iron wagons down the streets. They wore great red-patched woolen gloves and swaddled their heads with flannel shawls knotted under their chins. Rough coffee sackings were tied around their waists. Their trousers and vests were several layers thick. Slowly, all day long, they sifted through the tin cans, paper, and bits of slop and offal.

All of it overwhelmed his senses. It appalled him and it fascinated him. He felt like a character in one of Stephen Crane's stories—

> He had begun to look at the great world revolving near to his nose.
> He had a vast curiosity concerning this city in whose complexities he
> was buried. It was an impenetrable mystery, this city.[14]

He paused for soundings. He took his own emotional and spiritual pulse. Was all this just a "lawless, godless" chaos, an "absence of intelligent comprehensive purpose in the huge disorder"?[15]   Indeed, he thought, "there are things here which one must admire and others which I would rather not see, but what can you do, everywhere there is something."[16]

Perhaps it was in the late evening hours of 21 October, long after the excitement of the Music Hall concert held in his honor had died down, that he walked, stunned, toward the East River. This had been another one of those evenings, like the concert held for him earlier on the 9th, where everybody hailed him as the "savior" of American music.[17] He had even been presented a silver wreath to the tumultuous applause of the audience. This particular evening there had been a grandiose oration delivered by Colonel Thomas Wentworth Higginson, founder of the Boston Symphony. He had compared the discovery of the New World four hundred years ago to the promise Dvořák now represented as the discoverer of a *new American music.* Dvořák shivered in the late night mists. Suddenly he felt inadequate to the expectations heaped upon him. What was he doing here? How could he be this "saviour of music" everyone claimed him to be?

The lights of Brooklyn twinkled muzzily 'way off in the booming distance. The steaming tugs came up the river hauling great freight barges. He scowled and regarded the ash of his cigar. He usually liked to come here and watch the great ships. Sometimes he went aboard and chatted with the passengers and ship's masters. But tonight the air was only damp and cold, and the moaning monsters out there in the dark sounded sad and lost. Tonight he felt devoured by this great hollow darkness. He felt an intense longing for Bohemia, for the rest of his children . . . so far away. . . . He shrugged finally and turned away. It was late. Time to go home.

Dvořák was only one of many interested and curious observers who wandered the teeming streets of New York, Philadelphia, and Boston in the fall of 1892. Some of them protested the growing urban squalor. Jacob Riis was a Dutch immigrant who guided young Teddy Roosevelt, then an assemblyman, through the Lower East Side, Five Points, and Hell's Kitchen. With his camera and pen, Riis was documenting slum conditions, the baby farms, the street gangs, and the exploitation of child labor. His illustrated book, *How the Other Half Lives* (1890) had created a sensation.[18] The Reverend Dr. Parkhurst, a mild-mannered leader of the Madison Square Presbyterian Church, was attacking the corrupt power figures in the city—including Mayor Hugh J. Grant and Tammany Hall chief Richard Croker. That "lying, perjured, rum-soaked and libidinous lot," accused Parkhurst, was protecting the lawbreakers, not prosecuting them.[19]

Others were content with recording the rough, strange, and hitherto unsuspected beauty they found in the prosaic details of city life. Journalist Stephen Crane roamed the Bowery, startling the readers of the *Tribune* and the *Press* with his unusually direct and uncompromising street sketches.[20] Photographer Alfred Stieglitz, a native of Hoboken, had just returned to New York after nine years in Germany studying photography. With his tripod and camera he took to the streets, capturing fugitive moments in the lives of the horsecar drivers and the rag pickers. "I loathed the dirty streets, yet I was fascinated," he wrote. "There was a reality about them lacking in the artificial world in which I found myself."[21] Playwright James A. Herne, meanwhile, was busily revolutionizing the American drama. In association with Hamlin Garland and William Dean Howells, he had just scandalized audiences in Boston and New York with his play, *Margaret Fleming*. Here was something new on the American stage, an unusually frank indictment of society's repressive double standards toward women.[22]

In nearby Philadelphia a number of young painters and newspaper illustrators, some of them just returned from study in Europe, were also fascinated by the urban sprawl of the streets. Rejecting the staid and conservative ideals of the Pennsylvania Academy, Robert Henri, John Sloan, George Luks, Everett Shinn, and others sought to capture what Henri called "a personal confession of life as he feels it." Within a few years all would relocate to

"The Terminal" (1892) by photographer Alfred Stieglitz. Horse-drawn omnibuses and carriages were still prevalent in Dvořák's time. (Courtesy Photography Collection, Spencer Museum, University of Kansas.)

New York where they would foment a revolution in "realist" painting.[23]

These were important responses to fundamental changes in American life in 1892. The official end of the American frontier, as proclaimed at this time by historian Frederick Jackson Turner, triggered a growing American ambivalence about Old-World traditions and inherited ways. Colliding with a new nostalgia was a sense of release from a now irrelevant past. While some Americans thought America should fall back upon itself and consolidate its gains, others argued a case for imperialism and territorial acquisition. Blacks were speaking out for "black nationalism," although they disagreed about what that meant. Booker T. Washington sought an integration into the American society. Bishop Turner, on the other hand, urged a wholesale emigration back to Africa.[24] While some Native Americans were coping with their enforced migration west and into the government reservations, others rebelled, leading to the massacre at Wounded Knee the year before. The Carnegies and Rockefellers were praised and damned as philanthropists and pirates. Every contradiction and excess had somehow grown *conspicuous*, as Thorstein Veblen was saying, especially the disparity between the nouveau riche in their brownstones and the poor in their tenements.[25]

Prevalent notions about societal evolution were being questioned. A challenge was being flung at the faces of those who called themselves "social Darwinists." They had applauded the new wealth and opulence. They thought the wealthy industrialists were where they were supposed to be, according to prevalent notions of evolutionary processes. Likewise, the poor and sick were in the slums where *they* were supposed to be. "If they are not sufficiently complete to live, they die; and it is best they should die," said Herbert Spencer and his American disciple John Fiske. According to this philosophy, social improvement, government intervention, and public education were "interferences" with natural processes. Andrew Carnegie, a disciple of Spencer, agreed that what was happening was a natural development of the Republic as it evolved from a pastoral to a civilized state. The problems that arose were only natural and should be accepted as the inevitable results of an evolving society.

By contrast, the "reform Darwinists," such as Lester Frank Ward, Jacob Riis, and the Populists, rejected these laissez-faire attitudes and advocated reform. Ward's major work *Dynamic Sociology* (1883) and Riis's *How the Other Half Lives* (1890) documented the conditions of poverty and excess and indicted them as the causes of crime and corruption. These truths, they said, can be tested by their consequences. The proof was in the streets: poverty bred only more poverty if allowed to go unchecked.[26]

This spirit was essentially pragmatic. Philosopher William James, who in 1892 was teaching at Harvard, held that the truth of a thing or an idea resides in that which grows out of it. Truth is valid inasmuch as it is *validated*; its verity is, in fact, a process of verifying itself. This view holds, therefore, that a truth is always tentative and provisional, in a state of flux, not absolute or final.[27]

In this respect the reformers and artists of Dvořák's New York were joined at the hip. They insisted on looking past what James called the "thin and noble abstractions" of the philosophers to observe and record the sheer sensory nature of the street. They waded into the large embrace of the real, what James called the "big blooming buzzing confusion" of the world. It was the only way, albeit a painful one, to discard the fixed and moribund social and artistic standards of the past. As Lewis Mumford later observed:

> The genteel standards that prevailed were worse than no standards at all: dead objects, dead techniques, dead forms of worship, cast a morbid shadow on every enterprise of the mind, making mind itself a sham, causing vitality to seem somehow shameful.[28]

If chaos and confusion were the alternatives, let them come. Looking back upon this age, Henry Adams flatly said, "Always and everywhere the Complex had been true and the contradiction had been certain. . . . In plain words, Chaos was the law of nature; Order was the dream of man."[29]

And what of Dvořák and music? In the streets of New York he was testing ideas that had long been percolating in his brain. The notion that a country's truest musical expression should derive from its diverse ethnic groups seemed never more incontrovertible than here in America. It was an idea as revolutionary as the goals of the painters, playwrights, photographers, and artists who were already exploring the immediate, prosaic realities of the streets. It forced one to value the black plantation spiritual, the Indian chant, the Hebrew song, and other expressions hitherto overlooked by the musical establishment. Music, like the other arts, had been held in the hegemony of hand-me-down European traditions. For the last thirty years the New England Conservatory in Boston, the musical paper *Dwight's Journal,* and the so-called Second New England School of composers (led by John Knowles Paine) had dictated that American music should find its examples and precepts in Central Europe, particularly Germany. This attitude discouraged any indigenous "American" musical expression. It was a discriminatory agenda only thinly veiled by a smoke screen of economics and tradition. A student's tuition at home and abroad was expensive, therefore available primarily to the wealthy and privileged classes. Enrollment policies of the academies and conservatories were selective in terms of race, social position, and gender. But what if you enabled students, regardless of their background and status, to explore and express their own cultural roots? This would be difficult under prevailing conditions—unless the federal government's laissez-faire attitude toward the arts could be confronted and changed. Dvořák was a pragmatist and an activist. Like Mrs. Thurber and her National Conservatory, he fought to mobilize the forces of federal and state governments in support of a new music movement here, as had been done in Prague. "Just as the State here provides for its poor industrial scholars and university students," he realized, "so should it help the would-be students of music and art. . . . If schools, art museums and libraries can be maintained at the public expense, why should not musical conservatories and playhouses? . . . Is it not in the interest of the State that this should be done?"[30]

He tilted his head to the side, listening intently to the noisy world around him. What if . . . , indeed. When he first came here he had felt it was inappropriate to comment on American institutions. After all, he was only a foreigner. Now he realized that they were all immigrants in this vast city, all of them citizens of a new home:

The germs for the best in music lie hidden among all the races that are commingled in this great country. The music of the people is like a rare and lovely flower growing amidst encroaching weeds. Thousands pass it while others trample it underfoot. The chances are that it will perish before it is seen by the one discriminating spirit who will prize it above all else."[31]

Here, at the curb, in the saloons and variety houses, overhead on the Els, down in the docks and train yards, through the plain inflections of a diverse population—in short, here, in the chaotic confusion of the new American street, Dvořák heard America singing.

SOURCES AND ACKNOWLEDGMENTS

Among the many books consulted for this composite portrait of New York in the fall of 1892 are Oliver E. Allen, *New York New York* (New York: Atheneum, 1990); Henry Collins Brown, *In the Golden Nineties* (Hastings on Hudson: Valentine's Manual, Inc., 1928); Susan Edmiston and Linda D. Cirino, *Literary New York* (Boston: Houghton Mifflin Company, 1976); Lewis A. Erenberg, *Steppin' Out: New York Nightlife and the Transformation of American Culture* (Westport CT: Greenwood Press); David Jasen, *Tin Pan Alley* (New York: Donald L. Fine, Inc., 1988); Jeff Kisseloff, *You Must Remember This: An Oral History of Manhattan from the 1890s to World War II* (New York: Harcourt Brace Jovanovich); New York City Landmarks Preservation Commission, *Stuyvesant Square Historic District Designation Report*, LP-0393 (New York, 1975); Richard O'Connor, *Hell's Kitchen* (Philadelphia and New York: J. B. Lippincott Company, 1958); and Otakar Šourek, ed. *Antonín Dvořák: Letters and Reminiscences*, trans. Roberta Finlayson Samsour (Prague: Artia, 1954). I am also indebted to Mr. Jack Taylor, Dvořák Designation Coordinator for the "Dvořák American Heritage Association" and member of the Stuyvesant Park Neighborhood Association. His editorial advice in the preparation of this article and his assistance in obtaining information about the environs of the Stuyvesant district is greatly appreciated.

NOTES

1. Dvořák letter to Dr. Emil Kozanek, 12 October 1892; in Otakar Šourek, ed., *Antonín Dvořák: Letters and Reminiscences*, 149.

2. Between 1879, when Theodore Thomas had conducted his Slavonic Dances, and Dvořák's arrival in 1892, at least thirty-six of Dvořák's compositions had

been performed in New York, Boston, and Chicago. The Slavonic Rhapsodies, the String Sextet, two Piano Trios, the D Major Piano Quartet, the Sixth Symphony, the *Scherzo capriccioso*, and the choral work *The Spectre's Bride* had all been greeted with enthusiasm. "No one can doubt," writes John Clapham, "that Dvořák's music had already struck a sensitive and sympathetic chord in the hearts of American music lovers; he had already won them over." See "Dvořák on the American Scene," *Nineteenth Century Music*, vol. 5, no. 1 (Summer 1981), 20.

3. Dvořák letter to Dr. Emil Kozanek, 12 October 1892; in Otakar Šourek, ed., *Antonín Dvořák: Letters and Reminiscences*, 152.

4. Dvořák to Mr. and Mrs. Hlavka, 27 November 1892; in Otakar Šourek, ed., *Antonín Dvořák: Letters and Reminiscences*, 153.

5. The land for Stuyvesant Square had been donated to the City of New York by Peter Gerard Stuyvesant in 1836. The Stuyvesant Park was created in 1846. After Stuyvesant's death in 1847, his heirs divided his land holdings and leased them for development in the 1850s. By the end of the decade Stuyvesant Square had become a fashionable residential neighborhood. Dvořák's home at No. 327 stood on a lot sold by Stuyvesant's niece, Catherine Ann Catlin, to one John S. Cocks in 1851. For a detailed history of this area, see NYLPC, *Stuyvesant Square Historic District Designation Report* (LP-0393); Schacter/Edelman Urban Research, report prepared for Stuyvesant Park Neighborhood Association, November 1989, copy in LPC research files; and M. Christine Boyer, *Manhattan Manners* (New York, 1985), 43–129.

6. Quoted in Joe Chiffriller, "The Life and Local Times of Antonín Dvořák," *Town & Village*, 15 December 1983, 16.

7. Dvořák to Dr. Emil Kozanek, 12 December 1892; in Otakar Šourek, ed., *Antonín Dvořák: Letters and Reminiscences*, 149.

8. William Dean Howells, *A Hazard of New Fortunes* (New York and London: Harper & Brothers Publishers, 1911), 67. The story of Basil March and his family moving to New York in 1890 to begin a publishing venture is semi-autobiographical. The Stuyvesant Square area is an important location in the novel. When the book appeared two years before Dvořák's arrival, it was widely acclaimed as one of the first "realistic" popular novels of life in New York City.

9. Theodore Dreiser, *Sister Carrie* (New York: The Heritage Press, 1939), 360. The rambles through the New York streets by the character Hurstwood are recounted with an almost documentary precision. They provide an invaluable view of city life in all its aspects in the 1890s.

10. William Dean Howells, *A Hazard of New Fortunes*, 83–84.

11. William Dean Howells, *A Hazard of New Fortunes*, 84.

12. For more information and statistics on the boom in songwriting, the proliferation of publishing houses, and the securing of copyright laws in 1891–92, see David A. Jasen, *Tin Pan Alley*, 6–8.

13. Antonín Dvořák, "Music in America," *Harper's New Monthly Magazine*, vol. 90, no. 537 (February 1895), 429.

14. Stephen Crane, *George's Mother*. In *"The Red Badge of Courage" and Selected Prose and Poetry* (New York: Holt, Rinehart and Winston, 1968), 222–223.

15. William Dean Howells, *A Hazard of New Fortunes*, 211.

16. Dvořák to Mr. and Mrs. Hlavka, 27 November 1892; in Otakar Šourek, ed., *Antonín Dvořák: Letters and Reminiscences*, 151.

17. Dvořák to Dr. Emil Kozanek, 12 October 1892; in Otakar Šourek, ed., *Antonín Dvořák: Letters and Reminiscences*, 150.

18. For Riis's own account of these activities, see Jacob A. Riis, *The Making of an American* (New York: The Macmillan Company, 1960, 170–231.

19. A colorful account of Parkhurst's adventures is included in Richard O'Connor, *Hell's Kitchen*, 99–115.

20. See especially the following works by Crane, in chronological order: "Travels in New York: The Broken-Down Van" (the New York *Tribune*, July 10, 1892), "When Everyone Is Panic-Stricken" (the New York *Press*, November 25, 1894), *Maggie: A Girl of the Streets* (1893), and *George's Mother* (1897). For an overview of Crane's New York years, see R. W. Stallman, *Stephen Crane* (New York: George Braziller, 1968), 44–128.

21. Quoted in Dorothy Norman, *Alfred Stieglitz: An American Seer* (New York: Random House, 1973), 36. Cited are the following photographs by Stieglitz: "The Terminal" (1893), "Winter—Fifth Avenue" (1893), and "The Rag Picker" (1893). For reproductions see William Innes Homer, *Alfred Stieglitz and the Photo-Secession* (Boston: Little, Brown and Company, 1983), 16–30. Stieglitz's formation of the so-called Photo-Secession group lay a decade in the future.

22. For a discussion of the controversy surrounding Herne's *Margaret Fleming* (1890), see Alice M. Robinson, "James A. Herne and His 'Theatre Libre' in Boston," *Players*, vol. 48, no. 5–6 (Summer 1973), 202–209. For Herne's own account, see James A. Herne, "Art for Truth's Sake in the Drama," *The Arena*, February 1896, 362–363.

23. By 1908 when they exhibited at the Macbeth Gallery in New York, these painters were dubbed, variously, the "Ash-Can School," "The Apostles of Ugliness," "The New York Art Anarchists," and the "City-Veritists." The best historical overview is in Bennard B. Perlman's *The Immortal Eight: American Painting from Eakins to the Armory Show, 1870–1913* (New York: Exposition Press, 1962).

    A fictional recreation of the work of these artists can be found in Theodore Dreiser's novel, *The Genius* (Cleveland and New York: The World Publishing Company, 1943). It was first published in 1915 but is set principally in the 1890s. For a discussion of the links between the novel and the artists, see Joseph J. Kwiat, "Dreiser's 'The Genius' and Everett Shinn, the 'Ash-can' Painter," *Modern Language Association Bulletin*, March 1952, 15–31.

24. A good discussion of this polarization among the blacks of the 1890s is found in Edwin S. Redkey, "Bishop Turner's African Dream," *The Journal of American History*, September 1967, 271–290.

25. See Thorstein Veblen, *The Theory of the Leisure Class* (New York: The New American Library, 1953).

26. For an especially lucid examination of the "Reform" and "Social" Darwinist philosophies in the late nineteenth century, see Paul F. Boller, *American Thought in Transition: The Impact of Evolutionary Naturalism, 1865–1900* (New York: University Press of America, 1981), 47–69.

27. James wrote about the nature of truth: "The truth of an idea is not a stagnant property inherent in it. Truth *happens* to an idea. It *becomes* true, is *made* true by events. Its verity *is* in fact an event, a process: the process namely of its verifying itself, its veri*fication*. Its validity is the process of its valid-*ation*." (Quoted in Paul F. Boller, *American Thought in Transition*, 140)

     For a discussion of the impact of James's pragmatism upon American art see Algis Mickunas, "Philosophical Pragmatism and American Narrative Film," *Wide Angle*, Spring 1976, 13–21.

28. Mumford is quoted in Waldo Frank, ed., America and Alfred Stieglitz: *A Collective Portrait* (New York: The Literary Guild, 1934).

29. Henry Adams, *The Education of Henry Adams* (Boston: Houghton Mifflin Company, 1961), 451–455. As a personal document of some of the main philosophical and scientific questions of the late nineteenth century, this book is, of course, indispensable. Adams also writes: "Man had translated himself into a new universe which had no common scale of measurement with the old. He had entered a supersensual world, in which he could measure nothing except by chance collisions of movements imperceptible to his sense, perhaps even imperceptible to his instruments, but perceptible to each other." (381–382)

30. Antonín Dvořák, "Music in America," *Harper's New Monthly Magazine*, 430–431

31. Antonín Dvořák, "Music in America," *Harper's New Monthly Magazine*, 433.

CHAPTER SIX

Dvořák at the National Conservatory

Emanuel Rubin

Although Antonín Dvořák's American adventure has been documented and discussed for almost a century, surprisingly little is known about the National Conservatory of Music of America, for which he served as director for almost three years. Since its opening in 1885, it had been the outstanding institution for professional musical preparation in the United States. At its height in the 1890s it boasted a faculty of international renown, including Dvořák, and initiated a course of study whose features became a basis for the curriculum now taken for granted in the colleges and conservatories of the United States. In recognition of its artistic and educational attainments, the National Conservatory won a Congressional Charter in 1891, the only such acknowledgment ever conferred on a school of the arts in America. As recently as 1955 it was praised by Victor Herbert's biographer, who wrote that it "boasted a truly brilliant faculty, offered comprehensive curricula, and proved itself a vital force in this country's musical development. To this day no institute of musical instruction can be said to have surpassed it in potentialities."[1]

The National Conservatory was supported by a wealthy, idealistic New Yorker named Mrs. Jeannette Meyer Thurber, who devoted most of her time and money to its activities. She has been described as "one of America's greatest music patrons, one of her great visionaries, one of her most imaginative cultural leaders."[2] Her coup in bringing Dvořák to America as its director can scarcely be overestimated. Later in her life, almost twenty years after Dvořák had come and gone, she reflected, "In looking back over my thirty-five years as president of the National Conservatory of America, there is nothing of which I am so proud as having been able to bring Dr. Dvořák to America."[3]

On her death, just short of her ninety-sixth birthday,[4] an editorial in the *New York Times* credited her with preparing a national climate for the advanced study of music and inspiring the emulation of her school and its high standards by other educational institutions.

However, Mrs. Thurber and her school have slipped into undeserved obscurity, overshadowed by the surge in post-secondary music education that followed World War I. Her personal papers and records have disappeared. All that remain are two scrapbooks of clippings apparently maintained by Mrs. Thurber herself, which are now in the New York Public Library (cf. n. 12), and an account book for the earliest years of the school that I found at the New York Historical Society among the papers of Richard Irvin, controller for both the Conservatory and the American Opera Company until 1898.

Our story properly begins with Jeannette Meyer. She was born in Delhi, New York, on 29 January 1850 and died at her daughter's home in Bronxville, New York, almost 96 years later, on 7 January 1946. The daughter of Henry Meyer, an enthusiastic amateur violinist who had immigrated from Copenhagen, and Annamarie Coffin Price, she was sent to the Paris Conservatory to study music while still in her teens. After her return she married the wealthy wholesale food merchant Francis Beattie Thurber, of New York, on 15 September 1869. Her husband, who matched her in idealism and shared her interests, provided financial backing for her enterprises. Not only did Mr. and Mrs. Thurber make separate personal contributions and loans to the National Conservatory, but Francis Thurber's firm, Thurber, Whyland & Co., was also a major donor.

She was strikingly beautiful, with a light, glowing complexion magnificently set off by dark hair and eyes. Pianist and writer James Gibbons Huneker, her secretary at one time, wrote many years later,

> She was a picturesque woman, Gallic in her "allures," but more Spanish than French in features. She spoke French like a Parisian, and after thirty years, I confess that her fine, dark eloquent eyes troubled my peace more than once.[5]

Her activities as a music patron would have earned attention for their impact on concert life in the United States even if she had not gone on to found the National Conservatory. In 1883 she underwrote Theodore Thomas's notable concerts for young people in New York City; and in 1884 she provided the city with its first Wagner festival.[6] She founded the American

Jeannette M. Thurber, founder of the National Conservatory of Music and creator of the American Opera Company. She was responsible for bringing Dvořák to New York. (Courtesy Onteora Club Library.)

Opera Company in 1885[7] specifically to give outstanding productions of the standard repertoire in good English translations at affordable prices. The troupe went on national tours in an attempt to bring the best in opera to every part of the country. In 1888–89 she sponsored the debut of the Boston Symphony Orchestra in New York.

Francis B. Thurber, Jeannette's husband, was an avid patron of the arts and supported her various projects, including the Conservatory. (Courtesy Onteora Club Library.)

In 1885 Jeannette Thurber persuaded Andrew Carnegie, William K. Vanderbilt, Joseph W. Drexel, and August Belmont to join with her in establishing a school of music modeled after the Paris Conservatory.

While studying in France she had been impressed by the French conservatory system, which provided musical education to talented students at government expense. As a result, when she founded the National Conservatory she insisted that any student with sufficient talent should be subsidized in the finest education possible. The National Conservatory was the first such institution in the United States to make a special mission of seeking out and encouraging women, minorities, and the handicapped, and it soon earned a reputation for being "specially successful in helping students of foreign birth and certain special classes, like the blind and those of negro blood."[8] Thus, neither race nor gender, both of which placed insurmountable hurdles before applicants at other conservatories, played a part in the selection of students at Mrs. Thurber's school. Black pupils made up a significant percentage of the Conservatory's student body at every level. The African American composers Will Marion Cook, Edward or Paul Bolin (sometimes spelled Bohlen),[9] and Maurice Arnold (Strothotte) were all students there, and the great black soprano Sissieretta Jones performed with the Conservatory's orchestra and chorus. At one of the school's orchestra concerts a critic noted in wonder, "The violins, especially, *among whom there is a sprinkling of girls,* covered themselves with credit" (emphasis added).[10] All this, it must be remembered, was at a time when women were not employed by respectable orchestras, and nonwhite musicians could gain neither recognition nor engagements in the concert world.

On 21 September 1885 Mrs. Thurber's group obtained a Certificate of Incorporation from the State of New York and chose the celebrated baritone Jacques Bouhy as Director at a lavish annual salary of $9,000.[11] Mrs. Thurber served as president and the eminent retired jurist William Gardner Choate as vice-president. The incorporators on the original petition constituted a select list of New York's most prominent industrialists and musicians: Mr. and Mrs. August Belmont, Mrs. William T. Blodgett, Andrew Carnegie, William G. Choate, Joseph W. Drexel, Parke Goodwin, William R. Grace, Mr. and Mrs. Richard Irvin, Jr., Henry G. Marquand, Jesse Seligman, Theodore Thomas, Mr. and Mrs. Francis B. Thurber, Mrs. T. W. Ward, and William K. Vanderbilt.

The institution opened its doors in the fall of 1885 with eighty-four pupils in two converted homes at 126–128 East Seventeenth Street, near Irving Place, in New York City. There was some initial confusion about the identity of the new institution because two different names were attached to it in quick succession. At first, it was called The American School of Opera, reflecting the school's earliest intent, the training of talented young people as apprentices for Mrs. Thurber's American Opera Company. The school operated under that name until it was legally changed by petition of Mrs. Thurber on 15 April 1886 in a flurry of activity to detach assets from the

This is the location, near the corner of East Seventeenth Street and Irving Place, where the National Conservatory resided during Dvořák's time. No trace of the original building survives. (Courtesy John C. Tibbetts.)

American Opera Company (which then was facing bankruptcy).

Mrs. Thurber's original idea of admitting students on the basis of talent alone relied on private funding. The plan fell victim to the vagaries of patronage and the realities of operational expenses, which combined to produce financial difficulties from the very beginning. Mrs. Thurber was reported to have donated $100,000 herself to get the project started.[12] Not all her supporters, unfortunately, were equally reliable in addressing those responsibilities, and the fiscal shortfall frequently had to be met from the pockets of the Thurbers themselves. Her report to the trustees during the second year of operation reminded them pointedly that they had an "honorable obligation" to cover the debt of $15–$20,000 "due to teachers only."[13]

Whether or not the school charged tuition is a question on which otherwise reliable sources are sometimes unclear. The 1920 American Supplement to *Grove's Dictionary of Music and Musicians* stated that tuition was free, while George Martin, in his book *The Damrosch Dynasty* (1983), wrote that the National Conservatory charged no tuition until 1915, "but it was frequently in financial difficulty."[14] As an advertisement in the *Musical Courier* of 1892 indicates, general tuition was not free, but was $100 per semester.[15] In fact, "free tuition" had from the beginning been intended for only the most talented and needy students in the "artist" course. For them, Mrs. Thurber developed what appears to have been an ingenious, self-perpetuating loan scheme by which a student's education could be funded, and within a few years that same student would begin to provide funds to continue and enlarge the scholarship program. Gifted students who could not afford to pay signed an agreement that read, in part:

> Students are bound, on the completion of their studies, to assist in carrying on the National Educational work of the Conservatory, by contributing, for a specified time in each case, one-fourth of all monies earned professionally by them over and above the sum of one thousand dollars per annum.[16]

The policy amounted to a "talent" or "service" scholarship with a repayment provision that would maintain the scholarship pool for other students yet to come. The reality, though, fell short of the intent. In the first place, the clause was not enforceable, because most students were minors at the time they entered into the contract. Secondly, many of those students were women or members of minority groups, and their earnings after graduation were very limited. Lastly, for most young women at that time marriage meant the end of a career and, consequently, the abrogation of ephemeral obligations such as this.

In November 1887, advertisements for the National Conservatory began appearing in the New York area, listing the following original faculty whose areas of specialization clearly reflect the school's original purpose as an opera training institute: Ilma di Murska (voice), Gertrude Griswold (voice), Frida Ashforth (voice), Christian Fritsch (voice), Ferdinand Q. Dulcken (repertoire, piano), F. F. Mackay (elocution), C. Bournemann (solfeggio), Alberto Francelli (solfeggio), Fred Rumpf (solfeggio), Mamert Bibeyran (stage deportment and choreography), Regio Senac (fencing), and Pietro Cianelli (Italian).

The following year, according to advertisements of 1888, the faculty was enlarged. Romualdo Sapio, new director of opera studies, had alternated with Luigi Arditi in conducting Adelina Patti's last performances in New York, and the critics had declared him the better of the two. W. V. Holt was employed as an expert in diction, and two additional teachers, Miss Eleanor Warner Everest[17] of Philadelphia and Madame Elena Corani, appeared on the voice faculty. There were still three teachers of solfeggio (Leila LaFetra, Johannes Wershinger, and Alberto Frencelli), but now separate dictation sessions were supervised from the piano by a Signor Pizzarello. Perhaps most significant was the addition of lecturer Henry T. Finck (music history) and instrumentalists Rafael Joseffy (piano), Adele Margulies (piano), Victor Herbert (cello), James G. Huneker (piano), Leopold Lichtenberg (violin), and Oscar Klein (piano, organ, and composition), which signaled a philosophical change toward a more comprehensive adacemic program.

The Conservatory was advertised aggressively. Its secretary, Charles Inslee Pardee, sent announcements to the newspapers trumpeting each new faculty acquisition. Mrs. Thurber's scrapbooks include the following letter of 23 September 1889, sent to editors throughout the New York area:

> Dear Sir:
>
> It may interest your musical readers to learn that the president of the National Conservatory of Music of America [Mrs. Thurber] who is now abroad, has secured the services of the eminent artist M. [Theophile] Manoury as Director of the Vocal Department. He will arrive in this country the 6th of October and will enter immediately upon his duties.
>
> He comes highly recommended by Ambroise Thomas, Gounod, Saint-Saens and Massenet. The latter writes a letter concerning his artistic career in Europe, a copy of which you will find enclosed, as also a summary of the principal roles in which he has distinguished himself.
>
> I would ask some kind mention of M. Manoury as you may think is merited by an institution established for the advancement of musical art and not for pecuniary profit.
>
> Yours very truly,
>
> Charles Inslee Pardee

The Conservatory's scope was truly national. As *Harper's Weekly* reported:

> It is the intention of Mrs. Thurber to follow the example of the [Paris] Conservatoire . . . in establishing branches of the National Conservatory, and tributary to it, in other large American cities. . . . These need not necessarily be newly founded schools, but of the already existing schools the best might be brought into connection with the National Conservatory, sending their advanced pupils to receive their "finishing touches" in the centre of American musical activity.[18]

Besides notices in national journals, like *Etude, Musical America, Musical Courier*, and so on, announcements and paid advertisements of the school's New York auditions appeared in local newspapers all across the country—not only in large metropolitan centers, but in many smaller cities as well.[19]

By 1890–91 more than forty personnel were on the faculty and the student body had increased proportionately, with 207 students registered in piano classes alone. The Conservatory claimed with some justification to be "the only musical institute in America in which the groundwork of a thorough musical education is laid, and its structure afterward carried to completion".[20]

> Among the few music schools in this country which really merit the name of conservatory, the National Conservatory of Music of America in New York deserves special attention because it was not organized as a money-making institution, but as a sort of musical high-school where pupils could prepare themselves for the career of concert, church, or opera singers, of solo or orchestral players, or of teachers, for a merely nominal sum, or if talented, without any charge for tuition. . . . The National Conservatory is not, however, intended solely for those who wish to devote themselves to music as a profession, but also for amateurs. Indeed, there are four special courses in the vocal department, among which students have their choice. . . .
>
> The *Concert* and *Oratorio Course* embraces Singing, Solfeggio, elocution, Italian and the History of Music, and Chorus.
> The *Artist's Course* embraces Singing, Solfeggio, Deportment, Opera, Repertory, Fencing, Italian, Elocution, and the History of Music, and Chorus.
> The *Amateur Course* has been established for the benefit of the many applicants desirous of profiting by the teaching of the Conservatory, without intending to utilize the same in view of any public career. The course includes Singing, Solfeggio, and Theory of Music, Italian, Elocution, and the History of Music, Deportment, Fencing, and Chorus. Similarly, the Piano, Organ and other instrumental classes have each a preparatory and an advanced course. . . . Church-choir singers who have passed through the [solfeggio] course will never thereafter experience any difficulty in singing at sight the most difficult harmonic parts of a sacred composition.
> There is also a solfeggio class for children.[21]

The forward-looking academic program of the National Conservatory played an important but little-acknowledged role in developing the profile of unified technical and humanities-oriented courses that came to typify later college-level music programs in this country. At that time history of music was most often taught, as is still the case in some other countries, in university courses separated from performances or theoretical studies, which take place at a specialized music conservatory. At the National Conservatory, though, Henry Theophilus Finck, music editor of the New York *Evening Post* from 1881 to 1924, began lecturing on music history in 1888 and continued to do so until his death in 1926. "The founder's cardinal precept," noted one laudatory writer, "is that general culture should go hand in hand with special training. There must be, insists Mrs. Thurber, a counterpoise to the severe technical drill of the classrooms."[22] Indeed, this has now become a basic premise of American music schools.

The introduction of solfeggio (sight singing and ear training) was another such innovation. In 1890 *Harper's Weekly* hailed the National Conservatory as the "first to introduce [solfeggio] into this country in 1885,"[23] an approach most certainly influenced by Mrs. Thurber's own experience at the Paris Conservatory. Frank Damrosch, who had surveyed the programs of leading European conservatories in planning the opening of the Institute of Musical Arts in 1905, also became an advocate of its inclusion in the curriculum, and in a 1912 article spoke forcefully about the need for such study with justifiable pride in his own institution's course, which had been instituted not too many years later.[24]

Other features of the National Conservatory curriculum now considered standard in American music schools included required piano study for all students, "for the reason that it gives a solid basis to one's harmonic knowledge," and a supervised "practice teaching" experience:

> Teachers are literally made and by beginning their duties in preparatory classes by a system of logical evolution, they become the masters of a singularly clear and inevitable method.[25]

As early as the Conservatory's third season, when over 220 students had passed through its doors, Jeannette Thurber submitted to Congress a plan for securing a federal endowment for the Conservatory. Had it been passed as submitted, it would have made the school truly a *national conservatory*, chartered and subsidized by the federal government. As it was, her proposal triggered a debate that has not yet been silenced. In a petition of 1888 addressed to the Senate and the House of Representatives, she asserted, "Among the arts the first rank is held by music." She noted the near-universal subsidization of that art in Europe and felt that a similar step was "inevitable" for this country. She argued that it must be taken at once:

> America has, so far, done nothing in a National way either to promote the musical education of its people or to develop any musical genius they possess, and that in this, she stands alone among the civilized nations of the world.

The crux of her proposal was to have a line item in the federal budget to fund the National Conservatory:

> It is in all respects desirable that your honorable body should include in the Appropriations Bills for the current year the sum of $200,000

to be used under the direction of the trustees of the said institution in extending its usefulness, and upon the condition that each Senator and Member of the House of Representatives shall have the privilege of nominating one pupil who, upon passing the requisite examination as to talent, shall be taught free of charge.

The petition was also disseminated to the public at large by means of a pamphlet. Her prose was sweeping, the arguments convincing, and the circumstances propitious: a large and embarrassing tax surplus existed and Congress was looking for a politically expeditious way to spend it. However, political support for her cause was weak, and the petition failed.[26]

Within a short time she rallied her forces for another attack. The ground was laid with a concert of American music in Washington on 26 March 1890. The program included music by John Knowles Paine, Dudley Buck, Frank Van der Stucken, and Arthur Weld. The following year, with a new administration in place, she mustered support from the political and legal communities as well as the worlds of finance and the arts and achieved partial victory in the form of a Congressional charter. While there was no grant of funds, the prestige alone was an enormous boost for the school's image.

Mrs. Thurber's new strategy revolved around an appeal to make the nation's capital the home of the National Conservatory. She included in the proposal a clause that read, "Said corporation is hereby empowered to found, establish and maintain a national conservatory of music within the District of Columbia."[27] The District of Columbia, which was then, even more than now, seen as a provincial outpost, could not help but be attracted by the idea of capturing an institution with the panache of the National Conservatory. The bill for the charter was first introduced into the Senate on 8 December 1890 by Randall Lee Gibson (D., Louisiana) as S 4557, and was brought to the House of Representatives on the same day by William H. Lee (D., Virginia).

The House referred it to the Library Committee, which passed it in turn to the Committee on the District of Columbia for study on 6 January 1891. Chairman John J. Hemphill (D., South Carolina) made a favorable report on the bill only three days later (Report no. 3402) and it was duly put on the calendar for action. Speaking on behalf of the bill, Representative Benton MacMillin told the House:

> Mrs. Thurber . . . is engaged in a noble exertion to advance music and art in this country and desired to make that exertion in this capital city. . . . I hope there will not be a single objection to its passing.[28]

There were few objections. The bill passed the House on 2 March 1891, and the Senate approved it the next day on the motion of James R. MacMillan (R., Vermont). There was an amendment by George F. Edmunds (R., Vermont) to the effect that "the power to amend or repeal this act is hereby reserved." President Harrison signed it into law later that same afternoon, 3 March 1891.

As might be imagined, passage of the bill was hailed by musicians and patrons of the art as a major step in raising the musical standards of the entire country. The prospect of moving the National Conservatory to Washington, though, seems to have lost its appeal almost immediately, if indeed it had ever been more than a ploy. There was not much sentiment in New York for giving away what appeared to be a valuable cultural asset to provincial Washington. The New York *Post*, for example, acclaimed the event as a cultural triumph, although it viewed the proposed relocation with a bit more reserve:

> On the same day that the International Copyright Bill was passed in the Senate, another bill of importance from an intellectual point of view was signed, incorporating the National Conservatory of Music. . . . [This is] the first instance of anything being done by the National Legislature on behalf of music. That the National Conservatory will not abuse this privilege may be hoped from the high character of its instructors. . . . Hereafter the National Conservatory in New York will be nominally only a branch of the central establishment at Washington, but in reality it will continue, for some time, at least, to be of more importance than the Washington school.[29]

Although the corporation was specifically empowered to "found, establish and maintain" a site in the District of Columbia, that never became a reality, despite introduction of another bill in 1894 to fix a location there. The Committee on the District of Columbia reported negatively on the proposed site, receiving suspiciously little opposition, or even attention, from the charter's sponsors. This particular plan never again received serious Congressional consideration.

Whatever else the charter of 1891 accomplished, it did not solve the continuing financial problems inherent in the very design of the Conservatory. There could be no attempt to raise money by the sale of shares or securities, as the Conservatory was a not-for-profit institution.[30] The financial burden of the school and its programs, then, fell almost entirely on incorporators and donors, especially on Mrs. Thurber and her husband. In addition to an original sum rumored to have been $100,000, Francis Thurber contributed $5,000 in 1885 and again in 1886, and the Conservatory's account books show several loans "to be repaid when in funds": one of $2,000 on 26 February and another on 2 April 1886. Mrs. Thurber obtained another such open-ended loan of $5,000 (2 April 1886) from Mr. L. Horton, which enabled the Conservatory to balance its books. But except for an initial $5,000 check from Andrew Carnegie, the books of those first years are silent about the other members of the board. Within a few years, however, the picture changed appreciably as the school's fame grew. Following the orchestral concert of American music in Washington, account books for May and June of 1890 show over $14,000 in gifts, mostly in checks for $100 or less.

Mrs. Thurber was well aware that the key to the school's quality and prestige lay in its faculty, and she herself made the principal appointments on the basis of prospective teachers' professional reputations rather than through open advertisements or auditions. Her own trips abroad were often invested in identifying and interviewing prospective teachers, and it was not uncommon for her to impress current faculty into that service as well, when they were on tour.

Her strong personality and idealism inspired them to feel individually responsible for the success of her endeavors. An example of that can be seen in an exchange of letters from December 1889, made public by Charles Inslee Pardee, dean and secretary of the Conservatory. Seven of the best-known members of the faculty submitted a letter with the proposal that, "[recognizing] how hard and successfully you are laboring to establish a United States Conservatory which shall be truly national in character," they would volunteer their services for a scholarship fund-raising concert. The offer was quickly accepted.[31] Normally, she included the faculty as allies rather than employees, and members of the staff were made to feel privileged to have been chosen for their post.

Some, for example, regarded Victor Herbert's faculty appointment in 1889 as "tacit recognition that he was the country's leading cellist."[32] Immediately upon joining the faculty, Herbert became one of the founders of the National Conservatory Trio Club, together with pianist Adele Margulies and violinist Leopold Lichtenberg. The Trio Club's first season was 1889–90. A typical concert seems to have featured the three performers as soloists and in various combinations as well as in the Trio.[33] When Herbert left the Trio in 1892, he was replaced by Leo Schulz, principal cellist of the New York Philharmonic from the 1899 to 1906. Schulz had been on the faculty since at least 1890, and the following year, according to one of Charles Inslee Pardee's ubiquitous press releases, "the celebrated violoncello virtuoso" Fritz Giese was added to round out the staff.[34]

Other faculty members included:

Ferdinand Q. Dulcken (piano)—English pianist who had studied with Mendelssohn and Moscheles.

Henry Theophilus Finck (music history)—Music critic for the *Nation* (1881–1924) and the *Evening Post* (from 1888). He was a Wagner-Liszt advocate and an influential writer on musical and historical subjects.

Rubin Goldmark (piano, harmony, chorus)—Nephew of the composer Karl Goldmark. His music once caused Dvořák to exclaim, "Now there are *two* Goldmarks!" He studied at the National Conservatory from 1891–93 and continued there as a faculty member. In 1924 he became head of the Composition Department at Juilliard.

James Gibbons Huneker (piano)—Pianist and well-known writer on music. He was music critic for a succession of New York papers from 1891 to 1921 and the author of entertaining and perceptive books about music and musicians. He taught piano at the Conservatory from 1888 to 1898.

Rafael Joseffy (piano)—Hungarian pianist, dubbed by Louis Elson "The Genius of the Piano." He had been a student of Moscheles and Tausig before coming to the United States in 1879. He taught at the Conservatory from 1888 to 1906.

Horatio Parker (organ)—Composer of the popular *Hora Novissima* (1893) which led to his appointment in 1894 as the Chair of the Music Department at Yale University.

Anton Seidl (opera conductor)—Conductor of German opera at the Metropolitan Opera since 1885. He became permanent conductor of the New York Philharmonic from 1891 until his death from ptomaine poisoning in 1898. Seidl conducted the premiere of Dvořák's "New World" Symphony on 16 December 1893.

Frank Van der Stucken (conductor)—Presenter of the Sunday Steinway Hall concerts in New York since 1885. He was conductor of the Cincinnati Orchestra at the time he was appointed to the Conservatory in April 1890. After the death of Anton Seidl he took over the New York Philharmonic.[35]

Jeannette Thurber's designee as Conservatory director in 1885 was the famous baritone Jacques Bouhy (1848–1929). Bouhy was a product of the conservatories of Liège and Paris and had established an outstanding international reputation on the opera stage. He was best known for creating the role of the fiery Escamillo in Bizet's *Carmen*, which had premiered only a decade earlier. Under his direction the curriculum for the first years of the Conservatory was dominated by solfeggio (required for instrumentalists and vocalists alike), voice training, and opera. To assist in carrying out those last two, he brought in the renowned soprano, Mme Emma Fursch-Madi, also a graduate of the Paris Conservatory. The opera department, as might be imagined, was very active under his leadership.

After Bouhy returned to Paris in 1889, there was a period of three years during which the school functioned without a nominal director. During that period, at the same time she was petitioning Congress for a national charter, Mrs. Thurber searched for a new director whose prestige would be irresistible on the floor of Congress. Her choice finally fell on the Bohemian composer Antonín Dvořák. "[She] wanted a big name for her National Conservatory and she was prepared to pay for it," asserted biographer Alec Robertson.[36]

A kind of folktale has grown up around this invitation. The story goes that Jan Sibelius was initially considered, but the envoy chosen to deliver the invitation, pianist Adele Margulies, preferred not to make the long trip north. Margulies had already planned to visit her parents in Vienna, however, which would make a trip to Prague no great inconvenience. So, because of her unwillingness to travel, preliminary negotiations were conducted with Dvořák.[37] While attractive, the story is probably apocryphal. Sibelius, who was only twenty-six years old and studying with Karl Goldmark at the time, is unlikely to have been seriously considered for such an important post. Dvořák, by contrast, was fifty years old and at the height of international acclaim.[38] On the other hand, there could be a kernel of truth in the story. Decisions were often made informally at the Conservatory, and it is not inconceivable that Margulies's travel plans factored in some way into the choice of Dvořák. Then, too, the exact role of Dvořák's English publisher, Alfred Littleton, still remains to be explored. He certainly played a role in the correspondence between Dvořák and Thurber. (See Graham Melville-Mason's essay, Chapter 4, on the Littleton/Dvořák connection.)

In any event, Mrs. Thurber cabled Dvořák in the late spring of 1891 and offered him $15,000 for each year of a two-year contract, with the added stipulation that he was to conduct ten concerts of his own works.[39] Dvořák, who had little inclination to travel to America, at first declined. Like so many other frustrations in her life, that only inspired Mrs. Thurber to renew her efforts. She besieged him with communications and emissaries from America. His trepidation and indecision during that summer are recounted by his biographers,[40] while Merton Aborn, in an unpublished dissertation, established the chronology of events and documents pertaining to Dvořák's correspondence with Mrs. Thurber via the publisher, Littleton.[41] Dvořák proved to be no match for the indefatigable Thurber, and when he inquired whether it might be possible to reduce the number of concerts he would have to conduct, she answered with a firm "no" and enclosed a complete contract for his signature.[42]

Dvořák arrived in New York on 27 September 1892 to become the second director of the National Conservatory. He brought his wife and two oldest children, leaving the other family members at home for the time being with his mother-in-law. During his three-year tenure, the school undoubtedly reached its apex. He developed a superb working relationship with Mrs. Thurber, who neither exceeded nor demanded in full the liberal terms of his contract. Although Dvořák was required to set aside one hour three times weekly for administrative meetings, for example, there is little evidence that this was exacted from him with any rigor. Mrs. Thurber also saw to it that "only the most talented students" were allowed into his composition class, as he had requested.

Mrs. Thurber's solicitude provided Dvořák with the resource most valuable to any composer: time to concentrate on his music. During the National Conservatory years he created some of his most important works. Of the dozen or so compositions that came out of this productive period, four should be mentioned here as having specifically American connections. The first year he completed work on *The American Flag*, Op. 102, an obligatory piece called for in his contract and written with his usual craftsmanship but apparently no special enthusiasm. (The libretto had not reached him in time to have the cantata prepared for his first appearance in New York in October of 1892.) In the second half of that same academic year, though, he completed what is probably his best-known work, the great E Minor Symphony (No. 9), which seems to have been written at the encouragement of Mrs. Thurber, who may also be credited with its subtitle, "From the New World." During an idyllic summer of 1893 in the predominantly Czech settlement of Spillville, Iowa, he completed two of his best-loved chamber works: the "American" String Quartet in F Major, Op. 96, and the beautifully lyric String Quintet in E-flat Major, Op. 97, which has moments of similarity with the E Minor Symphony. It was that same summer in Spillville, too, that he orchestrated the symphony. There should be no doubt that these works were deeply influenced by his experience on this side of the Atlantic. "I should never have written these works 'just so' if I hadn't seen America,"[43] he wrote to friends in Prague.

Anticipating that Dvořák's presence would attract a group of talented young composers and national attention to the school, Mrs. Thurber established in 1892 a $500 prize for "American" compositions. This was a feature of a projected Conservatory Orchestra concert in Washington in observance of the four hundredth anniversary of Columbus's voyage. Dvořák and a panel of seven judges, including Dudley Buck, John Knowles Paine, and Benjamin Johnson Lang, named several winners, including Henry Schoenefeld's *Rural Symphony*, Frederick Field Bullard's Suite for Strings, Horatio Parker's cantata *The Dream King and His Love*, and a piano concerto by Josuhua Phippen. In the next few years other winning compositions included George Whitefield Chadwick's Third Symphony and Marguerite Merington's opera libretto, *Daphne*.[44]

Dvořák expanded the Conservatory's composition department and acted as mentor to many young American musicians. His composition students included Laura Sedgewick Collins, William Arms Fisher, Edwin Franko Goldman, Rubin Goldmark, Harry Patterson Hopkins, Edward H. Kinney, Harvey Worthington Loomis, Harry Rowe Shelley, Maurice Arnold (Strothotte), Henry Waller, and Camille W. Zeckwer. He also influenced many other young Americans with whom he came into contact—Harry T. Burleigh (see the essay by Jean Snyder, Chapter 9), Will Marion Cook, who may have been in his composition class (see the essay by Dr. Adrienne Block, Chapter 11), Horatio Parker, and Alois Reiser, who studied with Dvořák after his return to Prague and subsequently came to America as a composer for motion pictures.

These students and colleagues in turn influenced American music for decades to come. Consider the example of Rubin Goldmark, a student who became a noted composer. As the head of the composition department at Juilliard from 1924 until his death in 1936, he counted among his students Henry Brant, Aaron Copland, Abram Chasins, Lehman Engel, and George Gershwin.

Dvořák met three days a week with his students for two hours, and twice a week he rehearsed the student orchestra, a post for which he was perhaps less well suited. Instead of the six—originally ten—concerts mentioned in his contract, he presented only one with Conservatory forces, and that one seems to have been a financial debacle. A memo from Mrs. Thurber says, in part, "[Dvořák] gave one concert, which was not a success financially. Fearing that he might not wish to return, it was decided to give up the other concerts."[45]

The concert was a powerful demonstration of the school's philosophy.

It took place at the Madison Square Garden Concert Hall on Tuesday evening, 23 January 1894, as a benefit for the New York *Herald's* Free Clothing Fund, to which it turned over $1,047 in net proceeds. Operatic soprano Sissieretta Jones (the "Black Patti") and black baritone Harry T. Burleigh were featured in Rossini's Stabat Mater with "the colored male choir of St. Phillip's Church under the direction of Edward H. Kinney, the organist and choirmaster of the church and a pupil in Dr. Dvořák's composition class." Also on the program was Dvořák's own arrangement of Stephen Foster's "Old Folks at Home" for soloists, chorus, and orchestra (see Deane Root's article, Chapter 18.)

"Long before the hour fixed for the opening the hall was filled with an immense throng," the *Herald* crowed. "It was a unique program. Each soloist, with one exception, belonged to the colored race. This idea was due to Mrs. Thurber." Dvořák was presented with a gold-mounted ebony baton. Black composer Maurice Arnold, another composition student, conducted the premiere of his own Plantation Dances, a work based on African American folk rhythms.[46]

What kind of teacher was Dvořák? Two of his students, Harry Rowe Shelley and Camille W. Zeckwer, have left fascinating portraits of life in the Conservatory with him.[47] Both attest to his fierce, almost intimidating presence. He made great demands upon them and refused to waste time on preliminaries, insisting that before coming to him they already possess a high degree of technical competence and compositional skill. "He stipulated the right of command," explained Shelley, "either to teach a pupil or to dismiss him because of the lack of talent in composition, saying, 'this heartache is only one: it will save you many, by-and-by.'" When auditioning for him, Zeckwer described his own trepidations:

> He glowered at me as if I were a bill collector, or a book agent, and, without a word of greeting, he commanded me to play my sonata. By this time my small reserve of courage had well-nigh completely oozed away, and I played in nervous desperation. I gained some small amusement by counting the bars as I played, to see how far I should get without being stopped or even bodily ejected.

Zeckwer was astonished when he was allowed to finish. Dvořák's "Jovian frown relaxed and gave way to expressions of mild approbation." So complete was the change that he offered him a scholarship and urged him to take up residence in New York in order to study with him daily.

The schedule was rigorous. He insisted upon continuous work and demanded a close acquaintance with the great masters. He declared American students lacked the proper respect for them. Students were made to work continuously, sometimes reworking their scores dozens of times along the example of Beethoven or Schumann. One pupil was kept at work for forty weeks on a particular thematic development until it was right. Yet if a student's music betrayed signs of overt imitation and borrowing, he flew into a rage of indignation. "YES, BUT IT IS NOT YOURS!" he would cry. "If you imitate any composer, you are a bad musician. Now go your own way." A particularly offending page drove him into a fury. He was known to throw the manuscript onto the floor and grind it under his heel, "punctuating the performance with grunts like unto those of a wild boar." But then his temper would evaporate and he would tenderly retrieve the papers and compliment some passage that had escaped the "devastating heel."

His opinions were absolute and final. He disdained the pedagogical treatises and followed his own instincts. He disliked fugues, for example. "Why bore your listeners by telling them the same thing over and over again?" he asked. "They should feel insulted!" Schubert was the great prophet, he would say. You could find the music of the future only by going back to Schubert.

When he shared his own music with the class, it was always an unforgettable experience. On some days he took pupils with him to rehearsals of his works; at other times, as Shelley recalls, he would play or sing his new themes to them in the class. Once he auditioned the newly written theme of the Largo of the "New World" Symphony and

> [sang] the immortal theme with great passion and fervor, his eyes bulging out; his blood purple red in the neck veins . . . his whole body vibrating as he played this music to his first listeners. . . .

It was not unusual, apparently, for him to get lost in his own composing and forget all about his Conservatory duties. Zeckwer remembers being told at the Conservatory one day that Dr. Dvořák was ill. Suspicious, he walked over to Dvořák's house where he found the composer busily working on his own music. "His only illness was a fever of composition," he wrote. "The remains of many past meals were strewn around the room, where he had been barricaded, probably for several days."

There is no question, in the final analysis, that this quirky, irascible, but essentially good-hearted man was an enduring example to his pupils. "No other teacher was ever such an inspiration to me," concluded Shelley. "He always seemed to me like a second father. . . . Simple as a child he was, but ever with a confidence in his own opinions that proved his unaffected consciousness of his own deep and rich authority."

As the end of his two-year contract drew near, financial pressures forced Mrs. Thurber to offer him less favorable terms for a renewal. Financial reverses in the Panic of 1893 had created both business and personal problems for her husband, Francis. To make matters worse, Congress, as we have seen, had not provided the expected budget; and other major contributors balked in the face of the bleak economic situation. Salary checks had appeared erratically during the second year, which created some friction between the composer and Mrs. Thurber. In short, the Conservatory could no longer afford the exorbitant salary of $15,000 offered for 1892–94. After his return from his summer vacation in Spillville, Omaha, and St. Paul, he learned that his contract for 1894–95 offered only $8,000.

Mrs. Thurber used all her powers of persuasion to get him to accept. She explained the nature of the school's difficulties and promised more dependable payments in the future. Dvořák capitulated, perhaps as much out of his regard for Thurber as anything else, and returned for a third year. It became clear, though, that growing dissatisfaction with the Conservatory's fiscal instability, coupled with Dvořák's increasing homesickness, made his departure inevitable. At the conclusion of the academic year 1894–95 Dvořák returned to Prague to accept the directorship of the Bohemian Conservatory of Music. Mrs. Thurber made several efforts to get him to return to New York, but without success. In 1897 she advertised that he would be returning for the 1897–98 academic year, and Aborn even reproduces a copy of a cable dated 25 August 1897 in which Dvořák advises Mrs. Thurber, "YES YOU CAN USE MY NAME AS DIRECTOR OF NATIONAL CONSERVATORY."[48] In fact, though, Dvořák never returned to America.

The National Conservatory continued to be a force in American music for another thirty-five years. After Dvořák's departure, there was no replacement director until Emil Paur's tenure, which began in 1898.[49] By then Mrs. Thurber could boast that "nearly 3,000 music students have received their sole tuition at the National Conservatory." Emil Paur was more skilled as a conductor than Dvořák, and consequently he produced far more polished performances with the students. The critics of both the New York *Post* and the *Daily Tribune* concurred. The *Post* described a concert on Wednesday, 22

February 1899:

> Last night's fourth concert of the National Conservatory was by far
> the best given by the pupils and teachers of that organization. . . . An
> audience filled every seat in Madison Square Garden. [They played]
> the prelude to Humperdinck's "Hansel & Gretel," [and the] Ballet
> Divertissement from Saint-Saens' "Henry VIII". . . . In the Humper-
> dinck one got the impression that a professional band was playing, so
> true was the intonation, so mellow the tone, so musicianly the
> phrasing. . . . In Handel's Largo Miss Emerson played the solo violin.
> Another pupil . . . Miss Ray Whitlock, played the first movement of the
> Schumann [Piano] Concerto with intelligence and good technique.[50]

Paur continued as director of the Conservatory until 1902 and later
became director of the Pittsburgh Symphony from 1904 to 1910. He was
succeeded by Vassily Safonov in 1906. Safonov had come to New York as a
guest conductor of the Philharmonic on 4 March 1904 and made such a
dazzling impression that he was asked to remain for three more years. He
headed the Conservatory until 1909. In 1913 Engelbert Humperdinck
accepted the directorship but was forced to renege when he could not obtain
a release from his duties in Berlin. After that date, no one can be identified as
director, and many daily management decisions must have been relegated to
Mrs. Thurber, who was nearing seventy years of age.

The address of the Conservatory, meanwhile, had changed several
times. In 1902 a program for a concert gives the address as 128 East Seventeenth Street, indicating that the other house was no longer part of the institution.[51] It was listed in the *Musical Blue Book* of 1919–20 as being at 126
West Seventy-ninth Street.[52] The *Blue Book* of 1921–22, however, has no
listing of a "National Conservatory," although the school appears under
Jeannette Thurber's name at 621 West Seventy-ninth Street. Unfortunately,
that was the last *Blue Book*. The Manhattan telephone directory for the winter
of 1929–30 provided the last known address, 53 West Seventy-fourth Street.

The decline of the Conservatory is difficult to trace, if not so hard to understand. After the turn of the century, the number and quality of competitor
institutions increased. The most important of these was the Institute of
Musical Arts of the City of New York, chartered on 27 June 1904, with
Frank Damrosch as director and Andrew Carnegie, one of Mrs. Thurber's
original backers, as a patron. Under Damrosch's imaginative guidance the
Institute received an award of $23 million from the Juilliard Foundation in
1923, when it was renamed the Juilliard School of Music. By that time, of

course, the most dedicated of the National Conservatory backers were well along in years. Some others who had joined Mrs. Thurber withdrew from philanthropic activity as they turned their businesses over to the next generation or pulled back when their own priorities changed.

It is strange that during these years the Conservatory's name occasionally disappears from public view. Elson's *National Music of America*, written in 1899, fails to mention it, and there is no reference to it in Waldo Selden Pratt's *History of Music* (1907).[53] Yet the school was still advertising nationally and enrolling hundreds of students. In 1918 the *New York Times* reported that a bill had entered the House of Representatives advocating the formation of *another* "National Conservatory."[54] The article, which was devoted principally to deprecating the current state of music teaching in America, nowhere mentions that a concurrent, or even recent National Conservatory of Music was already in place. Further, at the hearing of the bill on 17 June 1918 there was again no mention of Mrs. Thurber's National Conservatory. With a war in progress in Europe, the idea of a national conservatory was hardly a priority, apparently, and the bill died. Yet the "National Conservatory" file at the New York Public Library indicates that the school was very much alive—there is a brochure advertising its 1928–29 academic year. The tuition for advanced vocal and/or instrumental courses was set at $300. Adjusting for inflation in the intervening years, that was just slightly above par with the $100 tuition charge in 1892.

Articles favoring a federally funded conservatory continued to appear throughout the 1920s, omitting any reference to the fact that one already existed, de jure as well as de facto. Even the *Musical Courier*, which earlier had carried advertisements for Mrs. Thurber's institution, blandly contemplated in 1925 the need for such a new school.[55] The decade is full of confusing references to newly proposed national conservatories, as well as to the existing one, so that it is often difficult to tell what is intended by the term, "national conservatory."

The stock market crash of 1929 and the ensuing withdrawal of funds that afflicted so many private institutions at the time were the final death blows to Mrs. Thurber's Conservatory. No record of its operation exists after 1930. Continued agitation to create or re-create such a school, however, attests to the void created by its absence.

Characteristically, Mrs. Thurber never relinquished her dream of a federally funded conservatory. As late as January, 1939, at the age of eighty-eight, she wrote to Congressman James W. Wadsworth, representative of the thirty-ninth district of New York, with a plan to once again introduce legislation on behalf of a national conservatory. He advised against it. "Such an attempt," he wrote, "I am sure, would fail, and through such failure the prospect of its success some time in the future would be diminished."[56]

That future never came. The moment had passed when the government would consider funding a national conservatory.[57] Throughout the 1930s and 1940s, articles advocating the revival or new creation of such an institution occasionally appeared in music journals and the general press, but the growing community of American music schools had no interest in a federal centralization.[58] After the Second World War, as the country became entangled in its own fear of the Communist menace, anything that even implied "nationalization" or "federal funding" was doomed to failure. The last nail was driven into the coffin of the National Conservatory when it was declared officially defunct by the state of New York on 15 October 1952, under section fifty-seven of the Membership Corporations Law, for failure to file mandatory operational reports.[59]

A handful of loyal supporters continued to contact various officials during the 1950s in the hope of reviving the idea. As late as 1960 attorney William R. Bays, of the law firm of Choate, Mitchell, and Bays, made one more effort, hoping to interest Charles Garside, of the Ditson Fund of Columbia University. While the attempt bore no fruit, Bays's legal opinion of the status of the school at that time is interesting:

> I am a surviving member of the Board of Trustees and, as I understand it, would be in a position to appoint Associate Members to the board, which might include the persons who may, at this time, become interested in carrying out the purposes of the conservatory, not alone because of its name, but because of the power conferred by these two congressional enactments.[60]

But by then no one was left to take up the fight. The National Conservatory of Music of America is now forgotten by all but a handful of historians. The principals are all passed away and the records scattered and lost. It might seem a dead issue, but its impact on American music was considerable. Under Mrs. Thurber's leadership, it set the pace and standard for postsecondary music education in the United States; it established a curricular philosophy that still remains the infrastructure of every American music school; it assailed the barriers that kept minorities and women from advanced education and professional engagements in music; and it brought Antonín Dvořák to America.

NOTES

This material is based on an article by the present writer, "Jeannette Thurber and the National Conservatory of Music," *American Music*, vol. 8, no. 4 (Fall 1990), 294–325. It has been revised especially for this volume. Although her middle name has been usually cited as "Meyers," I am now persuaded that it is M-E-Y-E-R. In a recently discovered typescript account of her family background that she wrote herself, she omits the "*s*" from the name. The corrected spelling of "Meyer" now seems certain.

1. Edward N. Waters, *Victor Herbert, A Life in Music* (New York 1955), 53.

2. Edward N. Waters, *Victor Herbert, A Life in Music*, 52–53.

3. Jeannette M. Thurber, "Dvořák As I Knew Him," *Etude* (November 1919), 693.

4. "Friend of Music," *New York Times*, 12 January 1946, 14. In the *New Grove Dictionary of Music and Musicians*, 4, Emile Serposs gives the date of her death as 2 January 1946 (393); however, the New York Times editorial of 12 January 1946 gives the date as 7 January, and the obituary notice marks it as 8 January.

5. James Gibbons Huneker, *Steeplejack* (New York 1925), 65–66. Pictures of Mrs. Thurber appear in the *Cyclopedia of American Biography*, vol. D, plate facing p. 216; in the *American Art Journal*, Saturday, 4 January 1902; and in *The Illustrated American*, 4 August 1894, 133.

6. This constituted the first full-scale production of Wagner's major works as a series in the United States. Excepting the presentation of excerpts, the only prior Wagner opera presentations were Carl Bergmann's American premiere of *Tannhäuser* at the old Stadt Theatre in the Bowery, with the assistance of the Arion chorus, and A. Neuendorf's premiere of *Lohengrin* in 1870 at the same hall.

7. The first productions took place in the 1885–86 season, according to numerous newspaper reviews and Nicolas Slonimsky's "Plush Era in American Concert Life" in *One Hundred Years of Music in America* (New York, 1961), 109–127. Emile Serposs in the *New Grove Dictionary of Music and Musicians*, 4, is mistaken in writing that the first season was 1886–87. Some confusion may be attributed to the troupe's temporary new name, the National Opera Company, for 1886–87, when it undertook a second transcontinental tour.

8. Waldo Selden Pratt (ed), "National Conservatory," in *Grove's Dictionary of Music and Musicians*, 3d ed. (American Supplement, 1920), 6:306.

9. I am indebted to Ms. Josephine Harrold Love for bringing Edward Bolin's name to my attention, but he remains an elusive subject. There is no mention of him in any currently available biographical list, and checking with Dominique DeLerma at the Black Music center in Chicago produced no results; however, Thomas Riis, who has researched Dvořák's students, called my attention to the fact

that J. G. Huneker mentioned a "Paul Bolin" having been a piano student at the National Conservatory. As with Will Marion Cook, there is no conclusive evidence that this person studied composition with Dvořák.

10. "National Conservatory Concert," [New York] *Evening Post*, Wednesday, 22 February 1899.

11. Bouhy was paid in bimonthly installments of $1,500 beginning 6 February 1886, according to the Conservatory's account books, found among the papers of its treasurer, Richard Irvin, in the library of the New York Historical Society. By comparison, the average annual earnings of nonfarm workers in 1880 was about $588 (about $2.26 per day). Its equivalent today would be approximately $100,000 as calculated from figures given in the tables of "Series D and E" in *Historical Statistics of the United States Colonial Times to 1970* (Bureau of Census, 1975).

12. "Mrs. Thurber Talks: Gives Plans for Future," Boston *Daily Globe*, 11 Jan 1887. Clipping pasted into a scrapbook marked "National Conservatory of Music" in the New York Public Library. Several scrapbooks, probably kept by Mrs. Thurber herself, are in the New York Public Library filed under "National Conservatory of Music." These are referred to as the "Thurber scrapbooks."

13. Quoted in Merton Robert Aborn, *The Influence on American Musical Culture of Dvořák's Sojourn in America*, Indiana University unpublished Ph.D. dissertation, 1965, 70

14. Merton Robert Aborn, *The Influence on American Musical Culture of Dvořák's Sojourn in America*, 233.

15. As an exercise in relative economics, in 1892 coal was $3.94 a ton, bacon 11 cents a pound, eggs 22 cents a dozen, and sugar 44 cents a pound.

16. *The National Conservatory of Music*, 1887–88. Pamphlet in the New York Public Library "National Conservatory" file.

17. I am indebted to Wayne Shirley, editor of *American Music*, for pointing out that Miss Everest would later become well known as the composer Eleanor Everest Freer.

18. "The National Conservatory of Music of America," *Harper's Weekly*, vol. 34, no. 1773 (13 December 1890), 970.

19. Such publications included the *Crescent* (Corwith, Iowa), *Farmer's Advocate* (Malone, New York), *Weekly News* (Chester, New York), *Daily Patriot* (Concord, New Hampshire), *Brighton News* (Illinois), *Sibly County Independent* (Henderson, Minnesota), *Princeton Press* (New Jersey), *Herald* (Tonawanda, New York), *Osceola Gazette* (Kissimee, Florida), *Hokah Sun* (Minnesota Sun), *Hayes Company Times* (San Marcos, Texas), the *Esoteric* (Boston), the *Maple Leaf* (Albert, Alberta); and notices in some fifteen or twenty other cities, like Antioch, Illinois; Topeka, Kansas; Oakland, California; Chippewa Falls, Wisconsin; Toledo, Ohio; Meadville, Pennsylvania; and Hutchinson, Kansas. Copies of these advertisements have been carefully clipped and pasted into the Thurber scrapbooks in the New York Public Library.

20. Quoted from an advertisement printed on the back of the National Conservatory Trio Club program of 18 February 1890 in the "National Conservatory" file of the New York Public Library.

21. "The National Conservatory of Music of America," *Harper's Weekly*, vol. 34, no. 1773 (13 December 1890), 970.

22. Unsigned article in the *Musical Magazine and Musical Courier*, 4 July 1898, 117.

23. "The National Conservatory of Music of America," *Harper's Weekly*, vol. 34, no. 1773 (13 December 1890), 970.

24. Cf. "America's Growth in Music Schools," *Musical Leader*, vol. 24, no. 15, 24–25.

25. "The National Conservatory of Music of America," *Harper's Weekly*, vol. 34, no. 1773 (13 December 1890), 970.

26. It was also a question of bad timing. President Cleveland had opposed "pork-barrel" increases in government spending and only months before had specifically charged Congress not to use the tax surplus for new projects. Then, too, in 1888 everyone's attention was riveted on election politics. A heated contest was running between Benjamin Harrison and the incumbent Grover Cleveland, largely over tariffs and taxes.

27. *Congressional Record*, 51st Congress, Second Session (Washington, 1981), 3804. To trace the history and discussion of this bill more fully, see also: pp. 197, 234, 956, 1121, 2579, 3821, 3854, 3916.

28. Congressional Record, 51st Congress, Second Session, 3804.

29. New York *Post*, 18 March 1891. This article is cited at length in Edward N. Waters, *Victor Herbert, A Life in Music*, 54–55.

30. The *Fisher Manual of Valuable and Worthless Securities* (New York, 1957) has no record of any securities having been offered by the National Conservatory or the American School of Opera.

31. The exchange of letters is quoted in Edward N. Waters, 55–56. Faculty members signing the initial letter of 24 December 1889 were Rafael Joseffy, Theophile Manoury, Leopold Lichtenberg, Adele Margulies, Christian Fritsch, Jessie Pinney, and Victor Herbert. Mrs. Thurber's reply of acceptance is dated from Washington only one week later, 31 December 1899.

32. Edward N. Waters, *Victor Herbert, A Life in Music*, 55.

33. A program from the Trio Club's first season, dated Tuesday, 18 February 1890, illustrates this (New York Public Library, item MED):

    1. SONATA No. 2 for Violin and Piano (Op. 19) . . . . Rubinstein
                 Miss Adele Margulies and Mr. Leopold Lichtenberg

    2.a. "MEMOIRE" . . . . Popper
       b. MOMENT MUSICALE . . . . Schubert
       c. "AT THE SPRING" . . . . Davidoff
                            Mr. Victor Herbert

3.   Tarantelle "Venezia e Napoli"..........................Liszt
Miss Adele Margulies

4.a. Aria.......................................Bach-Wilhelm
  b. Mazourka ....Wieniawski
Mr. Leopold Lichtenberg

5.   Trio No. 2, F Major, Op. 72..........................Godard
Miss Adele Margulies and Messrs. Lichtenberg and Herbert

34. Cf. letter typed on National Conservatory letterhead in the Thurber scrapbooks:

New York, Nov. 1, 1893

My Dear Sir:

Will you kindly call the attention of your readers to the fact that the National Conservatory of Music has added to its faculty Fritz Giese, the celebrated violoncello virtuoso?

Yours very sincerely,
Charles Inslee Pardee

35. The faculty for 1893 were listed in the school's regular advertisement in the *Musical Courier* (which always appeared in the upper right-hand corner of page 3). There are, however, some discrepancies between that list and other information available. Mme Fursch-Madi is not listed, for example, though Pratt's American Supplement to the third edition of *Grove's* gives her tenure at the Conservatory as 1885–94. Neither is cellist Leo Schulz listed, though he was supposed to have replaced Victor Herbert before this date. Frank Van der Stucken, still formally conducting the Cincinnati orchestra at this time, is cited as the orchestra director, but Dvořák, of course, conducted the weekly rehearsals of the student orchestra during the period when he was there. Dvořák was also cited as nominal director of the chorus, although it appears that most of the rehearsal work was done by Rubin Goldmark. Finally, Henry W. Cannon is shown as treasurer, but the books continued to be maintained by Richard Irvin, who also signed the checks.

36. Alec Robertson, *Dvořák* (London, 1945), 60.

37. For two versions of this story see Alec Robertson; and Paul Stefan, *Anton Dvořák* (New York, 1941), 186.

38. There is an interesting sidelight to this which has an ironic twist. In the unlikely eventuality that Sibelius might have come to America, he would have had as a student Rubin Goldmark, the nephew of his own teacher.

39. This translates into about $175,000 per year in today's dollars.

40. The interested reader is referred to two biographies: Hans-Hubert Schonzeler, *Dvořák* (London, 1984), especially pp. 135–167; and John Clapham, *Dvořák* (London, 1979), chapters 7–9, 100-141.

41. Merton Aborn, *The Influence on American Musical Culture of Dvořák's Sojourn in America.*

42. A detailed account of those negotiations, together with Dvořák's letters to acquaintances expressing some of his misgivings, can be found in Merton Aborn, 52 ff.

43. Otakar Šourek, ed., *Antonín Dvořák: Letters and Reminiscences,* trans. Roberta Finlayson Samsour (New York: Da Capo Press, 1985), 167.

44. Chadwick was notified of his award in a telegram from Dvořák dated 12 April 1894.

45. Quoted in Merton Aborn, *The Influence on American Musical Culture of Dvořák's Sojourn in America,* 140. This undated memo, which Aborn places sometime around the middle or end of April 1894, must certainly refer to the January 1894 concert.

46. "Dvořák Leads for the Fund," New York *Herald,* 24 January 1894.

47. The recollections of student days by Harry Rowe Shelley and Camille W. Zeckwer are in "Dvořák as I Knew Him," the *Etude,* November 1919, 694 and 700.

48. See Merton Aborn, *The Influence on American Musical Culture of Dvořák's Sojourn in America,* 312.

49. Paur's appointment may have been made for the 1898–99 concert/academic year, although it is given as 1899 in *Grove's* American Supplement (1920). He was identified as orchestra director for at least one of the school's concerts in 1898–99; however, at the fourth concert on 22 February 1899, the critic of the *Daily Tribune* noted, "The audience was numerous, Conductor Emil Paur being an interested listener."

50. See note #47.

51. Another possibility, of course, is that the building at #126 was in use, but not listed as an external address because it did not house the offices.

52. This must be an erroneous transposition of the digits of the earlier address, since the 600 block of West Seventy-ninth Street would be located under the Hudson River.

53. Pratt's *History* was revised in 1927, and again it failed to mention the National Conservatory.

54. The *New York Times,* 18 September 1918 (sec. 6), p. 4, col. 1. The article cites it as HR 6443. Actually, it was HR 6445, introduced in October 1917 by Representative Bruckner of New York: "To establish a national conservatory of music and art for the education of advanced pupils in music and art in all its branches, vocal and instrumental, as well as painting, drawing and etching." Bruckner had retired, though, before the bill reached hearings. The principal sponsor of the bill became Jerome F. Donovan, also of New York City.

55. See Kenneth Bradley, "National Conservatory," *Musical Courier,* 10 February 1925, 56.

56. Correspondence of the author with the office of the Honorable Caroline K. Simon, Secretary of State, New York.

57. Nonetheless, Mrs. Thurber's forays into Congressional action precipitated use-

ful public debate over the appropriateness of a federally funded Conservatory in a capitalistic society. One of her supporters in this cause was Oscar Sonneck, head of the Music Division of the Library of Congress, who in 1904 was quoted to the effect that "such an institution [as] an outlet for thousands of home-trained musicians would become imperative—symphony orchestras and chamber music organizations would spring up everywhere by sheer force of economic necessity. . . ." ("Should Our Government Establish a National Conservatory of Music?" *Musical America*, 4 September 1904, 17)

Directors of private music schools and conservatories across the country did not find such a prospect attractive in the least. They were, in fact, appalled at the spectre of federally funded competition, resenting the downgrading of their schools to "feeder" status.

Of course, Dvořák supported Mrs. Thurber's view. In 1895, when he made some remarks in *Harper's New Monthly Magazine* in favor of a national conservatory with a federal subsidy, the New England Conservatory reacted heatedly. Claude M. Girardeau complained: "Indeed, we do not think that a single musical school in America is endowed in the way and to the extent that many in Europe are. Nor do we today think that state aid is the method best suited to the American nation." (Editorial, *New England Conservatory Quarterly*, May 1895, 90; quoted in Edward John Fitzpatrick, Jr., "The Music Conservatory in America," dissertation submitted to the Faculty of Fine and Applied Arts at Boston University, August 1916, 507.)

58. This discussion followed the rejection in the 1920s of several attempts to present bills in Congress regarding the federal subsidy of a Conservatory of Music—including HR 11243 (1923), HR 7011 and S 1320 (1924), HR 266 (1926), HR 7755 and S 1477 (1926), and HR 8894 and HR 12290 (1928).

59. See Note #54.

60. Letter dated 22 June 1960. Reproduced in Merton Aborn, *The Influence on American Musical Culture of Dvořák's Sojourn in America*, 318.

Dvořák's Spillville Summer
An American Pastoral

John C. Tibbetts

*E*arly in 1893 Antonín Dvořák was anticipating a return to Bohemia for the summer. However, when his secretary, J. J. Kovařík, proposed instead a trip across the American prairies to the town of Spillville, Iowa, the composer was intrigued. Kovařík had grown up there, and his father, Jan Josef, was the town's bandmaster and choirmaster. Dvořák would be among his Czech compatriots and hear his native tongue again. The name "Spillville," Kovařík explained, was derived from its founder, Joseph Spielmann, a Bavarian, who built a mill on the Turkey River in 1854. The majority of its four hundred inhabitants were from Bohemia, from towns and villages like Cermna, Varvasov, Purkarec, Temelin, and Zverkovice. Furthermore, Dvořák could take advantage of the journey to visit other locations he was interested in—Omaha, Nebraska (whose newspaper editor was a former citizen of Bukovany); the World's Columbian Exposition in Chicago in August; St. Paul, Minnesota; and the fabled Niagara Falls.

At that time there were an estimated 300,000 Czechs living in the states of Illinois, Wisconsin, Minnesota, Iowa, and Nebraska. Most of them were working in the industrial centers of Chicago, Milwaukee, St. Paul, and to a lesser degree, Cleveland, Cedar Rapids, and Omaha. A smaller percentage were landowners in self-contained village communities like Spillville.

In their native land, generations of peasant families occupied the same home (*dům*) or farmstead (*hospodářství*) but remained only tenants under obligation to the lord or cleric who owned the land. In the late 1840s serf-

Joseph Spielman was the first settler and founder of Spillville, Iowa. (Courtesy Cyril Klimesh Collection.)

dom was abolished in Bohemia, and for the first time in two hundred years, the restrictions on travel and land ownership were lifted. The Austrian-controlled government, however, was in disarray, and poverty and unemployment among the peasants were severe. As historian Cyril M. Klimesh writes, "With such unsettled conditions, it did not take too much deliberation for some of the peasants to see the opportunity which lay across the seas and forsake the country which they loved but whose government they hated."[1] They knew through letters and newspapers that the American plains west of the Mississippi were being opened up to white settlement. Ironically, this was the result of government treaties that pushed the Native Americans farther westward. For the Czechs, at least, if not for the Native Americans, the time was right to seek new opportunities in America.

The state of Iowa was an especially attractive area. Originally a portion of the Louisiana Purchase of 1803, it had been included in, successively, the Indiana Territory, the Territory of Louisiana, the Territory of Missouri, the Territory of Michigan, and the Territory of Wisconsin before it achieved statehood in 1846. In 1854 Czech immigrants, lured by glowing tales of the Turkey River Country in northeast Winneshiek County, came overland by wagon train, crossed the Mississippi by mule-powered ferry, and reached Ft. Atkinson. By occupying their claims they qualified for "squatters rights,"

Dvořák's secretary, Josef Jan Kovařík, was a citizen of Spillville. (Courtesy Dvořák House, Spillville.)

allowing them to purchase the land at $1.25 per acre. By 1885 the census revealed that 888 Bohemians had settled in Winneshiek County.

Dvořák made his decision in mid-February 1893 to remain in America that summer and make the journey to Spillville. Whimsically, he referred to it as his "summer Vysoka." In a letter back home he enthused: "Everything is Czech. I shall be among my own folks and am looking forward to it very much. . . . How grand it will be. The priest has two pairs of ponies and we shall ride to Protivin, a little town near Spillville. Here in America there are names of towns and villages of all nations under the sun!!"[2]

With a draft of the "New World" Symphony score completed, he sent for his other four children, Anna, Magda, Otakar, and Zinda, their aunt Terezie Koutecka, and a maid. They arrived in New York on the ship *Havel* out of Bremen on 31 May 1893, and after a joyful three days of family reunion, the party of eleven ventured inland. They left in the early morning of Saturday, 3 June, with Kovařík shepherding everybody to the Pennsylvania Railroad Harbor Terminal in New Jersey. Dvořák was delighted to learn that they were taking the Chicago express, the very train he had seen speeding away from the city so many times during his trips up to 155th Street. After brief stops in Philadelphia and Harrisburg, they raced along the main range

Antonín Dvořák during his stay in Spillville, Iowa, in the summer of 1893. (Source unknown.)

of the Allegheny Mountains, where the terrain reminded Dvořák of the Böhmerwald and the Erzgebirge back home. From Pittsburgh there was a fast run across the level plains of northern Ohio and Indiana, through Lima and Fort Wayne to Chicago, where they stopped long enough to visit with Kovařík's brother. After making arrangements for him to join the group in Spillville later in the summer, they resumed the journey at nine o'clock that evening, taking eleven hours to cover the 250 miles to MacGregor, Iowa, on the banks of the upper Mississippi.

"The Master took an immense interest in everything on the journey," reported Kovařík. "I had constantly to explain what country we were passing through etc. The journey passed pleasantly, everything went smoothly, the train was up to time and the Master's interest kept growing."[3] For the final leg of the trip, they took a branch line inland to a hilly region called "Little Switzerland," spanning regions in Wisconsin, Iowa, and Minnesota. At Calmar, Iowa, they met Father Thomáš Bílý, the parish priest, Jan Kovařík (Josef's father), and a priest from the neighboring Czech settlement of Protivin. Kovařík junior remained at Calmar to take care of the luggage, while on the morning of 5 June, two buggies took the group the remaining five miles to Spillville. They settled into the top half of a two-story brick house owned by one Jacob Schmidt.

It is easy to imagine Dvořák rising at four o'clock the next morning, 6 June 1893, to a dawn full of birdsong. The recent winter months in New York had afforded him few opportunities to hear his beloved birds. But here, outside his second-floor window, there were robins and blue jays and cedar waxwings aplenty—and a strange red bird with black wings that had a peculiar, rapid little song. . . . One can see the composer in the half-light, quickly shrugging on his clothes and boots and stealing out of the house without waking his wife and children. With pipe and notebook, he strides along the main street bearing northward toward the edge of the town. The muzzy early-morning light turns the nearby Turkey River, a tributary of the upper Mississippi, into molten silver. This area, it is said, was once so full of wild turkeys and passenger pigeons you had only to fire your rifle out your cabin door to bring one down. But today, the composer is hunting only with his ears. . . . "Imagine," he wrote, "I was walking there in the wood along by the stream and after eight months I heard again the singing of birds! And here the birds are different from ours, they have much brighter colours and they sing differently, too. And now I am going to have breakfast and after breakfast I shall come again."[4]

After his walk that first day, Dvořák joined his family at St. Wenceslaus Church on the hill for seven o'clock morning mass. Unseen by the congregation, he seated himself at the organ in the loft and began playing the Czech hymn "*Bože, před tvou velobností*" (God, Before Thy Majesty). In the pews below, his family began singing. The rest of the congregation, according to Kovařík, turned their heads, startled. They were not accustomed to being disturbed at "silent mass." But past traditions can change, and every day thereafter Dvořák sat at the organ while the congregation sang. "The old women got used to the Master's 'disturbing them'," recalled Kovařík, "and began to sing too, which pleased the Master very much; things progressed so far, indeed, that after mass some granny or granddad ventured to address him: 'Mr. Dvořák, the singing was fine today,' and 'What will you be playing us tomorrow?'"[5]

Dvořák loved his walks down the hill from the church. He was especially moved by the odd little graveyard with its curious baroque cast-iron crosses covered with silver paint. There Joseph Spielman was buried. "He died four years ago," reported Dvořák. "And in the morning when I went to church, my way took me past his grave and strange thoughts always fill my mind at the sight of it as of the graves of many other Czech countrymen who sleep their last sleep here."[6]

View of Spillville with St. Wenceslaus Church in the distance at the extreme left, ca. 1900. (Courtesy Cyril Klimesh Collection.)

The St. Wenceslaus parish was one of only a handful of Czech-speaking parishes in the United States at the time of Dvořák's visit. Many of the American Czechs had had to abandon Catholicism in the later years of the nineteenth century because there were so few priests who could speak or understand their language. In Dvořák's day only a few Czech-speaking priests were left. When Spillville was granted a Czech parish of its own in 1859, a two-acre plot midway between the east and west reaches was selected for construction of a church. The project went on for most of the remaining years in the century. The bell tower was completed in 1869, and a magnificent clock with four faces was installed in the steeple sixteen years later. It was an amazing achievement—out of only seventy-two Czech families dispersed over a 144-square-mile area, perhaps no more than sixty active parishioners ever worked on the building at any given time. As Cyril Klimesh says in his history of the town, the citizens can be proud: "St. Wenceslaus stands as a monument of their determination, their devotion, and their success."[7]

It was a magical summer for Dvořák—filling his ears with a weird mix of Native American stamping rhythms and the sprightly kick of Czech dances. Unfamiliar birds sang overhead and faraway locomotives hooted at the distant horizons. Electrical storms, which always frightened him, stitched the sky with a violent needlepoint. The pungent aromas of fertile soil twitched the nostrils. There was the river at dawn, the early masses, work at the piano at home, games of *darda* after supper, and musical evenings with the Kovaříks. The villagers, who quickly accepted him as one of their own, helped him celebrate his fifty-second birthday on 8 September. And there were long conversations with the elder settlers at Joe Kapinos's or Casper Benesh's saloon. His new friends Mathias Bílý (from Sepekov), John Klimesh

Looking along Main Street toward St. Wenceslaus Church in the distance, Spillville, ca. 1900. (Courtesy Cyril Klimesh Collection.)

(from Zverkovice), and John Kovařík (from Vsetec) told him about their bitter and difficult beginnings, how many of the Czechs had suffered in the winter snows of Minnesota and Iowa and had had to dig tunnels in the frozen ground while they awaited the spring thaws. The old men proudly boasted that they had helped build the railway forty miles away.

Music was never long absent from this place. As Cyril Klimesh has reported,

> When the immigrants came to Spillville, they brought with them a great fondness of music and a tradition of choral singing and small orchestras. No special public gathering—social, religious or political, a wedding, funeral, church or state holiday, or even an ordinary Sunday afternoon event such as a glass ball and pigeon shoot—was complete without the *muzikanti* (musicians).[8]

On one occasion Dvořák played the organ for a Czech-American marriage; on another, for a funeral. The Kovařík family were the town's most prominent musicians. Nicknamed "Volynka" (after the locality in Bohemia where they had lived), J. J.'s father and uncle kept Czech musical traditions alive with their church choir and the public band and orchestra. So renowned were these organizations that their doings were reported in Bohemia in the Prague musical publication, *Dalibor.*

Immediately on his arrival Dvořák began composing, elated because, as he put it, he was "composing now, thank goodness, only for my own pleasure." He worked on the town's only piano, a dilapidated dinosaur that Joseph Kovařík referred to as "old, antediluvian, square cornered and yellowing."[9] If he needed to work out a harmony, there were Wenzil Kovařík's parlor organ across the street and Stephen Kruchek's reed organ next door. Within five days of his arrival, at 6 P.M. on 10 June 1893, Dvořák completed the sketch of his Quartet in F Major, Opus 96. "Thanks to the Lord God," he wrote that evening, "I am satisfied. It went very quickly." He intended to call it "Spillville," but later it was dubbed "American." Nonetheless, it reveals close associations with the village—including in the Scherzo a subsidiary idea purportedly based on the strange bird Dvořák heard in the nearby woods—a bird indigenous to the area called a scarlet tanager (see Alan Houtchens's essay, Chapter 16).

His "try-outs" of the work were held in the Kovařík home, where Dvořák played first violin.[10] One can imagine the scene as described by Kovařík, a musical evening in the warm, humming twilight as the instruments tuned up in competition with the cicadas:

> The whole family was mobilized for it. Dvořák played the first violin, my father the second, my sister the viola and I the cello. We went at it full steam. It wasn't easy, but we finally succeeded. . . . We felt it to be glorious to play Dvořák's chamber pieces, and he himself was able to hear them immediately after composing them. The whole family was delighted, even if it was a drudgery. Our house echoed with Dvořák's music.[11]

Between 26 June and 12 July he composed another chamber work, the Opus 97 String Quintet. Commentators disagree as to the extent it was influenced by the Native American music that Dvořák may have heard that summer. The Scherzo movement of the Opus 97 Quintet, for example, contains what to many listeners are distinctive Indian idioms—an underlying, monotonous "drum rhythm," for example, and a spare, simple melody tied to a downward scale. And there are some commentators who point to the many pentatonic scales in all the music Dvořák was writing at the time. In rebuttal, other scholars, such as John Clapham, insist that beyond some superficial correlations between Dvořák's music and certain idioms of the Iroquois and Algonquin there is no conclusive evidence of any significant cultural borrowing. (See the essays by John Clapham and Alan Houtchens, Chapters 9 and 15.)

The Indian frontier had been moving north and west. During the three decades before mid-century, the area of the future Winneshiek County had been in the hands of the Sioux, Sauk, Winnebago, and Fox. Recurring

During the first four decades of the 1800s, northeast Iowa was the hunting grounds for the Sioux and Fox tribes. (Courtesy Cyril Klimesh Collection.)

hostilities among the tribes led, in 1825 and 1830, to treaties sponsored by the federal government. Boundaries were established among the tribes, but the incursions of white settlers and the construction of Fort Atkinson (ostensibly to protect the Winnebago from hostile neighbors but actually to prepare the way for more white settlements) complicated the situation. Although a school was provided for them, the Indians gradually began to disperse. In June 1838, as a result of a treaty concluded in Washington, the remaining tribes were forced to emigrate from Iowa to Minnesota. Some loaded their lodges and possessions onto wagons and left the area under military escort. Others launched their dugout canoes on the Turkey River and paddled downstream to the Mississippi where they boarded a steamer for the rest of the journey. Thus the way was cleared for more white settlers who, like the Spielmans in 1850, benefited from the cultivated land that had been abandoned.

By Dvořák's time the Kickapoo, a part of the Algonquin linguistic group of tribes, had resided primarily in northeast Kansas and Oklahoma, but there may have been a few tribal remnants that reached the Iowa area. That could explain why the Native Americans who visited Spillville in July 1893—Big Moon, John Fox, and John Deer—have been identified by some observers as Kickapoo and Yankton Sioux.[12] At any rate, the troop set up tents for fourteen days in a field across the creek from Nockle's brewery, and Dvořák attended several "performances," which included tribal dances and healing ceremonies. In other words, these gentlemen were pitchmen selling herbal medicines. Klimesh writes:

> It is not known if Dvořák purchased any of the four types of "medicine" the Indians were selling. Their nostrums included a salve they claimed would cure anything from a wart to an ingrown toenail. But at one of the performances Anton [*sic*] did try the ointment for a slight headache; when the compound was rubbed on his forehead, he exclaimed: *"Pali to jako hrom"* (It burns like thunder)![13]

Some villagers say they saw his daughter, Otilka, walking evenings with Big Moon. Others claimed she took nocturnal strolls with Dvořák's secretary, Kovařík. Could any of these occurrences—if indeed they were true—have influenced Dvořák's departure in September?

If New York City had appealed to Dvořák's cosmopolitan tastes and sophistication, Spillville brought out contrasting qualities—his identity as a Bohemian villager and traditionalist. Here, thanks to his salary from Mrs. Thurber, he could lead an independent life, free from the congestion and the "American push" of the city streets. He did not have to consort with critics, reporters, bureaucrats, or other musicians. He suffered none of the "nerve fevers" he habitually complained of in Prague and New York. He was content at times to walk alone; at others to go fishing, play with the children, or just walk along the streams. If there were no locomotives or steamships immediately at hand, there was the great broad prairie country that exerted its own peculiar, unique effect on him. As time went on, however, as had happened in New York, he began to perceive a disturbing undercurrent to the American experience. In New York it was the desperation of poverty and the shame of corruption in the crush of the city streets. Here he felt something else entirely, and in an eloquent passage he described these disturbing sensations. It is worth quoting at length:

> It is very strange here. Few people and a great deal of empty space. A farmer's nearest neighbour is often 4 miles off, especially in the prairies (I call them the Sahara) [where] there are only endless acres of field and meadow and that is all you see. You don't meet a soul (here they only ride on horseback) and you are glad to see in the woods and meadows the huge herds of cattle which, summer and winter, are out at pasture in the broad fields. Men go to the woods and meadows

Dvořák conducted his music on 12 August 1893 ("Bohemian Day") at the World Columbian Exposition in Chicago. This is a view of the Court of Honor built in Jackson Park on Lake Michigan. (Courtesy Adrienne Block.)

The World Columbian Exposition, view of the Music Hall with the 60-foot-tall statue of the Republic on the right. (Courtesy Adrienne Block.)

where the cows graze to milk them. And so it is very "wild" here and sometimes very sad—sad to despair.[14]

Spillville was no arcadian pastoral. Perceptively, he knew this to be a different kind of space—not a picture on a wall sampler, something trim, tidy, benign, and enclosed but rather a boundless topography under an overwhelming sky, a crushing force that leveled the numberless immigrants of all nationalities. If the big cities compacted them into the crowded tenements, this land stretched and pulled them apart, dismembering them with its sometimes cruel indifference.

But, after all, the great world beyond the prairies still beckoned. There were side trips for Dvořák during the summer. Early in August he took his two eldest daughters, Otilie and Anna, on a week's trip to the World's Columbian Exposition Quadricentennial in Chicago. Dignitaries President Grover Cleveland and Chicago Mayor Carter Harrison had opened the Fair on 1 May, and it was nearing the end of its six-month run.

The contrast between the realities of Chicago and the sights of its Exposition was emblematic of what was wrong and what was right with America. Chicago itself was second only to New York in size and notoriety. The slum population was estimated at 162,000 citizens, and there was a saloon for every two hundred people. The Chicago River was polluted with thick grease, and the air was clouded by smoke from the overcrowded factories. Trains and streetcars clanged and screeched their way through inner-city mazes at all hours of the day and night.

Yet in nearby Jackson Park on Lake Michigan was a weird caricature of American dreams and American pretensions. The "White City" was a preposterous aggregate of palaces, canals, and gondolas that encased the Gilded Age with a coat of plaster. Along the midway the ethnic diversity Dvořák had noted in the crowded New York streets and the desolate midwestern plains was compressed into a microcosm, a sideshow of multicultural and ethnic mix. Persian, Japanese, and Indian bazaars rubbed shoulders with other exhibits—a Chinese village, a Hungarian Orpheum, a Lapland village, an African Dohamony village, and an Irish industrial village. Towering high over everything was the newest rage, a 264-foot-high Ferris wheel.

The arts were showcased in classical frames. The architectural shapes were copied from the arcade, the triumphal arch, the saucer dome, and the pediment. Statues and images of nudes were discreetly draped and covered. A sixty-foot-tall statue personified the Spirit of the Republic as a virginal,

The chief attraction along the World's Fair midway was the 264-foot-high Ferris wheel. (Courtesy Adrienne Block.)

monumentally idealized American Woman. (To be sure, women did have their own building, in which Susan B. Anthony and Jane Addams helped celebrate advances in their cultural and economic status.) On a less elevated level were the daily shows by entertainers as various as Lillian Russell, Scott Joplin, and Buffalo Bill with his Wild West Show. And showman Florenz Ziegfeld came to unveil the prototype for what would become, a decade later, his annual "Ziegfeld Follies."

Somewhere in the middle of this bizarre bazaar stood a bewildered and bedazzled Dvořák. After a warm welcome on 12 August by the eminent conductor Theodore Thomas and a delegation of local Czechs, he joined in the "Bohemian Day" celebrations by conducting his Eighth Symphony in Jackson Park to an audience of twelve thousand people. Earlier there was a huge procession wherein thirty thousand Czechs and Moravians marched the three miles from the downtown district to the fairgrounds. "The Exhibition itself is gigantic," he noted, "and to write of it would be a vain undertaking. It must be seen and seen very often, and still you do not really know anything, there is so much and everything so big, truly made in America."[15] Commentator Henry Adams was less impressed. "Since Noah's Ark," he wrote, "no such Babel of loose and ill-joined, such vague and ill-defined and unrelated thoughts and half-thoughts and experimental outcries . . . had ever ruffled the surface of the Lakes."[16]

At the beginning of September Dvořák left Spillville on another trip, this time to Omaha, Nebraska, where he was again received by another lavish (if less overwhelming) banquet and concert. His host was an old friend from Bohemia, Edward Rosewater, the proprietor of the *Omaha Bee*. Then, at the invitation of Father J. Rynda, whom Dvořák had met in Chicago, he went on to St. Paul, Minnesota, another city with a large Czech population. Rynda took him to see the Minnehaha Falls. So busy was Dvořák, he could not have known of the ominous events taking place in New York. In June the stock market had collapsed, precipitating the Panic of 1893. The Thurber grocery firm was in jeopardy and Dvořák's salary would be endangered. He had been paid only half the agreed-upon sum and the remaining seventy-five hundred dollars was not immediately forthcoming.

But that bad news was still in the future. For now, as the summer drew to an end, Dvořák was pleased about his Spillville adventure. "The three months spent here in Spillville will remain a happy memory for the rest of our lives," he said. "We enjoyed being here and were very happy though we found the three months of heat rather trying. It was made up to us, however, by being among our own people, our Czech countrymen, and that gave us great joy."[17]

Today, a hundred years later, the Winneshiek County area has become a tourist attraction for an estimated twenty-five thousand visitors every year. Spillville still numbers approximately four hundred citizens, while Decorah, the first Norwegian settlement beyond the Mississippi, is now the largest town in the area with a population of eighty-five hundred. It is the site of the Vesterheim Norwegian-American Museum, America's oldest and largest museum devoted to one immigrant ethnic group, and Luther College, a four-year liberal arts Lutheran institution. Nearby Burr Oak, Ft. Atkinson, and Calmar are homes to the Laura Ingalls Wilder Museum, the Atkinson State Preserve (site of the 1840 frontier outpost), and the historic railroad depot, respectively.

I have come to Spillville on assignment from *Classical* magazine and the *Christian Science Monitor* Radio Network to retrace Dvořák's footsteps through the region.[18] There have been plane delays from my home base in Kansas City to Chicago and more delays by prop shuttle to La Crosse, Wisconsin. After renting a car, I drive the remaining eighty-five miles in the dark. I had thought to accompany this leg of the trip with the cassette tapes of Dvořák's "American" music I had brought with me, but the rental agency had no cars with tape decks. On the radio are only broadcasts of baseball games. Nothing for it but to settle back with my own thoughts and follow the twin headlight beams that frame Highway 35. It is late at night when I arrive in Decorah, just thirteen miles northeast of Spillville.

Next morning a light, misting rain spatters the windshield as I get my first real look at the northeastern Iowa countryside. The terrain is quite hilly and the terraced meadows form graceful, curved patterns and stripes of deep green and pale yellow. The crops are primarily beans, corn, and hay. The silos are probably all filled by now. These days the third crop of hay is being cut and harvested. The bean harvest will have to wait until the first frost. Flecking the prairie grasses with vivid spots of red and yellow are goldenrod, milkweed, asters, sunflowers, and prairie roses. From a distance the blue-gray pasqueflowers look like prairie smoke. Rain spatters the windshield—

It's purely a fancy, of course, but somewhere I hear in my mind the vivid opening measures of the "American" Quartet, that vigorous, arching melody that rises like birds from the prairie grasses, . . .

—and along Highway 9 the morning mists roil up from the Mississippi tributaries and creeks. For miles at a time the milky-white streams flow and twinkle in the brightening light along one side of the highway. Towering limestone rock formations on the right pierce the tendrils of low-hanging clouds—

The second theme from the Largo of the "New World" shivers with the chill of the early frost. . . .

—then I make a sharp turn onto Highway 325 and sprint the last leg toward Spillville. The land is flattening and the rain is ending. "Vítáme Vás," reads the friendly sign rushing toward me—"We Welcome You"—

Stamping dances—from the Scherzo of the Opus 97 Quintet and the A Major Piano Suite—pound with the insistence of Indian tom-toms. . . .

—and passing quickly by are red barn roofs, neatly stacked piles of firewood, cows and horses on the raw green slopes. Harvest time is almost here. The beans, corn, and hay will soon swell the silos. Across the broad fields wails a distant train—

The trotting rhythms of the "American" Quartet's finale . . . steamboat whistles and train pistons blowing and clacking in a mesh of gears and wheels. . . .

Spillville is like a quilted fabric, a collage of contrasting colors, shapes, and textures stitched together. Stand at the venerable wooden dome of the Inwood Pavilion, a beautifully crafted structure that has been the site for weddings and festivals for generations, and you can just see through the trees

Spillville's Main Street in Dvořák's day. His house is visible in the distance, third house from the left. (Courtesy Cyril Klimesh Collection.)

another, more modern dome, the geodesic-dome dwelling of ex-mayor Ed Klimesh. You can walk from Cathy's Quik-Mart at one end of Main Street to the 130-year-old St. Wenceslaus's Church on the hill in just a few minutes, walking 150 years back in time in just a few strides. Midway down Main Street is the trim brick house where Dvořák and his family lived. The large sign posted on the front might confuse you at first, however. It proclaims: "Bílý Clocks." The Bílý brothers, Joseph and Frank, bought the structure early in this century, preserved the Dvořák rooms upstairs, and used the ground floor to house their world-famous collection of twenty hand-carved clocks. In all of America there surely is nothing like these intricately designed and fashioned clocks.

The brothers were farmers and carpenters, and in 1913 they began their winter hobby of clock-making. Joseph designed them and took charge of the joining of the woods they imported from all parts of the world. Frank did most of the carving. With homemade tools they constructed mechanisms of great sophistication, some of them nine feet high and featuring many moveable, individually carved figures and musical chimes. Each illustrates a theme of religious piety, patriotism, or local history. The Parade of Nations clock, for example, rotates against a globe of the world a series of thirty-six figures, each clothed in its native costume. The Apostles Clock, in

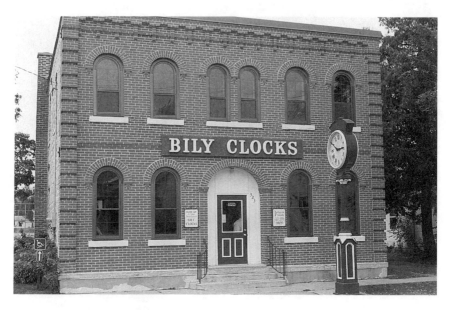

The Dvořák House as it looks today. The rooms occupy the upper story, and the Bílý Clocks are housed on the lower story. (Courtesy Cyril Klimesh Collection.)

Closer view of the façade of the Dvořák House. (Courtesy John C. Tibbetts.)

addition to the figures of the twelve disciples, displays at its base relief views of the Prague town hall and the Spillville church. The Hall Clock, carved in 1913, has imported Swiss chimes that accompany a display of carved figures representing the old Spillville village band. The Violin Clock, carved in 1948–49, commemorates Dvořák's visit. The face of the composer is inset into the base of a violin fashioned from hard maple wood. These industrious brothers arranged after their deaths that all the clocks would remain the property of Spillville, never to be broken up or dispersed.

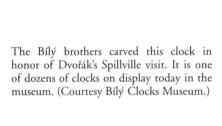

The Bílý brothers carved this clock in honor of Dvořák's Spillville visit. It is one of dozens of clocks on display today in the museum. (Courtesy Bílý Clocks Museum.)

The clocks create a mechanical web of sound that pervades the Dvořák rooms upstairs—a clockwork counterpoint of gongs, chimes, and clicking gears. For eighteen years Rosalind Proshusta has guided tourists through this ticking house, amiably explaining the local history and winding the clocks. Now, coming up the stairs to join me after showing some tourists through the collection, she admits that many more people come here for the clocks than out of interest in Dvořák. "But I always tell them about him and some go on up out of curiosity."[19]

Of course, she amends, there have been many Dvořák enthusiasts as well. Although Dvořák himself never returned, his son, Otakar, came back to reunite with the friends of his youth. Violinist Josef Suk, a descendant of Dvořák's son-in-law, has been here; and the eminent Czech pianist Rudolf Firkušný. Others, like me, have come armed with notebooks and tape recorders, searching for the same sights and sounds Dvořák looked for— radio broadcaster William Malloch of Los Angeles, noted Dvořák scholars like John Clapham, and novelists and poets like Joseph Škvorecký and Patricia Hampl. Would that we all had the same kind of magical shirt cuffs Dvořák used upon which to inscribe our own findings!

Meanwhile, Mrs. Proshusta begins her tour through the rooms. "This is a brick building with fourteen-inch walls and many windows," she gestures around her. "At the time Dvořák came here the window framing was all made of wood. But about ten years ago we changed it to steel frames. We're

Three photographs of Dvořák—from left, as a youth, a young man, and the mature composer. (Courtesy Dvořák House, Spillville.)

not sure which room was the kitchen, or the living room, or the bedroom. But he did have the upstairs for the family and the nanny. Mr. Kovařík stayed with his family." In one of the rooms she unlocks a glass case and proudly shows me an old book. "This is a postal ledger. Here is his signature in receipt of a package." The strokes of the pen dash boldly across the paper. In other rooms a number of display cases reveal a bewildering array of donated items from friends and guests—stones, buttons, clocks, wooden shoes, butter churns, an ancient phonograph, old flatirons, and a wooden cradle. This part of the house is a museum dedicated not so much to Dvořák as to the desiderata of centuries and of the Czechs who lived with or alongside him.

I pause at the doorway of a small room whose window faces out toward the street. Mellow sunlight splashes the walls and floor. Placed along one wall beneath a triptych of Dvořák portraits is a modest pedal–pump organ. Mrs. Proshusta explains it is a relic of Dvořák's stay; he played on it frequently. Unable to resist the temptation (and with an approving nod from my host) I seat myself before the keyboard. Someone has thoughtfully provided sheet music of the famous *Humoresque* (the one supposedly composed here). Pumping and playing is hard work—rather like rubbing the stomach and patting the head at the same time—and producing the wheezing notes

This small room in the Dvořák House contains the composer's pump organ. The music of the *Humoresque* No. 7 is kept on the console. (Courtesy John C. Tibbetts.)

Another view of Dvořák's pump organ in the Dvořák House. (Courtesy John C. Tibbetts.)

works up a sweat. Some aspects of music history are, perhaps, better left alone.

Later that afternoon, the westering sun at our backs, a local woman named Rebecca Neuzil guides me across some of the countryside Dvořák came to know so well. Rebecca is one of those civic volunteers every small community depends upon for a thousand chores, ranging from church work to fund-raising and festival-planning. She and her husband own a small farm several miles outside of Spillville. "This is where Dvořák used to go for morning walks and to listen for the birds," she explains as we leave the main road and pick our way through the dense underbrush toward the banks of the Turkey River. A racket of birds quickly envelops us. "I imagine that from where he lived, he went down in the morning and went to the tavern, got his little pail of beer, walked around the back of the tavern, up to the Turkey River, and along the river, and ended up at the park at the edge of town."

The Turkey River lies quietly, flanked by thickets and dense patches of trees that arch protectively over it. I try not to look beyond the tree line at the hulks of rusting cars and farm machinery in the distance. Somehow, they diminish the quiet poetry of the area.

I prefer to imagine Dvořák's figure silently standing here on this very spot, the scene limned in that stark light that only imagination can provide. His head is slightly cocked to one side, intently listening to something. He bends to his notebook. "An odd-looking bird," he writes hastily; "—red-plumaged; but the wings are black." He tries to whistle the notes he has just heard. He looks again and there it is—a small bird perched high in the trees above. The bird resembles a robin, but robins don't have that kind of red color. . . . He decides he must include this curious little song in the new string quartet he is writing. . . .[20]

Skirting the river is Riverside Park, a natural bower that contains a round stone monument erected in Dvořák's memory in 1925. A metal plaque bears the inscription:

IN COMMEMORATION OF THE VISIT

OF

ANTONÍN DVOŘÁK

RENOWNED COMPOSER

TO

SPILLVILLE IN 1893

THIS TABLET IS ERECTED BY

HIS FRIENDS

AND

THE IOWA CONSERVATION ASSOCIATION

1925

After a stroll through these peaceful, well-tended grounds, we head back for the main road and continue southward past the public square's charming bandstand, built at the end of World War I in honor of American soldiers and sailors. The names of the war dead on the shell are, by now, familiar—Kovařík, Barta, Sabelka, Balik. Then, on we go to the old Spiel-man Mill. (Actually, Spielman's mill, which was located on the banks of the creek just north of Ed Klimesh's dome house, no longer exists. The mill now standing on the Turkey was constructed by a trio of men from Decorah.) The broad stony shoulder of the road affords a view of the foamy river roaring below us. The current is quite strong. The mill still functions, although the wheel is gone. It is a lovely, quiet spot on a mild fall afternoon and a good time to catch up on some of the local legends about Dvořák.

The Turkey River looks today very much as it did in Dvořák's time. He walked along these banks, scribbling notes for works like the F Major Quartet. (Courtesy John C. Tibbetts.)

Everyone is gone now who had direct contact with the Dvořáks. But only thirty years ago you could still talk to Mrs. Anna Benda, who as a girl did the family's baking and cleaning. She remembered pausing to listen to the composer working on his music during her visits to the house with freshly baked rye bread. It was difficult to launder Dvořák's shirt cuffs, she claimed, because of his habit of scribbling notes on them. She and her husband, a cobbler, accepted Dvořák as "just another neighbor, kind and simple, for whom she did laundry for four dollars a week."

As recently as 1964 there were village elders alive who could recall their boyhood days during the Dvořák summer. When they drove the cows to pasture, cracking their willow whips, they saw the Master in the woods at work in his notebook. Frank Kapler and Joe Kohout had been thirteen-year-old youngsters then. Kapler could remember playing with the Dvořák children and pumping the church organ for the Master. Sometimes in the woods Dvořák would ask the boys to chase the birds from the trees and bushes in his direction so he could jot down their sounds. When they offered to take him fishing, he accepted only if they agreed to bait his hook for him. Upon reaching the river, however, he would hear a new bird sound, and fishing was promptly forgotten. There was a favorite place he liked to sit while making his notes—the stump of a great white oak tree that had been blasted by lightning. Other memories included the image of Big Moon fashioning

Spillville mill, ca. 1910. (Courtesy Cyril Klimesh Collection.)

The Spillville mill as it looks today. (Courtesy John C. Tibbetts.)

arrows that the Dvořák children took back to Bohemia with them; the unforgettable taste of the rye bread and beer that the kids would bring him at lunchtime; and the day Dvořák rushed to the river to watch a herd of cattle being driven across. Another time, the boys took Dvořák at his request to see a skunk. After uncovering a nest, they were all "baptized" by the stink— except for Dvořák, who ran away at top speed. In general, said Kapler, the "old man" was kindly and quiet, although he "didn't have a very good look."[21]

The afternoon sun is waning and there is just enough time to walk the short distance to the Sportsman's Bar. This is where Dvořák drew his pail. The original taproom has been converted into a dining area. Spillville had been "dry" in 1893, but it bootlegged its beer in from nearby Decorah. It is here, Rebecca admits, that folks still speculate about the reasons for the rather sudden departure of the Dvořák family for New York in September 1893. "Some of us think that Dvořák's daughter [Otilka] fell in love with one of the Indians who came here. He was named Big Moon. The old man was furious and yanked the family out of here!" I tell Rebecca that Cyril Klimesh has refuted that theory. She shrugs. The Big Moon story is old news around here. (See Josef Skvorecky's essay, Chapter 24.)

My nostalgic tour notwithstanding, there is a no-nonsense attitude in Spillville about its Czech past and, particularly, its most famous citizen. A television report several years ago on "CBS Sunday Morning" led you to believe that all of Spillville is spending its dotage either dancing in quaint Czech costumes or sighing in its beer over a vanished past.

"Oh, we learned those dances for the TV crew," laughs Rebecca Neuzil. It is the next morning and we are having breakfast at the Old World Inn.[22] "I love the dancing and the costumes and all of that, but there are probably a lot of Czechs here who don't speak or read the language anymore. My own children are Czech, but they don't speak it. We never taught 'em. Our mistake."

Beulah Sindelar comes out from the kitchen to join us. She's been hovering over the big cooking pots all morning long, presiding like a genial wizard over the wonderful aromas filling the place. "I think we take Dvořák with a grain of salt," she says. (As the former proprietor and present cook, sharing the responsibilities with Ellen Soukup and Lillian Karnik, she's an expert on seasoning!) She pauses while I dive appreciatively into a breakfast of *jaternice* (pronounced YI·TER·NITS'·CHUH) and *rohlický* and *kolache* pastries. With her husband, she and Juanita Loven opened the Old World Inn on 1 April 1987. They had always wanted to run a place serving authentic Czech food. The building had been built as a general store in 1871 and over the years has served the community as a pool hall, butcher shop, residence, and warehouse. Now it's a tidy, cozy place with a restaurant and four rooms upstairs (each with a private bath). The tables are covered with crisp red-and-white tablecloths, and imported Czech lace curtains frame the windows. Paintings and handiwork are on display, including an assortment of decorated eggs, rosemalings, and quilted fabric pieces. (At this writing the owner-ship of the place has been passed on to Ed Klimesh and his wife, Linda.)

"*Jaternice* is boiled pork, ground after it's boiled," Mrs. Sindelar is explaining. "Then you season it and add cooked pearl barley and then you form it into rings like a baloney. The *rohlický* is a crescent-shaped roll, usu-ally with poppy seed or sesame seed on it. The Czechs are great for seeds in everything. They make their kraut with caraway, you know. The *kolache* are cookies filled with prunes, apricots and cherries. And, of course, more poppy seeds! Mildred [Riehle] makes them and she sends them to customers all over the country."

Sitting around the table we talk about the importance of the Dvořák legacy to Spillville.

"It's like anything you live with," says Mrs. Sindelar. "You live next to the river, you take the river for granted. You don't pay a great deal of atten-tion to it. I'm not Czech by ancestry, but I guess I've become a Czech by osmosis. Before we opened this building, it had fallen into disrepair. At dif-ferent times it had been a general store, a living residence, and other things. It was supposedly built in 1881, and it was new when Dvořák came to town."

Just then Fritz Kala wanders in. Rebecca has asked him to come over and bring his family scrapbook. Fritz, or "Fred," as he is called around here, is over eighty years old. He used to own the Sportsman's Bar. Although he cheerfully admits he has no great love for Dvořák's music, he cherishes a col-lection of letters between members of the Dvořák family and his parents. "Here you see all the letters—my dad used to correspond with Otakar, who was Antonín Dvořák's son. They wrote back and forth for quite a few years. They even kept in touch during World War II. And when Otakar came back to visit, he came to see my folks." I ask Fritz to translate the letters, which are written in Czech. He shakes his head wistfully—no, he can't read the close print anymore. I stare at the handwritten sheets covered with a bewildering maze of unfamiliar letters and symbols.

Rebecca Neuzil speaks up. "Gee, Fred, what would you say?—Are there many anymore who can read them?" Fritz pauses a moment. "Well, it's fading out; but we still have a few that will talk the Czech, who still can ram-ble along with it." Obligingly, Fritz agrees to sing the Czech national anthem for me. I set up my tape recorder and the Czech words, sung in his softly rasping voice, float with a simple elegance through this quiet little inn. . . .

Later at the home of Russell Loven, one of the former proprietors of the Inn and current superintendent of schools for South Winneshiek Community Schools, I learn that some of Spillville's citizens fear the memory of the Czech language and customs in general and Dvořák's memory in particular may pass away completely. "I would say the younger generation now doesn't understand much about the Dvořák story," says Mr. Loven. "Once a journalist was here and asked one of the local kids what he knew about Dvořák. The only thing he could say was that he liked his suds. All he knew was that Dvořák drank a lot of beer. But everybody had their beer by the bucket back then."

That evening I meet some of my new friends for a wedding dance at the old Inwood Pavilion. It would be like any noisy party in any small town, except that a rock band called "The Buck Hollow Gang" is belting out some mighty peculiar polkas while young people, grandparents, and excited children in exotic costumes spin and whirl in a variety of dance steps on the polished wooden floor. I am reluctant to leave, but I have one last appointment with Ed Klimesh in his fabulous geodesic-dome dwelling. For eight years he was the Mayor of Spillville. Now he teaches and preserves the fabulous collection of slides and historical information about the town left him by a cousin, Cyril Klimesh. Still a young man and a former candidate for the state senate from the thirty-first district, he describes himself as a prodigal son come home. "Like most people growing up in the sixties, I couldn't wait to disconnect as much as I could from the area and its heritage." He continues: "It took a few years of being away to decide that there was a lot there worth reconnecting with. But now, as fewer and fewer people speak the language and fewer and fewer read it, it's tough to backtrack and make those connections." We spend a couple of delightful hours looking at slides of Spillville as it looked a hundred years ago. These images are now part of the Cyril Klimesh collection.

The sometimes uneasy truce between Czech tradition and contemporary American life-style that exists in Spillville today is, perhaps, no different than it was in Dvořák's time. By the end of the nineteenth century most of the Czechs had applied for American citizenship while retaining their pride in their Bohemian heritage. The two most important holidays balanced old and new worlds—the Fourth of July and the Feast of St. Wenceslaus (28 September). The Czech language was, of course, spoken by the adults, although, as Dvořák noted, the younger generations were becoming more interested in English:

> [The] children go to an American school, but they are still Czechs and their language is that of the Czechs. Some of the old people can speak nothing else, but the younger ones, most of whom have grown

St. Wenceslaus Church, ca. 1910. (Courtesy Cyril Klimesh Collection.)

View of St. Wenceslaus Church today. (Courtesy John C. Tibbetts.)

up in America, speak English as well as Americans. The children, I have noticed, speak nothing else, although they can answer one in Bohemian when spoken to.[23]

When Spillville celebrates in 1993 the centennial of Dvořák's visit, the town will once again be caught in the cross hairs of American and Czech traditions, past and present. Chaired by Mrs. Amy Balik, Spillville's postmaster, the Remembering Dvořák Committee is planning an enormous festival and musical celebration for 6–8 August. She promises it will be even bigger than

The console of the organ that Dvořák played in St. Wenceslaus Church. It is still used in services today. (Courtesy John C. Tibbetts.)

the Spillville Conference that convened in 1979 to mark the seventy-fifth anniversary of Dvořák's death. Among the distinguished guests for that event had been the eminent Czech pianist Rudolf Firkušný, who performed Dvořák's Piano Concerto with an orchestra composed of the best high school musicians in the tri-state area, and cellist Nathaniel Rosen, who performed the Cello Concerto. Thousands are expected for the 1993 celebration, and plans are now being completed. Ed Klimesh and his wife, Linda, are preparing the Old World Inn at this writing. But there are only four rooms there. If you haven't made your reservations yet in Spillville or nearby cities like Decorah, you are advised to bring sleeping bags.

Saturday night. Twilight. My last night in Spillville. The church of St. Wenceslaus sits gracefully atop the hill at the northwest end of town. The lemon-yellow glow in the sky has the luminosity of a lamp. They say this is the most beautiful church in northeast Iowa. I believe it. Inside the main door, immediately to the right is a narrow, spiral staircase that winds upward to the organ loft. I emerge into a small chamber filled with a rich, ruby-red light cast from a high, round stained-glass window. Sitting at the organ, preparing for the Saturday evening mass, is Mrs. Doris Thompson. She's expecting me.

This organ is special, you see. It is the very instrument that was installed here in 1876, which Dvořák played for daily morning mass.

"I started playing this organ for church services about eighteen years ago," she whispers, one eye on the pews below us filling with people. Some of them are wearing Czech folk costumes. "A few years ago we thought we should replace it with a newer instrument, a Lowry organ. But it didn't last and we went back to this old one. It sounds like it did a hundred years ago—except for the leathers that have been replaced and the pipes that have had to be vacuumed every once in a while."

It is time for the service to begin. "You know," says Mrs. Thompson as she prepares herself, "I guess it's true I don't appreciate this organ like I should. I know it was Dvořák's instrument and that he played it. But I've lived here all my life and I'm used to it. Sure, the first few times I played it I thought—Oh, if I pull these stops out too much the organ will come down on me. But the pastor just laughed at me. It hasn't come down yet. I guess it'll stand for a while!"

The music begins: "*Bože, před tvou velebností*" . . .

SOURCES AND ACKNOWLEDGMENTS

The author is indebted to the good citizens of Spillville for their hospitality and assistance in the preparation of this article. Special thanks go to Rosalind Proshusta, Amy Balik, Rebecca Neuzil, Fritz Kala, Beulah Sindelar, Doris Thompson, Mr. and Mrs. Russell Loven, and Mr. and Mrs. Ed Klimesh (and their sons, Simon and Lew!).

Other sources for the history of the town and environs include, in alphabetical order: W. A. Dostal, "Dvořák's Visit to Spillville," *Iowa Catholic Historical Review,* 1933, 5–15; John Karras, "Spillville's Czech Treat," the *Iowan,* vol. 39, no. 1 (Fall 1990), 62–65; Cyril M. Klimesh, *They Came to This Place: A History of Spillville, Iowa and Its Czech Settlers* (Sebastopol CA: Methodius Press, 1983); Walter Nugent, "Dvořák: An American Interlude," *Timeline,* October-November 1986, 2–13; and Otakar Šourek, ed., *Antonín Dvořák: Letters and Reminiscences,* trans. Roberta Finlayson Samsour (Prague: Artia, 1954). Special acknowledgment and thanks are also made to Mr. William Malloch, a Los Angeles radio broadcaster, whose radio series "They Remember Dvořák" was produced for Los Angeles radio station KPFK in 1964–66. Mr. Malloch interviewed several citizens of Spillville who recalled their childhood days during the Dvořák visit. I am indebted to Mr. Malloch for the opportunity to hear these tapes. They are an extraordinary document of a past recaptured.

NOTES

1. The most important information resource for the settlement of the area is Cyril M. Klimesh, *They Came to This Place*, Chaps. 1–3.

2. Dvořák to Dr. Kozanek, 12 April 1893, quoted in Otakar Šourek, ed., *Antonín Dvořák: Letters and Reminiscences*, 158.

3. From *J. J. Kovařík's Reminiscences*, quoted in Otakar Šourek, ed., *Antonín Dvořák: Letters and Reminiscences*, 160

4. From *J. J. Kovařík's Reminiscences*, quoted in Otakar Šourek, ed., *Antonín Dvořák: Letters and Reminiscences*, 160

5. From *J. J. Kovařík's Reminiscences*, quoted in Otakar Šourek, ed., *Antonín Dvořák: Letters and Reminiscences*, 161

6. Dvořák to Dr. Kozanek, 15 September 1893, quoted in Otakar Šourek, ed., *Antonín Dvořák: Letters and Reminiscences*, 165–66.

7. Cyril M. Klimesh, *They Came to This Place*, 138.

8. Cyril M. Klimesh, *They Came to This Place*, 148.

9. Cyril M. Klimesh, *They Came to This Place*, 154.

10. In *They Came to This Place*, Cyril Klimesh recounts the later fortunes of the Kovařík family: "All of J. J.'s six children received thorough musical training. Four of them adopted music as their life's work. Two years after his return to the United States following completion of his schooling in Bohemia, Joseph joined the New York Philharmonic Orchestra. He continued to be a member for over forty years. The Russian conductor Safanov declared that Joseph was the best violist he had ever heard. Frank Kovařík played with the Minneapolis Symphony for twenty-five years, later taught at several of the colleges in St. Paul. On 17 September 1933, Frank conducted the Capital City Symphony Orchestra when it played at Spillville to commemorate the fortieth anniversary of Anton [*sic*] Dvořák's visit to the village. Cecelia and Anna followed in their father's footsteps by becoming professional music teachers, and like their father, both served their parish as church organists," 153.

11. Quoted in Cyril M. Klimesh, *They Came to This Place*, 155.

12. See John Clapham, *Dvořák* (New York: W. W. Norton and Company, 1979), 124. Dr. Clapham disputes Kovařík's claim that the Native Americans who came to Spillville were Iroquois. In *They Came to This Place*, 155, Klimesh identifies them as one Sioux and two Algonquin.

13. The fullest account of this curious "healing" incident is in Cyril M. Klimesh's *They Came to This Place*, 155. Other sources omit it entirely—including John Clapham's *Dvořák*, Neil Butterworth's *Dvořák: His Life and Times*, Alec Robertson's *Dvořák*, and Gervase Hughes's *Dvořák: His Life and Music*. However, in

his interview with Walter Malloch, Frank Kapler gives an eyewitness account of the "healing" episode.

14. Dvořák to Dr. Kozanek, 15 September 1893; quoted in Otakar Šourek, ed., *Antonín Dvořák: Letters and Reminiscences*, 166.

15. Dvořák to A. Rus, 17 August 1893; quoted in Otakar Šourek, ed., *Antonín Dvořák: Letters and Reminiscences*, 164.

16. Quoted in R. Reid Badger, *The Great American Fair: The World's Columbian Exposition and American Culture* (Chicago: Nelson Hall, 1979), *xiii.*

17. Dvořák to Dr. Kozanek, 15 September 1893; quoted in Otakar Šourek, ed., *Antonín Dvořák: Letters and Reminiscences*, 165.

18. See my "Dvořák in the New World: A Spillville Adventure," *Classical*, vol. 3, no. 2 (February 1991), 32–36.

19. These and other remarks by Spillville citizens are taken from interviews with the author in October 1990.

20. John Clapham maintains that there is no question the bird was a scarlet tanager, which frequents the Spillville area. After listening to recordings of the bird's song, he writes: "The recorded song resembled Dvořák's sketch in general style, with some differences. . . . The song is extremely rapid and might well have provoked Dvořák to describe the scarlet tanager as a 'damned bird.'" See *Antonín Dvořák: Musician and Craftsman* (New York: St. Martin's Press 1966), 181.

   In his radio broadcast "They Remember Dvořák," William Malloch compares a recording of the scarlet tanager's song with one of an excerpt from the Scherzo in the F Major Quartet. By slowing down the birdsong and speeding up the music, a convincing comparison is made.

21. These anecdotes are drawn from Cyril M. Klimesh's *They Came to This Place* and Walter Malloch's radio interviews with Mary Klimesh and Frank Kapler. There are striking consistencies.

22. A charming history of the Old World Inn is in John Karras, "Spillville's Czech Treat," the *Iowan*, vol. 39, no. 1 (Fall 1998), 62–65.

23. Quoted in Cyril M. Klimesh, *They Came to This Place*, 189.

CHAPTER EIGHT

Dvořák and the American Indian

John Clapham

$\mathcal{A}$n American reporter once told me that the most valuable talent a journalist could possess was a "nose for news." Just so the musician must prick his ear for music. Nothing must be too low or too insignificant for the musician.[1]

With these few words Dvořák summed up in a vivid manner his personal attitude to some of the new musical experiences that flooded in upon him during the first two years of his stay in the United States. His keen interest ranged on the one hand from "Negro melodies, the songs of the creoles, the red man's chant, or the plaintive ditties of the homesick German or Norwegian" to the melodies of whistling boys, street singers, and blind organ grinders. In all of these he believed he heard "the voice of the people," an entity he valued very highly; for as he asserted in the same article:

> This music of the people is like a rare and lovely flower growing amidst encroaching weeds. Thousands pass it, while others trample it under foot, and thus the chances are that it will perish before it is seen by the one discriminating spirit who will prize it above all else.

Since Dvořák undoubtedly saw the article "Songs of the American Indian"[2] written by his friend V. J. Novotný, editor of the periodical *Dalibor*, and it is also possible that he may have encountered Theodore Baker's *Über die Musik der Nordamerikanischen Wilden*, it is reasonable to assume that American Indian music was not completely outside his ken before he crossed the Atlantic for the first time. Naturally the impact upon him would have been much stronger if he had seen and heard the small group of Indians who performed in Prague, and whom Novotný reported to be Iroquois and

Comanche, but we have no grounds for making such an assumption. Like others of that period, Novotný automatically attempted to relate what he heard to the music which was already a part of his experience, and so he noticed resemblances to European folk song and Jewish chant. His brief transcriptions also suggest he was thinking in terms of European scales and rhythmic patterns.

Judging by the characteristics of this music—for instance, the comparatively small pitch range, the choice of notes and melodic intervals, the absence of long terraced descents that are so typical of music of the plains tribes, and the inclusion in one case of double drone accompaniments—it seems likely that the melodies he noted down were [more] Iroquois than Comanche.[3] But since Novotný stated that the songs were accompanied by a tambourine, which is not an Indian instrument, we are justified in questioning the authenticity of the music performed. We also observe that, in contrast with some remarks Dvořák made in America on the nature of Indian song,[4] only two fragments quoted by Novotný can be regarded as pentatonic.

A tiny handful of melodies such as these—even if genuine and accurately transcribed, which is extremely doubtful—gives a totally inadequate idea of Indian song. Baker's collection, on the other hand, comprises some fifty songs, almost all of which are from the eastern woodlands and plains of the United States, regions that Dvořák was to visit. At the time they were published scientific methods for notating primitive song had not been developed, yet they inspire a little more confidence than Novotný's amateurish attempts. Nevertheless, they can give to the uninitiated no idea of how the songs would sound when sung according to native custom.[5]

If, then, Dvořák had only the haziest impression of the nature of North American Indian song when he arrived in the United States, his chances of learning rather more soon increased a little. Since Mrs. Thurber was extremely eager for him to compose an opera on Hiawatha, she decided to provide him with some fruitful ideas for the ballet by taking him to Buffalo Bill's Wild West Show. At these shows audiences witnessed episodes from the savage historic intertribal warfare, reconstructed for their benefit by Colonel Cody's Oglala and Brulé Sioux and supplemented at times by a few leading Crow, Cheyenne, Arapaho, and Shoshone Indians.[6] Since all of these share the culture of the plains area it may be confidently assumed that any music Dvořák heard that was not drowned by the din of battle would have been closely related to types of song to be found in the large collection of music of the Teton Sioux and their enemies the Ojibwa.[7]

When adjudicating for a composition prize at the National Conservatory of Music, certain aspects of the music he was examining forcibly attracted Dvořák's attention. Describing this he said, "here and there another spirit, other thoughts, another colouring flashes, in short, Indian music, something à la 'Bret Harte.'"[8] It is possible that Dvořák might have been shown some published transcriptions of American Indian songs, for although only a limited amount of detailed work had been attempted at that time, Franz Boas, J. Owen Dorsey, Benjamin Ives Gilman, Alice C. Fletcher, Francis La Flesche, Carl Stumpf, and others had begun to be active in this sphere. Nevertheless, since this is a specialized field and none of those with whom Dvořák was in close contact appears to have been a member of the American Folk-Lore Society, it is not at all certain that the learned journals in which the articles appeared[9] would have come his way. Possibly he was shown Theodore Baker's study. It may have been at about this time that Krehbiel gave him transcriptions of three Iroquois songs from the Six Nations Reserve, Canada (Example 8-1), for we know that a friend gave him a number of Indian melodies before he wrote the "New World" Symphony.[10] Even if the transcriptions are slightly suspect, Dvořák would undoubtedly have accepted them as genuine. Owing to the primitive character of these songs, however, they seem to offer very little that might have been of value to Dvořák in one of his compositions.[11]

The evidence of newspaper interviews leads one to conclude that until the summer of 1893 Dvořák was far more strongly drawn to Negro spirituals and plantation songs than to Indian music, but that after this he modified his attitude. It is curious that when his symphony was about to be performed he let it be known that "the work was written under the direct influence of a serious study of the national music of the North American Indians"[12] and that it expressed the spirit of that music without quoting any actual themes. It is not easy to explain this. When he wrote the symphony his knowledge of such music was limited, and it is certain he had made no "serious study" of the music. It was not until his summer vacation that he came into close contact with Indians. Perhaps in an unguarded moment he saw an opportunity to give a boost to his desire and Mrs. Thurber's dream to create a national school of composition, but he would have had a better chance of carrying conviction had he recommended Negro music rather than Indian, in conjunction with folk songs of the white races of the United States, as the basis for a national music. Dvořák's apparent failure to notice that his symphony does, in fact, show some signs of the influence of Negro music but none at all of Indian music was due to a misunderstanding on his part. Based on the slender grounds that pentatonic melodies are to be found in the music of

Example 8-1. Transcriptions of three Iroquois songs given to Dvořák by Henry E. Krehbiel, who provided the last two songs with key signatures of one sharp.

both races, together with a few other small points of resemblance, he had deluded himself into thinking that "the music of the Negroes and of the Indians was practically identical."[13]

    It is important, however, not to discount Dvořák's statement that the middle movements were inspired by the *Song of Hiawatha* and that the Scherzo represented the dance of Pau-Puk-Keewis.[14] (See Michael Beckerman's essay, Chapter 15.) According to the New York *Daily Tribune*, Hiawatha's wooing served as the basis for the Larghetto, with "possibly also a suggestion of the sweet loneliness of a lovely night on the prairies."[15] But Dvořák's biographer Šourek, without offering his reasons, was under the impression that the composer may have had Minnehaha's funeral in mind. Possibly the information came from Kovařík.

    Krehbiel admired the symphony, but he was sceptical about its Indian spirit. In describing the first movement in his review of the work he said, "What the spirit of Indian music may be I do not know. If this movement which is now going on breathes the genuine native atmosphere, then certainly the future of music is in the hands of the red man."[16] Considering the work as a whole, Krehbiel conceded that it might be Indian in spirit, but he was clear-sighted enough to recognize that it was Bohemian in atmosphere. For, as he said, "Dr. Dvořák can no more divest himself of his nationality than the leopard change his spots."

Since I have already attempted to investigate the problem of the identity of the Indians who visited Spillville, Iowa, during Dvořák's stay there,[17] I will merely summarize the main points and concentrate attention on new facts that have come to light. Jan Josef Kovařík's statement that the Indians were "Kickapoo and belonged to the Iroquois tribe"[18] and the similar statement made by his son Josef Jan in unpublished correspondence with Šourek immediately put me on my guard, for the Kickapoo are Central Algonquins, not Iroquois, and the latter are not a tribe but a confederation of five, and later six, nations. In 1890 most Kickapoo were on reservations in Kansas and Oklahoma.[19] In correspondence, Frances Densmore informed me that since the Indians were selling fresh medicinal herbs in summer they could not have traveled from as far away as Kansas. Furthermore, because they were a small and unimportant tribe, she believes that they could hardly have assembled a large enough group for singing and dancing without including members of other tribes. It seems probable that the leader of the group, Big Moon, was Kickapoo, but we cannot be so certain that his wife, Large Head, was also.

Otakar Dvořák, who was at Spillville with his father, told me that his family came into contact with the Indians daily and that, at his father's request, the whole group assembled at the inn on two or three occasions for performances of native singing and dancing.

The identity of the Indians has a direct bearing upon the style of music that Dvořák heard during these evenings, for the style of Indian music varies from tribe to tribe and especially from one cultural area to another.[20] Among neighboring tribes, similarities of style may be found when several of them share the same ceremony, yet within a single tribe, marked differences are seen in the style of music associated with each of their ceremonies. It may perhaps be true that there are almost as many different styles in North American Indian music as in the folk songs of Europe.

It seems reasonable to assume that since the Indians at Spillville appear to have been members of different tribes, they comprised representatives of some of the numerous Algonquin, Siouan, and perhaps Caddoan tribes, and that the music they performed would generally have conformed to that of the eastern woodlands and plains. Thanks to the horse, all these tribes were highly mobile, thus making it easy for them to adopt ceremonies and customs, and the songs and dances associated with them, from their neighbors, whether friends or foes. The Rockies to the west were a formidable barrier across which their culture and that of the northwest coast tribes did not pass. And in any case, the seagoing Indians had entirely different patterns of culture.

We must recognize, however, that during Dvořák's time Indians could travel more easily. Antonín Sychra draws attention to an interesting similarity between a theme in Dvořák's F Major Quartet and a Kwakiutl (Vancouver Island) Woman's Song that was published at the end of 1893;[21] but since Dvořák wrote his theme several months earlier, we are obliged to conclude that the resemblance is fortuitous. The only Kickapoo song that appears to have been published can be ignored, for it belongs to the peyote cult, a modern Indian religion with its own characteristic style of music that did not reach the Kickapoo until 1906.[22]

We can obtain a good idea of the types of song that Dvořák might have heard at Spillville by turning to the various general collections of music of the plains and eastern woodland Indians.[23] We learn from an unpublished letter from J. Comfort Fillmore to Dvořák (11 August 1893) that he and Alice Fletcher sent the Czech composer a copy of her recently published *Study of Omaha Indian Music* when he was in Chicago, but this was after he had written the E-flat String Quintet, the only work of his that bears unmistakable signs of Indian influence. (See Jan Smaczny's essay, Chapter 17.) Without knowing anything about American Indian music, Šourek and others have imagined that they detected its influence in his music where none exists. The G minor theme of the Quintet's finale is in fact far closer to themes of Smetana and Schubert than to Indian music, and the second viola's rhythmic pattern on a monotone in the Scherzo, which it is so tempting to regard as a drum rhythm, is much more complex than any drum rhythm Dvořák could conceivably have heard at Spillville.[24]

But it is a different matter when we come to the second subject of the first movement. Dvořák's theme (Example 8-2a) is obviously "primitive," and is basically a short motif founded on four notes, which is immediately repeated and followed by sequential repetitions. The dotted rhythm that accompanies it and permeates so much of the movement is not far removed from a type of drum rhythm that occurs in Algonquin music, even if one might often expect an Algonquin drum rhythm to proceed at a slightly faster pace than that of the melody it accompanies.

Example 8-2a. Dvořák, String Quintet, Opus 97, first movement, second subject.

Example 8-2b. Closing song of the Menominee drum ceremony.

Example 8-2c. Indian motive heard by Dvořák at Spillville, notated by Kovařík.

Dvořák's theme also appears to have a family resemblance to the closing song of the Drum Ceremony of the Menominee of Wisconsin (Example 8-2b),[25] a song that it is most unlikely Dvořák would have heard. However, Josef Jan Kovařík noted down, presumably from memory, an Indian melodic fragment that they heard at Spillville (Example 8-2c) and which he thought might have served as the melodic basis for the Czech composer's theme.[26] Reference to the three themes leads us to the conclusion that Dvořák molded his theme to suit himself.

Apart from this one instance of undeniable Indian influence, it may be reasonable to suggest that in certain of the other works Dvořák wrote in America, such as the Sonatina, Opus 100, and the Suite in A, Opus 98, in particular, the composer may have wished to express "something primitive," but I am inclined to think that Indian influence in these cases can only have been indirect. It is clear that certain of his pentatonic themes were Negro inspired, yet often these are more characteristic of Dvořák himself.

As we have seen, there have been misunderstandings concerning the presence of Indian elements in Dvořák's music for which he himself was originally to blame. It is true that Dvořák was influenced by Indian music, but only very slightly. Greater use was made of Indian material by MacDowell and Busoni.

NOTES

This chapter is based on an article originally printed in the *Musical Times*, 107 (1966), 863–867. It has been slightly altered by the editor with permission of Dr. Clapham.

1. Antonín Dvořák, in collaboration with E. Emerson, "Music in America," *Harper's New Monthly Magazine*, 90 (February 1895), 428–434. Abridged reprint in *Composers on Music* (New York: Pantheon, 1956), ed. Sam Morgenstern, 258–266. The quotation appears on page 265.

2. V. J. Novotný, "Písně amerických Indianů," *Dalibor* 1, nos. 24–25, Prague, 1879.

3. Gertrude P. Kurath's "Iroquois Music and Dance," *Bureau of American Ethnology Bulletin* 187, Washington 1964, is the most important study of Iroquois music.

4. "Dvořák on His New Work," New York *Herald*, 15 December 1893.

5. [Editor's note—Dr. Clapham has more to say about the Iroquois music elsewhere: "Unlike some American Indian songs, most Iroquois songs appear to fit fairly satisfactorily into the European major and minor diatonic systems, with due prominence given to a tonic; but it should be realized that the Indians never had a musical theory or a musical notation, and by fitting their songs into our own system we are to some extent distorting the image. Notes are sometimes sung sharp or flat, deliberately in all probability, and are approached with graces and glides, so that the songs inevitably sound peculiar to the ears of a westerner. The use of a complete scale is comparatively rare, most Iroquois songs being based on five notes or less, but it would be inaccurate to say the songs are predominantly pentatonic. In the two hundred or so Iroquois songs the writer has encountered, the combination of notes that occurs most frequently corresponds with the major pentatonic scale (C, D, E, G, A, C), but these only represent twelve percent of the total. Besides this, other pentatonic forms appear; six percent of the songs adopt the thirdless 'Chinese' form (C, D, F, G, A, C), five percent use the minor form (A, C, D, E, G, A), and three percent are in the thirdless form suggested in parts of Vaughan Williams's *The Lark Ascending* (C, D, F, G, B flat, C). In all, these amount to a little more than a quarter of the songs examined. . . . Iroquois songs are not melodic in the sense

that Negro spirituals and European folk-songs are melodic, partly because there are frequent repetitions of single notes or groups of notes, and there is much less sense of movement away from one note towards another, and less feeling for melodic curve. Rhythm is a prominent feature; a single short rhythmic figure is often repeated a number of times during the course of a song. Irregularities of meter occur from time to time, which make it impossible to give some melodies any regular barring in transcription. Judged by European standards the rhythm is apt to sound monotonous or arbitrary. A compass of an octave is seldom exceeded, and it is normal for the last note of a song to be lower than the first, except when the termination is a whoop or a call." (See John Clapham, "Dvořák and the Impact of America," *Music Review,* 15, no. 3, 1954, 204–205.)]

6. I am grateful to R. I. Frost, Curator of the Buffalo Bill Historical Center, Cody, Wyoming, for this information.

7. Frances Densmore, *Teton Sioux Music,* 2 vols. (Washington, 1918) and *Chippewa Music,* 2 vols. (Washington, 1910 and 1913). The Oglala and Brulé belong to the Teton group of Sioux.

8. Letter to Mr. and Mrs. Hlávka, 27 November 1892.

9. The newly founded *Journal of American Folk-Lore, Journal of American Ethnology and Archaeology,* and *American Anthropologist,* the publications of the Bureau of American Ethnology and of the Peabody Museum, and even *Vierteljahrsschrift für Musikwissenschaft.*

10. "Dvořák on His New Work," New York *Herald,* 15 December 1893.

11. The songs are quoted here from Krehbiel's MS by kind permission of Dvořák's heirs. The third song is one of three Krehbiel transcriptions that Tiersot included in his study "La musique chez les peuples indigènes de l'Amérique du Nord," *Sammelbände der Internationalen Musikgesellschaft,* 11 (1909–10). He entitled it "Chant de guerre." Mrs. Kurath assures me that the Iroquois have no Man-eating Song.

12. "Dr. Dvořák's Great Symphony," New York *Herald,* 16 December 1893.

13. "Dvořák on His New Work," New York *Herald,* 15 December 1893.

14. "Dvořák on His New Work," New York *Herald,* 15 December 1893.

15. New York *Daily Tribune,* 15 December 1893.

16. "Dr. Dvořák's Great Symphony," New York *Herald,* 16 December 1893.

17. "Dvořák and the Impact of America," *The Music Review,* 15, no. 3 (1954), 203–211.

18. Hazel G. Kinscella, "Dvořák and Spillville, Forty Years After," *Musical America,* 25 May 1933, 4.

19. *Report on Indians Taxed and Indians Not Taxed in the United States at the 11th Census,* 1890 (Washington, 1894).

20. Helen H. Roberts, *Musical Areas in Aboriginal North America,* Yale Univ. Publ. in Anthrop., 1936. Bruno Nettl, "North American Indian Musical Styles," *Journal of American Folklore* 67, nos. 263, 265, and 266 (1954).

21. *Estetika Dvořákovy symfonické tvorby,* Prague, 1959. J. C. Fillmore heard it at the Columbian Fair Grounds, Chicago, on 3 September 1893 and published it in the *Journal of American Folklore* 6, 23.

22. David McAllester, *Peyote Music* (New York, 1949).

23. The most important are: F. Densmore's two works already cited, together with her Washington publications: *Menominee Music* (1932), *Mandan and Hidatsa Music* (1923), and *Pawnee Music* (1929); A. C. Fletcher's *A Study of Omaha Indian Music,* Peabody Museum, Cambridge, Mass., 1893, and "The Omaha Tribe," in *Bureau of American Ethnology 27th Report,* Washington, 1905–1906; and F. La Flesche's "The Osage Tribe" in the *BAE 36th Report,* 1914–1915.

24. [Editor's note—In "Dvořák and the Impact of America," Clapham discusses Kickapoo songs further: "Speaking generally the music of the Wisconsin-Iowa area tends to have a greater compass and to have a more pronounced downward tendency than Iroquois songs, and the major pentatonic scale occurs among the Menominee in as many as thirty percent of their songs. Time changes are very frequent when the music is transcribed into European notation. Some three-quarters of the songs use five notes of the scale or less, and where six notes are used, the missing note is more likely to be the seventh than any other note of the scale." (207)]

25. Frances Densmore, *Menominee Music.*

26. Otakar Šourek, *Život a dílo Antonína Dvořáka* 3, 2d ed. (Prague, 1956).

CHAPTER NINE

A Great and Noble School of Music

Dvořák, Harry T. Burleigh, and the African American Spiritual

Jean E. Snyder

When Antonín Dvořák sailed back to Bohemia from New York in the spring of 1895, a prominent journal commented, "No sum of money was large enough to keep Antonín Dvořák in the New World. He left us his New World Symphony and his American Quartet but he took himself away."[1] For Harry T. Burleigh, however, the legacy of Dvořák's American sojourn extended farther and deeper than a handful of "American" compositions. For Burleigh and other African American composers of his time and since, Dvořák's example affirmed the intrinsic value of the folk music created by African Americans. Dvořák's departure from America was a deep personal loss to Burleigh, as was his death in 1904; but the honor Dvořák had paid him and his heritage inspired Burleigh throughout his career.

A few images and incidents in Burleigh's story have become familiar: Burleigh's arrival at the National Conservatory with little money but ample determination; his singing of "Swing Low, Sweet Chariot" to a fascinated Dvořák; his performances at St. George's Episcopal Church and his popularization in art song form of the African American spiritual tradition. He became Dvořák's friend, sometime secretary, and copyist. He was present at the genesis of the "New World" Symphony. He sang the baritone solo at the premiere of the Dvořák arrangement of Foster's "Old Folks at Home." And perhaps better than anyone else, he extended by example and spirit Dvořák's musical legacy. It was, in short, a unique friendship that spanned continents and cultures. Its consequences are still being felt today.

Harry T. Burleigh was born in Erie, Pennsylvania, in 1866. He was the third generation of his family to be free. The setting of his early life was not the stereotypical community of newly emancipated slaves. Rather, he is representative of the clusters of free African Americans in both the North and the South who, long before the Emancipation Proclamation, were aligning themselves with mainstream American values, following the paths of upward mobility. Through their creative industry and ingenuity, they won the respect of their white neighbors, though they seldom reaped economic and social benefits commensurate with their efforts.[2]

Burleigh's grandfather, Hamilton Waters, had been a slave in Somerset County, Maryland. He purchased his freedom and that of his mother, Lovey Waters, in 1832.[3] With his wife, Lucinda Duncanson Waters, he settled in Erie after the birth of their first daughter Elizabeth. Nearly blind, Waters nonetheless earned the respect and admiration of his wealthy white neighbors for his "originality, versatility and patient toil." He supported his family in several jobs, as a clothes presser, town crier, and lamplighter. He purchased a lot and built a home on East Third Street near Lake Erie to bring up his two daughters, Elizabeth (Harry's mother) and Louise. He and his wife devoted themselves to providing their daughters the best education possible.[4]

Erie was at the time an important junction on the Underground Railway for slaves fleeing to Canada, and Waters's blindness did not prevent him from assisting them on their way.[5] His connections with western Pennsylvania's active abolitionist community provided his daughter Elizabeth the opportunity to study at the first chartered college for African Americans in the United States, the Allegheny Institute and Seminary (popularly known as Avery College) in what is now Pittsburgh's North Side. Though it later became a trade school similar to Tuskegee Institute and other schools for African Americans in the South, Avery College was first established "for the education of colored Americans, in the various branches of science, literature, and ancient and modern languages."[6] Elizabeth Waters studied Greek, Latin, and French at Avery College. Amelia Freeman, one of Elizabeth's teachers, was later recommended by black abolitionist Martin Delany for her qualifications to give "instruction in painting, drawing, music, writing, etc., . . . which are necessary and useful accomplishments for both ladies and gentlemen."[7]

Elizabeth Waters was an apt student. At her graduation exercises in

A young Harry Burleigh with his grandfather, Hamilton Waters. (Courtesy Harry T. Burleigh, II.)

July 1855 she was described as "a very intelligent young lady in appearance" who "delivered an address—*La Salutation*—in French," showing "an excellent knowledge of the tongue." She also delivered "a very neat essay on 'American Institutions,' in the course of which she adverted in terms of sorrow to the enslaved condition of so large a portion of her race. She thought slavery the only stain upon our country's fair name."[8] Although the Erie *Weekly Gazette* reported that Miss Waters was now qualified to teach "in the first Seminary in the land," the Erie public school administration was not progressive enough to hire her as a teacher.[9] The 1860 census records listed her as a school teacher, but it was not until more than a decade later, after the death of her first husband, Burleigh's father, that she found employment at the Erie Public School No. 1—as a janitor.

Young Harry's closest tie to the slavery experience came through his grandfather. Harry and his older brother Reginald spent many hours with him, accompanying him on his early-morning and evening rounds as lamplighter, hearing his stories about plantation life and learning the songs Waters sang in his "exceptionally melodious voice." Harry also led his grandfather to the Himrod Mission, a black congregation, on Sunday afternoons after attending morning services at St. Paul's Episcopal Cathedral, a predominantly white congregation, with his mother.[10]

The family were active church members. In the 1830s Hamilton Waters had helped form a short-lived Wesleyan Methodist congregation,[11] but in 1869 he and daughter Elizabeth joined the St. Paul's Episcopal Church, where a charismatic young rector, John F. Spalding, was challenging his wealthy parishioners (more of whom had been slaveholders than former slaves)[12] to open their doors to the wider community. According to parish records, two-year-old Harry and his four-year-old brother were baptized on 27 March 1869.

Elizabeth taught the largest Bible class in Erie, a Greek New Testament at her side. From age two and a half Harry grew up in a congregation known for its fine singing of hymns and liturgical responses.[13] In his childhood there were Easter Sunday processions of six hundred children marching to the Cathedral with banners and carols.[14] Burleigh was a charter member of the St. Paul's Boys' Choir, formed while he was in high school. The choir assisted the professional soloists, and it became the pride of the congregation. The music then in use represented a wide range of classical American, English, French, and German composers.[15]

Singing was a family tradition at home. The family held frequent parlor concerts, and it is likely that Stephen Foster songs, which Burleigh later sang to Dvořák, were among the songs in his mother's repertoire. She was a natural singer, he later recalled. Foster's career was at its height when she had studied in Pittsburgh. Because Foster's best friend was abolitionist Charles Shiras, who knew the college's founder, Charles Avery, and lived near the college, it is possible that she met Foster personally.

Burleigh's Aunt Louise arranged for voice lessons from local teachers. Both his mother and his aunt encouraged him to pursue his unlikely dream of becoming a professional singer. And later it was his mother who, when lucrative vaudeville offers tempted him in New York, urged him to stay in the more secure and dignified environment at St. George's Episcopal Church as he built his career in art music.[16]

Harry never lost an opportunity to absorb music. He once hid all afternoon in the balcony of the Park Opera House to hear the great Campanini sing. He listened to the songs of stevedores while working as pantryman and deck steward on the Lake Erie steamers. He practiced the piano in a warehouse of the Colby Piano Company while working there as a stenographer.

And he was always singing. He sang wherever he went, whether tending horses with his stepfather, delivering newspapers at four o'clock in the morning, or lighting the street lamps as his grandfather had done (Hamilton Waters had died when Harry was ten years old). In his early twenties he appeared as church soloist at Park Presbyterian Church where his parents' employers attended, at First Presbyterian Church, and at the Hebrew Synagogue.

Through his mother Burleigh made some important professional contacts. Though racial discrimination kept her from the professional career for which she had prepared, her sophistication and competence brought her into contact with Erie's wealthy social elite. Elizabeth (Mrs. Robert) Russell, the daughter of the banker for whom Burleigh's father had worked, held a series of musicales in her home that attracted several famous musicians to Erie. Burleigh's mother was often employed as a maid for such functions. On one occasion the Hungarian pianist Rafael Joseffy, friend of Franz Liszt, appeared. Young Harry was so eager to hear the concert that he stood outside in the snow listening at the window, nearly catching pneumonia from the cold. Alarmed, his mother asked her employer if Harry could be given some job in the house where he could hear the music. He was appointed doorman for the next musicale. This time the pianist was the Venezuelan virtuoso, Teresa Carreno, who had taught Edward MacDowell and would later introduce many of his compositions in her recitals. Her traveling companion was MacDowell's mother, Frances Knapp MacDowell. Years later in her role as registrar of the National Conservatory Mrs. MacDowell would help secure Burleigh's admission.

In January 1892 Burleigh left Erie to pursue a musical career in New York City. He had just passed his twenty-fifth birthday. Promptly on his arrival he applied for admission at the National Conservatory. It had a policy which attracted gifted students, men and women, regardless of their ethnic background or ability to pay.[17] He auditioned for a committee that included Rafael Joseffy, whom Burleigh had seen and heard play through the window of the Russell home in Erie. When Burleigh learned that his audition had been judged slightly below the admission standard, he appealed to the registrar, Frances Knapp MacDowell, "the kind-faced lady" he remembered as Teresa Carreno's traveling companion. His letter of recommendation from Mrs. Russell persuaded Mrs. MacDowell to intercede on his behalf, and he was admitted. In time Burleigh became clerical assistant to Mrs. MacDowell and would become acquainted with her son, Edward.[18]

Burleigh entered the National Conservatory of Music just a few months before Dvořák became its director. Though he was not among the more advanced composition students, he was prepared by family background and previous musical experience as well as by aptitude to make the most of the rich musical environment. Burleigh won the respect of numerous other colleagues and musicians who would play a significant role in his later career. Horatio Parker taught organ and hired Burleigh as occasional soloist at Holy Trinity Episcopal Church.[19] Burleigh got to know cello instructor Victor Herbert during his first summer job as wine steward at the Grand Union Hotel in Saratoga Springs, where Herbert played cello and was assistant conductor of the hotel orchestra. During the second summer, when Burleigh returned to Saratoga Springs as baritone soloist at the Bethesda Episcopal Church, he also sang with Herbert's orchestra. (Later, in 1914, Herbert invited Burleigh to be one of the charter members of ASCAP.[20]) Max Spicker, one of Burleigh's counterpoint teachers, was organist at Temple Emanu-El, the wealthiest synagogue in the United States where Burleigh was hired as soloist in 1900.

His most important job came through the assistance of Jeannette Thurber, the founder of the National Conservatory. When she heard of a need for a baritone soloist at St. George's Episcopal Church, located near the Conservatory, she prevailed upon Rector Dr. William S. Rainsford to hear Burleigh's audition. Burleigh, who at the time was considering an offer of employment from a minstrel company, auditioned from behind a blind, as did his sixty fellow applicant-competitors. He won the audition and worked there as soloist and choir member for fifty-two years, the first African American in the choir.[21] In 1896 he left a position as voice teacher at the Conservatory to pursue his voice-teaching and recital career. His sacred choral compositions and his arrangements of many spirituals became an important part of the church choir's repertoire. His singing of Jean-Baptiste Faure's *The Palms* became a Palm Sunday tradition. Through the 1930s and early 1940s the yearly service of spirituals, which organist George Kemmer had instituted in 1924, were annual attractions, drawing overflow crowds. For taxi drivers and others thronging the city, St. George's came to be known as "Mr. Burleigh's church."

The wealthy parishioners of St. George's were soon obtaining Burleigh's services on numerous occasions. He was in demand in the home of J. P. Morgan, who as chief vestryman at St. George's had cast the deciding vote to hire Burleigh. (Burleigh sang Morgan's favorite song, "Cavalry," at his funeral.) He sang at the Vanderbilts' and at the homes of many other wealthy New Yorkers. On some occasions he sang for visiting English and European royalty at their receptions. Among his own students were children from the wealthiest homes in the city.

One reviewer described Burleigh's voice as "a rather high baritone of

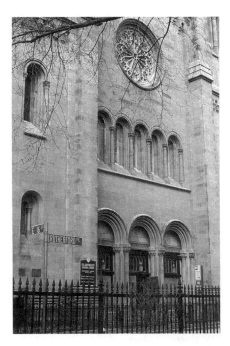

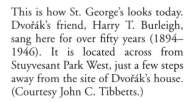

This is how St. George's looks today. Dvořák's friend, Harry T. Burleigh, sang here for over fifty years (1894–1946). It is located across from Stuyvesant Park West, just a few steps away from the site of Dvořák's house. (Courtesy John C. Tibbetts.)

great power and pleasing quality and capable of the gentlest modulation." Another commented that he seemed to have "a special tone color for every emotion."[22]

It was a hectic, busy world in which young Burleigh found himself in New York in 1892. But nothing could compare to the excitement generated by the Conservatory's new director, Dvořák. Everything he said and did made headlines. On 21 May 1893, the New York *Herald* published an interview in which Dvořák commended African American music as an invaluable resource for creating an American school of music. His words, which stirred bitter controversy, rang out with a proud affirmation for African Americans: "In the negro melodies of America I discover all that is needed for a great and noble school of music. They are pathetic, tender, passionate, melancholy, solemn, religious, bold, merry, gay or what you will. . . . There is nothing in the whole range of composition that cannot be supplied with themes from this source."[23] To African Americans accustomed to hearing slave music described as "barbaric," "savage," "weird," and "primitive," Dvořák's statements must have been electrifying.

Throughout his life Dvořák had drawn creative energy from the ordinary people of his native country and from their music, as well as from the ordinary people he met wherever he traveled. A friend of Brahms, hailed by Hans von Bülow as "next to Brahms the most God-gifted composer" of his time, he relished his Slovak peasant heritage. He was inspired by its folk melodies and rhythms to write music whose inexhaustible spontaneity belied its painstaking effort.[24] It is not surprising, therefore, that Dvořák, accomplished composer of art music, equally valued the music of ordinary people. His frank public acknowledgment of its influence on his own compositions proved the sincerity of his words. His "American" compositions, moreover, demonstrated a sophisticated approach to the use of folk music, and the enthusiastic public reception of these works fostered an openness among some of his admirers to receive the work of young African American composers as well.

The profound impact of these words on African American composers such as Burleigh can scarcely be overestimated. Dvořák's pronouncements presented a sharp contrast to the prevailing social, political, and cultural attitudes in American society at the time. Post-Reconstruction racism was sweeping away the hard-won social, political, and economic gains of African Americans. Lynching proliferated, and the doctrine of African American racial inferiority was being "scientifically" established. Popular culture glorified the "good old plantation" life, and minstrel songs and the more degrading "coon" songs demeaned African American culture and character even while they drew their most engaging musical elements from the culture they caricatured. Against this background Dvořák's assertion was revolutionary.

Burleigh soon became friends with the fierce-looking Czech master. A spurious part of the Burleigh/Dvořák legend holds that the young man studied composition with him. Indeed, Victor Herbert, Henry Finck, and James Gibbons Huneker all referred to him as Dvořák's composition student, and Herbert called him "one of Dvořák's best students." However, as Burleigh himself explained on a number of occasions, he studied with another teacher, Rubin Goldmark, because he was not advanced enough to be admitted to Dvořák's composition class: "I didn't even dream of being a composer—at least not out loud. I was going to be a singer and I am."[25]

It was his singing that drew Dvořák's interest. James Gibbons Huneker introduced Burleigh to Dvořák, and when the composer heard him sing, he invited him to come to his home to sing the plantation songs Burleigh had learned from his mother and his stepfather and from his grandfather.[26] Burleigh has left a vivid description of the evenings he spent in Dvořák's home on East Seventeenth Street. "He was in his shirtsleeves, with

Harry T. Burleigh at the time he knew
Dvořák at the Conservatory, ca. 1892.
(Courtesy Harry T. Burleigh, II.)

all his kids round him," remembered Burleigh. Moreover,

> he had bird cages all over the house with thrushes in them. He kept
> the cage doors open so the thrushes flew about freely and joined in
> the singing. I'd accompany myself at the piano. Dvořák especially
> liked Nobody Knows the Trouble I've Seen, and Go Down Moses.
> He asked hundreds of questions about Negro life.[27]

Once after Burleigh had sung "Go Down, Moses," Dvořák exclaimed, "Burleigh, that is as great as a Beethoven theme!"[28]

Another of Dvořák's favorites was "Swing Low, Sweet Chariot," the second and third measures of which, as Burleigh often pointed out, Dvořák used almost note for note in the second theme of the opening movement of the symphony "From the New World." However, direct quotation of folk melodies was not Dvořák's method for creating a nationalist style—in either Bohemia or America. That had been done before he arrived, by George Chadwick in the Scherzo of his Symphony No. 2, and Edward MacDowell employed the technique in his *Indian Suite* (first performed in New York in 1896). Instead, as Burleigh recalled, Dvořák "literally saturated himself with Negro song. . . . I sang our Negro songs for him very often, and before he wrote his own themes, he filled himself with the spirit of the old Spirituals." From the ordinary Dvořák created something extraordinary, music in which Americans of all ethnic backgrounds found a familiar resonance.[29]

Burleigh was frequently in Dvořák's company during the time the "New World" Symphony was being written. As he later remarked, he saw

more of Dvořák than most of the students who were in the advanced composition class. Burleigh, who was a trained stenographer (he took his class
notes verbatim in shorthand), wrote music manuscript with an engraver's
hand. Dvořák turned more and more of his manuscript copying over to Burleigh. "'Make the notes as big as my head, Harry, so I can see them,'" Burleigh remembered Dvořák saying.[30] An avid student, Burleigh absorbed a
great deal from this exposure to Dvořák's methods of composition. He even
received the dedication of Dvořák's choral arrangement of Stephen Foster's
"Old Folks at Home," singing in its premiere at Madison Square Garden on
23 January 1894, and he told an interviewer in 1941 that he had the manuscript (see Dr. Deane L. Root's essay, Chapter 18.)[31]

But it is his association with the "New World" Symphony for which
he will forever be remembered. Not only did he acquaint Dvořák with
"Swing Low, Sweet Chariot," but he participated in the scoring as well. "I
copied many of the orchestra parts of the 'New World' Symphony from his
original *partitur*," he recalled, "getting it ready for its first performance by the
Philharmonic."[32] According to an early biographer, H. C. Colles, Dvořák
changed his orchestration of the famous melody in the Largo from clarinet
and flutes to the *cor anglais*, or English horn, "because of all the instruments
it resembled the quality of Burleigh's voice most closely."[33] This melody, to
which William Arms Fisher, another student in Dvořák's composition class,
set the words "Goin' Home," has become so familiar that many people
believe it originated as a plantation song. The popular misconception suggests that Dvořák successfully captured the characteristic idiom of the songs
Burleigh sang to him.

From time to time after Dvořák's death, Burleigh was called upon to
comment about the extent to which Dvořák had consciously used African
American and Native American folk music as creative resources in his
"American" compositions. As early as 1893, a debate was raging. Philip Hale,
music critic of the Boston *Transcript* had scoffed at the notion of an African
American source for the "New World" Symphony. Eighteen years later, in
1911, Hale wrote Dvořák's sons, asking them to settle the question. The
sons replied that, although their father had been interested in "American
Negro airs, which abound in melodic particularities," and had studied their
scales, the Symphony's themes, "which as some pretend have been taken
from Negro airs, are absolutely our father's own mental property; they were
only influenced by Negro melodies." He had accomplished a similar transformation in the use of Slav idioms in his songs. Indeed, they claimed that all
of Dvořák's American works responded to Slavic origins,

and anyone who has the least feeling will proclaim this fact. Who will not recognize the homesickness in the largo of this symphony? The secondary phrase of the first movement, the first theme of the scherzo, the beginning of the finale and perhaps also the melody of the largo which give a certain impression of the groaning Negro song, are only influenced by this song and determined by change of land and the influence of a foreign climate."[34]

Taking a counterposition was W. J. Henderson, music critic of the New York *Sun*. He retorted that Hale had only succeeded in proving "the cause of his adversaries." He added sarcastically that Hale and his cohorts would probably "continue to insist that Dr. Dvořák never made any study of Negro themes, that he never asserted that upon them might be reared a distinctly American type of music, that he made no endeavor to do anything of the kind, that he never told any New York critic that he did, and that all New York critics are habitual evaders of the truth."[35]

When the "New World" Symphony was first performed in Hamburg, Germany, a clarinet player there had claimed that the Symphony was "an early work, composed by Dvořák in Europe and retouched for American consumption, dubbed 'New World' by him to please this country's public."[36] While American audiences enthusiastically welcomed Dvořák's contribution to American musical culture, the critics argued venomously over how much of America could actually be heard in it, and if American it was, whether that identity could or should be traced to Dvořák's use of African American or Native American themes.

Burleigh and Camille W. Zeckwer, a Dvořák composition student, attempted to clarify the issues. Their response was published in the Philadelphia Orchestra program for performances of the "New World" Symphony (conducted by Carl Pohlig) on 24 and 25 February 1911. Zeckwer verified that Dvořák had talked freely with his composition students about "what he was doing and what he thought they ought to do." Dvořák had played through the entire score for Zeckwer and had repeatedly spoken of his intention to use African American melodies as his inspiration for the Symphony. Moreover, Zeckwer described rehearsal discussions between Dvořák and conductor Anton Seidl about how the Symphony should be interpreted in its first performance "in order to bring out these American characteristics." In particular, Seidl had made "certain suggestions as to tempi, which Dvořák accepted, which suggestions were intended to give the full exotic effect of the so-called negro tunes." Furthermore, according to Zeckwer, those who heard the first performance believed that "its message from the 'New World' is only fully delivered when these ideas are revealed in the interpretation."[37]

Anton Seidl was a pupil of Richard Wagner and, as the conductor of the New York Philharmonic, a champion of Dvořák's works. He conducted the premiere of the "New World" Symphony at Carnegie Hall, 16 December 1893. Drawing by John C. Tibbetts.

Although Burleigh reiterated that Dvořák, for the most part, had "just saturated himself with the spirit of these old tunes and then invented his own themes," he questioned the prevailing tendency to "ignore the Negro elements" in the Symphony. He wondered why "many of those who were able in 1893 to find traces of Negro musical color all through the Symphony . . . now cannot find anything in the whole four movements that suggests any local or Negro influence." He verified that while "the workmanship and treatment of the themes was and is Bohemian," without a doubt Dvořák had been deeply influenced by Negro spirituals and by the songs of Stephen Foster, which Burleigh had also sung to him. Burleigh provided musical examples demonstrating the similarity between "Swing Low, Sweet Chariot"—"the old melody as the slaves sang it"—and the second theme of the first movement. He commented on Dvořák's use of the flatted seventh, a characteristic of many of the slave songs Burleigh had sung to him. On hearing the flatted seventh, Dvořák would jump up and ask, "Is that really the way the slaves sang it?" He continued at some length:

> I have never publicly been credited with exerting any influence upon Dr. Dvořák, although it is tacitly believed that there isn't much doubt about it, for I was with him almost constantly, and he loved to hear me sing the old melodies. Walter Damrosch once alluded to my having brought these songs to Dvořák's attention, but there was so much discussion and difference of opinion as to the value of the intimation that in the songs of the Negroes lay the basis for a national school of music and the controversy waxed so hot that all reference to the real source of his information was lost sight of.[38]

Burleigh declared that the introduction of the Symphony and the first theme of the opening movement was "pervaded with syncopation common to Negro song." The flatted seventh of the minor mode contributed to the "colorfulness" of the music, which he found "suggestive of the strangeness of the new country." On other occasions Burleigh acknowledged Native American influences on the Symphony. During its composition Dvořák had read the famine scene in Henry Wadsworth Longfellow's *Hiawatha.* "It had a great effect on him," Burleigh said, "and he wanted to express it musically" in the Largo. (See also Michael Beckerman's article, Chapter 15, on the *Hiawatha* references in the Symphony's scherzo.)[39]

Thanks to the inspiration of Dvořák and the practical assistance of others, including none other than Edward MacDowell, Burleigh brought the traditional spiritual into the arena of the art song. Dvořák had urged him to "give those melodies to the world."[40] Although Dvořák took himself away in 1895, Burleigh said "he left behind a richer appreciation of the beauties of Negro song, of its peculiar flavor, its sometimes mystical atmosphere, its whimsical piquancy, and its individual idiom, from all of which many other artists have already drawn inspiration."[41] Near the end of his life, when he made his last concert appearance in Erie, Burleigh said, "Under the inspiration of Dvořák, I became convinced that the spirituals were not meant for the colored people, but for all people."[42]

Edward MacDowell remains to this day the best-known American composer of the late nineteenth century. Although he objected in print to many of Dvořák's pronouncements regarding the roots of a new American music, in practice he was sympathetic to the incorporation of Native American and African American elements into his compositions. Drawing by John C. Tibbetts.

When Edward MacDowell heard Burleigh sing "Swing Low, Sweet Chariot" in a simple, traditional version, he said, "Burleigh, why not give that melody a setting that will make it available to all musicians and music lovers—to the Caucasian interpreter as to the Negro creator?" This from the composer who had rejected Dvořák's call for a nationalistic American music, even going so far as to demand that his compositions be dropped from a concert of American music![43] Burleigh reported that when he took him an early sketch of his setting of the melody, MacDowell helped him increase the sophistication of his arrangement.[44]

Years before he began publishing his solo arrangements of spirituals (beginning with "Deep River" in 1916), he performed them while traveling with Booker T. Washington through the resort areas of New England to raise funds for the Tuskegee Institute.[45] While he was recognized in the elite African American communities of metropolitan New York, Boston, Washington, D.C., Philadelphia, and other Eastern communities, and as far west as Chicago, as "the leading baritone of the race," some of these audiences were less than charmed by his use of dialect songs and spirituals. As he later recalled, "Audiences in Boston and Cleveland criticized me severely for singing these songs before white people." But Burleigh insisted that "these songs are our heritage and ought to be preserved, studied and idealized."[46]

In addition to his own performances, Burleigh collaborated with Kitty Cheatham in presenting a number of his arrangements before they were published. Cheatham was a storyteller-singer who, in the first decade of this century, created an extraordinary career telling children's stories and singing children's songs from every country. Her sensitive, carefully researched and beautifully staged performances were as enchanting to adults as to children. Her particular specialty was African American songs and stories, "without which no recital of hers would be complete."[47] Burleigh helped her prepare his spiritual arrangements for performance, and on numerous occasions he accompanied her on the piano. She also introduced Burleigh's arrangements to many audiences in Europe before they were published in the United States.[48]

New York audiences had heard Burleigh and several white singers perform songs from his 1901 collection, *Plantation Melodies, Old and New.*[49] Several of Burleigh's arrangements for Henry E. Krehbiel's *Afro-American Folksongs* (1914) were also used in recital by singers. And the Philharmonic Society of New York performed two of these arrangements in their 1913–14 concert season.[50] In 1913 his first two choral arrangements of spirituals, "Deep River" and "Dig My Grave," were premiered by Kurt Schindler's

Schola Cantorum. But with the publication of his 1916 solo arrangement of "Deep River," Burleigh's career moved into a new phase.[51] Thus, at age fifty, twenty years after Dvořák's departure, Burleigh had found the medium through which he would do his part to fulfill Dvořák's commission to "build a great and noble school of music" from his African American music heritage.

The success of Burleigh's solo arrangement of "Deep River" caught the attention of concert reviewers. Several critics observed that it appeared on more recital programs in New York City and Boston than any other song.[52] G. Ricordi, Burleigh's publishers, capitalized on its popularity, publishing advertisements in music journals listing the names of singers who performed it. The cover of the 1917 edition listed twenty-one singers who were using it.[53] President Woodrow Wilson's daughter Margaret Wilson sang it; composer Dudley Buck's voice students sang it; African American tenors Roland Hayes and Sidney Woodward sang it; and Boston critic Hiram K. Moderwell commented that "Deep River" had "justly brought [Burleigh] into prominence which he has long deserved."[54] Burleigh issued twelve spirituals for solo voice in 1917 and twenty more in the following five years, in addition to a number of critically acclaimed secular art songs.[55]

As Burleigh's arrangements of spirituals became standard fare for concert performers, white and black, controversies arose. When the white baritone, Oscar Seagle, ended a concert in Brooklyn in May 1917 with a group of Burleigh's spirituals, an advertisement in the Musical Courier hailed him as "the only vital interpreter of the negro spiritual."[56] As other singers followed Seagle's example and spirituals came to be in "in vogue," many African Americans were gratified to see spirituals gain wide acceptance. But for others, hearing these slave songs sung by white performers bore a distasteful irony. Both black and white reviewers noted the difficulty white singers often had in presenting spirituals convincingly. And a number of critics, black and white, protested that Burleigh's arrangements violated the essence of the original music sources. Spirituals had derived from group performance in particular contexts and were the product of artistic procedures rooted in an African music aesthetic. European solo performance practices, like the ritualized protocol of the concert stage where the distance between performer and audience is preserved, violated that aesthetic.[57]

From the beginning of his career as a singer and arranger of African American folk songs, Burleigh was careful to present these songs with dignity and according to the highest artistic standards, as he defined art. The struggle for dignity in the face of the popular portrayal of African American character and musical culture in minstrel and coon-song performance was relentless, Dvořák's 1893 affirmation (see Appendix A) notwithstanding. Most white art musicians of the first quarter of the twentieth century also railed against ragtime and jazz as musical travesty. But Burleigh's rejection of these emerging popular African American music forms gained special force from the need to defend the artistic value of African American music against demeaning stereotypes.

From 1917 on, Burleigh devoted himself to giving lecture-recitals on spirituals to educate both white and black audiences on the history of spirituals, their artistic value, and how they should be performed. As the Preface inside the cover of every Burleigh arrangement stated, "Success in singing these folk songs is primarily dependent upon deep spiritual feeling," and "their worth is weakened unless they are done impressively." The spirituals had originated as "the spontaneous outbursts of intense religious fervor"[58] and therefore they should be sung with reverence. To Burleigh, the "debasement" of this musical heritage in ragtime or jazz versions was a violation of their artistic and religious essence. Worse, for African American musicians to misuse spiritual melodies by "ragging" or "jazzing" them represented a betrayal of their most precious artistic heritage.

In 1922 two young African American Broadway musicians, Henry S. Creamer and J. Turner Layton (the son of John T. Layton who had conducted Burleigh's performance years before in Samuel Coleridge-Taylor's *Hiawatha*), used the melody of "Deep River" for their popular song "Dear Old Southland." Burleigh wrote a letter of protest to the NAACP, which was published by the New York *News* and carried in other papers as well. Burleigh charged that "delinquent musicians contemptuously disregard" the "mine of musical wealth" in spirituals. He deplored "the growing tendency of some of our musicians to utilize the melodies of our spirituals for fox trots, dance numbers and semi-sentimental songs." He alleged that they did so for "personal, commercial gain." He continued:

> Their work is meretricious, sacrilegious and wantonly destructive. It offends aesthetic feelings of all true musicians—white and black—and because some of us have endeavored never to sink the high standard of our art nor commercialize the sacred heritage of our people's song, but rather revere it and exalt it as a vital proof of the Negro's spiritual ascendancy over oppression and humiliation, we feel, deeply, that the willful, persistent, superficial distortion of our folk-songs is shockingly reprehensible.[59]

One of Burleigh's major concerns was that young people would be misled by this "pernicious musical trickery." As folk music was in the public domain and the perpetrators did not seem to realize the seriousness of their offense, he appealed to pride of race to convince these musicians to "forgo the cheap success and the easy money." Not only was their work in bad taste, they were "polluting a great, free fountain of pure melody."

Several years later when two other African American composers, his friends J. Rosamond Johnson and Lawrence Brown, published arrangements of spirituals in their *Book of American Negro Spirituals* (1925) that were intended to reproduce more accurately the harmonies of oral performance in African American communities, Burleigh criticized their work. In his review of the book, R. Nathaniel Dett wrote that "the use of jazz, the 'Charleston,' and other dance-like motifs in the accompaniment threaten[ed] seriously the spirit of nobility and dignity" that was appropriate for the spirituals. Like Dett, Burleigh felt Rosamond Johnson and Lawrence Brown had betrayed their responsibility to present the spirituals in a form representing the highest standard of musical excellence. Though he would probably not have used the term, this constituted for him a "black aesthetic."[60]

From a late twentieth century perspective, one could argue that the black aesthetic of the Harlem Renaissance—which freed African Americans to take pride in their traditional heritage through forms closer to their folk origins, without needing to transform them—represented a more valid African American aesthetic than Burleigh's insistence on a standard of musical excellence shaped by Euro-American music traditions. But it seems clear that Burleigh's path-breaking work helped to make that Renaissance possible. As James Weldon Johnson wrote in his preface to the *Second Book of American Negro Spirituals* (1926), the affirmation of a black aesthetic among literary artists of the Harlem Renaissance arose partly out of their awareness of the spirituals as a unique artistic heritage. "Almost suddenly the realization broke upon the Negro that in the Spirituals the race had produced one of the finest examples of folk-art in the world. The result was a leaping pride, coupled with a consciousness of innate racial talents and powers, that gave rise to a new school of Negro artists."[61]

In the years before his arrangements of spirituals were published, Burleigh had built a solid reputation as a composer of art songs. Some of them, like songs by his friend Victor Herbert, were light romantic ballads—the sort of thing in demand as encore pieces. Others were regarded by singers and music critics as among the best American art songs of their time. In

1915 *Musical America* ran a column listing "Some Compositions by Americans Which Are Worthy of Recognition" for the benefit of teachers and performers. The first column listed Burleigh's "Jean" (1903) and his song cycle *Saracen Songs* (1905). Subsequent issues named "Ethiopia Saluting the Colors" (1915), "He Sent Me You" (1915), "Just You" (1915), and "The Glory of the Day Was in Her Face," from the cycle *Passionale* (1915). In May of the same year *Musical America* asked twenty-seven opera and recital singers to list their ten favorite American songs. Six, including Eleanora de Cisneros, Mary Jordan, John McCormack, Dan Beddoe, Paul Althouse, and Herbert Witherspoon, listed songs by Burleigh, including two of the before-mentioned songs and "The Grey Wolf" (1915), "Her Eyes Twin Pools" (from *Passionale*), and "The Hour Glass" (1914). In February 1916 contralto Zabetta Brenska, who often performed with her husband, tenor Paul Althouse, replied when asked to name her favorite American song, "If I had to narrow my choice down to one composer, I should select Harry Burleigh's songs."[62]

Burleigh's more serious art songs tend to be shorter and more compressed than the lighter romantic ballads, the emotional intensity of their texts reflected in explorative harmonizations and in their concern for the compositional expression of mood, individual words, and phrases. His "Ethiopia Saluting the Colors" was described by critic Hiram K. Moderwell of the Boston *Evening Transcript* as demonstrating "the robust spirit . . . that is much needed to lift American song-literature from the deadly average of mediocrity which now holds it fast."[63]

Burleigh's skill as a music editor facilitated the publication of his own songs. He did free-lance editing for his publisher, William Maxwell, for several years. In 1913 Maxwell's brother George asked Burleigh to join the editorial staff of the New York branch of Ricordi and Company. From that time on, access to the publication of his songs was virtually assured.[64] From 1896 through 1913 he had published over sixty songs, including art songs, plantation songs, sacred solo songs, sacred choral anthems, and a set of piano sketches.[65] Ricordi was to publish over one hundred additional songs, including three song cycles, a set of violin and piano pieces, and more than seventy solo arrangements of African American spirituals and secular songs (many of which were also arranged for a variety of choral ensembles). For many years a substantial portion of Ricordi's song catalogue was devoted to Burleigh's music.

The success in 1917 of his solo arrangement of "Deep River" and eleven other spirituals began to eclipse his reputation as a secular art song composer. In the disillusionment following the First World War, the taste for the Romantic art song faded. Ragtime, blues, and jazz were finding their way into the instrumental compositions of American and European composers. But Burleigh had brought into American art song a new voice, the voice of the African American slave.

H. L. Mencken wrote in a 1917 article, "The Hoe-Down Begins to Soar," that Burleigh was one of the African American composers who would lead the "new flowering of American music which promises to be a part of the general intellectual reconstruction" that followed World War I. Mencken charged that white composers had hitherto only showed "a childish pedantry which fills the most hopeful with doubts and maketh the judicious to grieve." When they ignored their cultural roots and imitated the music of the immigrants, they produced "second-rate German music of the stupidest Kapell-meister type, or fourth-rate French music that is neither French nor music." Burleigh and his colleagues, by contrast, were "vastly more talented." Burleigh was noteworthy not just as a consequence of his African American heritage, but

> because he is one of the few Americans who have ever learned how to write a sound song. Moreover, the thing he achieves is an American song—not a limp reboiling of a German song or French song or a Russian song, but an American song, racy of the soil in its whole cut and color. In brief, the man writes music like Schubert, because music is always bubbling infernally within him, and not simply because he has learned how to make the pothooks and to copy harmonies out of books.[66]

Among all his works, including the art songs and the piano and violin pieces, Mencken concluded that the spirituals were his best work. "The negroes imagined these incomparable songs to begin with; now they have a composer to do for them what Silcher did for the German folksong."

In the final analysis, Burleigh did not see himself as the quintessential American composer Dvořák had envisioned or Mencken described. He was too modest for that. But though Burleigh viewed nationalism—black or otherwise—as too limiting for the artist, he nonetheless remained proud of his role in preserving the heritage of the spirituals. "We have not yet developed a distinctive national literature or art," he said in 1924; "we have not made American music. It will come, but it will take a long time. When it does, I think it will show the influence of the Negro spirituals. . . . They have

Harry T. Burleigh, ca. 1935. (Courtesy Harry T. Burleigh, II.)

not yet affected American music. They will not, until America is willing to admit that Negroes can be artists." As he often said, "in [spirituals] our race has pure gold."[67]

Near the end of his long life, Burleigh paid one last public tribute to the composer and friend who had so profoundly affected his life. On 13 December 1941, in celebration of the one hundredth anniversary of Dvořák's birth, Burleigh joined a group of dignitaries and musicians at the Dvořák home at 327 East Seventeenth Street in New York. Other guests included Jan Masaryk, the Czech Minister of Foreign Affairs; J. G. Kovařík, the student/ secretary who had accompanied the composer on his travels to New York and Spillville; conductor Bruno Walter; violinist Fritz Kreisler; and New York Mayor Fiorello La Guardia. At the suggestion of Kovařík and Burleigh, a commemorative plaque was affixed to the housefront. In spite of heavy rains the house was "so crowded that some feared it would collapse," according to one account. Further,

> it was a moving ceremony. . . . Kovařík was so deeply moved that he was unable to speak. Burleigh took over, with emotion and sensitivity. . . . Oh, how Burleigh did speak! . . . Burleigh paid tribute to the greatness, simplicity and humane charm of Master Dvořák and thanked him not only for having made the black folk melodies capable of artistic rendition, but for making them into spokesmen of the black people, that stand firmly against oppression and humiliation.[68]

In accepting Dvořák's challenge to "build a great and noble school of music," Burleigh had helped to coin the "pure gold" of the spirituals in universal currency. Dvořák, "the ordinary Czech musician," had given to ordinary African Americans a gift of their own musical heritage. As Burleigh said at the time of Dvořák's centennial, "Dvořák, a Czech with a great love for the common people of all lands, pointed the way."[71]

NOTES

1. Harry T. Burleigh, "The Negro and His Song," in *Music on the Air*, ed. Hazel Gertrude Kinscella (New York: The Viking Press, 1934), 186–189.

2. Lawrence W. Levine, *Black Culture and Black Consciousness: Afro-American Folk Thought from Slavery to Freedom* (New York: Oxford University Press, 1977), 138.

3. Copies of the manumission papers are in the Erie County Historical Society Burleigh Collection.

4. See the following: S. B. Nelson, "The Waters Family," in *Nelson's Biographical Dictionary* (Erie, Pennsylvania: S. B. Nelson, 1896), 742; Anne Keye Simpson, *Hard Trials: The Life and Music of Harry T. Burleigh* (Metuchen, New Jersey: The Scarecrow Press, Inc., 1990), 3; and Records of the 1850 U.S. Census.

5. For a record of Waters's Underground Railway activity, see Frank H. Severance, "Underground Trails," in *Old Trails on the Niagara Frontier* (Frank Severance, 1899), 255.

6. Saul Sack, *History of Higher Education in Pennsylvania*, 2 vols. (Harrisburg: Pennsylvania Historical and Museum Commission, 1963), vol. 1, 167.

7. Quoted in Alexander L. Murray, "The Provincial Freeman: A New Source for the History of the Negro in Canada and the United States," *Journal of Negro History*, 44 (1959), 133. See also Saul Sack, *History of Higher Education in Pennsylvania*, 2 vols. (Harrisburg: Pennsylvania Historical and Museum Commission, 1963), 167.

8. "Commencement of Avery College," Pittsburgh *Gazette*, 12 July 1855.

9. "Commencement at Avery College," Erie *Gazette*, 18 July 1855.

10. Letter from Fannie Moorhead to Anne K. Simson, 1 January 1986, Erie County Historical Society. See also Erie, "Harry Burleigh, Tenor [*sic*], Is Son of Former Slave," 10 April 1931.

11. Laura G. Sanford, *The History of Erie City, Pennsylvania* (New York: J. B. Lippincott & Co., 1861), 176.

12. In the first decades of the nineteenth century Pennsylvania had instituted a gradual emancipation act, so by 1825 slaves were free by law. But as late as 1819 P. S. V. Hamot, in whose home the founding members met in 1826 to form the St. Paul's Episcopal congregation, advertised an announcement of a runaway slave.

13. "The Churches of Erie," *Erie Weekly Dispatch*, 5 August 1865.

14. See, for example, "Easter Sunday School Celebration," *The Parish Guide*, 2:4, April 1873, 29.

15. Information on the St. Paul's Church repertoire was gathered by examining service bulletins from 1899. Burleigh left Erie in 1892, but the choir director and organist with whom Burleigh had sung were still in charge of the music at that time.

16. His Aunt Louise's part in arranging for lessons is reported in "How Harry T. Burleigh Rose to Fame and Fortune," the *New Deal*, an undated Erie black newspaper, ca. 1930, 9, Erie County Public Library Burleigh Collection. See also Lester A. Walton, "Harry T. Burleigh Honored To-Day at St. George's," 30 March 1924, reprinted in *The Black Perspective in Music*, 2:1, Spring 1974, 83.

17. Merton Robert Aborn, "The Influence on American Musical Culture of Dvořák's Sojourn in America," Ph.D. dissertation, Indiana University, 1965, 63.

18. Lester A. Walton, "Harry T. Burleigh Honored To-Day at St. George's," 82. See also Charlotte W. Murray, "The Story of Harry T. Burleigh," *The Hymn*, 17 (1966), 103.

19. William K. Kearns, *Horatio Parker, 1863–1919: His Life, Music and Ideas*, Composers of North America, no. 6 (Metuchen, New Jersey: The Scarecrow Press, Inc., 1990), 13.

20. Lester A. Walton, "Harry T. Burleigh Honored To-day at St. George's," 83.

21. Nora Douglas Holt, "Henry Thacker Burleigh," the *Chicago Defender*, 27 December 1920, 12; Lester A. Walton, "Harry T. Burleigh Honored To-day at St. George's," 83–84; Burleigh's grandson, Dr. Harry T. Burleigh II reports that the applicants sang behind a blind.

22. Unnamed, undated paper, Hartford, Connecticut, 16 December 1902; and F. R. Burton, unidentified paper, Yonkers, New York, 12 May 1903; both clippings courtesy of Dr. Harry T. Burleigh II.

23. Quoted in John Clapham, *Antonín Dvořák: Musician and Craftsman* (New York: St. Martin's Press, 1966), 3–5.

24. Barrymore L. Scherer, "A New Wave of Interest for a Beguiling Melodist," *New York Times*, 9 April 1989, H25.

25. Victor Herbert is quoted in Edward N. Waters, *Victor Herbert, A Life in Music* (New York: Macmillan, 1955), 88. See also "New York Church Pays Tribute to Burleigh," *Musical America*, 12 April 1924, 21; A. Walter Kramer, "H. T. Burleigh: Composer by Divine Right and the American Coleridge-Taylor," *Musical America*, vol. 23, no. 26 (29 April 1916), 25; and Harry T. Burleigh, "The Negro and His Song," 188.

26. John Clapham, "The Evolution of Dvořák's Symphony 'From the New World,'" *Musical Quarterly*, vol. 54, no. 2 (April 1958), 168.

27. "'Sweet Chariot' Inspired Anton Dvořák to Immortalize Negro Spirituals," New York *World Telegram*, 12 September 1941. See also Charlotte W. Murray, "The Story of Harry T. Burleigh," *The Hymn*, 17 (1966), 104.

28. Charlotte W. Murray, "The Story of Harry T. Burleigh," 104.

29. Harry T. Burleigh, "The Negro and His Song," 188.

30. A. Walter Kramer, "H. T. Burleigh: Composer by Divine Right and the American Coleridge-Taylor," 25. See also the following sources: Henry T. Finck, *My Adventures in the Golden Age of Music* (New York: Funk and Wagnalls, 1926), 279; Nora Douglas Holt, *New Amsterdam News*, 30 November 1946, 12; and Lester A. Walton, "Harry T. Burleigh Honored To-day at St. George's," 82.

31. "'Sweet Chariot' Inspired Anton Dvořák to Immortalize Negro Spirituals," New York *World*, 12 September 1941.

32. A. Walter Kramer, "H. T. Burleigh: Composer by Divine Right and the American Coleridge-Taylor," 25.

33. John Clapham. *Antonín Dvořák: Musician and Craftsman* (New York: St. Martin's Press, 1966), 90.

34. "Negro Music," *The Crisis*, vol. 1, no. 4, February 1911, 12.

35. "Negro Music," *The Crisis*, 12.

36. A. Walter Kramer, "H. T. Burleigh: Composer by Divine Right and the American Coleridge-Taylor," 25.

37. W. M. H., "Henry T. Burleigh's Contribution to the Discussion of the True Meaning of 'The New World Symphony,' The Philadelphia Orchestra Program, 24–25 February 1911, courtesy of Dr. Harry T. Burleigh II; see also Camille W. Zeckwer, "Dvořák as I Knew Him," the *Etude*, November 1919, 694.

38. Some of Burleigh's remarks from the 1911 Philadelphia Orchestra program were reprinted in March 1918 in the New York Philharmonic Society program. This source was often cited in later renewals of the discussion.

39. Harry T. Burleigh, "The Negro and His Song," 188; "New York Church Pays Tribute to Burleigh," *Musical America*, 12 April 1924, 21; see also Joan Foster, "The Negro Spirituals—Fad or Folk Music?" the *Musical Digest*, April 1928, 17, courtesy of Patricia Turner.

40. "'Sweet Chariot' Inspired Anton Dvořák to Immortalize Negro Spirituals," New York *World*, 12 September 1941.

41. Harry T. Burleigh, "The Negro and His Song," 189.

42. "Harry Burleigh Returns to Erie for Sunday Concert," Erie *Times*, 9 June 1944.

43. As early as 1891 MacDowell expressed his opposition to all-American concert programs (see his letter to Frederick Grant Gleason, 10 April 1891). His most notorious protest was his letter to Felix Mottl in February 1904, demanding that any work of his be dropped from an all-American concert at the Metropolitan Opera House. He offered to pay the cost of crossing his number off the program. MacDowell's letter is quoted in Alfred Frankenstein, "American Music at Home," *Juilliard Review* 3:1, Winter 1955–56, 3.

44. *New York Age*, 12 November 1927.

45. Burleigh's son Alston Waters Burleigh is quoted on this in "Burleigh Sings Spirituals amid Church Honors," New York *Herald Tribune*, 22 May 1933. Numerous items of correspondence relating to these appearances are in the Booker T. Washington Papers, Manuscript Division, Library of Congress.

46. Alain Locke in the Baltimore *Afro-American*, 16 June 1917, quoted in Anne Keye Simpson, *Hard Trials: The Life and Music of Harry T. Burleigh*, 291.

47. This was a common phrase. See, for example, H. F. P., "New Glories in the Art of Kitty Cheatham," *Musical America*, 29 March 1913, 40.

48. A. Walter Kramer, "Kitty Cheatham's Summer Abroad," *Musical America*, 5 November 1912, 36.

49. For example, David Bispham, an American baritone who staunchly supported American composers and who often performed songs in character costume, performed several of these songs in the United States and London. A reviewer for the London *Star* commented, "Why, when the originals are so priceless, should

anyone be at pains to produce imitations which have no merit?" (10 July 1901, Brooks & Denton publicity brochure. See also Metropolitan Opera House program, 22 February 1903. Both items are in the Burleigh Papers, courtesy of Harry T. Burleigh II).

50. These were "I'm a-Seekin' fo' a City, Hallelujah," and "I'm Gwine to Alabamy," which were performed under the title *Old Negro Folk Songs and Tales.* James Gibbons Huneker, *The Philharmonic Society of New York and Its Seventy-Fifth Anniversary: A Retrospect* (New York: New York Philharmonic Society [1917]).

51. Burleigh issued two solo versions of "Deep River" in 1916 and a third in 1917. His first version ended on the phrase "deep river," omitting the final "I want to cross over into camp ground," which ended the version published in the Fisk collection. His second 1916 version provided a more satisfying ending by adding a countermelody above the final "deep river" and one repetition of the phrase, "I want to cross over into campground." In the 1917 version Burleigh simplified the accompaniment, bringing the harmonization more in tune with the pentatonicism of the melody. The author is indebted to Wayne Shirley of the Library of Congress for alerting her to the second 1916 version.

52. See the New York *Tribune*, 24 November 1916; A. Walter Kramer, *Musical America*, 10 February 1917, 40; and Hiram K. Moderwell, "'Deep River' Popularizes a Composer," Boston *Evening Transcript*, 10 March 1917, reprinted in *The Black Perspective in Music*, vol. 2, no. 1, Spring 1974, 75.

53. The present author has documented thirty-four nationally and internationally known white singers who used Burleigh's "Deep River" during the 1916-1917 season, and a study of the use of Burleigh's music in Pittsburgh indicated a similar trend during that year.

54. Hiram K. Moderwell, "'Deep River' Popularizes a Composer," 75.

55. Burleigh's unique contribution was to pioneer the arrangement of spirituals for solo voice in art song form, but he also arranged many of these songs for mixed, men's, and women's choral ensembles. Later, other arrangers published choral versions based on Burleigh's harmonizations for solo voice.

56. *Musical Courier*, 3 May 1917, 18 (courtesy of Anne Keye Simpson). It should be noted that Roland Hayes was not widely known among white audiences outside of Boston until his return from Europe in 1923. His performances of spirituals, as well as those of Paul Robeson and Marian Anderson, redefined in their own way what a "vital interpretation" of spirituals could be.

57. In a 1919 New York *Tribune* review, Henry E. Krehbiel contrasted two arrangements by white folklorist Natalie Curtis Burlin with two "beautifully and reconditely arranged by Mr. Burleigh." Krehbiel said Burlin's arrangements "made a good and convincing demonstration of the proper treatment of folk-songs of this character" and warned that "a good folk-song can be spoiled by too much sophistication." (Quoted in *Southern Workman*, vol. 49, no. 1, January 1920, 6). See also Carl Van Vechten in *Keep A-Inchin' Along*, ed. Bruce Kellner (Westport, Conn: Greenwood Press, 1979), 38, and Alain Locke, *The Negro and His Music* (Washington D.C.: The Associates in Negro Folk Education, 1936), 23.

58. This phrase originated in Thomas F. Seward's "Preface to the Music," in the Fisk Jubilee collection, *The Jubilee Singers and Their Campaign for Twenty Thousand Dollars* (Boston: Lee & Shepard, 1872), 163.

59. "Eminent Musician Assails Misuse of Spirituals in Dance Tunes," New York *News*, 18 November 1922. Burleigh had used the melody of "Somebody's Knockin' at Your Door" in "Ahmed's Farewell," the last song in his cycle *Saracen Songs* (1914), but this use as an art song theme fit Burleigh's definition of the appropriate artistic development of spiritual melodies.

60. Burleigh's criticism was reported in a letter from Carl Van Vechten to Paul Robeson's wife, Eslanda, 9 October 1925; quoted in Martin Bauml Duberman, *Paul Robeson* (New York: Alfred A. Knopf, 1988), 594. See also R. Nathaniel Dett, review of *The Book of American Negro Spirituals* in *Southern Workman*, 54 (December 1925), 564.

61. James Weldon Johnson and J. Rosamond Johnson, *The Second Book of American Negro Spirituals* (New York: The Viking Press, 1926), 19.

62. "Some Compositions by Americans Which Are Worthy of Recognition," *Musical America*, 5 June 1915, 21; 17 July 1915, 35. See also "Their Ten Favorite American Songs," *Musical America*, 16 October 1915, 3–5.

63. Hiram K. Moderwell, "'Deep River' Popularizes a Composer," 75–79.

64. Burleigh's first publication was the 1896 song "Christmas Bells," written for use at St. George's Church. This song, which is not mentioned either by Roland Allison or Anne Simpson, is in the Burleigh music collection at the Library of Congress.

65. A set of violin and piano pieces apparently written in 1901 has not been traced and may not have been published.

66. H. L. Mencken, "The Hoe-Down Begins to Soar," unidentified paper, November 1917, courtesy of Dr. Harry T. Burleigh II.

67. "New York Church Pays Tribute to Burleigh," 27.

68. Quoted in Anne Keye Simpson, *Hard Trials*, 141.

69. "'Sweet Chariot' Inspired Anton Dvořák to Immortalize Negro Spirituals."

CHAPTER TEN

Dvořák, Stephen Foster, and American National Song

Charles Hamm

$\mathcal{T}$here were no courses in American music or popular music when I was a student, to my knowledge, and ethnomusicology was in its infancy in this country. But the proliferation of such courses in the past two decades has been little short of amazing. At my school, Dartmouth College, more than half of all music courses now deal wholly or in part with American, popular, or non-Western music, and no more than a third deal solely with the Western European classical repertory. In my opinion, though, the pendulum hasn't swung far enough in this direction. It's a simple matter of percentages: if there were any way of measuring the amount of music performed and listened to in the contemporary world, we would see that only a tiny fraction is Western art music, and limiting one's knowledge to this fragment alone is an act of blatant ethnocentricity. Quite beyond that, study and increased awareness of popular, traditional and non-Western musics has the potential of opening up new perspectives on even the canonical repertory of classical music.

A case in point involves the study and interpretation of Dvořák's visit to the United States. When he arrived in New York, the city was seen by certain "older" Americans as being overrun by hordes of immigrants from undesirable national backgrounds who couldn't speak English and weren't even Protestant. The fact that Dvořák went to that city rather than to Boston, and that he soon suggested that American composers might draw on the culture of ethnic groups outside the traditional New England establishment, surely had something to do with the suspicion directed toward him in certain conservative musical quarters, particularly in New England.[1]

Dvořák's attitudes toward the music of minority national groups had been anticipated by Stephen Foster. I devote an entire chapter to Foster in my book *Yesterdays: Popular Song in America*,[2] developing a rather elementary argument that hadn't, however, been put forward before: that Foster was a professional songwriter rather than merely a talented amateur; a composer who had studied a wide range of music including some of the classical repertory and opera; and a songwriter who wrote popular songs from choice, not from poverty of intention or absence of musical taste as some people would have us believe.

As an important part of his musical education, Foster mastered a wide range of national song styles. He knew German songs, including some by Schubert and Abt. He certainly knew Irish songs, many of them. He knew the Italian vocal style very well, from exposure to both song and opera. He had some contact with the music of black Americans, though it's not altogether clear what and how much. One can see Foster's knowledge of various bodies of music in his arrangements in *The Social Orchestra* and in his direct emulation of one or another national song style in some of his earliest songs. (See Deane Root's article, Chapter 18.) The central point of my chapter is that, as a professional musician who had made it his business to absorb these various styles, Foster then proceeded to bring aspects of them together into his own style. If one understands all this and knows what to look for, one can take any later song by Foster, including the well-known ones, and say, "Well, yes, that phrase draws on Irish melody," or "That turn of phrase derives from Italian opera," or whatever. Foster incorporated these various elements into a style that became his own and, in time, came to be heard as "American."

In the last years of his life, Foster was making enough money from his songwriting—from royalties on his older songs and the sale of new songs to various publishers—to sustain him. He didn't manage his money well, and he died in virtual poverty, but he was a professional songwriter—the first American to make a living this way, though there were no effective copyright laws at that time and he was victimized by publishers who brought out many of his songs in editions from which he collected no fees and no royalties. It would be half a century before Irving Berlin and other Tin Pan Alley songwriters succeeded in setting up structures giving them control over their products.

In Foster's day, in both the home parlor where people gathered to sing and play for one another and in public performances, distinctions between "popular" and "classical" music were much less rigid and important than they were to become later. Selections from opera and classical song repertory were often published in simplified arrangements for performance by amateurs. One could say, in fact, that Italian opera by Bellini and Donizetti became popular music, since selections were sold in large quantity, to be performed and listened to by a "mass" of amateurs. Collections of nineteenth-century sheet music often mixed arias from Italian opera, art songs by Schubert and other classical composers (in English translation), and songs by Foster and his peers, which today would be classified as popular music.

A more rigid division between popular and classical music began to take shape shortly after mid-century, perhaps especially in *Dwight's Journal of Music*, published between 1852 and 1881 by John Sullivan Dwight, a Harvard-educated musical amateur devoted to the music of Beethoven, Schubert, and other early nineteenth-century European composers. Dwight saw his mission as "correcting" and "elevating" the musical taste of America by encouraging the performance and understanding of classical music. In doing so, he felt that he was promoting a body of music that was morally and spiritually uplifting, in contrast to the more popular genres.

Dwight's attitude was part and parcel of the emergence of more tightly stratified class structures in the United States. In the second half of the nineteenth century, classical music became more and more associated with the cultural and economic elite; the very notion that one body of music is superior to all others and can be understood and "appreciated" only by a small, privileged segment of the population is in itself elitist. The American people were perceived as being split into "us" and "them," and in a way that was judgmental: we have our music and they have theirs; and our music is better than theirs. Less remarked was the fact that this cultural divide corresponded to ethnic and national divisions as well: most of the elite were of Anglo-Saxon descent, most "others" were Irish, Italian, black, German, Scandinavian, and soon Central European and southern Mediterranean.

It's no accident that the most important patrons of classical music in New York, the people who funded opera companies and symphony orchestras and attended their performances, were the Carnegies and other "robber barons." What does this mean? Quite simply that at certain points in the history of our country, classical music has been an instrument of power—social power, economic power, political power. In this connection, Elise Kirk has published a most interesting book about music in the White House,[3] underlining how certain presidents have used classical music to make statements and to create specific images of "culture."

On the other hand, America's emerging and vital popular music scene, soon to be called Tin Pan Alley, was dominated by people who were not in positions of economic and social power, at least in part because they were Irish, German, and above all, Jewish. Drawing on a variety of popular and traditional musical styles brought by successive waves of immigrants, and blending these with older popular strains of American popular music (which had themselves been forged largely from many different ethnic traditions), popular songwriters created a repertory which soon swept over the entire country, and much of the rest of the world as well. This style drew on Italian, Irish, black, and other national elements, but it was perceived as distinctively "American" because it was only in the United States that all these different strains came together. One doesn't need to talk about pentatonic scales and such things in discussing this music. The social fact comes first and is most important.

Given this context, one can better understand how Dvořák's suggestion that a truly American music might be based on the music of socially and politically marginal groups was given a negative reception in certain quarters. New England, for instance, had become a veritable hotbed of social conservatism. A most interesting book by MacDonald Smith Moore, *Yankee Blues*,[4] argues that such New England composers as George Chadwick, Daniel Gregory Mason, and Charles Ives felt that they had inherited a mission to preserve "true" American culture and art (see Stuart Feder's "psychoanalytical" discussion of Dvořák and Ives, Chapter 12 in this volume). Two separate issues were at stake: the survival of classical music in the face of the growing threat posed by popular music, and the survival of Anglo-American people and their culture in the face of the growing threat posed by increasing tides of immigration from non-British lands. But in the minds of these composers, the two issues were, in fact, closely related. Classical music was first and foremost the province of upper-class Anglo-Saxons (though Germanic elements dominated in other parts of the country), and popular music was the province of the lower classes, mostly of non-British descent. Thus the split between classical and popular music also had racial and ethnic dimensions.

The later nineteenth century witnessed the emergence of the concept of "national race," which held that each large nation-state had a dominant "race" with a common language, history, and culture. Anyone living within such a nation-state who did not share its ethnicity was regarded as marginal and suffered cultural exclusion. Richard Wagner wrote, for example, that it was impossible for a Jewish person to speak the German language authoritatively and that German culture would forever remain foreign to the German

Jew, who would always remain alienated in a society he could never fully understand. Thus, in Wagner's opinion, no Jew could ever write "German" music. Similar arguments were put forward in the United States. John Powell, a composer from Virginia, insisted that everything fine and progressive in America's past and present, its sportsmanship and sense of fair play and justice, was derived from Anglo-Saxon culture. Thus, Anglo-Saxon models were the only fitting basis for American music. Daniel Gregory Mason saw the Anglo-American New England individual as fully representative of the "American temper," and he and his New England peers were convinced that their own music, with its Anglo-Saxon roots, could redeem the American spirit and help audiences understand what it meant to be an American.

Doubts were expressed by such people that "alien races" could ever become integrated into American culture. John Powell insisted that "Americans" were no more "black Africans" than they were "red Indians." Gilbert Seldes questioned that the music of such people could ever be considered our national music. Mason wrote that Jews, who were coming to America by the millions, constituted a menace to our culture, threatening to corrupt or debauch public taste, since Hebrew art juxtaposed violent extremes of passion with strains of eroticism and pessimism; such "exaggerations" were in conflict with Anglo-Saxon sobriety and restraint.

I number myself among those who believe that the cultural history of our country is written largely in the statistics of immigration. Patterns changed dramatically in the two decades after Dvořák's visit, as a result of what we today would call backlash from many people, not least politicians, who began viewing with alarm a situation whereby the United States was being so largely peopled by "undesirable" ethnic and national groups as a result of several decades of relatively unrestrained immigration. By the second decade of the twentieth century, the flow into America of central European and Mediterranean peoples, most of them Catholics or Jews, had come to a virtual halt as the result of new immigration laws. This is a common first step when the "older" population of a country begins to be concerned about new arrivals: they take steps to stem the flow. This had happened in the nineteenth century, for instance, with the Chinese Exclusion Laws, once cheap labor was no longer needed to build the transcontinental railway lines.

The "Yankee" composers, who were convinced that classical music in European style written by Anglo-Americans should be *the* American music, wanted to stop all immigration from Russia, Poland, Turkey, southern Italy, and Greece, and to keep ex-slaves in their place in the South. How could the Negro and the Jew speak for America? After all, according to their way of thinking, these people did not belong to the "American race" and never would.

The irony, of course, is that the culture of the United States had been, and continued to be, incredibly enriched by such people. They *did* become Americans, and through such composers as Irving Berlin and Duke Ellington and George Gershwin they *did* speak to and for America.

When Dvořák arrived here in 1892, this debate over American character and musical style was in its first stages. It's usually claimed that he suggested the possibility of a distinctive American music built on Indian and Negro melodies, but in fact he proposed something quite different. Most often quoted in this connection is his essay entitled "Music in America."[5] (See Appendix A for the complete text of this article.) As found today in several anthologies, the piece has been cut to no more than two-thirds of its original length, with omissions that alter its sense.

In the original, Dvořák begins with the disclaimer that as a recent arrival in the country he isn't really qualified to speak about American music. He's been struck, however, by how America's population is so varied, made up of the "commingling of so many different national races," and how music from other parts of the world reaches the United States so quickly, given the modern capability for instantaneous transmission. Some people have argued on these two grounds, he says, that no distinctively American music can come into being.

But in his opinion there already exists a body of "national song" in the United States, the "plantation songs" of Stephen Foster and his peers. Dvořák recognizes that those were composed by white professional songwriters, not by Negroes themselves. But he believes that it matters little if existing and future American "national songs" derive from the music of the Creoles, the black man, or the homesick German or Norwegian, no more than it matters that Shakespeare borrowed his plots from other writers. What does matter is that such "lovely songs" exist and are accepted by Americans as their own.

In this essay, then, Dvořák denied that the music of any one national group could be considered the true American style, but suggested rather that such a style could come about from integration of the musics of the various nationalities making up the country's population. In his opinion this had already happened with the plantation songs of Foster and other songwriters, which he knew were contemporary products of professional songwriters, not the folk songs of black slaves and ex-slaves; and he predicted that other American "national song" styles would be forged in similar fashion from the music of other groups.

In this essay Dvořák didn't urge American composers to draw on the folk songs of one group or another, and in fact he wasn't concerned with "folk song" at all, never using the term. He predicted a continuing school of American national song, drawn from elements of the country's diverse population, and he thought that America's composers of classical music might well draw on such material, much as he himself had drawn on the popular dance music of his native land in some of his compositions written before he came to the New World. And his prediction indeed came true in the decades following his visit to America, when music by immigrant, urban, Jewish composers with names like Irving Berlin, George Gershwin, and Aaron Copland—borrowing elements from black, Irish, Jewish, Italian, and Anglo-American styles—was perceived at home and abroad as a distinctive American music. The New England Anglophiles' worst nightmare was realized. One could argue that this came about, at least in part, because these men had been preceded by a Stephen Foster and an Antonín Dvořák who had suggested and demonstrated that various national and ethnic styles could become part of an American style.

Perhaps Dvořák's most important contribution to American music was his foresight and audacity in suggesting that contemporary, commercially produced popular music could be the national song of the United States. Not blinded by the ethnocentricity or elitism of his peers in America, he was able to see that a nation's distinctive classical repertory might be built, not on its "folk music," whatever that term means, but on its "commercial" popular music. And in this connection it should be noted that a melody from his "New World" Symphony, fitted with words by one of his students, William Arms Fisher, and titled "Goin' Home," became an American popular song after he returned to Europe.

NOTES

This article is based on the editor's interview with Prof. Charles Hamm at the Dvořák Sesquicentennial Conference and Festival in New Orleans, 14–20 February 1991. The interview has been subsequently revised by Professor Hamm especially for this volume.

1. For an invaluable documentation of the New England response to Dvořák's pronouncements, see Adrienne Block, "Boston Talks Back to Dvořák," *I.S.A.M. Newsletter*, vol. 18, no. 2 (May 1989), 10–11, 15.

Dvořák's article in the New York *Herald* of 21 May 1893 was reprinted in the Boston *Herald,* and a number of Boston musicians responded to his remarks. Those that questioned Dvořák's assertions regarding the importance of the black musical heritage to an American national expression were John Knowles Paine, head of the Music Department at Harvard University, George Whitefield Chadwick, and Mrs. H. H. A. Beach. Paine retorted that Dvořák "greatly overestimates the influence that the national melodies and folksongs have exercised on the higher forms of musical art"; Chadwick stated, "Such negro melodies as I have heard . . . I should be sorry to see become the basis of an American school of musical composition"; and Beach said, "I cannot help feeling justified in the belief that they are not fully typical of our country. The African population of the United States . . . represents only one factor in the composition of our nation. Moreover, it is not native American[;] the Africans are no more native than the Italians, Swedes or Russians."

2. Charles Hamm, *Yesterdays: Popular Song in America* (New York: W. W. Norton and Company, 1979).

3. Elise K. Kirk, *Music at the White House: A History of the American Spirit* (Urbana: University of Illinois Press, 1986).

4. MacDonald Smith Moore, *Yankee Blues* (Bloomington: Indiana University Press, 1985). Moore points out that Mason, Ives, and their "Yankee" peers referred to their Anglo-Saxon heritage as a racial inheritance that had sired "a neighborly sense of moral community peculiar to old New England." They believed their generation "was the last generation of composers to retain a semblance of ethnic unity." Moore continues: "The diversity of the younger generation encouraged the Yankees to define themselves by what they were not: not recent immigrants, neither Catholics nor Jews, seldom enthusiasts of the emergent ethnic, industrial, urban America, not Southerners, and surely not Negroes." (4–5)

5. "Music in America" was published in *Harper's New Monthly Magazine*, vol. 90, no. 87 (February 1895), 428–434, and reprinted in abridged form in *Composers on Music*, ed. Sam Morgenstern (New York: Pantheon, 1956), 258–266.

CHAPTER ELEVEN

Dvořák's Long American Reach

Adrienne Fried Block

*I*n the introduction to an edition of Edward MacDowell's *Historical and Critical Essays*, Irving Lowens wrote: "In 1912 Dvořák's reputation was at its zenith in America, and his viewpoint in regard to the sources of our national music was very popular."[1] Not only was his influence still strong two decades after he left the United States, but there is also considerable evidence that his definition of Americanism in music determined the parameters of the debate over nationalism for almost half a century. Dvořák's immediate influence is hardly news to American scholars; indeed, it is acknowledged in most discussions of nationalism in histories of American music.[2] What has perhaps been less generally recognized, however, is the lengthy duration of Dvořák's influence.

The first task of this essay is to put the pieces together—including ideological precepts and musical examples—so that the larger picture can emerge. The second task is to show how folk music research in the United States affected and was affected by the nationalist movement in American music, something not heretofore considered. Along the way, I will also consider—albeit all too briefly—perceptions and misperceptions concerning folk music and its role in the creation of a distinctive national style.

Dvořák came to the United States in 1892 not only to head the National Conservatory of Music in New York and teach composition to the students there but also to stimulate American composers to create a national style. As his own awareness of American music evolved during his three-year sojourn, he made a series of public statements on how to do this. His first statement appeared on 21 May 1893, eight months after his arrival. He told composers that an American national style should be based on the music of African Americans. He himself stated that his just-completed symphony "From the New World," his first American work, was founded largely on plantation, Creole, or southern tunes (see Michael Beckerman's essay, Chapter 15, for a different reading of the work) and that while there were no direct quotations, he had imbued the symphony with "characteristics that are distinctly American."[3]

He heard black spirituals sung by Harry Thacker Burleigh, a student at the National Conservatory and a professional singer, composer, and arranger. Burleigh gave an estimate of his own influence on the "New World" Symphony: "[Although] the workmanship and treatment of the themes [of the symphony] was and is Bohemian . . . there is no doubt at all that Dvořák was deeply impressed by the old Negro 'spirituals' and also by Foster's songs. It was my privilege to sing repeatedly some of the old plantation songs for him in his house, and one in particular, 'Swing Low, Sweet Chariot,' greatly pleased him, and part of this old spiritual will be found in the second theme of the first movement of the symphony" (see Jean Snyder's essay, Chapter 9, on Burleigh).[4]

At the time of the premiere of the "New World" Symphony in December 1893, Dvořák amended his prescription: now he suggested that composers create a national style from Native American as well as black folk music. During the previous summer Dvořák had heard Native American music while on vacation in Spillville, Iowa (see John Tibbetts's essay, Chapter 7, on Spillville).[5] He also had attended Buffalo Bill's Wild West Show in which Indians danced and sang;[6] and he may have examined Theodore Baker's dissertation on the music of the North American Indian.[7]

Dvořák also changed his story about the sources of inspiration for the "New World" Symphony. Now he said that there were two primary influences—black melodies for the outer movements and Indian melodies for the two inner ones, adding that the two bodies of folk music "bore a remarkable similarity" to each other—and to Scottish and Irish melodies as well[!][8] (The illustration on page 159, executed by James Hadley in 1934, reflects this revised view.) Ironically, the theme of the second movement became famous when Williams Arms Fisher, a composition student of Dvořák's, added a text and turned it into a pseudo-spiritual, "Goin' Home."

Dvořák's last statement about musical nationalism in the United States came in May 1895. About to make his final departure for home, he tacitly admitted that his original prescriptions were based on incomplete

Antonín Dvořák by James Hadley in an unidentified publication (1934).
Courtesy of the Iconography Collection, New York Public Library.
Used with permission.

knowledge of musical traditions in the United States and that now he believed that "the germs for the best of music lie hidden among all the races that are commingled in this great country" (see Appendix A for these texts).[9]

Many people ignored that last statement. Rather, they accepted Dvořák's previous suggestions, often choosing between Indian and black traditions as a basis for national music. Louis Elson, writing twenty years later, believed that the music of African Americans was more likely to be that basis.[10] Charles Sanford Skilton, an Indianist and student of Harry Rowe Shelley (who in turn had been one of Dvořák's students at the Conservatory), told the Music Teachers' National Association in 1918 that tribal music "possesses elements of vitality and interest that opened an unique though limited field to the American composer."[11]

When he prescribed tribal music and plantation songs, Dvořák was choosing traditional music of the most downtrodden and oppressed or, as Hitchcock has phrased it, of the "folk," identified as "national or regional or even racial children."[12] Here, for example, is historian Rupert Hughes writing in 1899: "All national musics are founded on the groundwork of humble and unlettered musicians, whose only thorough-bass was natural talent and emotion."[13] Carl Dahlhaus questioned the validity of such a choice in his excellent essay on European musical nationalism:

> It was the nineteenth century which chose to believe—on very shaky grounds—that national character was the primary and essential quality of folk music, and that folk music expresses the spirit of a people (understood as the spirit of the nation, first and most clearly manifested in the culture of the lower classes).[14]

He also pointed out that the creators of folk music were separated by class from the composers who quoted folk music (e.g., Edward MacDowell and John Powell) and from their concert audiences as well. Nevertheless, he wrote, composers who base their works on folk elements hope to "reconcile artistic integrity with popularity." As these works show, and as Dahlhaus reminds us, the matter of class divisions did not make the use of folk music invalid or take away its power to influence composers, to enrich their writing, or in some cases to lead them to create new and distinctive styles.

There was still another misperception: eventually a grand assimilation of disparate population groups would occur, and a unified folk music tradition would evolve. This idea surfaced before Dvořák's American stay. Fanny Morris Smith wrote in 1888 that "the future music of America will have all the most sterling qualities, will lack nothing of this unique, priceless endowment of the musical inheritance of all constituent countries."[15] That opinion continued to be heard for decades. In 1917 the composer Henry Gilbert wrote,

> Our coming American music will perhaps not be built upon but will contain and reflect elements derived from all the folk-songs of the various races—fused together by the new and all-powerful element denominated American spirit: a mood of fundamental optimism and heroic valor; a will of accomplishment, laughing at death. For America is surely the great adventure of humanity in recent times.[16]

Gilbert reflected current opinion regarding the ultimate formation of a unified folk heritage, but he was prescient when he suggested the existence of an overarching "American" spirit. Today, of course, we have replaced the idea of the melting pot with the view that the many multiethnic strains will continue to coexist, each having its own special contribution to make.

Following Dvořák's catalytic statements, three overlapping waves of consciously nationalist art music arose in America. Each was dependent on the availability in print, in performance, and on recordings of a specific folk or traditional repertory. The first wave of art music was based on Native American music, the second on traditional black music, and the third—one that Dvořák did not foresee but that nevertheless was inspired through his students—on Anglo-American music.

Before considering these movements, I would like to call attention to a group of proto-Anglo-American works that may have been affected by Dvořák. Because I have discussed this music in an earlier article, only a summary is needed here.[17] As America's leading composers and members of the its first school of art composers, named by Hitchcock the "Second New England School," the Bostonians George Whitefield Chadwick, Arthur Foote, Amy Beach, and Edward MacDowell expressed opinions regarding Dvořák's recommendations, some in partial support, some clearly opposed.[18] The idea that they, rather than Dvořák, should be the ones to define an American style is implicit in their responses. This attitude later become explicit in the writings of Daniel Gregory Mason, also a product of the Boston school.[19]

Even more to the point, all wrote compositions influenced by folk music, especially music from Ireland and Scotland. As Charles Hamm has pointed out, Irish music had been an important influence in America from the seventeenth century on, first through the oral tradition and later, most powerfully, with the introduction (ca. 1810) of songs from Thomas Moore's *Irish Melodies*, a collection that "quickly entered the mainstream of music in America and stayed there throughout the nineteenth century."[20] Scottish popular songs also entered the American musical mainstream, especially through the publication of the songs of Robert Burns. Given that heritage, it is hardly surprising that American composers should quote the actual songs as well as write in those folk idioms.

But an added factor, noted by Victor Yellin, was that successive waves of immigration beginning in the second half of the nineteenth century eventually threatened the cultural dominance of the Yankee composers, and he suggests that compositions such as Beach's Symphony in E Minor ("Gaelic") (1894–96), Margaret Ruthven Lang's "An Irish Love Song" (1895) and "An Irish Mother's Lullaby" (1900), Foote's "Loch Lomond" (1895), MacDowell's "Keltic" Sonata (1901), Chadwick's *Four Irish Songs* (1910) and his symphonic poem, *Tam O'Shanter* (1914–15), grew out of their search for musical roots as well as a desire to reassert Yankee dominance.[21] Although all five composers used folk idioms before Dvořák's arrival in America, they increased their use of Irish and Scottish folk music significantly after 1893.

There may have been another contributing influence. Olin Downes suggested in 1943 that Gilbert's incidental music of 1903–04 for plays by Yeats and Synge, in which he quotes Celtic folk tunes, was a response to the Stateside performances of plays of the Irish Renaissance. But it also could have been an "American expression, if only because, from the standpoint of a believer in musical folklore as basic material for a national school of composition, [Gilbert] conceived of such a school as gradually emerging and taking shape from the melodies of the races settled on this soil, including the Celtic!"[22] But like many who were influenced by Dvořák, Gilbert's main preoccupation from 1898 on was the creation of American music out of the folk tunes of Native and African Americans.

THE INDIANIST MOVEMENT

While Irish and Scottish folk music was ubiquitous to the point of being taken for granted as "American" music, this was far from the situation with Native American music. For Caucasians it was as exotic as music from the Far East. Nevertheless, research into Native American cultural life, supported by the Federal Government as an adjunct to its political aims, began in earnest in the 1880s following the publication of Baker's dissertation. Soon thereafter, studies by ethnologists from the Smithsonian Institution, the United States Bureau of Ethnology, and the Peabody Institute of Archaeology and Ethnology at Harvard appeared, including Franz Boas's on the Alaskan Inuit and the Kwakiutl of Canada and Alice Fletcher's on the music of the Omaha.[23] Jessie Walter Fewkes and Benjamin Ives Gilman collected music of the Southwest Indians, also issuing their first reports before the advent of Dvořák.[24] The emphasis changed after Dvořák's arrival. Now a number of collectors stressed the usefulness of their publications for composers. Among them was Henry Edward Krehbiel, folklorist and music critic of the New York *Tribune*. Krehbiel, who had been collecting for two decades, was interested in all folk music but especially that of African and Native Americans. At the World's Columbian Exposition in Chicago in 1893, he appeared before the Musical Congresses to report on and sing an Indian Council chant that retells tribal history of the Iroquois.[25] On the other hand, a publication of 1895 for which Krehbiel was assistant editor includes a discussion of Americanism that focuses almost exclusively on black music as the source for art music.[26]

In 1899 Krehbiel began publishing a series of articles in the New York *Tribune* on folk music, emphasizing its use in art music "to show the bearing of folk-tunes upon national schools."[27] Krehbiel's articles are important not only for their information about folk music from many countries and their inclusion of notated music but also for his extensive bibliographies, which offer an excellent summary of work done to date.

Krehbiel recalled and refuted negative initial reactions to the use of Native and African American music in art music: "Dr. Dvořák . . . showed [in his American works] that the laughter of the skeptics was as 'the crackling of thorns under a pot' in the case of negro songs, and much of the ribaldry which greeted the Indian notion was silenced when Mr. MacDowell produced his 'Indian Suite.' "[28] This Suite, based on melodies found in Baker, was commenced but not completed before Dvořák arrived in 1892. Because Krehbiel's articles on music of the American Indian appeared, not in some obscure publication, but rather in a leading daily newspaper, they had a wide audience among many people for whom the information was entirely new.

At about the same time, Alice Fletcher responded to Dvořák's suggestions by producing, in 1900, a collection of music specifically for composers, *Indian Story and Song from North America.*[29] The melodies in this collection were harmonized, as were those in earlier collections, mostly by John Comfort Fillmore, despite the fact that harmony is not part of the Native American musical tradition. Fillmore justified the use of chordal accompaniments because he believed that Indians "heard" traditional Western harmonies as they sang their monophonic melodies—that they had "the natural, universal harmonic sense."[30] By extension, this notion became the justification for composers to provide not only simple but also harmonically rich and complex settings for Native American tunes, something Indianist composer Charles Wakefield Cadman later called "idealization."[31]

In 1901 Arthur Farwell became, in his own words, "the first composer in America to take up Dvořák's challenge . . . in a serious and whole-hearted way."[32] Unable to find a publisher for his *American Indian Melodies*, he established the Wa-Wan Press to support innovative composers working in a variety of traditions, including the European. However, many of his own compositions, as well as those by others that appeared in Wa-Wan publications, were based on melodies in Fletcher's collection of 1900. In his earliest Indianist works, Farwell was influenced by the simple harmonizations in Fletcher's edition, with only an occasional addition of an appoggiatura or a chromatic progression. Later he found more adventurous ways to set these tunes. He also published in the Wa-Wan Press a suite entitled *Lyrics of the Red Men*, by Harvey Worthington Loomis, who was a student of Dvořák. Loomis used an aharmonic style while exploiting some of the rhythmic interest of the piece.

Several Indianist composers also were collectors, among them Charles Wakefield Cadman, Arthur Nevin, and Thurlow Lieurance. Like the ethnologists, they felt it necessary to live among the various Native American tribes in order to understand the societal function of the Indian music they quoted in their compositions. Lieurance's first field trip was in 1895, when he was sent by the Federal Government to the Crow Reservation;[33] and Arthur Nevin spent the summers of 1903 and 1904 among the Blackfoot Indians collecting music for his opera *Poia* (1910).[34]

In October 1920 *The Etude* had a special issue on Indianist music. Charles Wakefield Cadman, who had been collecting Native American music for over a decade, asserted that "instead of dying out, the matter of Indian folk-themes and their incorporation into American music seems to be growing." While he did not believe this to be the American music of the future, "it is better and more American to make use of these indigenous themes in the composition, when the subject calls for it, than it is to add to the already large number of European works with folk themes from the soil of Europe."[35]

The need for context may also explain why there were so many "Indianist" operas. In addition to *Poia* there were *Atala* by Dvořák's pupil, Henry Schoenefeld, Frederick Shepherd Converse's *The Pipe of Desire* (1907), Victor Herbert's *The Sacrifice* (1910) and *Natoma* (1911), Mary Carr Moore's *Narcissa* (1912), Nevins's *A Daughter of the Forest* (1917), Cadman's *The Robin Woman* (*Shanewis*) (1918), and Charles Sanford Skilton's *Kalopin* (1927) and *The Sun Bride* (1930). Dvořák, who influenced Schoenefeld directly and Skilton indirectly, may have led others as well to this genre. He told the press in 1893 that opera is far superior to the symphony as a mode of expression for folk-based style[36]—even though he did not carry through his Hiawatha project, which had been suggested by Jeannette Thurber (See Michael Beckerman's essay, Chapter 15).

Others who have written on Indian themes include Frederick Ayres, Marion Bauer, Amy Beach, Ernest Bloch, Natalie Curtis Burlin, Frederick R. Burton, Carl Busch, John Alden Carpenter, Samuel Coleridge-Taylor, Henry Gilbert, Rubin Goldmark, Charles Tomlinson Griffes, Homer Grunn, Charles Ives, Frederick Jacobi, Ernest R. Kroeger, John Philip Sousa, Lamar Stringfield, and Carlos Troyer.[37]

Later string quartets on Indian themes display modernizing tendencies. Farwell's quartet "The Hako" (1922),[38] based on Fletcher's book of the same name, uses chromaticism and suggests nonfunctional harmonies. That same year Charles Tomlinson Griffes's *Two Sketches Based on Indian Themes* appeared. The first, marked *lento e mesto*, has as its theme a "Farewell Song" of the Chippewa. Its sparse textures and dissonant harmonies driven by contrapuntal logic nevertheless remain within a tonal frame (Example 11-1).

*Farewell Song of the Chippewas

Example 11-1. Charles Tomlinson Griffes, *Two Sketches Based on Indian Themes,* first movement, mm. 25–36. New York: G. Schirmer, 1922. Used by permission of the publisher.

Amy Beach's Quartet for Strings in One Movement, Opus 89 (MS, 1921–29) is based on melodies from the Alaskan Inuit. The composer transformed the first four measures of "Ititaujang's Song" (Example 11-2) to create the fugue subject in Example 11-3. Although the entire piece is in G minor, the fugue is written in dissonant counterpoint, with tonicizing passages but without a stable tonality. Most notable is the change from the late Romantic harmonic vocabulary usually associated with Beach, but in fact a feature typical of her earlier rather than her later works.

Example 11-2. "Ititaujang's Song," mm. 1–4. From Franz Boas, "The Central Eskimo," *6th Annual Report of the Bureau of Ethnology*, Smithsonian Institution. Washington, D.C., 1888, 655

Example 11-3. Amy Beach, Quartet for Strings in One Movement, Opus 89 (1921–1929), p. 15, mm. 261–279. Holograph at the University of New Hampshire, Durham. Reprinted with the kind permission of the MacDowell Colony Inc. and the University of New Hampshire. (© The MacDowell Colony Inc. 1993.)

The distance these composers traveled from Farwell's first Indianist works is great in terms of integration of theme and setting and the eschewal of late Romantic harmonies. The period from 1901 to 1930 saw the greatest production of Indianist works, but some appeared in the 1930s and 1940s as well. With few exceptions the compositional idiom was conservative, offering less adventurous listeners a respite from modernist works of the teens and twenties. Eventually, the Indianist movement was displaced by the last Americanist movement based on the recently collected Anglo-American folk music.

ART MUSIC ON BLACK THEMES

Music based on black idioms differed in several respects from that based on Native American music. Harmony is part of black folk tradition, and melodic structure is often close to Western art music, both formally and intervallically. Further, thanks to touring choirs like the Fisk Jubilee Singers and the Hampton Singers, audiences in the North and East were becoming familiar with plantation songs in Europeanized concert versions. And there was yet another difference: while Native American composers of art music were remarkable for their absence from the Indianist movement, African American composers were involved in composing music based on black themes from the very beginning, thanks in part to the tuition-free policy at the National Conservatory in New York and its quest for talented black students, among them Maurice Arnold (Strotthotte) and Will Marion Cook.

Will Marion Cook, an African American from Washington, D.C., studied violin in Berlin with Joseph Joachim and composition with Dvořák at the National Conservatory. His musical shows *Clorindy* and *In Dahomey* were among the first to bring black performers to Broadway at the turn of the century. His pupils included Duke Ellington and Harold Arlen. Drawing by John C. Tibbetts.

As we have seen, a few composers had found black idioms useful even before Dvořák gave his blessing to the practice. Louis Elson, writing in 1915, professed to find African American influences in Chadwick's Second Sym-

phony (1883–85). He made a point of the fact that the symphony predated
Dvořák's arrival and was "the first real effort of an American composer to utilize the only folk-song which our country possesses—the music of the
South, the themes of the plantation. This occurs in the scherzo, the second
movement," and features not only syncopations and suggestions of gapped
scales but also a certain jauntiness thought to be expressive of American
character.[39]

The first compositional evidence of Dvořák's influence on his students occurred during a short-lived period in which composers used songs of
the black Creoles. Although *Slave Songs of the United States* (1867) is an early
source for Creole melodies, Dena Epstein states that few people knew about
this collection.[40] A more accessible source appeared in 1886—George
Cable's two articles on Creole music in the *Century Magazine,* a much-read
literary journal.[41] Cable included some twenty melodies, a few of them harmonized by Krehbiel, with texts and descriptions of their performances in
New Orleans's Congo Square and in the context of Black Creole life.

Later sources reflected Dvořák's influence. In Clara Gottschalk Peterson's edition of twelve Creole Songs, she wrote that the songs were "practically unknown to the public save for two or three whose themes were made
use of by my brother, the late Louis Moreau Gottschalk." One of her aims
was transmission to composers: "If as Dr. Dvořák has claimed there is in
time to be a native School of American Music based on the primitive musical
utterances of the Red Man and the black among us, then truly these melodies of the Louisiana Negroes . . . are . . . of some interest."[42]

Krehbiel published eight Creole songs in his *Afro-American Folksongs*
of 1914.[43] Seven years later, in 1921, Maud Cuney Hare put out a collection
of six Creole songs, four of them previously published in Cable, two of them
new. Hare's approach differed from that of her predecessors because she
stressed the performance tradition of this music without reference to its use
in art music, implying that the music needs no "idealization" but is best presented as received.[44]

The American public heard art music based on Creole tunes even
before the end of Dvořák's first year here. In the summer of 1893, he
announced the upcoming New York performance of a suite of Creole dances
by "the most promising and gifted of [my composition] pupils . . . a young
Westerner, [Maurice Arnold] Stratthotte [*sic*] of St. Louis." Strotthotte's
Suite "contain[s] material that he has treated in a style that accords with my
ideas." In that same interview, Dvořák acknowledged for the first and perhaps only time Gottschalk's prior use of Creole music.[45]

Dvořák's influence was not confined to his students. The first work that might have been inspired by Dvořák was not by a student but by John A. van Broekhoven, whose arrangements of Creole tunes are found in *Slave Songs* of 1867. His *Suite Creole* for string orchestra was conducted at the Chicago Fair by Theodore Thomas on 4 August 1893. Thomas, perhaps in response to Dvořák's influence, may have chosen this work as an exemplar of the brand new movement in American music.

Among the later compositions based on black Creole themes is Henry Gilbert's *Dance in Place Congo* (1908, rev. 1916), a symphonic work produced at the Metropolitan Opera as a ballet pantomime. And Amy Beach, whose responses to Dvořák's suggestions I have examined elsewhere,[46] wrote "Cabildo" (1932), a one-act chamber opera set in New Orleans, that uses Creole tunes found in *Slave Songs* as well as in Cable, Krehbiel, Peterson, and Hare.[47] These tunes are quoted *in extenso* as themes besides being used developmentally as accompaniments to recitatives.

But the main line of development of nationalist music based on African American folk songs was the spiritual, introduced to concert audiences by the Fisk Jubilee Singers as early as 1871. Other groups followed, beginning with the Hampton Institute singers. The popularity of the several Jubilee choirs continued until well into the twentieth century.[48]

Concert versions of this music often changed its character. Locke complained not so much that the songs were being Europeanized as that, by the 1890s, some choirs were cheapening them by stressing their rhythmic values. But, he averred, it was the "New World" Symphony that rescued the spiritual for art. "Since then the spiritual and even the secular Negro folk melodies and their harmonic style have been regarded by most musicians as the purest and most reliable musical ore in America, the raw materials of a native American music."[49] That attitude was not confined to musicians. In 1906 students from the Industrial Institute of Manassas, Virginia, appeared at the White House before Theodore Roosevelt. The President stated after hearing them sing that "gradually out of the capacity for melody that the Negro race has, America shall develop some school of 'national music.'"[50] But Locke looked beyond the concert choirs, for he believed that African American sacred and secular songs "will find their truest development . . . in symphonic music, or in the larger choral forms of the symphonic choir . . . [when] they will reachieve their folk atmosphere and epic spirituality."[51]

In addition to performance, spirituals were also available in print. In 1872 the Fisk Jubilee Singers' arrangements of spirituals appeared with multiple editions to follow. *Cabin and Plantation Songs as Sung by Hampton Stu-*

dents was published in 1891.[52] Among the publications of black folk music after Dvořák were Krehbiel's three articles entitled "Slave Songs in America" that appeared in the New York *Tribune* in September 1899 as part of his series, "Folk Music Studies." His first is devoted to a discussion of the uses of black music as material for development in art music, with repeated references to Dvořák. In those that followed, Krehbiel discussed the music and its social context, giving a few musical examples.

Krehbiel later expanded these articles into a full-length study, *Afro-American Folksongs*. In the preface he writes: "This book was written with the purpose of bringing a species of folksong into the field of scientific observation and presenting it as fit material for artistic treatment."[53] The book features spirituals and other plantation music as well as Creole songs, but not ragtime, which Krehbiel considered their "debased offspring." There are over fifty musical examples, most with piano accompaniments.

There followed an impressive succession of editions of spirituals collected and arranged for choir and solo voice by African American composers—Will Marion Cook in 1914, John Wesley Work in 1915, and Harry T. Burleigh in 1916 (his edition offering the first arrangements of spirituals as art songs). Thanks to Burleigh it had become traditional for black concert artists to include a set of spirituals in concert arrangements on their programs. Others who followed in the 1920s were J. Rosamond Johnson, James Weldon Johnson, Clarence Cameron White, and R. Nathaniel Dett. By the 1930s and 1940s, most leading black composers had issued arrangements of spirituals—Edward Boatner, J. Harold Brown, William Dawson, Florence Price, Hall Johnson, and Margaret Bonds, among others.

Several composers who studied with Dvořák wrote orchestral works based on spirituals and other black folk songs. Among the compositions by whites were Harry Rowe Shelley's *Carnival Overture* and Henry Schoenefeld's Suite, Opus 15, which has a second movement entitled "March fantastico (Southern Negro Life)." These were played at the World's Columbian Exposition in Chicago on 7 July 1893, conducted by Theodore Thomas. Schoenefeld also composed a violin sonata based on spirituals (1899).

Rubin Goldmark is an important link between Dvořák and the "Americanist" movement of the late 1930s and 1940s. First a student of Dvořák's and then a teacher at the National Conservatory, he was the composer of a number of works that reflected Dvořák's influence. David Beveridge notes the lack of recordings of Goldmark's music and the difficulty of finding scores. But, he continues, "a large portion of his music written after

Dvořák's sojourn in New York utilizes descriptive titles referring to American subject matter, and sometimes specifically Indian or Negro subject matter."[54] Notable among his works is the *Negro Rhapsody* (1919), in which he quotes a Negro spiritual, features syncopations and flatted sevenths, and emphasizes the subdominant harmonies so frequently found in black folk music.

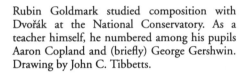

Rubin Goldmark studied composition with Dvořák at the National Conservatory. As a teacher himself, he numbered among his pupils Aaron Copland and (briefly) George Gershwin. Drawing by John C. Tibbetts.

Later, Goldmark became one of the most respected teachers of composition in America. Among his students were Frederick Jacobi, George Gershwin, and Aaron Copland, who studied with Goldmark for four years. Copland later asserted that Goldmark "really should get more credit than he has been given for my early training."[55]

Although Henry Gilbert was not a pupil of Dvořák, his choices of folk music—both Native and African American—suggest the Czech composer's influence.[56] His *Negro Episode* (1897) includes a tune from *Slave Songs of the United States*, "Nobody Knows the Trouble I've Seen," while his *Negro Rhapsody* (1912) is based on two ring shouts, traditional black worship music reflecting African influence, "Listen to the Angels" and "You May Bury Me in the Eas'."[57] Other composers who were among the first to write from this tradition are Dvořák's student William Arms Fisher, as well as Edward MacDowell, Ernest Richard Kroeger, Henry K. Hadley, and Ernest Bloch.

There was considerable negative reaction to the use of black folk idioms in art music. One of the more colorful criticisms simultaneously acknowledges the Bohemian composer's influence while mistakenly blaming his followers for the popularity of ragtime: "A horde of young American composers followed Dvořák's precept and example, and the result was a wholesale cabbaging of the Jubilee Singers and a riotous emission of suites and fantasies in the pentatonic scale, with fearful and wonderful eccentricities of rhythm. Out of this furious clash of meters and booming kettle drums arose ragtime, a new and horrible pestilence for a wicked world."[58]

Dvořák's influence also extended to composers active in the 1910s and 1920s, such as John Powell and Daniel Gregory Mason. Powell wrote several works for orchestra on black themes, including the Suite for piano *In the South* (1906) and *Rhapsodie nègre* (1918?). Mason's *String Quartet in G Minor on Negro Themes* (1922) is based on spirituals (Examples 11-4 and 11-5).

Example 11-4. "You May Bury Me in de Eas'," mm. 1–5. From Henry Edward Krehbiel, *Afro-American Folksongs.* New York: Frederick Ungar, 1962, p. 86. Used with permission of the Crossroad/Continuum Publishing Group.

Although both men demonstrated arguably racist attitudes, they were nonetheless drawn to this repertory for its musical potential. Other white composers who quoted spirituals and folk songs include Louis Gruenberg, Lamar Stringfield, Mary Howe, and Morton Gould, who wrote *Spirituals for Orchestra* (1941) and *Symphony of Spirituals* (1976).

As Eileen Southern has noted in *The Music of Black Americans: A History*, the first generation of black composers around the turn of the cen-

Example 11-5. Daniel Gregory Mason, *String Quartet in G Minor on Negro Themes,* first movement, mm. 19–37. Bryn Mawr: Theodore Presser, 1930. Used with permission of the publisher.

tury were conscious nationalists, several of them directly inspired by Dvořák's valuing of black folk music and his use of the idiom in concert music. It is striking that so many of this group drew on the spiritual for art music. In addition to Maurice Arnold (Strotthotte), there was Will Marion Cook who began an opera based on *Uncle Tom's Cabin* while a student of Dvořák's but did not finish it. He found he had to cross over into musical comedy to make a living.

Harry Burleigh's *Six Plantation Melodies for Violin and Piano* appeared in 1901. Other early twentieth-century black composers who drew on traditional black music were Nathaniel Dett, Harry Lawrence Freeman, and Clarence Cameron White. Trained in conservatories, both American and European, they aimed to integrate black folk music into the Western art tradition. Most were from the middle class, which may have influenced their choice of the spiritual rather than ragtime or later jazz.

White in his article, "The Musical Genius of the American Negro," written a few months after the first performance of Gershwin's *Rhapsody in Blue*, declared that the spiritual had made a tremendous contribution to American music. He also recounts with pride the achievements of African Americans in concert music while bemoaning their tragically limited opportunities. His account of several highly trained musicians who, shut out of symphony orchestras, were forced to play in jazz bands, suggests a desire to distance himself from jazz and its practitioners.[59]

George Gershwin studied briefly with Rubin Goldmark, a former pupil of Dvořák's at the National Conservatory. Drawing by John C. Tibbetts.

In the next generation of African American composers were J. Harold Brown, Edward Boatner, Margaret Bonds, William Dawson, Florence Price, and William Grant Still. Most quoted or wrote in the style of black folk music. Dawson, who was "directly inspired by Dvořák's views on nationalism in music" drew on black folk songs for most of his works.[60] Florence Price, like Dawson, joined European art music to themes of black derivation. Rae Linda Brown believes that the "New World" Symphony "provided a role model for many American composers in the use of American folk materials, and it is likely that Price used Dvořák's American works as a source of inspiration" for her Symphony in E Minor (1932). Written in the same key as Dvořák's "New World," it has a pentatonic theme in the first movement, an original "hymn" in the second, and a third movement based on the rhythms and melodies of "patting juba."[61] Also like Dvořák, Price wrote her own themes, something that Alain Locke may have found lacking, although he defended her freedom to choose her own way: "Mrs. Price's work vindicates the Negro composer's right, at choice, to go up Parnassus by the broad high road of Classicism rather than the narrower, more hazardous, but often more rewarding path of racialism."[62]

Historians have acknowledged Dvořák's profound influence on American music. Locke, for example, wrote that "there is no deep divide between our folk music and the main stream of world music."[63] John Tasker Howard wrote in 1941, "What Dvořák accomplished was to create our respect for the folksongs that existed in our own country. Since then we have had hundreds of concert settings of Negro songs, some sophisticated and others simple in treatment; choral arrangements; and developments and elaborations of Negro material in symphonic works."[64]

POSTSCRIPT

MUSIC IN THE ANGLO-AMERICAN TRADITION

Dvořák, like most of his contemporaries, subscribed to the notion that the English had no folk song tradition. He reported in May 1893:

> When I was in England one of the ablest musical critics complained to me that there was no distinctively English school of music. . . . I replied . . . that the composers of England had turned their backs upon the fine melodies of Ireland and Scotland instead of making them the essence of an English school.[65]

It was believed that not only was there no Anglo-American folk song tradition, but also that Americans of Anglo-Saxon heritage were as bereft of their own folk music as were their English cousins. Indeed, the belief extended to all ethnic groups in the United States—excepting the two ethnic groups that Dvořák chose. Louis Elson, for example, wrote in 1925 that the American folk music heritage was "rather barren. . . . American folk-song in its true sense can only be derived from Indian or plantation life."[66] And Marion Bauer, reporting on a meeting in Brussels of the International Society for Contemporary Music in 1930, noted with disbelief that European composers considered the only truly "American" music to be that which was based on Native and African American folk music.[67]

In fact, during the first half of the twentieth century, folklorists found a rich store of music in this country from many ethnic groups, including Anglo-American.[68] As a result of those discoveries, composers created art music based on Anglo-American folk songs. This movement, which Dvořák could not have predicted, was the culmination of the nationalist movement in the United States, ending at mid-century. Its practitioners were Ives, Powell, Virgil Thomson, Roy Harris, Deems Taylor, Gruenberg, Douglas Moore, and many others. As a leader in this movement, Copland—with Gershwin and Frederick Jacobi—provides the link to Dvořák through Goldmark, his teacher and Dvořák's student.

Aaron Copland studied music theory with Rubin Goldmark, one of Dvořák's Conservatory pupils. Drawing by John C. Tibbetts.

Had the Anglo-American folk heritage been discovered early enough to be available to the composers of the Second New England School, there might have been a direct line from their works to those of the Americanist school. Or Dvořák's prescriptions might have led composers to Native American and then to African American folk music anyway, because of the belief that the most direct expressions of the "folk" came from the most oppressed groups—a characterization that did not fit the people of Anglo-American stock who lived in the Appalachians.

Indeed, such was the influence of Dvořák that for years after 1893 a significant number of musicians, critics, and historians in Europe as well as the United States continued to define American folk music as primarily that of Native and African Americans; and "American" art music as that based on those two groups of folk and traditional music. To that extent, Dvořák determined the debate over the nationalist movement in music in the United States from 1893 almost to the middle of the twentieth century.

NOTES

1. Irving Lowens, Introduction to Edward MacDowell's *Critical and Historical Essays*, ed. W. J. Baltzell (New York: DaCapo Press, 1969), *xxiii–xxiv.*

2. See, for example, Charles Hamm's excellent summary of Dvořák's initial impact in his *Music in the New World* (New York: W. W. Norton, 1983), 410–413. Richard Crawford, at the Dvořák Conference in New Orleans in February 1991, presented a list of eight music histories from Elson (1904) to Hitchcock (1988) in which Dvořák's influence is discussed.

3. "For National Music: Dvořák, the Great Bohemian Composer," Chicago *Tribune*, 13 August 1893, 29.

4. Quoted in Maud Cuney Hare, *Negro Musicians and Their Music* (Washington, D.C.: Associated Publishers, 1936), 57.

5. John Clapham, "Dvořák and the American Indian," *Musical Times*, vol. 107, no. 1484 (October 1966), 866.

6. Jeannette M. Thurber, "Dvořák As I Knew Him," *The Etude*, vol. 37, no. 11 (November 1919), 693.

7. John Clapham, "Dvořák and the American Indian," 863. Theodore Baker, *On the Music of the North American Indians*, a republication of his dissertation published in Leipzig in 1882, with original German text and English translation by Ann Buckley (New York: DaCapo Press, 1977).

8. "Dr. Dvořák's Great Symphony," New York *Herald*, 16 December 1893, 6.

9. Antonín Dvořák (with the assistance of Edwin Emerson, Jr.), "Music in America," *Harper's New Monthly Magazine*, 40 (February 1895), 433.

10. Louis Elson, *The History of American Music* (New York: Burt Franklin, 1925; reprint 1971), 133.

11. Charles Sanford Skilton, "Realism in Indian Music," in *Proceedings of the Music Teachers' National Association: Studies in Musical Education, History, and Aesthetics*, 13th series (Hartford, Conn.: MTNA, 1919), 106.

12. H. Wiley Hitchcock, *Music in the United States: A Historical Introduction*, 3d ed. (Englewood Cliffs: Prentice-Hall, 1988), 155.

13. Rupert Hughes, "A Eulogy of Ragtime," *Musical Record*, no. 447 (1 April 1899), 157–159.

14. Carl Dahlhaus, "Nationalism and Music," in *Between Romanticism and Modernism*, trans. Mary Whittall (Berkeley: University of California Press, 1989), 94.

15. Fanny Morris Smith, "Peculiarities of the Growth of American Music," *The Etude*, vol. 6, no. 4 (April 1888), 68. For another discussion of the fusion theory, see Frederick Grant Gleason, "American Composers," written for the meeting of the MTNA in Detroit on 1–4 July 1890 (Gleason Collection of Clippings, 1872–1903, series 4, no. 3: 1880–1895, Newberry Library, Chicago).

16. Henry Gilbert, "Folk-Music in Art-Music—A Discussion and a Theory," *Musical Quarterly*, vol. 3, no. 4 (October 1917), 601.

17. Adrienne Fried Block, "Dvořák, Beach and American Music," in *A Celebration of American Music: Words and Music in Honor of H. Wiley Hitchcock*, ed. Richard Crawford, R. Allen Lott, and Carol J. Oja (Ann Arbor: University of Michigan Press, 1990), 256–280.

18. In "Dvořák, Beach and American Music" I noted that neither Foote nor MacDowell were among the ten Boston musicians whose opinions on Dvořák's prescription were printed in "American Music: Dr. Antonín Dvořák Expresses Some Radical Opinions," Boston *Herald*, 28 May 1893, 23. I conjectured that they may have been in Europe. However, both men were at the World's Columbian Exposition in Chicago during the week of 21–28 May to perform their own works and thus could not prepare statements for the *Herald*.

    Foote did answer a later inquiry, which was published along with that of E. R. Kroeger and several others in "Dr. Dvořák's Proposed School," the *Keynote*, 10 June 1893, 27. He wrote that African American music was either of the music hall variety or, regarding spirituals, indistinguishable from white models. He also found that composers from Bach to Wagner depended on nothing but "their own musical invention. . . . Can we have better models than they are?"

19. MacDonald Smith Moore, *Yankee Blues: Musical Culture and American Identity* (Bloomington: Indiana University Press, 1985), 128–161.

20. Charles Hamm, *Music in the New World* (New York: W. W. Norton, 1983), 46.

21. Victor Yellin, "Chadwick, American Musical Realist," *Musical Quarterly*, vol. 61, no. 1 (January 1975), 96.

22. Olin Downes, "Henry Gilbert, Nonconformist," in *A Birthday Offering to Carl Engel*, ed. Gustave Reese (New York: G. Schirmer, 1943), 92.

23. Franz Boas, "The Central Eskimo," *6th Annual Report of the Bureau of Ethnology*, Smithsonian Institution (Washington, D. C., 1888); repr. as *The Central Eskimo*, ed. Henry B. Collins (Lincoln, Nebraska: University of Nebraska Press, 1964). Alice Cunningham Fletcher, "A Study of Omaha Indian Music," *Archeological and Ethnological Papers of the Peabody Museum*, vol. 1, no. 5 (Cambridge, Mass.: Peabody Museum, 1893).

24. J. Walter Fewkes, "A Contribution to Passamaquoddy Folk-Lore," *Journal of American Folklore*, 3 (1890), 257ff.; Benjamin Ives Gilman, "Zuñi Melodies," *Journal of American Ethnology and Archeology*, 1 (1891), 63ff.

25. Louis Elson, *History* (1925), 126–129.

26. Anton Seidel, Fannie Morris Smith, H. E. Krehbiel, and W. S. Howard, eds., *The Music of the Modern World* (New York: Appleton, 1895), 233–236.

27. Krehbiel's articles on African American music include "Some Words on Negro Music," New York *Tribune*, 24 April 1899, 6–7; and two installments of a series under the general heading "Folk Music Studies" in the New York *Tribune*, "Illustrated Supplement," 10 and 17 September 1899, 15. Articles on Native American music appeared in the same series on 24 September and 1 and 8 October 1899, 15. In addition there were articles on biblical, Slavic, Hungarian, Russian, Scandinavian, and Asian music. In several articles Krehbiel reiterates that their primary purpose is to bring the music to the attention of composers, following Dvořák's advice.

28. Henry Edward Krehbiel, "Folk Music Studies III: Songs of the American Indians," New York *Tribune*, "Illustrated Supplement," 8 October 1899, 15.

29. Alice Fletcher, *Indian Story and Song from North America* (Boston: Small and Maynard, 1900), vii.

30. John Comfort Fillmore, "Scale and Harmonies of Indian Songs," *Music*, 4 (September 1893), 484. For a recent commentary on Fillmore's methods, see James C. McNutt, "John Comfort Fillmore: A Student of Indian Music Reconsidered," *American Music*, vol. 2, no. 1 (Spring 1984), 64.

31. Charles Wakefield Cadman, "The Idealization of Indian Music," *Musical Quarterly*, vol. 1, no. 3 (July 1915), 387–396; and "The American Indian's Music Idealized," *The Etude*, vol. 38, no. 10 (October 1920), 659–660.

32. Evelyn Davis Culbertson, "Arthur Farwell's Early Efforts on Behalf of American Music," *American Music*, vol. 5, no. 2 (Summer 1987), 167.

33. Thurlow Lieurance, "The Musical Soul of the American Indian," *The Etude*, vol. 38, no. 10 (October 1920), 655-656.

34. Arthur Nevin, "Impressions of Indian Music as Heard in the Woods, Prairies, Mountains and Wigwams," *The Etude*, vol. 38, no. 10 (October 1920), 663–664.

35. Charles Wakefield Cadman, "The American Indian's Music Idealized," 660.

36. "For National Music," Chicago *Tribune*, 13 August 1893, 29.

37. Most of these composers, together with their relevant works, are cited on "A Brief List of Composers Utilizing American Indian Music," Archive of Folk Song, Library of Congress, Washington, D. C.

38. MS at the Music Research Division, New York Public Library.

39. Louis Elson, *History*, 174.

40. However, in his article of 10 September 1899 (see note 27), Krehbiel both discussed *Slave Songs of the United States* and described it as "the first and the best contribution to the bibliography of American folk-song." His excellent list of books and articles appeared on 17 September 1899, with an addendum on 24 September.

41. George W. Cable, "The Dance in Place Congo," *Century Magazine*, vol. 31, no. 4 (February 1886), 517–532; and "Creole Slave Songs," *Century Magazine*, vol. 31, no. 6 (April 1886), 807–828.

42. Clara Gottschalk Peterson, *Creole Songs from New Orleans in the Negro Dialect* (New Orleans: L. W. Greenewald, 1902), Preface.

43. Henry Edward Krehbiel, *Afro-American Folksongs: A Study in Racial and National Music*, 4th printing (New York: Frederick Ungar, 1975; a reprint of the 1914 edition).

44. Maud Cuney Hare, *Six Creole Folks Songs with Original Creole and Translated English Texts* (New York: Carl Fischer [1921]).

45. "For National Music."

46. Adrienne Block, "Dvořák, Beach and American Music," 256-280; and "Amy Beach's Music on Native American Themes," *American Music*, vol. 8, no. 2 (Summer 1990), 141–166.

47. "Cabildo" (libretto by Nan Bagby Stephens), a chamber opera in one act for solo voices, chorus, speaker, and piano trio, is unpublished. The MS is at the University of Missouri, Kansas City.

48. Eileen Southern, *The Music of Black Americans: A History*, 2d ed. (New York: W. W. Norton, 1983), 228.

49. Alain Locke, *The Negro and His Music* (New York: Arno Press and the *New York Times*, 1969, a reprint of the 1925 ed.), 20–21.

50. Quoted from the *New York Times*, 15 February 1906 in Nicolas Slonimsky, *Music Since 1900*, 4th ed. (New York: Scribner's, 1971), 88.

51. Alain Locke, *The Negro and His Music*, 21.

52. *Cabin and Plantation Songs as Sung by Hampton Students* (New York: G. P. Putnam, 1891). Krehbiel notes that the songs are "arranged—in part, I fear, badly disarranged—by Thomas Fenner and Fredrick G. Rathbun. The volume also contains songs sung by the students of the Normal School at Tuskegee, Alabama, and a few specimens from the Indian, Chinese, Japanese, and Hawaiian." See Krehbiel's "Folk Music Studies II: Slave Songs in America," New York *Tribune*, "Illustrated Supplement," 17 September 1899, 15.

53. Henry Edward Krehbiel, *Afro-American Folksongs, v.*

54. David Beveridge, "Dvořák's American Pupil Rubin Goldmark," 5. Unpublished paper. I am grateful to David Beveridge for sharing this paper with me and allowing me to quote from it.

55. David Beveridge, "Dvořák's American Pupil Rubin Goldmark," 4.

56. Gilbert Chase finds another connection with Dvořák in Henry Gilbert's interest in Slavic music, which led the American composer to present concerts by Smetana, Dvořák, Mussorgsky, and Rimsky-Korsakov in Cambridge in 1894. See his *America's Music* (Urbana and Chicago: University of Illinois Press, 1987), 352.

57. Olin Downes, "An American Composer," *Musical Quarterly*, vol. 4, no. 1 (January 1915), 29.

58. See "The Trend of American Music," *Musical America*, vol. 11, no. 6 (18 December 1909), 22. This was a quotation from an article in the December

1909 issue of *Bohemian*. Edward A. Berlin states that the ragtime era began in Chicago at the time of the World's Columbian Exposition of 1893; see his *Ragtime: A Musical and Cultural History* (Berkeley: University of California Press, 1980), 25.

59. Clarence Cameron White, "The Musical Genius of the American Negro," *The Etude*, vol. 42, no. 5 (May 1924), 305.

60. Eileen Southern, *The Music of Black Americans: A History*, 419.

61. Rae Linda Brown, lecture on the life and music of Florence Price, given at the Graduate Center, City University of New York, 22 February 1990. Cited with permission.

62. Alain Locke, *The Negro and His Music*, 115.

63. Alain Locke, *The Negro and His Music*, 129.

64. John Tasker Howard, *Our American Music: Three Hundred Years of It*, 3d ed., rev. (New York: Thomas Y. Crowell, 1939), 404.

65. "The Real Value of Negro Melodies," New York *Herald*, 21 May 1893, 28.

66. Louis Elson, *History*, 123.

67. Marion Bauer, "Have We an American Music?" *Musical America*, vol. 60, no. 3 (10 February 1940), 22, 271–272.

68. For a description of the experiences of Cecil Sharp and others who collected folk songs in the Appalachian Mountains, see Richard Aldrich, "Folk-Songs in America," in *Music Discourse from the New York Times* (London: Oxford University Press, 1928), 56–72. Also see D. K. Wilgus, *Anglo-American Folksong Scholarship since 1898* (New Brunswick: Rutgers University Press, 1959).

CHAPTER TWELVE

Homesick in America

The Nostalgia of Antonín Dvořák and Charles Ives

Stuart Feder

*C*harles Ives (1874–1954) did not remember Antonín Dvořák kindly. When he dictated portions of his "auto-biographical scrapbook of reminiscence" in 1932,[1] Ives had not composed anything of significance in nearly a decade. Although he was only fifty-eight, he was ailing and crotchety;[2] and there is a note of asperity in his defense of his use of American vernacular tunes in the "Adagio cantabile" (he called it his "Largo") of his Second Symphony:

> Some nice people, whenever they hear the words "Gospel Hymns" or "Stephen Foster," say "Mercy me!" and a little high-brow smile creeps over their brow—"Can't you get something better than that in a symphony?" The same nice people, when they go to a properly dressed symphony concert under proper auspices, led by a name with foreign hair, and hear Dvořák's *New World Symphony*, in which they are told this famous passage was from a negro spiritual, then they think it must be quite proper, even artistic, and say "How delightful!" But when someone proves to them that the Gospel Hymns are funda-mentally responsible for the negro spirituals, they say, "Ain't it awful!"—"You don't really mean that!"—"Why, only to think!"— "Do tell!"—I tell you, you don't ever hear Gospel Hymns even men-tioned up there to the New England Conservatory.[3]

Ives's Gospel musicology aside, there is little question that at this point he disparaged Dvořák ("the name with foreign hair") and thought of himself as not only the better composer but the rightful heir to all music American. Ives never met Dvořák. When Dvořák arrived in New York in the

fall of 1892, the eighteen-year-old Ives was attending a preparatory school in
New Haven hoping to be accepted to Yale University. His compositions to
date were youthful ones, largely collaborations with his father, George
Edward Ives (1845–94), a village bandmaster in Danbury, Connecticut.
Dvořák, on the other hand, was a Czech, a middle-aged, professional musi-
cian, a composer already at the height of his creative maturity.

In spite of Ives's late-life hostility to Dvořák, there were many subtle
connections between them. Any significant influences—the taint of which
would have been vigorously disavowed—were, as with much in Ives's life
and music, arcane and unconventional. We will trace some of these here.

Perhaps the fundamental bond between the two composers was a
non-verbal one, a complex of memory, loss, and nostalgia. As children, both
were acutely sensitive to their auditory environments—Charles's Danbury,
Connecticut, and Dvořák's Nelahozeves, Bohemia. In Charles's case awareness of music dawned with his awareness of others, in particular his father
who, in a sense, *was* music for the young child. The language of music was
an alternative language for him that developed parallel to verbal language.
The tunes George Ives played on his cornet while practicing alone at home
or rehearsing the band in the back yard—a blend of European classics, Civil
War marches, patriotic and parlor songs, hymns and gospel tunes—became
young Charles's own musical vocabulary. In time, they would become deter-
minants of his musical style and be quoted in Ives's mature musical scores.
This bond is acknowledged in Charles's words for a 1917 song, "The Things
Our Fathers Loved":

> I think there must be a place in the soul all made of tunes, of the
> tunes of long ago. . . ."[4]

Indeed, of the more than 140 songs Charlie would quote in his works,
virtually all were the "tunes of long ago," associated with the nineteenth century rural milieu of his father. They make up a virtual anthology of the
everyday and holiday music of an American country town. Like Dvořák, Ives
also composed passages intended to sound like authentic quotations. Often
the tunes prevail as raw material in the forging of advanced compositional
devices like dissonance, polytonality, and polyrhythm. In that duality of
modern form and traditional song—not contradictory but rather mutually
supporting—lies the unique achievement of Charles Ives. "I feel that, if I
have done anything that is good in music," Ives wrote, "I owe it almost
entirely to [my father] and his influence."

Antonín Dvořák, or Tonik (Tony) also grew up in a small town, Nelahozeves, where he enjoyed an active musical life. Although his father, František, worked as a butcher, he was also a "country fiddler" of sorts and gave his son his first violin lessons. Tonik, like Charlie, grew up steeped in the rich folk heritage of his region, though for him it was polkas and church music. After some uncertainty about his career, he, too, broke away from the confining rural environment and headed for the big city—Prague. Like Ives, Dvořák concentrated much of his subsequent studies on organ music and organ performance. And, despite the sophistication of his musical accomplishment and the cosmopolitan character of his world celebrity, the simplicity and naiveté of his boyhood days were never far away.

It is also significant, I think, that Ives's advanced musical training at Yale came at the hands of a former associate of Dvořák's, Horatio William Parker (1863–1919), the Battell Professor of Music at Yale since 1893. Parker had studied with Josef Rheinberger in Munich and had taught at the National Conservatory in New York in 1892–93 during Dvořák's first year there. For a composition competition sponsored by Mrs. Jeannette Thurber, the Conservatory's patron and guiding spirit, Dvořák had given him first prize in the cantata category for *The Dream King and His Love*. A gala concert was held at Madison Square Garden, and the work was favorably reviewed by the press.[5] Parker was duly qualified, therefore, to connect the student Ives with the rich European and largely Germanic symphonic tradition.

That Dvořák had integrated national folk idioms with musical traditions could not have escaped the student Ives, although he was fitfully seeking a different kind of integration, one that was deeply personal and not at all nationalist in intention. Later in life, Ives would have wanted to claim as his own any achievement resembling Dvořák's precedent.

Ives had a propensity for what I have called "parallel enactments" of important events in the lives of those close to him, chiefly his father and, as I will demonstrate, Horatio Parker. The most striking example of this was the failure of creativity Ives experienced when he reached the age of forty-nine, the age at which his father died. Another instance occurred when Charlie was twenty-eight, one in which Dvořák may be seen as a silent participant-in-fantasy.

Following graduation from Yale in 1898, Ives followed his father's example at a comparable age and moved to New York City. He took a post as church organist; later, he took his first job in the insurance industry. He con-

Charles Edward Ives studied music composition at Yale with Horatio Parker, a former colleague of Dvořák's at the National Conservatory. Drawing by John C. Tibbetts.

Horatio Parker taught at the National Conservatory with Dvořák and later became the head of Yale University's music department, where he numbered Charles Ives among his pupils. Drawing by John C. Tibbetts.

tinued to compose, of course, and musical evidence suggests that he was following the example of Parker in the writing of works for choir and organ. This culminated in Ives's *The Celestial Country* (1898–1899), which was cast in the image of Parker's *Hora Novissima* in text, music, and poetic idea. In following the trail of the respected Parker, Ives was testing his own potential for a music profession. He premiered *The Celestial Country*, I suggest, as an attempt to gain from Parker the same kind of blessing that Parker had received from Dvořák.[6] But the magical expectation in fantasy failed to be realized. While Dvořák had attended Parker's performance, Parker had not been present at Ives's. I believe this accounted for Ives's deep disappointment, subsequent depression, and eventual irrational disparagement of Dvořák.

Ives's excessive and defensive idealization of his father made it impossible for him to fully acknowledge his debt to any other master. In his *Memos* Ives thoughtfully compares his father to Parker and concludes, gratuitously, "Father was by far the greater man." In Ives's eyes his father's relative failure conjured up thoughts of "what might have been." It was intolerable to Ives, therefore, that Parker should have enjoyed a success George Ives could not achieve. The same can be said of his attitude concerning Dvořák's success.

George's gifts and training were modest compared to Parker's, let alone Dvořák's, who was four years George's senior; but Dvořák's case was a special one because Ives perceived his "Americanisms" in general as a kind of foreign invasion. Specifically, he construed Dvořák's use of the Negro spiritual, as he understood it, as nothing less than plunder. Ives associated spirituals with gospel hymns and an attendant nostalgia about boyhood days with his father. They were part of the earliest musical vocabulary that bonded father and son together. They represented their private, shared world.

In spite of himself, however, Ives was affected, stimulated, and even inspired by Dvořák's music. In Parker's classes at Yale he learned some of Dvořák's songs. Ives composed an alternate setting to the text of Adolph Heyduc's "Songs My Mother Taught Me," which in German translation (*"Als die alte Mutter"*) had been the basis for Dvořák's Opus 55, No. 4. Ives's realization conveys an unabashed sentimentality couched in harmonies as much related to those of the American parlor song as to any of Dvořák's.

Although it was probably written as an assignment, here may be seen the propensity for grief and that distinctive amalgamation of memory and affect we call "nostalgia" that he had in common with Dvořák, as conveyed by these lines:

> Songs my mother taught me in the days long vanished,
> Seldom from her eyelids were the tear drops banished . . .
> Now I teach my children each melodious measure,
> Other tears are flowing, flowing from memory's treasure.[7]

Ives thought well of the song and included it in his diaristic collection, *114 Songs*, as well as in the selection of fifty songs he later reprinted. Moreover, like many of his more significant works, it persisted in his mind, somehow unfinished, and eventually appeared yet again in a chamber arrangement for clarinet (or English horn) and string quartet (1902). All the musical features of the songs remain unchanged without the benefit, or hindrance, of words. The new title, "An Old Song Deranged," may have been expressive of the disillusionment and bitterness he was enduring at the time, contributing to his growing ambivalence toward Dvořák.

The common bond between Ives and Dvořák is most apparent in Ives's Second Symphony (1899–1902), although of an unconventional nature. It was less the nuts and bolts of the music that were critical here—the technical details through which idea and style are realized, such as the quotations of Stephen Foster songs and other popular tunes—but more the *affect*, the emotional sense such details encoded and communicated. This was of a *feeling* nature that reached deeply into the personal past and current inner lives of both men. When these strong feelings are revived, conflict elements may arise that are normally unconscious. I believe this was likely the source of both Ives's early interest in Dvořák and his later hostility.

The predominant shared affect was that of nostalgia, a yearning for an idealized past and the human and nonhuman objects associated with it. Most commonly it is experienced as a sad and bittersweet feeling associated with the persons and artifacts of home. Ives could not have known that "the famous passage . . . from a negro spiritual" in the "New World" Symphony, about which he was later so sarcastic, had emotional roots in the makeup of its composer that strikingly corresponded to his own. Each composer suffered from his own form of homesickness and family disruption and loss.

Money, wanderlust, and a taste for fame were not the only factors that led Dvořák to accept Jeannette M. Thurber's invitation to come to America as director of the National Conservatory. Unconscious motivations inevitably played a part in the decision; perhaps Dvořák's turning fifty in September 1891 contributed. As composer and teacher he had already accomplished more than could be reasonably expected in a highly successful and acclaimed career. If Horatio Parker was the exemplary American composer of his time, what can one say of Dvořák? His fiftieth birthday was attended by the reception of an honorary degree of Doctor of Music from Cambridge University. Yet in the composition of his Requiem in 1890—which appears to be unrelated to commissions at the time—he was perhaps addressing emergent existential issues concerning his own life. Indeed the Requiem's first performance was given a month after his fiftieth birthday. Thus, the prospect of a new life in a new world may have carried a strong appeal to a man increasingly aware of his own mortality.

However, the gratification of such desires and fantasies did not come without a price. The American trip temporarily broke up the family. When he arrived with his wife and two of the children, he left behind the other four children, many friends, and an elderly father. František's death in Bohemia came in March 1894, just a few months before the death of Ives's father. Thus, despite gratifying work during the first year, Dvořák was moody and subject to episodes of intensely felt nostalgia.

It was in this emotional atmosphere that Dvořák began work on the "New World" Symphony. Indeed, a degree of energy must have come from the anticipated reunion of the family in Spillville in the summer of 1893. (See John C. Tibbetts's essay, Chapter 7.) The Symphony's Largo, in particular, is redolent with those yearning feelings. I believe it had a stylistic influence, albeit an unconventional one, on Ives.

Ives's initial encounter with Dvořák's Largo must have produced a shock of recognition within himself. It served, perhaps, as stimulant and official "permission" to incorporate literal vernacular material associated with affect and memory into a symphonic setting. This reaction was rooted, as we have seen, in the complex relationship with his father—particularly in a longing for an earlier, preconflictual period of boyhood and a reverence for their shared past.

To be sure, while Ives worked on his Second Symphony, he was not self-consciously writing a "national" music. This style was in *statu nascendi* during its composition from 1896 to 1902. Rather, his Adagio Cantabile, said to have stemmed from an earlier organ prelude,[8] may have been the result of Dvořák's occult influence in the respects considered above. At one point during the composition of the work, in perhaps an unconscious reference to Dvořák's Largo, Ives referred to his Adagio Cantabile movement as a "Largo" and quoted the tune "America" boldly and with strong sentiment in the earliest climax and final statement of its theme.[9] Here, the intensity of feeling relates not only to America as a fatherland but, quite literally, to Ives's father. It is part of a persistent train of musical thought harking back to one of the earliest and most successful musical collaborations of father and son in the *Variations on "America,"* written when Ives was about seventeen years old. It is also worth noting that Dvořák himself considered writing a setting of the "America" tune during his visit (see Jarmil Burghauser's essay, Chapter 14).

Elsewhere in the Second Symphony we find another example of what appears to be an imitation, or emulation, of Dvořák's Largo. In the otherwise athletic and vivid fifth movement is a cantabile passage for solo horn that seems to me the counterpart of the theme that has come to be popularly known as "Goin' Home."[10] Dvořák's melody is written in D-flat major, Ives's in A-flat major; Dvořák's is written for English horn, Ives's for French horn. Ives's pentatonic melody seems related to Dvořák's. Further, the accompanying figures in the violins are reminiscent of other motifs in the "New World"

Symphony. Beyond this, there is a commonly felt thread, or underlying feeling of nostalgia. (As an old man, long after he stopped attending concerts, Ives once remarked that he would listen to a concert performance of the Second Symphony only because it reminded him so vividly of the old days with his father in Danbury.) A flute obbligato soon joins the horn solo and carries the tune of T. H. Bayly's "Long, Long Ago." Its unsung words serve as a gloss on the human condition experienced by both Ives and Dvořák:

> Tell me the tales that to me were so dear,
> Long, long ago, long, long ago;
> Sing me the song I delighted to hear,
> Long, long ago, long, long ago.
> Now you are come, all my grief is removed,
> Let me forget that so long you have rov'd;
> Let me believe that you love as you lov'd,
> Long, long ago, long ago.[11]

A musical influence may be transmitted not only in technical terms but through the underlying human context that informs music. It is precisely this fundamental humanism that makes music such a universal phenomenon. It is therefore curious that Ives, steeped in his own personalized version of transcendentalism, failed to include Dvořák in its all-encompassing embrace. Rather, he viewed him as a rival and musical carpetbagger. But the aging Ives of the *Memos* was no longer the younger man of the Second Symphony, poised between the nineteenth and twentieth centuries. A growing suspiciousness and xenophobia conjured up for Ives a hostile image of "the name with foreign hair." He was no doubt thinking quite literally at this point of the un-American accents in the orthography of **Antonín Dvořák**.

The truth is that both men expressed in their music a profound nostalgia and yearning for family, homeland, and an idealized past. The words to an Ives song express it best: "I know not what are the words, but they sing in my soul of the things our Fathers loved."

Both men were homesick in America.

NOTES

1. Charles Ives, *Memos*, ed. John Kirkpatrick (New York: W. W. Norton, 1972), 52.

2. For a discussion of the context of the autobiographical *Memos*, as well as of Ives's mental state at the time, see my *Charles Ives: "My Father's Song"* (New Haven and London: Yale University Press, 1992), Chapter 22. My other writ-

ings on Ives include "The Nostalgia of Charles Ives: An Essay in Affects and Music," *The Annual of Psychoanalysis*, vol. 10 (June 1981), 301–332, and "Charles and George Ives: The Veneration of Boyhood," in Psychoanalytic Explorations in Music (Madison CT: International Universities Press, 1989), 115–176.

3. In these writings I wanted to examine the mental life of the artist. They constitute a "psychoanalytic biography" because I tried to apply the biographical approach to the methods of clinical psychoanalysis. Both methods share certain features. Initially there is much history-taking and data-gathering; and later, formulations and interpretations suggest themselves as lines of meaning coalesce. In the case of Ives (and here, by extension, of Dvořák), the sheer auditory aspects of their upbringing were also profoundly important. Ives and Dvořák afford a fascinating opportunity for the biographer to examine how auditory representation affects life and art.

4. Charles Ives, *Memos*, 135.

5. Charles Ives, *114 Songs*, No. 43.

6. William Kay Kearns, *Horatio Parker*, Ph.D. dissertation, University of Illinois, 1965. Ann Arbor: University Microfilms.

7. Stuart Feder, *Charles Ives: "My Father's Song,"* Chapter Two.

8. In Ives's case two other extremes might be noted—a tendency toward deep depression as well as optimistic elation. This perhaps is manifest in Ives's setting in which the second strophe—unlike Dvořák's version—is carried in an upwardly moving figure in the major key.

9. John Kirkpatrick, *A Temporary Mimeographed Catalogue of the Music Manuscripts of Charles Edward Ives*, 1955, 5; in the Library of the Yale Music School.

10. Charles Ives, Symphony No. 2, Full Score, New York: Southern Music Publishing, 1951. See III at measures 15 and 127.

11. Charles Ives, Symphony No. 2, V at measure 58. This theme is foreshadowed in I at measure 33.

12. T. H. Bayly, "Long, Long Ago," in *The Ideal Home Music Library*, vol. 10 (New York: Scribner's, 1913), 159.

Part Two

New American Songs

The "American" Compositions

Dvořák as he looked in 1894, just after his return from Spillville, Iowa. (Courtesy Cyril Klimesh Collection.)

CHAPTER THIRTEEN

The Choral Works

Te Deum and "The American Flag"

Nick Strimple

*W*hen Antonín Dvořák arrived in New York on 27 September 1892 to assume his duties as director of the National Conservatory, he had with him a new Te Deum and the piano sketch of a cantata, *The American Flag*. Both works were brain children of the Conservatory's benefactor, Jeannette Thurber. Mrs. Thurber had thought that her new director should provide some suitable new work for the Columbus Quadricentennial Celebration scheduled for 12 October. It was at that concert that Dvořák would be officially "introduced" to the New World. Even though she had hatched this idea in the autumn of 1891, she had not provided any concrete suggestions until June 1892. At that time, Dvořák was requested to set to music one of the great ecclesiastical texts of jubilation, since an appropriate patriotic text had not yet been found.[1]

On 25 June of that year Dvořák responded, "It is a great pity that I did not know it some time ago, but now it is too late—despite that I will try to write a 'Te Deum' for the occasion but even this, I doubt I shall be able to get it finished because the time is very short."[2]

Within a month he received a copy of Joseph Rodman Drake's poem, "The American Flag." On 28 July he again wrote Mrs. Thurber:

> In my last letter I informed you that I would write a "Te Deum" and now I am able to say that it is completed and in a few days I will send it to you.
>
> If you wish to have it performed on the occasion of my first appearance in New York, on October 12, together with my "Triple Overture" it would be necessary to get it copied immediately. As to

"The American Flag" by Joseph Rodman Drake (and the explanatory notes by his grandson Charles de Kay), I can tell you that I like the poem very much—it is really a grand poem—and your selection for a patriotic hymn—"Columbus Cantata"—is very well fitted for music.

But what a pity it is that you did not send me the words a month earlier. It is quite impossible to get ready a work which will take half an hour in performance in time for October, and so I was compelled to write a "Te Deum." I shall, however, go on with the work from which every musician must get inspired.

Meantime, with many kind regards, I am faithfully yours,

Antonín Dvořák[3]

Dvořák began work on *The American Flag* almost immediately; he completed the piano sketch before he left Europe on 17 September.

The Columbus Celebration Concert did not take place until 21 October, at which time the Te Deum was premiered to critical acclaim. H. E. Krehbiel, in the New York *Daily Tribune*, found it "impressive throughout and sometimes eloquently expressive."[4]

Shortly after the concert, Dvořák resumed work on *The American Flag*, completing the full score on 8 January 1893. He then began long and futile attempts to publish both the cantata and the Te Deum, offering them first to Novello and then to Simrock. Negotiations continued off and on for the duration of Dvořák's stay in America, but neither publisher was very interested. In April 1895, just before his return to Bohemia, Dvořák wrote to a friend in the Czech community of Spillville, Iowa:

> Kindly accept this remembrance. It is a composition which should have been performed at Carnegie Hall in New York the day of my first appearance in public in America, Oct. 12, 1892. This composition I composed before my first visit to America and so I was not able to finish it in time I had to compose another so I wrote the "Te Deum" which was actually produced for the first time on Oct. 21, 1892 when I had the honor to present myself to the New York audience. This year upon the request of my wife I decided to have this composition published at the publishing firm Schirmer. When the "Te Deum" will be published I will also send you a copy. I must wait until the publisher takes pity on the work and so please wait also.[5]

G. Schirmer had given Dvořák the handsome sum of $1,000 for *The American Flag*. Simrock eventually "took pity" and published the Te Deum in 1896.

TE DEUM

While it has never been as popular as his Stabat Mater or Requiem, the Te Deum is still one of Dvořák's most original and satisfying works. The content is rich and varied, and it is stamped throughout by the force of the composer's own personality. Structurally, it is quite unique. Dvořák ignores the natural divisions of the text, adds an "alleluia" at the end, and creates a four-part scheme that corresponds, in highly concentrated form, to the divisions of a symphony:

**I
Allegro moderato
maestoso**

Te Deum laudamus,
Te Dominum confitemur.
Te aeternum Patrem
Omnis terra Angeli,
Tibi omnes Angeli,
Tibi caeli et universae potestates,
Tibi Cherubim et Seraphim
Incessabili voce proclamant:
Sanctus, sanctus, sanctus Dominus Deus Sabaoth.
Pleni sunt caeli et terra
Majestatis gloriae tuae.
Te gloriosus Apostolorum chorus,
Te Prophetarum laudabilis numerus,
Te Martyrum candidatus laudat exercitus.
Te per orbem terrarum sancta confitetur Ecclesia:
Patrem immensae majestatis;
Venerandum tuum verum et unicum Filium;
Sanctum quoque Paraclitum Spiritum.

**II
Lento maestoso**

Tu rex gloriae, Christe!
Tu Patris sempiternus es Filius.
Tu ad liberandum suscepturus hominem
Non horruisti Virginis uterum.
Tu devicto mortis aculeo,
Aperuisti credentibus regna caelorum.
Tu ad dexteram Dei sedes
In gloria Patris.
Judex crederis esse venturus.
Te ergo quaesumus, tuis famulis subveni,
Quos pretioso sanguine redemisti.

**III
Vivace**

Aeterna fac cum sanctis tuis
In gloria numerari.

Salvum fac populum, Domine,
Et benedic hereditati tuae.
Et rege eos et extolle illos usque in aeternum.
Per singulos dies benedicimus te.
Et laudamus nomen tuum
In saeculum et in saeculum saeculi.

IV
Lento; Tempo I

Dignare, Domine, die isto
Sine peccato nos custodire.
Miserere nostri, Domine,
Miserere nostri!
Fiat misericordia tua, Domine, super nos,
Quaemadmodum speravimus in te.
In te, Domine, speravi:
Non confundar in aeternum.
(Alleluia.)

The first section is in G major and is in straightforward ABA form. A highly energized effect of mass jubilation is achieved at the beginning by presenting several thematic and rhythmic motifs simultaneously over a timpani pedal. The resulting cross-rhythms and static harmonies, considered "primitive" by some commentators, really have much in common with late twentieth century minimalist techniques. This effect is relieved by an expressive, arching soprano solo, quietly punctuated by woodwinds and chorus. With an abbreviated return of the opening material, the piece flies headlong into the second section.

This slow movement, a bass solo with two brief choral refrains, is a wonderful example of Dvořák's harmonic inventiveness. Following an introduction in E-flat, the music embarks on a mind-boggling series of modulations, which eventually return to E-flat. The return is short-lived, however, and the music finally settles into G-flat, the second refrain functioning additionally as a harmonic transition into the B minor scherzo.

The scherzo has much to recommend it. It is vital and attractive, and the diatonic melodies and slow harmonic rhythm provide welcome relief from the modulatory gymnastics of the previous section. Again, the composer's harmonic genius is displayed. For example, he deploys some arresting augmented chords at "et rege eos"; and the E major chord at "in saeculum saeculi" is like a sudden shaft of sunlight. In tone and spirit, this section is similar to the scherzo Dvořák would write the following year for the "New World" Symphony. In both instances, Dvořák has some problems with structure. Normally, a scherzo would be a closed form. In the case of the Te Deum, that expectation is reinforced by the forms and proportions of the previous sections, as well as by the musical substance. Thus, as the scherzo dissolves, one is certain that this music will be heard again. The transition, however, leads not to a trio and subsequent return, but directly to the Te Deum's final section. Thus, while the Te Deum overall is brilliant, the lingering impression of the scherzo is one of unfulfilled promise.

The fourth section begins with another highly expressive soprano solo, in B major, once again punctuated quietly by woodwinds and chorus. The orchestration conveys a sense of urgency, and when a wandering pizzicato bass line leads into a repeat of this section, a minor third higher, it becomes apparent that Dvořák has begun a deliberately paced buildup to the Te Deum's final ecstasies. The soloists intone "Benedicamus Patrem, et Filium, cum Sancto Spiritu," the chorus repeatedly interjects "Alleluia," one by one the thematic motifs are reintroduced (including the timpani pedal), the tonality returns to G major, and the work ends in a blaze of glory.

THE AMERICAN FLAG

Like the Te Deum, *The American Flag* is organized according to a compressed symphonic scheme: a rather spaciously designed opening section, a scherzo, a multi-faceted march, and a finale which recapitulates the opening material in a triumphant peroration. The poem by Joseph Rodman Drake (1795–1820) was written in honor of American soldiers in the War of 1812:

I
Lento maestoso

1. THE COLOURS OF THE FLAG
When Freedom from her mountain height
Unfurl'd her standard to the air,
She tore the azure robe of night,
And set the stars of glory there!
She mingled with its gorgeous dyes
The milky baldric of the skies,
And striped its pure, celestial white
With streakings of the morning light.
Then, from his mansion in the sun
She call'd her eagle bearer down
And gave into his mighty hand
The symbol of her chosen land.

II
Allegro Vivace

2. FIRST HYMN TO THE EAGLE
Majestic monarch of the cloud,
Who rear'st aloft thy regal form,
To hear the tempest trumpings loud,
And see the lightning lances driven,
When strides the warrior of the storm,
And rolls the thunderdrum of heaven.

3. SECOND HYMN TO THE EAGLE
Child of the sun! to thee 'tis given
To guard the banner of the free;
To hover in the sulphur smoke,
To ward away the battle stroke.

And bid its blendings shine afar,
Like rainbows on the cloud of war,
The harbingers of Victory!

III
Allegro giusto,
alla marcia

4. FIRST ADDRESS TO THE FLAG
(The Infantryman)

Flag of the brave! thy folds shall fly,
The sign of hope and triumph high!
When speaks the signal trumpet tone
And the long line comes gleaming on.
Ere yet the life-blood, warm and wet,
Has dimm'd the glist'ning bayonet;
Each soldier eye shall brightly turn
To where thy skyborn glories burn;
And, as his springing steps advance,
Catch war and vengeance from the glance.

5. SECOND ADDRESS TO THE FLAG
(The Cavalryman)

And when the cannon mouthings loud
Heave in wild wreaths the battle shroud,
And gory sabres rise and fall
Like shoots of flame on midnight's pall;
There shall thy victor glances glow,
And cow'ring foes shall shrink beneath,
Each gallant arm that strikes below
That lovely messenger of death!

Introduction:
Allegro

6. THIRD ADDRESS TO THE FLAG
(The Sailor)

Flag of the seas! on ocean wave
Thy stars shall glitter over the brave;
When death, careering on the gale,
Sweeps darkly round the bellied sail
And frighted waves rush madly back
Before the broadside's reeling rack,
The dying wand'rer of the sea
Shall look at once to heaven and thee,
And smile to see thy splendours fly
In triumph over his closing eye.

7. APOTHEOSIS

Flag of the free heart's hope and home,
By angel hands to valour given
Thy stars have lit the welkin dome,
And all the hues were born in heaven!
And, fixed as yonder orb divine
That saw thy bannered blaze unfurled
Shall thy proud stars resplendent shine
The guard and glory of the world!

The F minor opening gradually transforms into the relative major, a process that establishes the harmonic vocabulary and thematic motifs that permeate the work. Then comes a tune from the alto solo and chorus, which after reaching a mighty climax, relaxes into the scherzo.

The scherzo, scored for bass solo and chorus, strikes a better formal balance than the corresponding movement in the Te Deum. But the thematic material is less interesting, and the straightforward key of C minor is not enhanced by any bold harmonic strokes.

The situation changes dramatically with the ensuing March. Here Dvořák's personality begins to assert itself. The bright key of A major provides a welcome home for music that is boisterous and exuberant—real Fourth-of-July music, if you will, albeit with a European flavor. The inspiration sags somewhat when the singers return, but the March proves to be extremely pliable and expressive of a variety of emotions. It moves into D minor and quietly passes from view on an unresolved chord.

After a brief pause, the ocean waves begin to ripple, building quickly into stormy billows in the far-off key of E-flat minor ("Flag of the seas!"). This section does not fit neatly into the four-part symphonic scheme. Textually, it belongs with the preceding March (the "Soldier," the "Cavalryman," the "Sailor"). But Dvořák could not pass up so obvious an opportunity for text-painting. Besides, he was also trying to go with the flow of the text and not attempting, as in the Te Deum, to force it into some absolute form. His solution was to treat this section as a long, dramatic introduction to the finale, although the score is labeled according to the poem's divisions. He repeats the E-flat minor chord up a half step, in E minor, and lets it gradually wind down, eventually subsiding into a compacted and reorganized recapitulation, in A major, of the opening section.

The Finale is very grand. Of special interest is the incredible final cadence, which has become only too well known through years of imitation in the movie industry.

The American Flag was not premiered in America until 4 May 1895, almost three weeks after Dvořák had left America for the last time. (Indeed, he never heard the work in performance.) The occasion was not successful. The *Daily Tribune*'s H. E. Krehbiel felt "obliged to speak words of disappointment and dispraise of the work."[6] Ever since, *The American Flag* has languished in near oblivion. Most commentators either avoid serious discussion of it or condemn it outright. Otakar Šourek, for example, cited it as "the weakest of his works."[7] Schirmer's reissue of the vocal score and Michael Tilson Thomas's recording—both coinciding with the American Bicentennial in 1976—did little to improve its popularity.

Even though analysis reveals it to be a work of considerable interest, crafted by a master, it is still easy to identify at least three reasons for the public's indifference. First, for all its charm and craftsmanship, *The American Flag* does not particularly sound like Dvořák. It is saturated by Wagnerian harmonies, while the thematic manipulations are pure Liszt. Second, its sentiments might have been repugnant to Europeans. If Dvořák had interpreted its belligerent message as an outcry against the domination of Europe by the Germans, then, as Andrew Cosgrove speculates in his program notes for the Tilson Thomas recording, this might explain in part why the work has been neglected in Europe and why it was Dvořák's only work to be first published by an American firm. On the other hand, Dvořák may have felt no emotional attachment whatever to the text, simply writing it as a commissioned work. As Gervase Hughes has pointed out, Dvořák was perhaps better at spontaneous nationalism than at more self-conscious patriotism.[8] Besides, how does one write a patriotic work for a *foreign* country?

The third reason for the work's relative neglect, for general audiences at least, is the text. Dvořák's profession of faith in the poem notwithstanding, it is difficult to imagine anyone being inspired by Drake's overblown rhetoric. Charles Dickens, with his customary probity, had satirized such patriotic inflations in his novel *Martin Chuzzlewit* (1843). On his travels through America, young Martin had many opportunities to observe pompous patriots and windy orators. One such blustering citizen declared to Chuzzlewit that the true American is

> a true born child of this free hemisphere; bright and flowing as our mineral drinks; unspoiled by withering conventionalities. . . . Wild he may be. So are our Buffaloes. But he is a child of nature, and a child of freedom, and his boastful answer to the Despot and the Tyrant is, that his bright home is in the Settin' Sun.

The cantata, while obviously not so great a work as the Te Deum, occupies an important position in the development of the composer's symphonic thinking. Perhaps it and the Te Deum were two halves of an ongoing structural experiment. In the Triple Overture of 1891–92 (*In Nature's Realm, Carnival,* and *Othello*), we see Dvořák stretching sonata-allegro form to accommodate his programmatic intentions. Just a year after his departure from America, Dvořák composed four symphonic poems— *The Water Goblin, The Noon Witch, The Golden Spinning Wheel,* and *The Wild Dove*—

which abandon sonata form altogether in favor of structures generated quite literally by the programmatic content, namely, Karl Jaromir Erben's *Bouquet of Folk Tales* (1853). In between these works and the Triple Overture stand Te Deum and *The American Flag*. As in the Triple Overture, Dvořák's thinking in Te Deum is still guided by ideas of abstract muscial form. Ignoring the Latin hymn's natural divisions, he subjugates the text to the architecture, projecting broad emotions in general, though deeply felt, terms. In *The American Flag*, however, the form loosens to embrace the higher priorities of the text, portraying specific emotions and events through text-painting and thematic transformation—processes that are to figure prominently in the symphonic poems. Seen in this context, the two "American" choral works figure as an important pivot in the composer's shift toward a more overtly programmatic music.

NOTES

1. See John Clapham, *Dvořák* (New York and London: W. W. Norton, 1979), 109.
2. Milan Kuna, ed., *Antonín Dvořák: Korespondence a dokumenty* 3 (1890–1895), Prague: Edition Supraphon, 1989, 132–133.
3. Milan Kuna, ed., *Antonín Dvořák: Korespondence a dokumenty*, 135–136.
4. Henry Edward Krehbiel, "Review" in New York *Daily Tribune*, 24 October 1892.
5. Milan Kuna, ed., *Antonín Dvořák: Korespondence a dokumenty*, 394.
6. Henry Edward Krehbiel, "Review" in New York *Daily Tribune*, 6 May 1895.
7. Otakar Šourek, "Antonín Dvořák," in *Grove's Dictionary of Music and Musicians*, Fifth Edition, 2: 838.
8. Gervase Hughes, *Dvořák: His Life and Music* (New York: Dodd, Mead and Company, 1967), 159.

Dvořák's preliminary sketch for what he referred to as a "future American anthem"—a musical setting to the text of "My Country, 'Tis of Thee." It is dated 19 December 1892 and entitled "Motivy New York." (Courtesy Jarmil Burghauser.)

CHAPTER FOURTEEN

"My Country, 'Tis of Thee"

Jarmil Burghauser

mong Dvořák's "American" compositions, the least known is the unfinished (and unpublished) "My Country, 'Tis of Thee." Some detective work has been needed to bring this intriguing fragment to light.

Dvořák was fascinated by the intensity and scope of the Columbian festivities in New York that were approaching their peak in the fall of 1892. As his secretary, Josef Jan Kovařík, reported in a letter written years later:

> Maestro assumed his duties at the Conservatory the next day [28 September 1892] after his arrival, and—in spite of having nothing to do there, he dwelt at the Conservatory the entire day. The reason for this was . . . the grandiose celebrations of the 400th anniversary of the discovery of America.[1]

From the windows of the Conservatory at 126–128 East Seventeenth Street, he was able to observe the parades passing by on Third Avenue. He described the spectacle in a letter to his friend Karel Baštař, 14 October 1892:

> The Columbus celebrations finished just yesterday, and they were simply gigantic! We have never seen anything like this; and never has America had such an opportunity to show what it is capable of accomplishing. Imagine an incessant succession of grand parades— from the branches of industry, trades, gymnastics (including our Sokols), the arts, and everything—which lasted three days, from the morning until 2 o'clock at night. There were thousands and thousands of people; and always many, many other images. And what about the various music bands![2]

We have no direct evidence that Dvořák heard the two great patriotic

songs of the United States—the "Star-Spangled Banner" and "America"—
during these festivities, but it is very probable. Ironically, both of these patriotic ballads were derived from British tunes. The lyrics to "The Star-Spangled Banner" had been written by Francis Scott Key in the early morning
hours of 13 September 1814. After he set it to an English melody, "Anacreon
in Heaven," it achieved an enormous popularity in the years leading up to
the Civil War (although it would not be until much later, on 3 March 1931,
that "The Star-Spangled Banner" would be declared America's national
anthem by an act of Congress). The lyrics to "America"—"My Country, 'Tis
of Thee"—were penned in 1831 by clergyman Samuel Francis Smith to the
tune of "God Save the King," the British national anthem. The new American version was sung publicly for the first time on the Fourth of July that
year in Boston. We do know that "The Star-Spangled Banner" and "America" were performed, respectively, at the beginning and end of Dvořák's first
public concert appearance (at Carnegie Hall) on 21 October.[3] On this occasion, according to Kovařík,[4] the words of the two songs were handed out to
the public:

> I brought, then, several copies home,[5] and the next day, Maestro read
> the words of the anthems attentively and eventually remarked it was a
> shame for America to use an English tune to one of the anthems. He
> seated himself at the piano, improvised a tune, wrote it down into his
> sketchbook, and said: So! This will be the future American anthem,
> arranged for baritone solo, choir and orchestra! Alas, this never has
> been realized. After finishing the orchestration of *The American Flag*,
> Maestro began to prepare a new large work, the Symphony "From
> the New World." He had nearly forgotten the American anthem,[6]
> but he used the theme later in another work. (See Jan Smaczny's essay
> on the E-Flat Quintet, Chapter 17.)

Then Kovařík quotes the first six bars from "America," followed by a quotation of measures 17–24 from the third movement of Dvořák's String Quintet, Opus 97 (which he describes as "Maestro's 'America' that he intended to
compose"). The key is A-flat and the time signature is 3/8, but there are
rhythmic changes to fit the written-in words of lines 1–3 and 7 of "America."

Kovařík must have kept a diary, or at least a record of events at the
time, for his memoirs contain a wealth of relatively precise detail with only
minor discrepancies from historical fact. But although we have no reason in
general to disbelieve Kovařík's memoirs, the extant sketch includes neither
the text nor title of "America" but is inscribed "Motivy New York." Dated
19 December 1892, this sketch (the first written by Dvořák after he arrived
in New York)[7] is accompanied by another unidentified three-bar sketch in

pencil. The page has been reproduced in facsimile several times, but the pencil portion is usually omitted.[8]

The sketch in question begins with fourteen bars that correspond to the first fourteen bars of the theme for variations at the beginning of the third movement of the E-flat Quintet. The key is G minor and the time signature is 3/4. The second part of the sketch, in G major, corresponds to bars 17–24 in the Quintet—the part inspired by the tune of "America," according to Kovařík. A third part, which is a variant of the second, is also in G major but uses 2/4 time and is marked Allegro. This last part does not correspond closely to any passage, either in the Quintet or elsewhere, as far as anyone has determined.

Assuming the basic facts of Kovařík's memoir to be correct, we must disassociate the piano improvisation of "America" from the version in the sketchbook, for the sketch was evidently written down, not the day after the 21 October concert, but nearly two months later. Furthermore, Kovařík may have been wrong when he coupled the words of the poem only to bars 17–24 of the Quintet melody. Dvořák, who had composed a considerable number of songs, choruses, and other vocal works, could not have missed the fact that the first part of each stanza begins with only *three* lines rather than four, and that these correspond to the first *six* bars of the melody "God Save the Queen" rather than the more customary eight. If we also consider Kovařík's mention of a setting for baritone and choir (with orchestra), we must suppose that the composition would begin with a solo, after the usual few bars of introduction, and continue with the choir. Searching for the appropriate place in the sketch where the first three lines of the text could have been placed, we find such an irregular six-bar section just before the change to major mode, while the surroundings keep to a four-plus-four-bar regularity. In composing the Quintet, where words were not a factor, Dvořák changed the unusual six-bar formation to a regular eight-bar formation by repeating the last two bars. This would seem to corroborate the theory that the six-bar phrase in the sketch was conceived to accommodate the unusual grouping of the first three lines in "My Country, 'Tis of Thee."

Working from this hypothesis, I have reconstructed the whole [see page 209] by using the first eight bars for a solemn introduction, putting the first three lines of the text (for solo baritone) at the only viable place, and bringing in the choir when the mode changes, as was Dvořák's frequent custom in orchestration. I mostly followed the harmonic solution Dvořák used in the Quintet, including the rather harsh turn to the dominant seventh chord in bar 4 and the unison in bars 13–14. For the orchestration, I used the same instruments found in Dvořák's arrangement of Stephen Foster's "Old Folks at Home" (see Deane L. Root's essay, Chapter 18), with the addition of three trombones to give the proper solemnity to the beginning, which also acts as an interlude before each of the following stanzas. To avoid the high G at the melody's peak, I transposed the whole from G major/minor down to F.

As Šourek has indicated, the beginning of the sketch may also be regarded as the germ of the opening adagio theme in the "New World" Symphony. But nobody I'm aware of has yet pointed out that the first two bars (and their subsequent iteration) are very similar to the first bars of the Arapaho "Song for a Spiritual Dance," contained in a collection by Dr. A. C. Fletcher (1838–1923), about whose earlier studies Dvořák could certainly have known. (See Example 14-1.) Fletcher, the author of *Indian Story and Song from North America* (1900), was a renowned American ethnologist who became vice-president of the American Association for the Advancement of Science in 1896. It is likely that her work, in progress during Dvořák's visit, was known to him. He had been interested in the music of Native Americans since no later than 1879, when a troop of them toured Europe with their music and dances.[9] The question remains, who was the mysterious "friend" who gave Dvořák "a certain number of Indian melodies," reported in the article "Dvořák on His New Work" in the New York *Herald* on 15 December 1893? Dvořák's daring, if obviously erroneous, statement that "the music of the Negroes and of the Indians was practically identical" can be reconciled only in the sense that he found pentatonic principles in both of them, just as he did in the "music of Scotland," as was much more aptly expressed at the beginning of the same article. Pentatonicisms are present in the examples given by Novotný in the *Dalibor* article, and it is my firm opinion that the mysterious friend was none other than Novotný himself. Certainly it could not have been Harry T. Burleigh, who was most likely the one who acquainted him with the African American spirituals; and it could not have been James G. Huneker who, according to Kovařík's memoirs, also addressed Dvořák on behalf of the spirituals. (By the way, it is doubtful if Dvořák would have called Huneker his friend; the opposite is more likely, if we recall the poisonous stories that Huneker fabricated in connection with the premier of the "New World" Symphony and thereafter.) Dvořák's interest in Native American music can already be discerned in the "American" coloring of the Te Deum, composed in the summer of 1892 and intended to be a part of the Columbus festivities.

Whereas the influence of African American spirituals in the music of

Example 14-1. "Song for a Spiritual Dance," purportedly an Arapaho Indian dance with which Dvořák may have been acquainted, bears a resemblance to the introductory material of his "Motivy New York."

Dvořák's American period has always been generally accepted, the influence of Native American music is often debated.[10] To me, it is evident that Dvořák came into contact with the latter much earlier than with the former. But through what channels did these influences come to him?

Dvořák was a typical representative of the younger generation of Czech artists. After Bedřich Smetana's generation had forged a new Czech culture, Dvořák and his peers widened its horizons by introducing inspirations from the cultures of other nations. He achieved in music what his friends Zeyer, Vrchlický, and Sládek were accomplishing in literature and Mikoláš Aleš in painting.[11] We have learned only some of the ways by which Dvořák became acquainted with non-Czech cultures.[12] American scholars may find a challenge in seeking a wider and deeper knowledge of the various sources from which he learned about North American folk music of all denominations. In so doing, it must be clearly understood that for the artist (unlike the scholar) only a short glimpse is sufficient to release a rich flow of creativity.

NOTES

1. Between 1927 and 1930 Josef Jan Kovařík (1870–1951) provided an extensive mosaic of personal remembrances of Dvořák in the form of letters written to Otakar Šourek. This archive, a part of the personal estate of Šourek, is now kept by the author of this article. (This and all other English translations are by the author).

2. Letter from Dvořák to his friend, Karel Baštař, 14 October 1892 (trans. from the Czech by Jarmil Burghauser); in *Antonín Dvořák: Korespondence a dokumenty* 3, 1890–1895, ed. Milan Kuna. (Prague: Supraphon, 1989), 154.

3. The concert included the overtures *In Nature's Realm, Carnival,* and *Othello,* and the world premiere of the Te Deum (with a choir consisting of 250 singers). Colonel Thomas W. Higginson's welcoming speech celebrated Dvořák's arrival in America as a hope for promoting the development of American music.

4. Letter to Šourek, 27 July 1927, *vi–vii* (part of the collection cited in Note 1).

5. That is, to Kovařík's "home" in the Dvořák household, 327 East Seventeenth Street.

6. Not completely, however, for in a letter to Fritz Simrock, dated 13 October 1893, Dvořák wrote about a new Quintet that would contain an "Andante with Variations" (in the printed edition changed to Larghetto), based on a melody originally conceived to an English text. ["The melody itself is from an unfinished song composed to an English text, which I later incorporated into another composition." Ed.]

7. See Šourek's four-volume biography, *Život a dílo Antonína Dvořáka* 3 (Prague: Státni nakladatelství krásné literatury, hudby a umění, 1956), 129. It appears in full in my commentary to the facsimile edition of the autograph of the Symphony in E minor (Prague: Pressfoto, 1972). There I quote rather extensively passages from Kovařík's memoirs; the English text is on pp. 19–22.

8. See Note 7.

9. The Prague musical periodical *Dalibor* I (1879), 191–192, brought out a report on it from the pen of Dvořák's close friend Václav Juda Novotný (1849–1922) with nine shorter or longer musical examples, written down by Novotný (evidently from memory).

10. The most interesting dispute over the influence of Native American music on Dvořák is the one between John Clapham and Antonín Sychra. See Clapham's "Dvořák, Irokézové a kickapúové," *Hudební rozhledy* 9 (1956), 983–985, and Sychra's *The Aesthetics of Dvořák's Symphonic Works*, Prague (1959). [See also John Clapham's essay, Chapter 8 in this volume, for an account in English.] Sychra hypothesizes that Dvořák may have known Fletcher's first collection, *The Songs of Omaha Indians*, published by the Peabody Museum of Harvard University in 1893.

11. Mikolas Ales, for example, was inspired by Native American culture in one of his large pictorial cycles.

12. I found the evident source for Dvořák's dumka-type compositions in the collection of Kocipiński (see my paper, "Dvořák's and Janáček's dumka," presented at the IMS Congress, Melbourne, 1988). The channels are still unknown in the case of his *Irish Choruses, Lithuanian Choruses, Three Modern Greek Poems*, and other minor works.

America

Sketch by Antonín Dvořák

Realization by Jarmil Burghauser

Jarmil Burghauser's realization of Dvořák's setting of "My Country, 'Tis of Thee" (with the first verse). This is the first time the realization has appeared in print.

CHAPTER FIFTEEN

The Dance of Pau-Puk-Keewis, the Song of Chibiabos, and the Story of Iagoo

Reflections on Dvořák's "New World" Scherzo

Michael Beckerman

A debate raged in the press following the premiere of Dvořák's Symphony in E Minor "From the New World": just how American *was* the work? Two days after the premiere, on 17 December 1893, Henry Krehbiel wrote in the New York *Tribune*, "All that is necessary to admit is the one thing for which he [Dvořák] has compelled recognition—that there are musical elements in America which lend themselves to beautiful treatment in the higher forms of art."[1] James Huneker countered with what is doubtless a tongue-in-cheek bit of reportage that he published in an article on 20 December 1893 in the *Musical Courier*: "Its extremely Celtic character was patent to numerous people, and the general opinion seemed to be that Dvořák had not been long in discovering what a paramount factor the Irish were in the political life of the country."[2] Indeed, the disagreement even seemed to fly awfully close to home, with the composer saying that "anyone with a nose" could tell that the work was American,[3] while his loyal secretary, Josef Kovařík later suggested that using the expression "New World" in the title was one of the Master's "little jokes."[4]

Whether the work ought to be considered "American" and what such a designation might mean will be considered at the end of this study. But the work has at least two obvious American connections: it was composed in the

United States, almost entirely in New York City, and the two middle movements were based on passages from *The Song of Hiawatha*, Henry Wads–
worth Longfellow's long poem in twenty-two cantos.

The source for this proclamation is not hearsay, nor is it suspect in
any way—it comes from the composer himself. Quoting from Dvořák's
remarks in the New York *Herald* on 15 December 1893,

> The second movement is an Adagio. But it is different to the classics
> in this form. It is in reality a study or a sketch for a longer work,
> either a cantata or an opera which I purpose [*sic*] writing, and which
> will be based upon Longfellow's "Hiawatha." I have long had the idea
> of someday utilizing that poem. I first became acquainted with it
> about thirty years ago through the medium of a Bohemian transla-
> tion. It appealed very strongly to my imagination at that time, and
> the impression has only been strengthened by my residence here. The
> Scherzo of the symphony was suggested by the scene at the feast in
> Hiawatha where the Indians dance, and is also an essay I made in the
> direction of imparting the local color of Indian music to music.[5]

Before we explore the implications of these remarks, some background information is in order. *The Song of Hiawatha* was published in 1855
and became the equivalent of a runaway best-seller. Based on two rather disparate sources, the Finnish *Kalevala* and a series of American Indian legends
compiled by Schoolcraft, the twenty-two cantos of the poem tell the epic
story of the brave and wise Hiawatha, a member of the Ojibway tribe. In its
characteristic (some would say plodding) rhythm, exotic vocabulary, and
vivid imagery, it tells of the hero's birth and his struggles to achieve maturity.
The middle cantos portray Hiawatha's wooing of Minnehaha (a member of
the hostile Dacotah tribe), their wedding, and her death during the famine.
We shall see that it was this part of the poem which captured the attention of
the composer.

The Song of Hiawatha was not a newly acquired taste for Dvořák. As
the interview suggests, he had been familiar with it for quite some time, at
least since the early 1870s.[6] According to documents in the possession of the
Dvořák scholar Jarmil Burghauser, the composer's secretary, Josef Kovařík,
obtained a copy of the poem for the composer shortly after Dvořák's arrival
in the United States. This came as a result of Jeannette Thurber's suggestion
that the poem might make a fit subject for an opera. That Dvořák did
indeed think of writing a Hiawatha opera is clear both from remarks in the
interview and from subsequent material consisting of sketches for such a
project. But the first and most profound realization of his Hiawatha impulse
is to be found in the middle two movements of the Symphony in E Minor,

most explicitly the Scherzo.[7]

Shortly before the premiere of his new symphony, Dvořák told Krehbiel that the second movement, the Largo, was inspired by "Hiawatha's Wooing," Chapter 10 of Longfellow's poem.[8] But this chapter is over 280 lines long and contains many episodes; finding precisely which parts inspired Dvořák requires a good deal of detective work and a certain amount of speculation. Determining the exact relationship between *The Song of Hiawatha* and the Scherzo is both more and less challenging. Although Dvořák, in a rare burst of openness, told us almost exactly where to look, many questions still remain.

When Dvořák mentioned "the feast in Hiawatha where the Indians dance," he could only have been referring to "Hiawatha's Wedding Feast," Chapter 11 of *The Song of Hiawatha.* This chapter directly follows "Hiawatha's Wooing," which played a role in the shape and spirit of the Largo (see note 8). The chapter begins with this short introduction:

> You shall hear how Pau-Puk-Keewis,
> How the handsome Yenadizze
> Danced at Hiawatha's wedding;
> How the gentle Chibiabos,
> He the sweetest of musicians,
> Sang his songs of love and longing;
> How Iagoo, the great boaster,
> He the marvellous story-teller,
> Told his tales of strange adventure,
> That the feast might be more joyous,
> That the time might pass more gayly,
> And the guests be more contented.

These opening lines summarize not only Chapter 11 but also Chapter 12, "The Son of the Evening Star." Both chapters take place within the context of the wedding feast, and both feature songs by Chibiabos.

In the first part of Chapter 11, lines 13–35 describe the display of raiment, tableware, and victuals at the wedding; the polished bowls and ivory spoons, the robes of fur, the pemmican and bison meat. Hiawatha and Minnehaha serve their guests but do not eat. Old Nokomis, grandmother of Hiawatha, fills the pipes and calls on Pau-Puk-Keewis to dance "the Beggar's Dance." Lines 55–96 contain a description of Pau-Puk-Keewis as an athlete and a gambler, a charmer and a dandy. He is dressed in fine soft doe skin, with fringes, quills, beads, and feathers. His face is "Barred with streaks of red and yellow, / Streaks of blue and bright vermillion."

The description of the dance itself is only 22 lines long, 97–118:[9]

> First he danced a solemn measure,
> Very slow in step and gesture,
> In and out among the pine trees,
> Through the shadows and the sunshine,
> Treading softly like a panther.
> Then more swiftly and still swifter,
> Whirling, spinning round in circles,
> Leaping o'er the guests assembled,
> Eddying round and round the wigwam,
> Till the leaves went whirling with him,
> Till the dust and wind together
> Swept in eddies round about him.
>
> Then along the sandy margin
> Of the lake, the Big-Sea-Water,
> On he sped with frenzied gestures,
> Stamped upon the sand and tossed it
> Wildly in the air around him;
> Till the wind became a whirlwind,
> Till the sand was blown and sifted
> Like great snowdrifts o'er the landscape,
> Heaping all the shores with Sand Dunes,
> Sand hills of the Nagow Wudjoo!

It is easy to see why investigators exploring the link between the poem and the music have focused on these lines—there appears to be a clear connection between the events in the Scherzo and the unfolding of the dance. Both begin under control, measured, "treading softly." While the dance actually accelerates, the music creates an analog through dynamic changes and syncopation. A hypothetical model for the relationship between the poem and measures 1–59 of the Scherzo is shown on pages 214 and 215.

Of course, it would have been a far more literal interpretation if Dvořák had written a movement that had actually accelerated in tempo, but we acknowledge that a composer often works with multiple models. In this case, besides somehow depicting the activities of the poem, Dvořák clearly had to satisfy some of the parameters of a Scherzo. These include a specific meter and range of tempi, certain kinds of return, and a basic formal design. A literal interpretation of the quoted lines, beginning with a slow tempo and gradually accelerating, would be a faithful depiction of the text but probably a rather chaotic musical work, since it would have to keep accelerating and decelerating to stay within the Scherzo framework. Dvořák seems to have

Table 15-1. Author's correlations between the text of Longfellow's poem and the pertinent passages of Dvořák's music.

To the sounds of flutes and singing, To the sound of drums and voices, Rose the handsome Pau-Puk-Keewis.	mm. 1–8	woodwinds and drums; introductory
First he danced a solemn measure . . . Treading softly like a panther	mm. 13–20	pizzicato woodwinds, piano "panther-like"
Then more swiftly and still swifter, Whirling, spinning 'round in circles,	mm. 21–32	eighth-notes in second violin; "whirling" figure, crescendo
Leaping o'er the guests assembled, Eddying 'round and 'round the wigwam, Till the leaves went whirling with him	mm. 33–48	"leaping" up to an octave, *fortissimo* leading to tutti
Stamped upon the sand and tossed it Wildly in the air around him; Till the wind became a whirlwind	mm. 49–59	main theme to bass line; chromatic syncopation woodwinds; breakdown of coherence

mm. 1–4

mm. 13–16

mm. 21–24

mm. 35–38

mm. 49–52

chosen a strategy that gives the general *impression* of the dance of Pau-Puk-Keewis by increasing intensity while decreasing predictability.

In addition to an abstract Scherzo model, Dvořák may also have had a *musical* model in mind for the Scherzo: the second movement from Beethoven's Symphony in D Minor. Certainly the opening of the movement, with its off-the-beat timpani strokes on tonic and dominant would appear to be an almost direct quotation of that work.

Example 15-1a. Beethoven, Symphony No. 9, Scherzo, mm. 1–4.

Example 15-1b. Dvořák, Symphony No. 9, Scherzo, mm. 1–4.

Like Beethoven's movement, Dvořák's starts softly and builds. Can we argue that the Beethoven Scherzo is also part of the "program"? One can almost imagine the process taking place in Dvořák's mind. He reads a passage "with intent to commit the composition of a Scherzo." The passage describes an activity that begins in a "pantherlike" manner—that is, soft and graceful, seemingly delicate, but filled with the potential for energy and perhaps danger. In a few short lines, near chaos reigns, the potential has been realized. Dvořák seeks to translate this impulse into sound, recalling the Beethoven Scherzo, which for him may be the prototypical realization of the same process. Indeed, if we didn't have the reality of time's forward motion to stop us, we could almost argue that *Beethoven's* Scherzo was based on the Dance of Pau-Puk-Keewis!

There is one further question that is important to ask about the first part of the Scherzo. Wherein lies the Native American character? If this is an "essay in local color," as the composer said, where should we look? We will never try to say what is or is not Native American; and further, we know that Dvořák, despite his enthusiasm, was a true amateur as an ethnographer.

Since, however, he did make a point of mentioning the subject, it must have been important to him.

The main place to look for "Indian-ness" is in the incessant rhythm, pounding drum beats, and the exotic "minor drone" harmony. Whether or not any of it *sounds* Native American hardly matters. One might add that, for good or ill, most of us don't know any more about Native American music than Dvořák did, perhaps even less, and we would not be likely to recognize the genuine article even if we tripped over it. It is almost certain that these repetitive rhythms and "monotonous" harmonies—primitive and powerful—were those elements identified as "Indian" by the composer. This links Dvořák with a whole range of composers, from Rimsky-Korsakov to Saint-Saens, who used a minor-key drone as a virtual symbol for the exotic.

Most critics have been satisfied with the general connection between the poem and the symphony as articulated by the composer. Yet up to this point we have only dealt with the first fifty-nine measures of the Scherzo! Where does the rest of it come from, and does it also reflect the composer's fascination with Native Americans in general and *The Song of Hiawatha* in particular? Writing about the Largo in the interview cited above, Dvořák said that it was "different to the classic works in that form." By this he was certainly referring to departures from his "normal" practice mandated by the use of a program.[10] Are there any such departures in the Scherzo?

One of the peculiarities of this movement is the way the E major episode at measure 68 almost fools the listener into thinking that the Trio has arrived. Let us borrow the old formal model of the Minuet/Scherzo simply for reference purposes:

ABA   CDC   ABA

While it is possible for "B" to provide contrast to "A," they are much more likely to be closely related. For them to be almost antithetical, as in the Symphony in E Minor, and for B to function as a pseudo-Trio, is extremely rare.[11]

If we continue with *The Song of Hiawatha*, we see that the dance of Pau-Puk-Keewis is not the only event of the wedding and perhaps not even the central one. After the dance there is a call for another entertainment:

> Then they said to Chibiabos,
> To the friend of Hiawatha,
> To the sweetest of all singers,
> To the best of all musicians,

"Sing to us, O Chibiabos!
Songs of love and songs of longing!"

Chibiabos then begins to sing "in accents sweet and tender" and "in tones of deep emotion." His song is one of the most beautiful passages of the poem, mixing the exotic locale of the open prairie and imagery from the Song of Songs, with specific reference to *"Ani Shoshanah ha Sharon"* (I am the rose of Sharon and the lily of the valley):

Onaway! Awake, beloved!
Thou the wild flower of the forest!
Thou the wild bird of the prairie!
Thou with eyes so soft and fawn-like!
If thou only lookest at me,
I am happy, I am happy,
As the lilies of the prairie,
When they feel the dew upon them!

In all, the song of Chibiabos is thirty-five lines long and is, by turns, sensitive, sensuous, reflective, and erotic.

There is no doubt that Dvořák knew these verses well. There is a setting of them on page 25 of the fifth American sketchbook, and they were clearly intended for the Hiawatha opera (Example 15-2).

On - a - way   a - wake   be - lov - ed   thou the wild flo - wer   of the for - est

Example 15-2. Dvořák, American Sketch Book No. 5, p. 25.

This kind of evidence is tantalizing: on the one hand it is proof positive that Dvořák was attached to these lyrics. On the other, it must be noted that the musical line is different from that of the second part of the Scherzo. Would Dvořák have set the same text twice in different ways?

I am not convinced that we will ever have a definitive answer to that question, but there are several reasons I think it likely that the E major section was, in fact, based on the song of Chibiabos. First, and most obvious, it is bizarre to imagine Dvořák reading just until the end of the dance and stopping at that point; indeed, we know he read further. The unusual musical design and the transition to a completely different musical vocabulary suggest that he was mirroring the moods of the poem.

Second, it is not necessary to assume automatically that Dvořák was *setting* the text. He may have had in mind simply the contrast between the wild dance and a lyrical ballad—the former involving *process*, as it changes from one state to another; the latter being more static. Indeed, in keeping with the lyrics, the passage beginning at bar 68 has the characteristics of a pastoral love song, with very little tension, harmonic or otherwise. Though it does not contain the explicit "bagpipe" drone that characterizes many pastoral settings, the repeated pattern in the bass line, the B pedal, and the constant reiteration of E on the first beat of almost every measure conjure up a world of unchanging consonance, while the gradually building intensity of the passage is in keeping with its romantic character.[12]

Example 15-3. Dvořák, Symphony No. 9, Scherzo, mm. 68–71.

The pentatonic flavor of the melody may well be an attempt to depict some sort of "Indian music," but it is even more likely a way of evoking the wide spaces of the prairie.[13]

We may wish to go further, though, and see the E major section as more closely related to the poem. First, we should note that while Dvořák's setting in the American Sketch Book No. 5 is unmetered, it is clearly in duple or quadruple meter. The requirements of a Scherzo would mandate a different metrical strategy, which might in turn call forth a completely different musical image. In this case, the ideas share certain features: both begin with a leap followed by a pentatonic descent, and it is not so hard to hear the words, "Onaway, awake beloved!" embedded in the Scherzo (see Example 15-4).

Certainly there is ample reason to consider the likelihood that measures 68–99 of the score reflect the love song of Chibiabos. But still, we are only at the end of the Scherzo; there is a rather lengthy Trio remaining. So far I have suggested that Dvořák used a dance and a song as models for char-

On - a - way!____   A - wake   be - lov - ed____

Example 15-4. Dvořák, hypothetical text-music relationship.

acteristic passages from the third movement of his symphony. But we may remember that a third event occurs at the wedding feast: Iagoo's tale called "The Son of the Evening Star," also the title of Chapter 12.

"The Son of the Evening Star," at 375 lines, is the longest chapter in *The Song of Hiawatha*, and with the previous chapter, it forms a centerpiece to the poem as a whole. It begins with the fall of evening and the appearance of the evening star. Iagoo declaims:

> Behold it!
> See the sacred Star of Evening!
> You shall hear a tale of wonder,
> Hear the story of Osseo!
> Son of the Evening Star, Osseo!

His story is long and rather involved. In the Northland there lived a hunter with ten beautiful daughters. All of them married young and handsome warriors with the exception of the youngest, Oweenee, who wed an old man named Osseo ("Broken with age and weak with coughing, / Always coughing like a squirrel.") Though old and infirm, his spirit was beautiful because he had descended from the Evening Star.

The handsome young husbands, some of whom had been rejected by Oweenee, mock the old man. One day, while on the way to a great feast, Osseo looks up to the sky and says, "Pity, pity me, my father." The other couples laugh at him. But as they walk they come to an uprooted oak. Osseo walks into one end of it and comes out the other as a young man, his youth restored. At the same time, Oweenee is turned into an old woman.

During the feast Osseo sits silently, "looking dreamily and sadly." He hears a voice telling him the spells that bound him are broken. Suddenly the lodge begins to rise, and as it does, it is transformed, turning to silver and crimson. The couple who have mocked Osseo are turned into birds. Oweenee, however, remains an old woman until Osseo gives "another cry of anguish" and her beauty returns.

Osseo's father appears in a radiant halo and tells his son to hang a bird cage on the doorway of his wigwam. He warns Osseo about the evil magician who had turned him into an old man. By and by a son is born to Oweenee and Osseo. They make a toy bow and arrows for him and allow him to shoot at the birds. Finally he hits one, and it changes into a beautiful young woman with the arrow in her breast. When her blood spills upon the ground all spells are broken. The birds resume mortal shape, only now they are little people, like pygmies. On summer evenings they can still be seen flitting about the woodlands.

Iagoo finishes his story with an injunction to his listeners: "Let them learn the fate of jesters." The chapter ends with another song by Chibiabos, about a maiden's lamentation for her lover, an Algonquin.

There are two reasons for focusing on the song of Iagoo. First, if we argue that two out of the three main parts of the Scherzo are somehow based on successive parts of *The Song of Hiawatha*, it at least makes sense to explore the relationship between the remainder of the movement and subsequent actions of the poem. Second, I am very intrigued by a series of trilled chords that are conspicuously featured in the middle section of the Trio. To my ear they suggest birdcalls. We may remember that Dvořák was a bird lover who kept pigeons throughout his life. Furthermore, his sketches for the never-completed Hiawatha opera include bird trills, and as I have argued else-where, the C-sharp major section of the Largo represents bird song as taken from Longfellow's lines, "All the birds sang loud and sweetly." Since the chapter in question deals with a group of Indians who are turned into birds through magic spells, a detailed look appears to be in order.

One observation that militates against the use of Hiawatha material in the Trio is simply that it sounds more like a Slavonic Dance than any other part of the symphony.[14] Its major-minor tonality, mincing rhythms, and tri-adic motifs seem to recall the Bohemian pseudo-aristocracy rather than the American forests (Example 15-5).

But the ensuing section, though it maintains a Continental veneer, is filled with trills and piquant modulations (Example 15-6).
The trills finally take over completely at measure 215 and there is another exotic inflection from E major to D minor (Example 15-7). When the main material of the Trio returns, it takes over the trills as an accompaniment fig-ure in the violins.

Much of Chapter 12 does not really lend itself to musical treatment, but there is one place that could, I believe, be the source for the Trio. It begins at line 135. A voice is heard from afar, "Coming from the starry dis-tance / Coming from the empty vastness / Low, and musical, and tender"; it

Example 15-5. Dvořák, Symphony No. 9, Scherzo, mm. 175–182.

Example 15-6. Dvořák, Symphony No. 9, Scherzo, mm. 192–199.

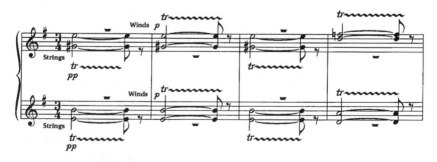

Example 15-7. Dvořák, Symphony No. 9, Scherzo, mm. 215–218.

announces that all old spells are broken. The voice goes on:

> Taste the food that stands before you:
> It is blessed and enchanted,
> It has many virtues in it,
> It will change you to a spirit,
> All your bowls and all your kettles
> Shall be wood and clay no longer;
> But the bowls be changed to wampum,
> And the kettles shall be silver;
> They shall shine like shells of scarlet,
> Like the fire shall gleam and glimmer.
>
> And the women shall no longer
> Bear the dreary doom of labor.
> But be changed to birds and glisten
> With the beauty of the starlight.
> Painted with the dusky splendors
> Of the skies and clouds of evening!
>
> What Osseo heard as whispers,
> What as words he comprehended,
> Was but music to the others,
> Music as of birds afar off,
> Of the whippoorwill afar off,
> Of the lonely Wawonaissa
> Singing in the darksome forest.

The first part of this passage, with its radiant message, could be related to the C-major section, with ensuing trills associated with the birds. Also intriguing in this passage is the reference to music, something which Dvořák could never resist.[15] The description continues as the prophecy is suddenly fulfilled.

> Then the lodge began to tremble,
> And they felt it rising, rising,
> Slowly through the air ascending,
> From the darkness of the tree-tops
> Forth into the dewy starlight,
> Till it passed the topmost branches;
> And behold the wooden dishes
> All were changed to shells of scarlet!
> And behold! The earthen kettles
> All were changes to bowls of silver!"

Then Oweenee's sisters and their husbands are transformed:

> All the sisters and their husbands,

> Changed to birds of various plumage,
> Some were jays and some were magpies,
> Others thrushes, others blackbirds;
> And they hopped and sang, and twittered,
> Perked and fluttered all their feathers,
> Strutted in their shining plumage,
> And their tails like fans unfolded.

Of course, the link between these lines and the Scherzo cannot be certain, but it is especially tempting to hear Example 15-6 as the hopping singing and twittering of the birds and Example 15-7, with its static and exotic trills, as the moment they begin to "perk and flutter," strutting "in their shining plumage . . . their tails like fans unfolded."

There are other features of the Scherzo, particularly the transition sections, that cannot easily be connected to the poem. Most notable is the motif from the first movement, which returns in all subsequent movements and occurs in bars 154 and 252 of the Scherzo. At this time there is no evidence to suggest a link between this idea and *The Song of Hiawatha*, but if my hypothesis is correct, it may be associated with the casting of spells.[16]

Let us now try to place these considerations in a broader context by returning to the query with which we began. To what extent, if any, *is* the work somehow "American," and what role does the Scherzo play in helping us to clarify the matter? I have two images in mind to help the inquiry along—a television ad and a landscape painting.

Beginning in the 1960s, a series of commercials showed a brand new television set with a picture variously claimed to be sharp, bright, clear, vivid, etc. These ads gradually became a kind of joke, because even the dullest of viewers figured out that the picture on the advertised set could not be any better or worse than the television in one's own living room. If one's own set had "snow," then so did the depiction of the set in the commercial, and so on. My second image comes from E. H. Gombrich's *Art and Illusion*.[17] On page 84 we find a reproduction of a watercolor, looking for all the world like a Chinese landscape. Yet we are informed that it is a view of the English country-side, painted by the Chinese artist Chiang Yee, who visited England in the 1930s.

Dvořák is like the viewer at home in the first analogy: his training attitude are his own television, and America is the newly advertised set. He can only see it through the mechanisms for perception he already has. Of course, he may notice certain things about the new product—perhaps it is handsome, the "picture" may be larger, the shape of the new cabinet different, and it may even evoke strong feelings; but it can only be perceived through a screen that conditions its effect.

Let us turn to the second image. Is the landscape Chinese or English? Obviously it is meant to be English. Does it *look* Chinese or English? It depends upon what one means by "look." Writing about the picture, Gombrich says:

> We see how the relatively rigid vocabulary of the Chinese tradition acts as a selective screen which admits only the features for which schemata exist. The artist will be attracted by motifs which can be rendered in his idiom. As he scans the landscape, the sights which can be matched successfully with the schemata he has learned to handle will leap forward as centers of attention. . . . Painting is an activitiy and the artist will therefore tend to see what he paints rather than to paint what he sees.[18]

Only when we understand this can we take true delight in a familiar landscape rendered in an exotic manner.

The symphony "From the New World" may be considered, at least in part, a "musical landscape" painted by a Czech. But almost all the evidence, including interviews with the composer, his letters to friends in Bohemia, and comments by those who knew him, reveals that its *subject* is America, and whether it "sounds" American or Czech to us doesn't really matter much. I am convinced, though, that any detailed analytic examination of the Symphony in E Minor in the context of Dvořák's other symphonic works will reveal a host of characteristics suggesting that the composer's creative vision had undergone a profound transformation.

In the particular case of the Scherzo, there is real evidence that Dvořák was painting an American musical landscape—and one which was quite intricate, involving forests, birds, the prairie, sand dunes, dancing, singing, and storytelling. Though Dvořák visited the United States one hundred years ago and even lived on the prairie, he saw no Indians who could have reminded him of Hiawatha. Apparently, he once met a ragged band, perhaps of Kickapoo, and he doubtless saw Native Americans in Buffalo Bill's "Wild West Show." But above all, in making his picture of America, he used his *imagination*, ignited by his reading of *The Song of Hiawatha* and expanded by his excitement and delight in the New World.

NOTES

1. This was the second of several forceful articles by Henry Krehbiel, who clearly considered himself Dvořák's champion. The first was a full-scale analysis of the symphony that appeared in the New York *Tribune* on 15 December, based on notes supplied by the composer. (An annotated version of this article, "Henry Krehbiel, Antonín Dvořák and the Symphony 'From the New World,'" appeared in *Notes*, vol. 49, no. 2 [December 1992], pp. 447–473.) The second article has not, to my knowledge, appeared previously in the Dvořák literature.

2. It is not clear to me that this article is known to Dvořák scholars, but it should be. Although it is unsigned, it is almost certainly by James Huneker, who was on the editorial board of the *Musical Courier*. Furthermore, the writer alludes to extended discussions with Dvořák, something we know Huneker had had. It appeared on 20 December 1893. Pages 36–37 were devoted to a reprint of Henry Krehbiel's analysis of the symphony, which had appeared in the New York *Tribune* on 15 December 1893. The second part of the article (pp. 37–38) was titled "The Second Philharmonic Concert—Dvořák's New Symphony."

3. In a letter to his friend Kozánek, 12 April 1893.

4. This passage is taken from Kovařík's memoirs, which are actually in the form of letters written to Otakar Šourek, Dvořák's first important biographer.

5. All the facts in the interview can be verified, and the grammatical lapses are characteristic of Dvořák's English. Although the article has no byline, the most likely person to have undertaken the interview would have been Steinberg, critic for the New York *Herald*.

6. Joseph Sládek, the man who translated the work into Czech, was a friend of Dvořák's.

7. The 1890s was a good decade for Hiawatha-related musical works. An article in the Boston *Transcript* on 6 October 1906 reported that Anton Seidl, conductor of the premiere of Dvořák's symphony, was working on a Hiawatha opera when he died in 1897. This work was not to have been based on Longfellow's poem but was to draw on the same legends. At the end of the decade, the black English composer Samuel Coleridge-Taylor wrote his most famous work, *Scenes from the Song of Hiawatha*, a choral trilogy based on Longfellow's work. The fact that Dvořák was Coleridge-Taylor's favorite composer may somehow explain the younger composer's choice of subject.

8. See my article "Dvořák's 'New World' Largo and *The Song of Hiawatha*" in *Nineteenth Century Music*, vol. 16, no. 1 (Summer 1992), pp. 35–48. Documentation in the Dvořák Archive in Prague makes it clear that Krehbiel and Dvořák were in close touch around the time of the symphony's premiere and that Dvořák made notes for Krehbiel about the work. Krehbiel does not specify which section of the chapter "Hiawatha's Wooing" Dvořák used for the Largo, but I contend it is most probably the last sixty lines, which describe the "pleasant homeward journey" of Hiawatha and Minnehaha. I also argue that the middle section of the Largo is related to the forest funeral of Minnehaha.

9. Several other scholars quoted this passage. Antonín Sychra reprints lines 92–124 of Sládek's Czech translation in his monograph *Estitika Dvořákovy symphonické tvorby* (The Aesthetics of Dvořák's Symphonic Works), Prague, 1959, 337. John Clapham also quotes these lines in several of his articles.

10. The features of the Largo that seem most atypical are the introductory chords (marked "Beginning of a legend" in the sketches), the bi-thematic quality of the middle section, the C-sharp major transition, which quotes material from the first movement, and the fact that the harmonic motion is only from major to parallel minor.

11. In a recent conversation, the Dvořák scholar Alan Houtchens suggested that this procedure is related to what might be called Dvořák's Dumky aesthetic. I am grateful to him for the observation. The juxtaposition of different vocabularies in the Scherzo may well have its roots in this practice while at the same time being a clear response to the poem.

12. This may be idiosyncratic, but I like to make a certain distinction between a "pastoral" and a "romance," seeing them as distinct topics. While the former seeks, as much as possible, to achieve the illusion of absolute stasis—an unchanging world of bliss—the latter, for obvious reasons, seeks some kind of fulfillment and resolution. In this case, the two impulses are linked.

13. I contend that one of the most distinctive components of Dvořák's "American" sound involves the use of what might be called "pentatonically inflected pastorals." Such moments as the Largo and the slow movement of the Sonatina in G, Opus 100, are explicit references to the American landscape..

14. Sychra points this out on pp. 337–338.

15. In an excellent paper at the International Dvořák Conference at Dobris, Czechoslovakia, Martin Chusid spoke about Dvořák's use of stage music. Stage music, of course, refers to all music in an opera, or even a tone poem, that is supposed to be a real musical performance in the context of the work. Dvořák never lost an opportunity to create stage music, and all his operas are rich in this aspect.

16. We may keep in mind, however, that such a connection would raise the spectre of something momentous. It seems clear that Longfellow's poem was quite an important part of Dvořák's creative process in the composition of the middle movements. Any attempt to link the first-movement motif with the poem would suggest that the entire work is, in reality, a giant "Hiawatha Symphony." The lack of documentary proof for this hypothesis is offset by the fact that the composer was passionately involved with the poem during the composition of the two inner movements. We must ask if it is likely that he simply banished it from his consciousness while composing the outer ones. A full consideration of this question—material for a separate study—would be essential for the deepest understanding of the symphony.

17. E. H. Gombrich, *Art and Illusion* (Princeton: Princeton University Press, 1972).

18. E. H. Gombrich, *Art and Illusion*, 85–86.

CHAPTER SIXTEEN

The F-Major String Quartet Opus 96

Alan Houtchens

*I*t was as if Dvořák's mind had unconsciously been working on a new composition while he was otherwise occupied with the trip to Spillville in early June 1893. He and his family had come by train from New York City to the Midwestern town; and no sooner had they settled into their summer home than, within the short span of just three days, 8–10 June, he composed one of his most popular—and, coincidentally, one of his very best—works. At the end of the sketch for the String Quartet in F Major, Opus 96, he wrote: "Thanks to the Lord God. I am satisfied, it went quickly." After "try-outs" with the Kovařík family in Spillville, the scoring was completed on 23 June. It was given its first public performance by the Kneisel Quartet (Franz Kneisel, Otto Roth, Louis Svecènski, and Alwin Schroeder) in Boston on New Year's Day 1894 and in New York on 12 January.

For the last eight months Dvořák had been living and teaching in New York; now, reunited with the whole family and away from the city's bustle, Conservatory duties, and the intrusive newspaper reporters, he greeted the freedom of country life with a flood of musical inspiration. The first movement of the work, Allegro ma non troppo, is cast in sonata form. Otakar Šourek suggests that there is a "smiling contentment of a bucolic existence" in its rustling tremolos, pizzicato touches, and airy principal theme.[1] The second movement, Lento, is a kind of arietta that presents a series of closely interrelated couplets within the broad scheme of AA BB CC A' Coda. Jarmil Burghauser finds here a "melancholy grandeur of the broad plains";[2] there is certainly a heartfelt intensity in the repetitions of the mournful melody against ceaseless, almost monotonous accompanying figures. The third movement, Molto vivace, is a scherzo with two trios, wherein the second trio is a variant of the first and both employ an augmented version of the scherzo theme. The association between the subsidiary idea in the high registers of the violins and the song of the scarlet tanager, a bird indigenous to the Iowa plains, is famous, even notorious. The last movement, Vivace ma non troppo, is a sonata-rondo. It is exceptionally vivacious and is animated by a skipping rhythm that pervades almost the entire movement. Clapham suggests that its choralelike central episode evokes the image of Dvořák improvising for mass on the little organ of the St. Wenceslaus Church at Spillville.[3]

As accessible and charming as this work is—making it by far the most popular of Dvořák's fourteen quartets—it is remarkable also in its unity of construction and its forward-looking manner of thematic treatment. The four movements are unified through a variety of means. For example, the first, second, and fourth movements begin in the same manner, with three instrumentalists playing music that is accompanimental in character (Examples 16-1a, 16-1b, and 16-1c).

The movements are also unified through key relationships. The first, third, and fourth movements begin and end in the home key of F major. The relative minor key, D minor (requiring the same key signature as F major), makes itself felt already by the thirteenth measure of the work and, along with its parallel key, D major, also serves as a complement to the principal key of F (major and minor) in the second movement, whose tonal center is, in fact, D. The importance placed throughout the entire quartet on mediant and submediant relationships (at the distance of a third above and below a given tonic) is made clear even melodically in the exposition of the first movement: the pitch D is stressed in the first theme (see Example 16-1a, m. 3) and the pitch F-sharp plays a prominent role in the closing theme, which is in the key of A major, the mediant of F major (Example 16-2, mm. 45 and 47). In addition, the key of the lowered submediant, D-flat minor/major, sometimes spelled enharmonically as C-sharp minor/major, figures prominently in the outer movements.[4]

All the movements are unified thematically as well. A figure consisting of the interval of a second followed by a third in the same direction, marked with an × in Example 16-1, reappears throughout the Quartet as a kind of leitmotif. A few of the many instances are shown in Examples 16-2 through 16-5. The triplet figure that makes its first appearance near the end of the exposition section of the first movement plays a structurally important role

Example 16-1a. Dvořák, F Major String Quartet, Opus 96, first movement, mm. 1–6.

Example 16-1b. Dvořák, F Major String Quartet, Opus 96, second movement, mm. 1–6.

Example 16-1c. Dvořák, F Major String Quartet, Opus 96, fourth movement, mm. 1–8.

Example 16-2. Dvořák, F Major String Quartet, Opus 96, first movement, mm 44–47.

in the development section. Subsequently this figure animates the second trio of the third movement and, more significantly, the last half of the finale, beginning in measures 193–198 where, it should also be noted, transformations of material drawn from the first and third movements are presented.[5]

In addition, the beginning of this second episode within the sonata-rondo structure of the last movement, with its choralelike presentation in imitative counterpoint, recalls portions of the development section in the first movement.[6] As tempting as it is to follow the cue of Šourek and Clapham and imagine this as an evocation of Dvořák at the St. Wenceslaus organ,[7] it seems more likely that this section reflects Dvořák's appreciation of similar contrapuntal passages written in a pseudo-Palestrina style found in Beethoven's last quartets.

Dvořák's aesthetic intentions with regard to the "American" Quartet have largely been misunderstood by writers who persist in ascribing to the music, for a variety of poorly articulated reasons, a certain "simplicity" (in contrast to "complexity," especially as represented by the music of Wagner), "primitivism" (presumably in contradistinction to urbanity), and "clarity" (as opposed to "confusion").[8] A statement made by Dvořák himself seems to support this view:

> Since I wrote that quartet in 1893 in the Czech community of Spillville (1200 miles distant from New York), I wanted for once to write something very melodious and simple, and I always kept Papa Haydn before my eyes; for that reason it turned out so simple.[9]

Yet, while the formal structures of the movements, the sequence in which they follow each other, and the harmonic relationships are not particularly adventuresome, in other, more significant respects this may be the most radical, forward-looking composition Dvořák ever wrote. As a piece of chamber music, it anticipates future trends to a degree beyond any contemporary work, save, perhaps, Debussy's String Quartet (1893). By considering four specific features of Dvořák's score—(1) the rarefied, concise nature of the melodic material and the corollary extreme compactness of form; (2) the highly sophisticated, complex manner in which thematic material and rhythmic motifs are treated; (3) the integration ad libitum, within a single melodic line or harmonic progression, of notes and chords belonging to both major and parallel minor keys, producing what, for lack of a better term, might be called integral bimodality; and (4) the intermittent stratification of individual components resulting in multilayered textures—one can arrive at no other conclusion.

One of the most striking examples involving the multilayering of textural components may be seen in Example 16-3, where four different rhythmic strata are operating simultaneously, and a fully formed melody in the cello line is complemented in the first violin part by motifs drawn from measures 11–14 of the exposition (the beginning of the transition section leading to the second key area).

Example 16-3. Dvořák, F Major String Quartet, Opus 96, first movement, mm. 123–127.

It was Josef Jan Kovařík who suggested that the tune which first appears in measures 21–28 of the scherzo was inspired by the song of a bird Dvořák had heard while walking in the countryside near Spillville[10] (see John C. Tibbetts's article on Spillville, Chapter 7); nevertheless, it would be folly to proclaim that this movement is, ipso facto, "primitive" or "mystical," thus using terms that are applied, with much more authority, to the music of Messiaen, for instance.[11] It would be more appropriate to presume that Dvořák included this bird call as part of a conscious effort to suffuse the Quartet with a pastoral mode, which for him, as for Haydn, must have connoted simplicity in the sense of rusticity. After all, Dvořák incorporated into the musical discourse of the "American" Quartet several other gestures and stylistic features traditionally associated with the pastorale, including bagpipelike drones and extended pedal points, the key of F major, and melodies that are predominately diatonic, triadic, and pentatonic.[12]

Moreover, there is nothing simple, primitive, or clear about the manner in which Dvořák's discourse proceeds; in the first movement, for example, consider how he derives—or to put it differently, *arrives at*—the cello melody in the recapitulation (Examples 16-3 and 16-4b) from the closing theme of the exposition (Examples 16-2 and 16-4a). (The cello tune in Example 16-4b has been transposed from D-flat major to the same key as Example 16-4a to illustrate their relationship more clearly.)

Example 16-4a. Dvořák, F Major String Quartet, Opus 96, first movement, mm. 44–47.

Example 16-4b. Dvořák, F Major String Quartet, Opus 96, first movement, mm. 123–127 (transposed).

By variation I mean a way of altering something given, so as to develop further its component parts as well as the figures built from them, the outcome always being something new, with an apparently low degree of resemblance to its prototype, so that one finds difficulty in identifying the prototypes within the variation.[13]

Although these are not the words of Antonín Dvořák, they are certainly apropos to the example just cited and to many others that could have been cited—to the whole of the second movement, for that matter. They are the words of Arnold Schoenberg (1874–1951), who was attempting to describe a process that he considered fundamental to his own compositional style and for which he coined the term "developing variation." Schoenberg felt that this process offered twentieth-century composers a fruitful alternative to the "model and sequence" method of melodic construction found in the music of Wagner who,

> in order to make his themes suitable for memorability, had to use sequences and semi-sequences, that is, unvaried or slightly varied repetitions differing in nothing essential from first appearances, except that they are exactly transposed to other degrees. . . . The damage of this inferior method of construction to the art of composing was considerable. With very few exceptions, all followers and even opponents of Wagner became addicts of this more primitive technique.[14]

In light of the manner, discussed earlier, in which some authors have described the music of Dvořák's "American" Quartet, it is all the more paradoxical that Schoenberg should have used the word "primitive" when describing this or any aspect of Wagner's music. Whenever he wrote about the process of developing variation and other stylistic tendencies in art music that he considered progressive, Schoenberg frequently cited examples from the works of Johannes Brahms; indeed, one of his most important essays, written in 1947, is entitled "Brahms the Progressive."[15] He never mentioned Dvořák's compositions in the same vein—not even the "American" Quartet, which obviously had a profound influence on him as he was composing his own String Quartet in D major (1897).[16]

Schoenberg did once acknowledge that he had composed this early work under the influence of Dvořák (as well as Brahms), but unfortunately he did not mention precisely what in Dvořák's music he found attractive.[17] We can only speculate that he was most impressed with the way Dvořák managed to produce vital offshoots from a minimal amount of melodic material and to condense his rhetorical arguments into the slightest amount of space (time). The Quartet in F major is by far the shortest of Dvořák's chamber works, and it is the most epigrammatic and aphoristic of all his compositions; as such, it presages techniques developed by many twentieth-century composers.

In describing his own development as a composer, Schoenberg notes that very early on he was driven by a compulsion to restrict both the content and form of his works. Only gradually did he become aware that restriction could be achieved through condensation and juxtaposition. He learned two important things: "first, to formulate ideas in an aphoristic manner, which does not require continuations out of formal reasons; secondly, to link ideas together without the use of formal connectives, merely by juxtaposition."[18] He may very well have been influenced along these lines by the integral bimodality found throughout the score of the "American" Quartet or by such sudden, unprepared juxtapositions of tonalities as occur in the last movement: F major to A-flat major at measure 69 (Example 16-5) and F major to D-flat major at measure 252. He likewise may have been struck by the manner in which Dvořák often juxtaposes different melodic ideas, sometimes simultaneously, sometimes one right after another.

Example 16-5. Dvořák, F Major String Quartet, Opus 96, fourth movement, mm. 69–75.

Šourek astutely gauged that the "American" Quartet "holds an important place in Dvořák's chamber music as a new and original work," though precisely what he meant by "new" is not certain; and he did not need to restrict his purview solely to the genre of chamber music.[19] While the work reveals new tendencies in the sense that these tendencies are progressive and forward-looking, it would not be correct to suggest that they show up for the first time in this composition to the exclusion of earlier works by Dvořák or other composers.

Twenty years earlier, Dvořák had already begun to experiment along similar lines. To cite just one example, his Piano Trio in B-flat major, Opus 21 (1875), has many stylistic features in common with the "American" Quartet: concision of formal design, pentatonic melodies, emphasis on submediant relationships, modal inflections, the process of developing variation, extreme rhythmic vitality, textural stratification. Like the Quartet, it even opens with two measures of accompanimental figuration. At this stage of his musical development, Dvořák's interest in dramatic music, which he maintained throughout his life, and his close personal and artistic association with

Leoš Janáček, provided important stimuli in his search for a "new" epigrammatic approach.[20]

Concurrently, Brahms was pursuing many of the same artistic goals, most notably in his First Symphony. The path he subsequently followed in refining the process of developing variation and honing an aphoristic compositional style runs nearly parallel to Dvořák's. In his F Minor Clarinet Sonata, Opus 120, No. 1 (1894), Brahms managed to create a work that, like the "American" Quartet completed one year earlier, marks the height of achievement. The two compositions are emblazoned on opposite sides of the same coin. It is a mystery why Schoenberg did not acknowledge the progressive nature of Dvořák's music alongside that of Brahms.

NOTES

1. Otakar Šourek, *The Chamber Music of Antonín Dvořák*, trans. Roberta Finlayson Samsour (Prague: Artia, [1956]), 98.

2. Jarmil Burghauser, "Antonín Dvořák: The String Quartets," liner notes to the Deutsche Grammophon recordings of the complete Dvořák String Quartets, DGG 429193-2.

3. John Clapham, *Antonín Dvořák: Musician and Craftsman* (New York: St. Martins Press, 1966), 181.

4. Compare mm. 68–77 and 123–135 in the first movement with mm. 155–169 and 252–262 in the finale.

5. In the first movement, triplet figures may be found in mm. 56–57, 74–75, and serving to articulate the beginning of the retransition, mm. 106–108.

6. Compare mm. 155–171 in the fourth movement with mm. 92–94 and 96–106 in the first movement.

7. Otakar Šourek, *Život a dílo Antonína Dvořáka* 3 (Prague: Státní nakladatelství krásné literatury, hudby a umění, 1956), 161. See also John Clapham, *Antonín Dvořák: Musician and Craftsman*, 181.

8. See, for example, David Beveridge, "Sophisticated Primitivism: The Significance of Pentatonicism in Dvořák's American Quartet," *Current Musicology* 24 (1977), 25–36, and Beveridge's "Romantic Ideas in a Classical Frame: The Sonata Forms of Dvořák," Ph.D. diss. (University of California, Berkeley, 1980); see also John Clapham, *Dvořák* (New York: W. W. Norton, 1979), 123.

9. Letter from Dvořák to Josef Bohuslav Foerster, 11 March 1895, in *Antonín Dvořák: Korespondence a dokumenty*, ed. Milan Kuna et al. (Prague: Editio Supraphon, 1989), 386. The translation is my own.

10. Josef Jan Kovařík, *Reminiscences*, quoted in Otakar Šourek's *The Chamber Music of Antonín Dvořák*, 102.

11. This is not to minimize Dvořák's sincere love of nature and her creatures, especially birds. He was an avid bird-watcher, and he raised pigeons as a hobby. It is worth noting in the present context that the informal list of the items in Dvořák's estate prepared by Josef Bachtík sometime during the 1940s and the more formal list prepared later by officials of the Museum Antonína Dvořáka in Prague indicate that he owned a copy of Simeon Pease Cheney's bird-watching guidebook *Wood Notes Wild* (Boston: Lee and Shepard, 1892). He must have obtained it during his sojourn in America. Unfortunately, none of the birdcalls notated by Cheney resemble the birdcall written out by Kovařík or the tune as it appears in the third movement of the String Quartet in F major. (For a different conclusion, see John C. Tibbetts's article on Spillville, Chapter 7.) John Clapham, in his *Antonín Dvořák: Musician and Craftsman* (London: Faber and Faber, 1966), 181, maintains that the call is that of the scarlet tanager, but this has yet to be convincingly demonstrated.

12. The fact that many of the melodic ideas are pentatonic does not necessarily make them primitive; nor does it necessarily imply that Dvořák was consciously trying to capture the spirit of the American and/or Bohemian geographical or cultural landscape, as many writers have suggested. Richard Graves, for instance, once playfully quipped during a BBC broadcast that listening to the Quartet in F major is "like eating Blueberry Pie and washing it down with Slivovic." (Americans know that he meant apple, instead of blueberry, pie.) Quoted in Hans-Hubert Schonzeler's *Dvořák* (London: Marion Boyars, 1984), 157.

13. Arnold Schoenberg, "New Music: My Music" (ca. 1930), in *Style and Idea*, ed. Leonard Stein, trans. Leo Black (Berkeley: University of California Press, 1975), 102–103.

14. Arnold Schoenberg, "Criteria for the Evaluation of Music" (1946), in *Style and Idea*, 129. See also "My Evolution" (1949), in *Style and Idea*, 80.

15. Arnold Schoenberg, *Style and Idea*, 398–441.

16. See Reinhard Gerlach, "Dvořákův vliv na mladého Schoenberga: Poznámky k Schoenbergovu smyčcovému kvartetu D dur," *Hudební rozhledy* 25, No. 2 (February 1972), 84–88; and "War Schoenberg von Dvořák beeinflusst? Zu Arnold Schoenbergs Streichquartett D-dur," *Neue Zeitschrift für Musik* 133 (March 1972), 122–127.

17. Arnold Schoenberg, program notes written in 1936 and 1937 for recordings of his five published string quartets, reprinted in *Schoenberg, Berg, Webern: The String Quartets, A Documentary Study*, ed. Ursula von Rauchhaupt. (Hamburg: Deutsche Grammophon Gesellschaft, 1971, 1987), 32–33.

18. Arnold Schoenberg, "A Self-Analysis" (1948), in *Style and Idea*, 78.

19. Otakar Šourek, *The Chamber Music of Antonín Dvořák*, trans. Roberta Finlayson Samsour (Prague: Artia, [1956]), 97.

20. After completing the Piano Trio in B-flat, Dvořák next composed the Serenade for Strings in E major, Opus 22, the Piano Quartet in D major, Opus 33, and the Symphony No. 5 in F major, Opus 76, then spent the rest of the year working on *Vanda*, the fifth of his eleven completed operas.

CHAPTER SEVENTEEN

E-flat Major String Quintet Opus 97

Jan Smaczny

$\mathcal{T}$he package of works that Antonín Dvořák offered his publisher Simrock after the summer of 1893 must have been among the most profitable ever acquired by the German publisher. Not only did Dvořák promise the "New World" Symphony and the Quartet, Opus 96, but he also announced that he was at work on a string quintet with two violas. Simrock accepted them all.

Relations between composer and publisher had been difficult in recent years. Simrock favored small-scale works that would sell well, while Dvořák's inclination was to write symphonies, operas, and other large works. "You counsel me that I should write small works," wrote Dvořák in October 1890, "but this is very difficult. . . . [A]t the moment my head is full of large ideas and I will do as the dear Lord wishes. That will certainly be for the best."[1] Dvořák did not write his publisher again until November 1891, when he promised some new works—a promise that didn't materialize until after the Spillville summer in 1893.

Spillville had undoubtedly stimulated some of his finest music. Dvořák had often been ill at ease working in New York without the chance of escaping to the countryside, as he often did at home in Bohemia. Now, with the family together again and time to walk, visit with friends, and compose in these broad open spaces, new works poured out of him. Although the E-flat Quintet took longer to compose than the Quartet, which had been completed within two weeks (see Alan Houtchens's essay, Chapter 16), it also went quickly and easily. He began it on 26 June (three days after completing the Quartet) and completed it on 1 August 1893.[2]

Šourek suggests that, whereas the Quartet portrays an "intimate spiritual experience," the Quintet reflects "the outward impressions made on the composer by the spirit of the new environment and by some of its very original characters, whose acquaintance the artist made on his frequent excursions into the surrounding forests and prairies."[3] Indeed, its exotic, occasionally rather florid harmonic plumage, drumbeat rhythms, and superb tactile qualities (ample use of tremolos, plucked strings, pizzicato passages, and tapping sounds) may evoke in the sympathetic listener a collage of Spillville's cricket-haunted twilights and blazing noonday suns. These are the sights and sounds the poet Milton described in "L'Allegro":

> Such sights as youthful poets dream
> On summer eves by haunted stream.

Some commentators prefer the Quintet to its more popular elder brother. Thomas Dunhill, for example, deplores its relative neglect: "It is an equally dextrous piece of writing, and is, in some ways, more satisfying, more concentrated, and, in places, more charged with sentiment."[4] It was premiered by the Kneisel Quartet (assisted by violist M. Zach) on 12 January 1894 in Carnegie Hall, eleven days after the premiere of the Quartet.

For many reasons, the epithet "American" can as easily be applied to the Quintet as to the Quartet. All the features associated with Dvořák's "American" style are felt as strongly in this work as in the "New World" Symphony, the Sonatina, and the piano Suite. Of course, the pentatonic melodies and motifs associated with this style exist in abundance in earlier works as well. For example, the pentatonic tendency—the casting of melodies which in the major mode avoid the fourth and seventh tones and in the minor mode use the diminished seventh—was present in the end of the A Major Piano Quintet, Opus 81. Indeed, one can look back to some of Dvořák's earliest works, such as the song cycle *Cypresses* (1865), and to works from his strongly experimental period in the late 1860s and early 1870s, including the Prelude to Act III of the first version of *King and Collier* (*Král a uhlíř*), and from the middle period that extended into the early 1890s. But there can be little doubt that his interest in pentatonic inflections was at its strongest in America.

Another influence can be seen in the Quintet. During Dvořák's stay in Spillville, a group of Native Americans visited the town. While their main purpose was to sell medicinal herbs (see John C. Tibbetts's essay on the

Spillville summer, Chapter 7), they were also able to perform tribal songs and dances for Dvořák at the local inn. Jan Kovařík took down some of the melodies they sang (see Example 17-1), and the pentatonic outlines bear a close resemblance to the second subject of the Quintet's first movement (Example 17-2).

Example 17-1. A Native American melody heard in Spillville
and notated by Jan Kovařík.

Example 17-2. Dvořák, E-flat Major String Quintet, Opus 97
first movement, second subject.

Dvořák seems to have dotted the eighth notes and altered the pointing to create a more fruitful compositional building block. The Quintet is strongly marked by a characteristic drum rhythm; it appears in all the movements except the Larghetto. To be sure, there has been a lot of debate about the extent to which Dvořák may have been influenced by these aural vernacular elements: Šourek claims that the Native Americans' music in Spillville did indeed affect Dvořák,[5] whereas Clapham rejects the supposition, or at least strongly qualifies it (see Clapham's essay, "Dvořák and the American Indian," Chapter 8). At the very least, as if intending to show pupils and future composers the way in which indigenous material might be used, Dvořák took the raw material offered by the Native Americans and created a plastic developmental unit suitable for use in a sophisticated modern genre. Dvořák was no musical snob, and he responded wholeheartedly to the popular national music of America—the songs of Stephen Foster, Native American chants and rhythms, and the black spirituals and plantation melodies. These traits would persist in the symphonic poems and operas written after his return to the Old World.

In addition to the twelve string quartets he had written up to that time and the Sextet in A-flat major, Opus 48, Dvořák had also composed two string quintets. The first was an apprentice work, Opus 1, written in 1861 and built on the body of work by older contemporaries like Vaclav Jindrich Veit, whose many quintets were current in Prague at the time. Dvořák turned again to the form in 1875 with the Quintet for String Quartet and Double Bass, Opus 77; his choice of two violas, instead of the two cellos used by Schubert and others, looks back to his first effort.

The opening viola solo of the E-flat Major Quintet consists of a pentatonic fragment that foreshadows the main theme of the Allegro non tanto. It sets in motion the kind of "in tempo" introduction Dvořák had cultivated so successfully in the finale of the Seventh Symphony and the first movement of the Eighth. There is also a novel harmonic piquancy throughout this first movement that is in part effected by some ear-catching false relations in the harmony a few measures after the beginning. Dvořák's concentration on melodic and rhythmic features in this work may account for the relative structural simplicity in three of its four movements. Once under way, the Allegro non tanto bounds along with enormous assurance: an uncomplicated transition, energized by excited dotted rhythms, not only leads to but anticipates the exotically colored second theme already mentioned. The working out of themes in the movement's development combines vigorous imitation in the latter stages with meltingly beautiful lyricism based on the first theme. The movement comes full circle in its final measures with reminiscences of the melodic fragments and the "bluesy" harmony of the opening. The close is exquisitely gentle.

In this first movement and the succeeding Allegro vivo (a rare example of the Scherzo movement in common time), Dvořák couples his lyrical imagination with a fine contrapuntal instinct. The result in the second movement is a strong sense of unity between the soulful theme of the first viola in the central section, Un poco meno mosso, and the delicately arching countermelody of the second violin heard after the opening. For all its openhearted qualities, the bustling vigor of the Allegro vivo conceals much care in the construction. A catchy, rhythmic ostinato underpins the simple pentatonic melody; in turn, these elements provide a background for both the sweeping melody in the violins and the exhilarating "hoedown" that eventually bursts upon the ear.

Like the F Major Quartet, the emotional heart of the Quintet is found in the slow movement. The Larghetto is an eloquent set of variations on a noble and expansive theme, the opening of which bears a family resemblance to the slow introduction to the "New World" Symphony. In fact, the melody can claim to be Dvořák's "American" signature since it was one of the first themes he sketched in the New World, on 19 December 1892. Dvořák also considered using the second part of the theme, a hymnlike melody in the major key, as an alternative melody for a setting of "My Country, 'Tis of Thee" (see Jarmil Burghauser's essay, Chapter 14). Throughout this remarkable movement Dvořák makes full use of the textural possibilities of the ensemble, producing some wonderful instrumental effects to complement his imaginative transformations of the theme. The end result is a movement of near-vocal quality, which the composer at one point considered as the basis for a larger work for voices and orchestra. A simple statement of the second part of the theme concludes the movement.

The Allegro giusto finale returns to the clear outlines of the preceding movements with its simple presentation of themes along a rondo plan. The opening melody has the dotted rhythms and infectiousness of the famous *Humoresque* No. 7. It also resists heavy-going development and leads with little elaboration to a second theme, which for all its apparent "Indian" qualities, can trace its ancestry back to the Rondo of Schubert's E-flat Major Piano Trio and the Finale of Smetana's G Minor Piano Trio. Whatever its pedigree, this passage, with its strangely spectral opening, makes for an interestingly exotic interlude during a stream of more familiar, though nonetheless entertaining, melodies. The Quintet ends in high spirits with a whirring string figure that looks forward to the magnificent conclusion of the B Minor Cello Concerto.

NOTES

1. See Milan Kuna, ed., *Antonín Dvořák: Korespondence a dokumenty* 3, 1890–1895 (Prague: Supraphon, 1989), 52–53.

2. See Milan Kuna, ed., *Antonín Dvořák: Korespondence a dokumenty*, 103.

3. Otakar Šourek, *The Chamber Music of Antonín Dvořák*, transl. Roberta Finlayson Samsour (Prague: Artia, 1956), 37–38.

4. See Thomas Dunhill, "The Chamber Music," in *Antonín Dvořák: His Achievement*, ed. Viktor Fischl. (London: Lindsay Drummond, 1942), 123.

5. Otakar Šourek, *Život a dílo Antonína Dvořáka* (The Life and Works of Antonín Dvořák), vol. 3, 165–166.

6. Otakar Šourek, *The Chamber Music of Antonín Dvořák*, 38.

CHAPTER EIGHTEEN

The Stephen Foster–Antonín Dvořák Connection

Deane L. Root

On Tuesday, 23 January 1894, during the fifth week of its clothing fund drive, the New York *Herald* printed an appeal for contributions:

HEAR THE "OLD
FOLKS AT HOME."

It Will Be Rendered to-Night
for Charity as It Has
Never Been Before.

DVOŘÁK'S OWN ARRANGEMENT.

It Will Be Sung Entirely by Negroes, of
Whom Mme. Jones, the "Black
Patti," Is Soloist.

AID FOR THE CLOTHING FUND.

Donations Are Still Coming in, but
There Is Still a Great Need
of Women's Wear.

The article named several patronesses of the National Conservatory of Music who promoted this charity by selling concert tickets. "Here is, indeed, a treat for all lovers of music, as well as for those who take interest in the development of our national schools of music and in the negro race." And the paper appealed to social status and societal duty at the same time: "Society, with its usual discrimination and goodness of heart, will be largely represented at the performance this evening."[1]

The *Herald*'s self-congratulatory review the next day reemphasizes the uniqueness of the performance forces:

> Each soloist, with one exception, belonged to the colored race. This idea was due to Mrs. [Jeannette] Thurber. She threw open the doors of her excellently equipped musical educational establishment to pupils of ability, no matter what their race, color or creed. Emancipation, in her idea, had not gone far enough. Bodies had been liberated, but the gates of the artistic world were still locked.
>
> Her efforts in this direction were ably seconded by Dr. DVOŘÁK. The famous Bohemian studied the race, their songs, their folk lore. He saw that in their intellectual make-up there lay, ignored or unknown, the germs of an original musical organization, the foundation of a truly national school of music.
>
> When the audience entered the hall last night the first thing which attracted attention was the gallery at the back of the stage, a gallery fitted with a chorus [of 130 members] composed entirely of colored pupils.[2]

Each work on the program was praised at length. Before naming some of the socialites present in the boxes of Madison Square Garden Concert Hall, the article reported the orchestra's presentation to its conductor of a gold-mounted ebony baton:

> Dr. Dvořák was too much overcome by his feelings to reply. He thanked the orchestra by gestures that were more eloquent of his appreciation of their kindness than any words could have been, and then taking up the beautiful present, he commenced to conduct. Appropriately enough, seeing that Dr. Dvořák is the apostle of national music, the first number he directed with the baton was his own arrangement of America's most popular folk song, "The Old Folks at Home," which he scored specially for this concert in aid of the HERALD's Clothing Fund.
>
> Mr. Harry Jones, barytone [*sic*], a pupil at the conservatory, and Mme. Jones sang the solos, the chorus being given by the colored choir. It is a very effective arrangement, quite a desolate character being imparted to it by the air being allotted to the flute in the prelude, with a very quiet and simple accompaniment.

Why did the Maestro select this song—which America's first professional songwriter, Stephen Collins Foster, had written for (and published under the name of) minstrel leader Edwin P. Christy in 1851[3]—for a perfor-

Portrait of Stephen Foster that hangs in the Foster Memorial in Pittsburgh, Pennsylvania. Dvořák admired Foster's work and applauded the example he set for later American song composers. (Photograph courtesy John C. Tibbetts.)

mance by African Americans? And what did this song symbolize for its audience, and for its musicians?

"Old Folks at Home," more commonly known as "Swanee River," may indeed have been the most widely known American song of the time. In the year before Dvořák's arrangement, it had been issued in at least two dozen different sheet-music editions, by the *Ladies Home Journal* with delicate true-to-life illustrations by Charles Copeland, as sets of variations for skilled pianists, in arrangements for chamber orchestra, as part-songs for German male choirs, as recital pieces of European opera stars, and in countless songbooks for use by churches, schools, and families. German travelers in the pre–Civil War American South had reported hearing slaves singing Foster's songs, speculating that perhaps he had merely arranged and claimed them for his own. Turn-of-the-century German publishers included "Old Folks at Home" in collections of "Negerlieder," showing that in the minds of Europeans it was firmly associated with genuine African American song.[4]

The evidence of manuscripts, publishers' records, royalty accounts, and family papers gathered in the Foster Hall Collection of the Stephen Foster Memorial at the University of Pittsburgh[5] allows us today to be far more sanguine about the origins of the song, penned by Foster in his second-floor songwriter's office in downtown Pittsburgh. But the trail from Foster's studio to Dvořák is not so clear.

As historian Jean Snyder has discovered (see her article, "A Great and Noble School of Music," Chapter 9), there may have been a connection through the family of Harry T. Burleigh, the baritone soloist in Dvořák's benefit concert. The singer's mother had been a student at Avery College in Pittsburgh during the years immediately following the song's composition and resounding early popularity; she could not have failed to have heard the song there, whether or not she ever met its composer. This and other Foster songs, introduced as "plantation melodies" by blackface minstrel performers, became familiar, not only as melodies for the home but also in public places of all types, and served as powerful themes for abolitionist meetings and antislavery theatrical presentations. No one, from the most ardent proponent of refined culture to the least-educated laborer, regardless of national, ethnic, or racial origin, whether of high or low social or economic standing, was unacquainted with "Old Folks at Home" in the 1850s.

Such universal familiarity was galling to some. As *Dwight's Journal of Music* reported,

> "OLD FOLKS AT HOME," the *last* negro melody, is on everybody's tongue, and consequently in everybody's mouth. Pianos and guitars groan with it, night and day; sentimental young ladies sing it; sentimental young gentlemen warble it in midnight serenades; volatile young "bucks" hum it in the midst of their business and pleasures; boatmen roar it out stentorially at all times; all the bands play it; amateur flute blowers agonize over it at every spare moment; the street organs grind it out at every hour; the "singing stars" carol it on the theatrical boards, and at concerts; the chamber maid sweeps and dusts to the measured cadence of *Old Folks at Home*; the butcher's boy treats you to a strain or two of it as he hands in the steaks for dinner; the milk-man mixes it up strangely with the harsh ding-dong accompaniment of his tireless bell; there is not a "live darkey," young or old, but can whistle, sing, dance and play it, and throw in "Ben Bolt" by way of good seasoning; indeed, at every hour, at every turn, we are forcibly impressed.[6]

The song was widely known and came to be treasured as it was passed along in the intimacy of families. Ms. Snyder reports that young Harry Burleigh learned the spirituals from his own family; might he also have learned Foster's songs in this way and conveyed them to Maestro Dvořák as well?

Dvořák's famous essay on nationalism in music, published in *Harper's New Monthly Magazine* in February 1895, a year after the *Herald*'s benefit concert, ties Foster's songs directly to the spirituals as being among the music nearest the hearts of the American people.

> The point has been urged that many of these touching songs [negro melodies], like those of Foster, have not been composed by the negroes themselves, but are the work of white men, while others did not originate on the plantation, but were imported from Africa. It seems to me that this matters but little. The important thing is that the inspiration for such music should come from the right source, and that the music itself should be a true expression of the people's real feelings.[7]

Whatever regard Dvořák and his protégé Burleigh held for "Old Folks at Home," we have the testimony of another participant concerning its selection for the benefit concert. A penciled note on both sides of a small (12.5 × 16.5 cm) piece of letter paper that was attached to the manuscript parts used by the orchestra in the concert reads:

> The enclosed will be of interest in case you wish to refer to the concert given by our students for the fund of the Silver Service for the Cruiser N.Y.
>
> I asked the Dr. to write "Old folks at home" for two v[o]ices. You will see that only one signature of the Dr. remains, the others were torn off by the pupils in the orchestra as autographs.
>
> This two-voice arrangement was sung on this occasion by *black Patti* and Harry Burleigh—and accompanied by the N.C. of A. orchestra conducted by Dr. D.

The author is undoubtedly Jeannette Thurber, and the context indicates that the manuscript parts remained in her possession for some years after 1894. She has confused the benefit recipient, and must not have had access to the full score (which proclaims the correct beneficiary at the very top of the first page). To whom this note was directed is a mystery; it accompanied the orchestral parts when they were offered for sale by Walter R. Benjamin Autographs to the Foster Hall Collection on 17 December 1946, within a year of Mrs. Thurber's death on 2 January 1946.

The parts are not in Dvořák's handwriting; in fact, there appear to have been at least two copyists. The Dvořák autograph that remains, in the bottom right corner of a second violin part, is dated 6 January 1894 (literally, "18 ⁶⁄₁ 94").[8] (See Figures 18-1 through 18-4.)

Examination of the parts reveals more than a facsimile edition can convey. An embossed stamp of G. Schirmer, New York, in some upper left corners shows the origin of the paper—sheets of lined music paper carefully torn in half. Far more telling, however, are the musicians' rehearsal markings.

Figure 18-1. Close-up of the Dvořák autograph signature on the second violin part.
(Courtesy Foster Hall Collection of the Stephen Foster Memorial, University of Pittsburgh.)

The first trumpet marks the last four measures of the chorus as pianissimo, adds a repeat for these measures, and lowers the final note from a D to an A above middle C, mirroring an alteration in the full score. A second violinist recorded the instruction for the last four measures of the chorus "*pp* last time." A violist, who kept the corner autograph, marked this passage "*p*" with a crescendo beginning the middle of the first measure. (The only other part checked by the arranger, apparently, was the cello, where a ragged lower right corner indicates the third autograph.) The most extensive, though cryptic, note is by another violist (see Sixty-Eight Publishers' facsimile edition, unnumbered page 55), who indicates the last four bars are "3 voices," then "3 time *ppp*, go 4 bars *ff*, tutti. Then Tutti from . . . ." What it all means, apparently, is that for the first and second times through the chorus (following the verses sung by the soloists), the orchestra accompanied softly; whether a third verse was sung, perhaps by both soloists, is not indicated, but at least the final four bars of the chorus were repeated on the last time through, at full volume.

    Unlike the orchestral parts, the full score has come down to us on a path that is not clear. No record has been found in the Foster Hall Collection of its acquisition. (None of Foster's biographers mentions the arrangement, even though John Tasker Howard took pains to list exhaustively other arrangements and artistic memorials to the songwriter.) And yet a small

Figure 18-2. Second violin part with Dvořák's signature at bottom right.
(Courtesy Foster Hall Collection of the Stephen Foster Memorial, University of Pittsburgh.)

typed slip of paper, clipped to the envelope in which the score was stored in the fireproof vault of the Collection, contains fresh information:

> Dvořák made this arrangement of "Old folks at home" for a concert given for the benefit of the New York Herald Free Clothing Fund in 1894. The Concert was given with the chorus and orchestra of the National Conservatory of Music, New York, Antonín Dvořák conducting. The soloists in "Old folks at home" were Sisseretta [*sic*] Jones ("The black Patti") and Harry T. Burleigh. Edwin Franko Goldman played the trumpet in the orchestra. Burleigh was the librarian of the orchestra, and at the concert Dvořák presented him with this manuscript.

In pencil at the lower left is written "From J. K. Lilly," the Indianapolis industrialist who assembled the Foster Hall Collection. Josiah Kirby Lilly gave his collection to the University of Pittsburgh in 1937; nowhere in the card index, acquisition records, or correspondence files that accompanied the holdings when they were transferred to Pittsburgh, however, is there reference to this manuscript. In an interview with the New York *World Telegram* in 1941, Harry Burleigh indicated that he still had the full score.[9] Since Mr. Lilly died 8 February 1948 the manuscript possibly passed through his hands sometime in the intervening six years, without trace in the Foster Hall Collection archives.

Before the manuscript was deposited in Pittsburgh, it was treated with

Figure 18-3. The full score, page 1.
(Courtesy Foster Hall Collection of the Stephen Foster Memorial, University of Pittsburgh.)

the intent of preserving it. Ragged edges and holes in the paper were filled in, and the whole was bonded to a reinforcing cloth on both sides of the paper. The preservation process, however, has actually accelerated the deterioration of the manuscript. The bonding agent has darkened and caused the paper to become extremely brittle. Where there were folds, the paper has begun to crack, and the leaves have split almost entirely apart. The bonding caused some bleeding of heavily inked spots. Moreover, the cloth is disintegrating, powdering away in places. After the cloth had been bonded to the paper, additional paper repairs were made on both outer edges, halfway down the page where the paper had once been folded. (This fold is barely visible in the facsimile edition, just below the timpani part on the first page and the chorus on the last page.)

Sometime before the manuscript was reinforced, photostats were made. The negative (often kept by repositories so that additional positives can be produced) has not been located, but a full positive copy is in the Foster Hall Collection, and the first three pages of a positive copy are in the New York Public Library Research Division at Lincoln Center. Although

Figure 18-4. Full score, first page; close-up of arranger's signature.
(Courtesy Foster Hall Collection of the Stephen Foster Memorial, University of Pittsburgh.)

Carleton Sprague Smith, who worked at the Library in the 1940s, does not recall the manuscript, Susan T. Sommer of the Library reports that the photostats were rediscovered at the Library by Richard Jackson in 1977. The photostat may have come to the Library through Sam Franko. Franko's sister was the mother of Edwin Franko Goldman, the famous composer, bandmaster, and pupil of Dvořák. Franko, a musicologist and conductor, gave most of his holdings to the Library upon his death in 1937.[10]

Whatever its route from Dvořák's podium to the Foster Hall Collection, the full score is a fascinating object, if only for its provenance from the Maestro himself. The paper, folded to create four pages (26.5 by 35.5 cm) of lined staves, bears a watermark of the Leipzig, Germany, firm of Breitkopf and Haertel, and the publisher's printed logo (B&H. Nr. 12. *C.*). The manuscript itself is quite clean, except for some minor stains that are not visible on the facsimile. At the bottom of page four is a partial sketch of an unidentified four-part work in F major in 2/4 time.

At the top of the caption title the year 1894 has been added in pencil. The manuscript itself is in two different inks or pens, with some additional pencil. On the last page the parts for winds and timpani appear to have been penciled in first, then inked over. This technique appears nowhere else in the score. One ink was used to write the full score as well as the title and attribution to Foster. Another, darker ink, applied with a finer point, was used to add the dedication and ascription in Dvořák's handwriting. Corrections to the score also appear to be in this darker ink. The individual parts reflect same changes; perhaps they were made during the first rehearsals.[11]

Whatever the inspiration for Dvořák's selection of this particular song, he must have had a copy at hand that was faithful to Foster's original edition. The key, D major, and the tempo, "Moderato," are Foster's. The text— words, spelling, punctuation, and capitalization—is nearly identical to Foster's. The original rhythms of the melody are retained, except that the last note of the verse is reduced to a half-note from a dotted half-note to accommodate the upward sweep of the string accompaniment. Perhaps most telling, Dvořák maintained the original accompanimental style—the somber bass unison on the first beat of the measure followed by repeated chords in the middle register on the final three beats of the measure. Even the original harmonies are preserved. Dvořák's own contributions, beyond the orchestration, begin to appear at the end of the first couplet of text (page 2, measure 8): a rising motif in the violins maintains momentum into the second half of the verse, then becomes a countermelody to the vocal soloist; this motion recurs in the middle of the second couplet, then gives flavor to the refrain.

The New York *Herald*'s article announcing the premiere on 23 January 1894—the only public performance until one was mounted in Pittsburgh in 1990—quotes Dvořák concerning "Old Folks at Home":

> It is a folk song and a very beautiful one. . . . The only difference it has from what normally comes under that head is that we know the composer's name. And that is only because he happened to write it at a period when the art of preserving music by writing it down existed, whereas most folk songs have been handed down from mouth to mouth until in later years they were copied in manuscript by some musician. But by that time the composer's name had been forgotten. American music is music that lives in the heart of the people, and therefore this air has every right to be regarded as purely national.

Although the music lasted only a few minutes in performance, the manuscript survives a century after its creation, a tangible link between one of the greatest nationalist composers of Europe and the sources nearest the heart of the American people whom he sought to inspire.

NOTES

1. "Hear the 'Old Folks at Home'," New York *Herald*, 23 January 1894.

2. "Dvořák leads for the Fund," New York *Herald*, 24 January 1894.

3. The standard accounts of Foster's life and music are found in the following works: William W. Austin, *"Susanna," "Jeanie," and "The Old Folks at Home": The Songs of Stephen C. Foster from His Time to Ours* (New York: Macmillan Publishing Company, 1975; 2d ed., Urbana: University of Illinois Press, 1989); John Tasker Howard, *Stephen Foster: America's Troubadour* (New York: Thomas Y. Crowell, 1934; 2d ed., 1953). For a more contemporary assessment, see Deane L. Root, "Myth and Stephen Foster," *Carnegie Magazine*, January–February 1987, 10; and Deane L. Root, "The Mythtory of Stephen C. Foster; or, Why His True Story Remains Untold," *American Music Research Center Journal* 1 (1991), 20–36.

4. For a fascinating account of how this and other Foster music has been absorbed into some other cultures, see Charles Hamm, "Way Down Upon the Yangtze River; or, American Music in the People's Republic of China," *Newsletter: Institute for Studies in American Music,* vol. 18, no. 2 (May 1989), 1–2, 7. The Foster Hall Collection contains other articles in Japanese, Chinese, Russian, and other languages attesting to the familiarity of Foster's songs in these countries.

5. The establishment and activities of the Stephen Foster Memorial and its Foster Hall Collection at the University of Pittsburgh are examined in the following: Fletcher Hodges, Jr., "The Research Work of the Foster Hall Collection," Reprint from *Pennsylvania History*, vol. 15, no. 3 (July 1948); Fletcher Hodges, Jr., *A Pittsburgh Composer and His Memorial* (Pittsburgh: University of Pittsburgh Press, 1951; reprinted from *Western Pennsylvania Historical Society Magazine*, vol. 21, 1938; and John C. Tibbetts, "In Search of Stephen Foster," *The World and I*, vol. 6, no. 7 (July 1991), 252–259.

6. *Dwight's Journal of Music*, 2 October 1852.

7. Quoted in Charles Hamm, *Music in the New World* (New York: W. W. Norton and Company, 1983), 411–412. For the complete text see Antonín Dvořák, "Music in America," *Harper's New Monthly Magazine*, vol. 90, no. 537 (February 1895), 428–434.

8. Dvořák's arrangement of "Old Folks at Home" was not performed publicly after its 1894 premiere until 18 April 1990, when the University of Pittsburgh and Department of Music presented it in concert in Pittsburgh. Kypros Markou conducted the University Community Orchestra, Demarius Cooper and Thomas Douglas were the soloists, and John Goldsmith prepared the Heinz Chapel Choir. The performance was broadcast the next day by WQED-FM.

   The manuscript full score and some of the parts were published in facsimile for the first time by Sixty-Eight Publishers in August 1991 as *Old Folks at Home: Ten, jehož dum tun Stal.* Included is a cassette tape containing versions in English (the Civic Orchestra of the Detroit Symphony conducted by Leslie B. Dunner) and in Czech (the Prague Philharmonic Players conducted by Bohumil Kulinský). An accompanying booklet contains the English and Czech texts and essays by Mrs. Josephine Harrold Love. Josef Skvorecký is the editor and publisher. It is available from Sixty-Eight Publishers Corp., Box 695, Postal Station "A", Toronto, Ontario M5W 1G2, Canada.

Leslie B. Dunner, Assistant Conductor of the Detroit Symphony Orchestra, spoke about the Dvořák-Foster recording in an interview with John C. Tibbetts, 20 December 1991:

> I didn't know about this work before Josephine Love told me about it. This was in the fall of 1990. She had known Harry T. Burleigh, who sang a solo part in its premiere in 1894, and she was most interested in having the music recorded. She lives in Detroit where she runs an organization called "Your Heritage House," where young people can learn about African American traditions in classical music. She also has connections with Sixty-Eight Publishers in Toronto.
>
> We secured the Detroit Civic Orchestra and were able to use the same recording equipment and engineer used by the Detroit Symphony Orchestra. We also contacted Brazeal Dennard, who is a choir director in Detroit, and he volunteered the services of his choir and of the soloists. Mrs. Love had gotten the photocopies of the orchestra parts, which were handwritten, from Pittsburgh, and we distributed them to the musicians. Our preparation and rehearsal time was very limited, just a few hours for run-throughs with orchestra and soloists. The performers were very young, from age 12 to 18. We used just one soloist, Samuel McKelton; in the other recording, the one in Czech with the Prague Philharmonic Players under Bohumil Kulinsky, they used two [Milada Cejkova and Vladimir Dolezal].
>
> We performed it last summer, playing it only in the recording studio in Detroit. There was no public concert. The players were shocked at learning of this work and also shocked that it had never been performed in almost a hundred years. Mrs. Love was present at the recording session and she was very moved at the experience. I'm very proud of it, and it was very exciting to help keep this music alive.

9. "'Sweet Chariot' Inspired Anton Dvořák to Immortalize Negro Spirituals," New York *World Telegram*, 12 September, 1941.

10. Telephone interviews by Deane L. Root with Carleton Sprague Smith, 17 December 1991, and with Susan T. Sommer, 13 and 17 December 1991. Smith was also a close friend of the Franko and Goldman families.

11. For example, in the flute part, measures 1 and 5, the half-note A above the treble staff is lowered to F-sharp and the first eighth-note F-sharp is crossed out and E is added. For the cello, measure 4, the dotted half-note and quarter-note D above the bass staff are lowered to A; in measure 6 the dot is removed after the first half-note, and the last quarter-note D is lowered to a half-note G. The second violin on page 2, measure 6, has the last quarter-note lowered from F-sharp to D, and in measure 9 the lower notes are removed. On page 3 the instruction *a due* has been removed from the flute line and a second part has been added beneath the first. Other more minor changes have also been made.

The "Biblical Songs," Opus 99

Daniel Jacobson

$\mathcal{T}$he months of late 1893 through early 1894 were productive and happy ones for Dvořák. Back in New York in late November 1893 after his trips through the Midwest, he began work on his Sonatina in G Major for piano and violin, Opus 100. He completed it on 3 December and inscribed it, affectionately, "Dedicated to my children Otilka and Tonik, Aninka, Mařenka, Otakar, and Zinda to commemorate the completion of my hundredth work." Three other new works were successfully premiered in Boston and New York in December 1893 and January 1894—the Ninth Symphony ("From the New World"), the F Major Quartet, and the E-flat Major Quintet.

Dvořák's joyful mood was shattered, however, when in February 1894 he learned of the death of his close friend and devoted supporter, the conductor Hans von Bülow. Soon after, he received word from Bohemia that his eighty-year-old father, František, was dying.[1] Longing for home but unable to leave America, he interrupted his work on the Piano Suite in A Major and began a cycle of ten songs derived from the Book of Psalms. For his *Biblical Songs*, Opus 99, Dvořák, although a devout Catholic, chose verse fragments from the traditional Czech Protestant Bible of Kralice (1613). He cleverly molded them into song texts that had more personal meaning for him than the original Psalms. The song cycle, for alto or baritone with piano accompaniment, was first published by Simrock in early 1895, with translations in German, English, and French.[2] He also fashioned an orchestrally accompanied version of the first five songs, scored for an ensemble of strings, two flutes, two clarinets, two horns, two trumpets, timpani, and triangle.[3]

Most of the *Biblical Songs* were sketched and completed with apparent

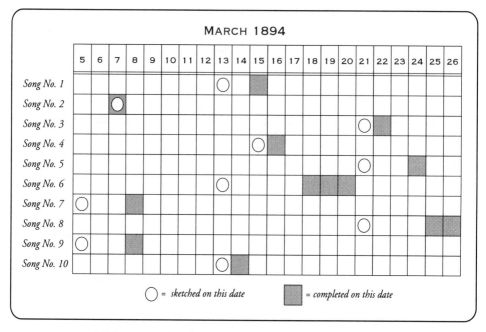

Table 19-1. Order of completion of the *Biblical Songs,* Opus 99.

ease (see Table 19-1); however, for either emotional or constructive reasons, Dvořák had particular difficulty finishing Nos. 6 and 8. As shown in Table 19-1, the songs were published in a much different order from that in which they were composed, indicating that Dvořák was particularly concerned with the structural significance of their final cyclical sequence. The outline of primary key relationships, seen in Figure 19-1 on page 257, reveals an intricate, religiously symbolic, series of keys derived from the Psalm texts themselves. The key of F is the focal center and ultimate goal of the cycle, representing "complete confidence in God." Dvořák's choice of keys betrays a belief that such "confidence" can be attained only if one both "fears God's wrath" and "joyfully trusts in His goodness." Throughout the cycle, the negative aspects of "fear," "doubt," and "anguish" are represented by tonalities below F (E minor, E-flat, D and C minor), while the positive aspects of "praise" and "trust" are signified through tonalities above F (G, A-flat, B-flat, and B).

This symbolic dichotomy allowed Dvořák to create a wavelike design (shown in Figure 19-1) that vividly depicts his own struggle to understand God's actions at this moment of personal crisis. As the cycle begins, "awe and fear of God's power" (songs 1 and 2 in G major and E minor) lead to a plea for mercy (song 3 in B-flat major) and eventually to a sense of "trust and joy-

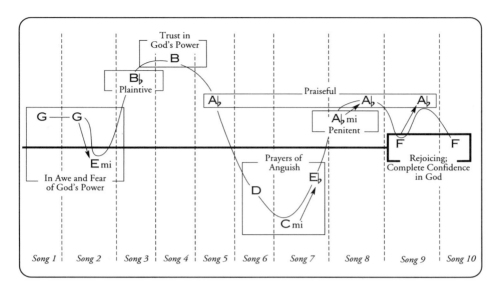

Figure 19-1. Outline of the primary key relationships in the *Biblical Songs*, Opus 99.

ful praise of His works" (songs 4 and 5 in B major and A-flat major). Song 5, the only slow song in the cycle, lyrically serves as the majestic focal point of the cycle's first half. The second half of the cycle begins as "trust" and "praise" are challenged by "doubt" and "desperation," depicted by an anguished descent to D major (a tritone from A-flat) in song 6 and to C minor in song 7. Song 8 starts penitently in A-flat minor but concludes praisefully in A-flat major. Songs 9 and 10 reconcile these structural extremes, as the "tonal wave" gradually subsides and the security of F major is reached. Song 10 also breaks free of the "andante" tempo that pervades the cycle, bringing the work to an exuberant conclusion.

As seen in Table 19-2, each of the *Biblical Songs* has a unique design, with greater diversity in meter and length of setting than are encountered in Dvořák's earlier song cycles. Word-painting is commonplace, and several songs are dramatized through the use of recitative. The harmonic language is also quite daring, with enharmonic and chromatic effects abounding. The overall complexity of these songs demonstrates Dvořák's affinity for the lieder of Schubert and Brahms and his mastery of Wagnerian counterpoint. Though elements of Dvořák's "American" style are evident in this cycle, the work primarily conveys a retrospective look towards the images and sounds of Bohemia.

	Text	Key	Meter	Tempo	Length
Song No. 1	Psalm 97	G	$\frac{3}{8}$	Andantino	50 mm.
Song No. 2	Psalm 119	G–Emi	¢	Andante	26 mm.
Song No. 3	Psalm 55	B♭–B–B♭	$\frac{3}{4}$	Andante	62 mm.
Song No. 4	Psalm 23	B	¢	Andante	32 mm.
Song No. 5	Psalms 144 & 145	A♭	¢	Risoluto, maestoso	53 mm.
Song No. 6	Psalms 61 & 63	D	¢	Andante	41 mm.
Song No. 7	Psalm 137	Cmi–E♭	$\frac{3}{8}$	Andante	60 mm.
Song No. 8	Psalm 25	A♭mi–A♭	$\frac{3}{8}$	Andante	38 mm.
Song No. 9	Psalm 121	F–Fmi–A♭	$\frac{3}{8}$	Andante con moto	45 mm.
Song No. 10	Psalms 98 & 96	F	$\frac{2}{4}$	Allegro moderato	72 mm.

Table 19-2. Structural Outline of *Biblical Songs*, Opus 99

Formal Design

Through-composed

Modified strophic

A1			Codetta	A2			Codetta
Verse 1a	Interlude	Verse 1b		Verse 1a	Interlude	Verse 1b	
mm. 1–4	5–6	7–12	12–13	14–17	18–19	20–25	25–26

Through-composed

Rondolike, highly modified strophic

A1		B1	A2	B2	A3	Codetta
Recit.	Verse 1	Verse 2	Verse 3	Verse 4	Verse 5	Intro
mm. 1–5	6–11	12–13	14–18	19–26	27–30	30–32

Modified strophic ternary

A1		A2		A3		B		A4	Codetta
Intro	Verse 1	Intro	Verse 2	Intro	Verse 3	Intro	Verse 4	Verse 5	Intro
mm. 1–4	5–10	11–14	15–20	21–24	25–30	31–32	33–40	41–47	48–53

cleverly reharmonized⤴

Modified strophic ternary

A1	A2	B	A3 (combines A1 and A2)
Verse 1	Verse 2	Verse 3	Verse 4
mm. 1–11	12–16	17–32	33–41

Modified strophic ternary

A1		A2	B	A3 (var.)	Coda
Intro	Verse 1	Verse 2	Verse 3	Verse 4	(restless)
mm. 1–2	3–14	15–28	29–36	37–43	44–60

Modified strophic

A1		A2 (expanded)		A3 (dev.)	
Intro	Verse 1	Intro	Verse 2	Intro (var.)	Verse 3
mm. 1–2	3–8	8–9	10–19	19–22	23–28

Through-composed

Modified strophic

A1		A2 (var.)		A3		Codetta
Intro	Verse 1	Intro	Verse 2	Intro	Verse 3	Intro
mm. 1–8	9–23	23–30	31–47	47–54	55–64	48–53

Example 19-1. Dvořák, *Biblical Songs*, Opus 99, No. 1
("Darkness and Thunderclouds"), mm. 22–35.

The first song, "*Oblak a mrákota jest vůkol Něho*" (Darkness and Thunderclouds Are 'Round About Him), is a dramatic, through-composed setting with considerable word-painting.[4] For example, at mm. 22–24 the agitated accompaniment depicts "thunder"; at mm. 26–34 tremolos illustrate "lightning and trembling"; and at mm. 34–35 the thick accompaniment disappears into complete silence, symbolizing "the mountains melt like wax" (see Example 19-1). Song two, "*Skrýše má a pavéza má Ty jsi*" (Lord,

Example 19-2. Dvořák, *Biblical Songs*, Opus 99, No. 2
("Lord, Thou Art My Shield"), mm. 18–26.

Thou Art My Shield), is at times reminiscent of Schubert's late strophic songs, especially mm. 20–26 with their thirds-related harmonies (see Example 19-2).[5] The opening phrases of its two verses (mm. 1–4 and mm. 14–17) bring to mind the gesture of a Negro spiritual. The third song, "*Slyš, ó Bože! slyš modlitbu mou*" (Hear My Prayer), pays homage to both Brahms and Schubert, especially with the daring tertian and chromatic modulations of its central section, mm. 22–42 (see Example 19-3 on pages 262 and 263).[6]

Continued on next page

Example 19-3. Dvořák, *Biblical Songs*, Opus 99, No. 3 ("Hear My Prayer"), mm. 22–42.

Continued from previous page

Srd - 'ce mé tesk-lí ve mně, a stra - cho-vé
Pained andsore is my heart, the fear of death

B   D   E♭maj7

smr - ti při - šli na mne, a hrů - za při-kva - či - la
lies hea - vy up on me And ter - ror o - verwhelms

C♯dim7   Dmi

Meno

mne.   I   ře - kl jsem:
me.   And thus I spake:

Aaug A   F7   B♭7

Song four, "*Hospodin jest můj pastýř*" (The Lord Is My Shepherd), is the most famous song of the cycle.[7] Its utter simplicity reflects a spiritual-like repose and childlike trust. The fifth song, "*Bože! Bože! Píseň novouj*" (I Will Sing Thee Songs of Gladness), climaxes the first half of the cycle.[8] It begins statically with three repetitive stanzas but ends with a flourish. Its fourth verse (mm. 33–40) is an intensely chromatic bridge section that presents eighteen different chromatic/enharmonic pitches in just six measures (see Example 19-4, mm. 36–39). In verse five, the final return of its "A" material is cleverly reharmonized (see Example 19-5). The opening phrase and recurring instrumental interlude of this song suggest the influence of both the Negro spiritual and American hymnody.

Example 19-4. Dvořák, *Biblical Songs*, Opus 99, No. 5
("I Will Sing Thee Songs of Gladness"), central bridge of verse 4, mm. 33–40.

The cycle takes a desperate turn in song 6, "*Slyš, o Bože, volání me*" (Hear, Oh Lord, My Bitter Cry)—a plaintive ballad in a strophic-ternary design.[9] The seventh song, "*Při řekách babylonských*" (By the Waters of Babylon) is one of the cycle's most remarkable settings.[10] It begins and ends in different keys (C minor and E-flat), and its intricate rhythms and striking modulations vividly depict the desperate overtones of the text. At mm. 1–28 the repeated chord figures of the accompaniment suggest the strumming of

Example 19-5. Dvořák, *Biblical Songs*, Opus 99, No. 5
("I Will Sing Thee Songs of Gladness"), comparison of verses 3 and 5.

harps. The jocular central section (mm. 29–36) illustrates the taunting of the captives, followed at mm. 44–60 by a cry of remembrance for their homeland. The eighth song, "*Popatřiž na mne a smiluj se nade mnou*" (Oh Lord, Have Mercy), starts in A-flat minor and proceeds with harmonic uncertainty, suggesting the restlessness of a lamenting soul.[11] It concludes joyfully in A-flat major, however, as trust in God is restored (mm. 33–38). The last two songs of the cycle continue in this positive vein. Song 9, "*Pozdvihuji oči svých k horám*" (My Eyes I Will Lift Up to the Hills), also begins and ends in different keys (F major and A-flat major).[12] Several instances of word-painting are evident in this setting. At mm. 24–27 an unyielding B-flat pitch in the vocal part depicts the words, "for He will not suffer thy foot to be moved." At mm. 28–29 the words "nor shalt thou fall" are illustrated by a carefully controlled descending line that ends unexpectedly with a "raised up" E-natural instead of an E-flat. At mm. 30–38, marking the words "He that keepeth thee slumbers not," the static accompaniment gives way to restless sixteenth-note figures with a sudden harmonic turn from F minor to A-flat major. Song 10, "*Zpívejte Hospodinu píseň novou*" (Oh, Sing a Joyful Song unto the Lord), is entirely pentatonic and is considered by many to be an actual spiritual.[13] Its lively dance rhythms and its faster tempo provide a fitting conclusion to the work, although its straightforward strophic form is the least inventive design of the cycle.

In summary, the *Biblical Songs* is unique among the works of Dvořák's American period. The cycle demonstrates Dvořák's ability to execute even the most difficult of details while maintaining a guise of utter simplicity and reverence—a feat rarely accomplished and the mark of a true master.

NOTES

1. Dvořák's father died on 28 May, two days after the completion of the last song.

2. Unfortunately, to accommodate the German translation, the rhythm and phrasing of Dvořák's original vocal line was ruthlessly altered. Oddly, the English and French translations were then fitted to the German versification—not to the original Czech. Thus, in most current non-Czech performing editions and recordings, the vocal line is not what Dvořák intended. The new Artia edition from Dvořák's Complete Works has remedied these problems.

3. Dvořák's orchestration of songs 1–5 was published in 1960 as part of the Complete Works edition. The score of songs 6–10, orchestrated by Jarmil Burghauser and Jan Hanuš, was published as a supplement to that edition.

4. Song 1 is based on Psalm 97, verses 2–6.

5. Song 2 is based on Psalm 119, verses 114, 115, 117, and 120.

6. Song 3 is based on Psalm 55, verses 2, 3, 5, 6, 7, 8, and 9.

7. Song 4 is based on Psalm 23, verses 1–4.

8. Song 5 is based on Psalm 144, verse 9 and Psalm 145, verses 2, 3, 5, and 6.

9. Song 6 is based on Psalm 61, verses 1, 3, 4, and 5, and Psalm 63, verses 1, 4, and 5.

10. Song 7 is based on Psalm 137, verses 16, 17, 18, and 20.

11. Song 8 is based on Psalm 25, verses 16, 17, 18, and 20.

12. Song 9 is based on Psalm 121, verses 1–4.

13. Song 10 is based on Psalm 98, verses 1, 4, and 7, and Psalm 96, verse 12.

CHAPTER TWENTY

Dvořák's Piano Works Opus 98a and Opus 101

John C. Tibbetts

*T*wo important though sadly neglected piano works that had their genesis in Dvořák's American sojourn are the "American" Suite in A major, Opus 98, and the *Humoresques*, Opus 101. In a letter to his publisher, Dvořák characterized the Suite as among the "best things I have done in these areas."

Performance neglect and critical indifference, however, have contributed to the problem. Among the biographers, Robertson says the Suite is "commonplace and lazily written." Gervase Hughes sneers that it is "a work of little character." Clapham, who prefers the orchestral version, describes it as generally "artless [and] unpretentious" music. Šourek ignores the Suite altogether and characterizes the *Humoresques* as "based on haphazard jottings." In her assessment of Dvořák's piano music, Harriet Cohen ignores both works altogether.[1] Indeed, until pianist Radoslav Kvapil and conductor Michael Tilson Thomas recorded, respectively, the piano and orchestra versions of the Suite in the 1970s, neither had been available on records. In recent years, only pianists Rudolf Firkušný and Kvapil have recorded the entire cycle of *Humoresques*.

Dvořák wrote the Suite early in 1894, the fifth work he completed in America. He began the final draft, as he noted, "in New York on the 24th of February, the day of St. Matthew, 11 degrees below zero," and completed it on 1 March. He orchestrated it a year later, at the same time he was working on the Cello Concerto. The orchestral version was neither performed nor published until after his death.

The five movements are marked Moderato, Molto vivace, Allegretto, Andante, and Allegro. The first movement is in A major and is in rondo form. The theme, a four-note descending figure (Example 20-1), is quite similar in contour—if distinctly different in effect—from the opening melody of another piano cycle, the *Poetic Pictures*, Opus 85, written five years previously. It is repeated ten times before the appearance of the first of two contrasting sections, a bubbly little confection that grows out of the cadence in bar 12. The second contrasting section reworks the opening theme into staccato sixteenth-notes and a repeating three-note "drumbeat." The opening melody returns in a broad, declamatory manner and finally dissolves into a tender cadence.

Example 20-1. Dvořák, Suite for Piano, Opus 98a, first movement, mm. 1–4.

The second movement's outer parts recall the scherzo of the Eighth Symphony. It opens with a veritable thunderstorm, in C-sharp minor, of swirling sixteenth-notes that plunge downward in furious scalar figures, capped by the same three-note drumbeat pattern heard in the first movement. The figures of two against three contribute to its propulsive drive. The descending scale of the middle section, a stripped-down variant of the preceding material, moves into D-flat major, where it is enlivened by piquant mordants and rhythmic activity. A headlong plunge in double octaves brings the movement to a peremptory close.

The third movement, another rondo in A major, has a good-humored polonaise character and could be a close cousin to the more famous *Humoresque* No. 7. Despite its apparent simplicity, its form is actually quite complicated. The opening theme yields to a richly chorded, hymnlike section full of dusky harmonies. A third theme, more like an episode, is tossed from hand to hand through several registers. Then, after a brief restatement of the opening theme (which contains a hint of the drumbeat pattern), we come to the emotional heart of the Suite: a rambling line spins out of the opening melody, stumbles, and seems to get lost (the inward discursiveness recalls Schumann), but it recovers at bar 73 and is magically transformed into an A minor variant of the second theme. This is a truly magical moment and is full of an almost unbearable longing (Example 20-2). Then, with scarcely a pause, the opening theme returns for the last time, concluding with the characteristic descending phrase in octaves.

Example 20-2. Dvořák, Suite for Piano, Opus 98a, third movement, mm. 73–75.

The fourth movement, the Andante, is dominated by a simple, almost stark, six-note melody against an arpeggiated figure in the left hand (Example 20-3). The tonal center seems ambiguous at first, and it is not until the end of the first phrase that it settles into C major. At bar 11 there is a breathless moment when the melody unexpectedly shifts into E-flat major. In its brief fifty-five measures, the melody is repeated no less than 28 times, always varied with infinitely subtle nuances and textures. For example, in bar 30 the swaying bell-like pattern in the left hand momentarily takes over (it is marked un poco marcato). In the concluding measures there is the faintest teasing echo of the theme before it is banished by three final chords.

The concluding A minor Allegro is full of those qualities that somehow seem so authentically "American."[2] The phrase lengths of the opening theme begin on the second beat of each bar, rather in the manner of a gavotte, and lead to a repetition of the melody in the left hand against right-hand triplets. The three-note drumbeat pattern dominates, with "scotch snaps" punctuating the downbeats. The second section eventually shifts into F-sharp major, and the upward leaps move against a droning "bagpipe" figure (Example 20-4). At the conclusion, after an emphatic restatement in A major of the first movement's opening theme, a series of trills ascend stepwise before sudden descending octaves hurry things to an end.

Example 20-3. Dvořák, Suite for Piano, Opus 98a, fourth movement, mm. 1–6.

Example 20-4. Dvořák, Suite for Piano, Opus 98a, fifth movement, mm. 41–45.

In his orchestration of the Suite, Dvořák employed a large orchestra for three out of the five movements, requiring—in addition to the normal woodwind in pairs, full brass, and percussion—a piccolo, triangle, and double bassoon. At times the textures are very spare, as when a solo oboe, over muted strings, takes the first entry of the theme in the fourth movement and the middle section of the last movement. At other times brass, piccolo, and triangle decorate the lines, adding a kind of overall sheen. Thicker orchestral textures are reserved for only a few occasions—the agitated passages in the second and last movements and the last few measures of the finale. While his transcription for orchestra is scrupulously faithful to the piano original, Dvořák has added a few judicious touches, pointing up the "tom-tom" effects with timpani, drumrolls, and cymbals.

Familiarity with the work confirms that, far from being randomly or loosely organized, it is quite tightly structured. All key areas exploited in the work derive from the notes of the opening theme, particularly the notes that are accented—F-sharp, C-sharp, and A. The theme itself, along with the three-note drumbeat figure, recurs in various guises throughout the entire work. Although there is a pause after each movement, the interconnections are obvious. The last note of the opening movement becomes the stepping-off point for the second. The double-forte descending octaves in the final bar of the third movement pivot seamlessly into the placid opening of the fourth. Indeed, that emphatic, descending scale in octaves appears throughout the entire work. And, of course, the reappearance in the finale of the opening theme serves as a closing bracket, or frame.

Another unifying characteristic, as Prof. Michael Beckerman has pointed out,[3] is a prevailing sense of motionlessness, a kind of musical and psychological *stasis*. Although this effect, which is achieved through constant repetition and a relative lack of tonal development, has not been lost on some other commentators, it has nonetheless been a source of exasperation. Gerald Abraham complains of Dvořák's "irritating" habit, of "naively repeating a short phrase or a mere motive like a child crooning to itself."[4] On the other hand, as Beckerman contends, the practice suspends our melodic and tonal expectations and compels us to concentrate instead on the infinite variety of color and texture. This is most apparent in the fourth movement, where the shifts in color and dynamics with each repetition of the melody express, by turns, plaintive, elegiac, tender, and consoling moods. Could this have been a response to the open American spaces Dvořák found in the great prairies? We recall Dvořák's words to Emil Kozanek upon arriving in Spillville (quoted at length in Chapter 7 on Spillville, Iowa):

> It is very strange here . . . especially in the prairies there are only endless acres of field and meadow. That's all you see. . . . You don't meet a soul, and you're glad to see the huge herds of cattle in the woods and meadows which in summer and winter are out to pasture in the broad fields. And so, it is very wild here, and sometimes very sad, sad to despair.[5]

Indeed, there is an ineffable quality of stillness, even sadness in the Suite. We stand outside of time, all forward motion stopped, alone in a contemplative trance.

The *Humoresques* began as scattered musical ideas during the Spillville months. They were developed the following December and completed in the summer of 1895 during Dvořák's return to Vysoka, near Pribram, in Western Bohemia. Clapham claims Dvořák originally intended to entitle them *New Scottish Dances*.[6] The eight pieces do not display the interlocking motivic and formal bonds of the Suite, although each is in a 2/4 dance meter. As in the Suite, there are frequent uses of pentatonic themes, although the general tone colors are generally more dissonant and exotic. As a whole the *Humoresques* come closer than the Suite to matching Oscar Wilde's description of Dvořák's piano music as "curiously coloured scarlet music."[7] The movements are marked, Vivace, Poco andante, Poco andante e molto cantabile, Poco andante, Vivace, Poco allegretto, Poco lento e grazioso, and Poco andante.

The first *Humoresque* is in E-flat minor and is windy and tumultuous, the forceful theme interrupted by shorter dancelike episodes in E-flat major and G-flat major. Number 2, in B major, alternates its perky hopping motifs with episodes that are more flowing and expansive. In bar 21 Dvořák gives us one of his enchanting birdcalls, two-note slurs in thirty-second notes that are repeated twelve times, modulating deliciously after every fourth repetition before returning to B major (Example 20-5). A plaintive musette with an interesting chromatic alto line concludes the piece. Number 3 is in A-flat major and is distinguished by a particularly delightful syncopated section in E major, beginning at bar 25, that eventually melts into a winding Schumannian tangle of chromatic colors.

Example 20-5. Dvořák, *Humoresques*, Opus 98a, No. 2, mm. 21–24.

One of the most enigmatic of the set is Number 4. The introductory two measures establish a very tentative F major tonality. This is followed by a scalar melody already started in bar 1, full of bluesy flatted thirds and sixths, concluding with an odd cadence of E major to F major over an F pedal (Example 20-6). (Clapham says the theme was originally conceived to represent Hiawatha as a child in Dvořák's projected opera on that subject.)[8] An episode of bright, high-stepping dance music appears in bar 33 and brings an emphatic F major relief to the rather murky tonal ambivalence. But this is only a temporary respite. A mysterious hush veils the descending triplets of the quadruple-piano close.

The boisterous Number 5 in A minor bears a thematic resemblance to (and presents the same kind of pounding drive as) the concluding piece of the Suite—although, in general, it is the happiest piece of the set. A particularly felicitous touch occurs in bar 137—the work has seemed to settle into a

Example 20-6. Dvořák, *Humoresques*, Opus 98a, No. 4, mm. 3–6.

cozy gemütlichkeit, when suddenly a high, warbling birdcall in A major soars happily skyward. We plunge back to earth in the concluding descending octave passage. Number 6 wears the most exotic plumage of the set. It withholds its tonal identity until after a tentative statement that encompasses two diminished seventh chords that bear no clear tonal relation to each other or to the eventual key. Finally, we reach B major, and gradually a rising-and-falling scalar melody pulls itself together and builds, at bar 29, into an unashamedly schmaltzy dance. But suddenly, unexpectedly, with no preparation whatever, the high jinks cease; in bar 25 we settle into a quiet, lovely passage of rich, dusky chords—the sort of magical intimacy that Schumann would have labeled *innig*. It is the still point of the entire work, and it lingers long in the memory. As if reluctant to finish, the piece concludes with a few hesitant diminished chords.

By far Dvořák's most popular piano work is the seventh *Humoresque* in G-flat major. It is the most formally simple work in the set. Although it is frequently characterized as possessing a syncopated character, it really consists of written sixteenth- and eighth-notes functioning as appoggiaturas (Example 20-7). Conductor Maurice Peress says the opening melody shares a kinship with a work by one of Dvořák's African American pupils. "It has the same phrase structure, the same cadence, the same stride of Maurice Arnold's 'Second American Plantation Dance,'" claims Peress. "Dvořák talks about

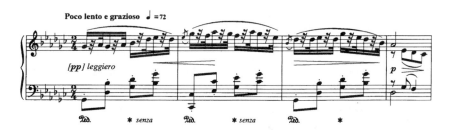

Example 20-7. Dvořák, *Humoresques*, Opus 98a, No. 7, mm. 1–4.

knowing Arnold's piece in December of 1893, and he included it in a program of music for the New York *Herald* Benefit in 1894 (see essays by Emanuel Rubin, Chapter 6, and Deane Root, Chapter 18). Arnold himself conducted these dances at that particular concert. Curiously, you can play Stephen Foster's 'Old Folks at Home' in counterpoint to it. I'm not saying that Dvořák copied Arnold's melody, or that he had the Foster thing in his mind, necessarily, but I think the musical process is like this: Artists like Dvořák will hear music and then it imprints itself onto the conscious and subconscious mind. It's no shock that some of it will reemerge in some form or another in Dvořák's later works. After all, he's standing on the shoulders of several generations of musicians. That's all right. That's good."[9]

The concluding Number 8 is dominated by a sturdy theme in B-flat minor which conveys a distinctly modal flavor. Quiet at first, but insidiously persistent, its stride bass punctuates it with plenty of swagger. After a contrasting, bustling theme that appears in bar 25, a quiet modulation leads to a concluding flourish.

Example 20-8. Dvořák, *Humoresques*, Opus 98a, No. 8, mm. 8–12.

Pianist Radoslav Kvapil has studied, performed, and recorded these and other Dvořák piano works. During his appearance at the Dvořák Sesquicentennial Conference and Festival in New Orleans, February 1991, he spoke to this writer about his lifelong efforts to bring them to wider audiences.[10]

Kvapil was born in Brno in 1934. He studied piano with Prof. Ludvik Kundera in Brno and followed him to the Janáček Academy of Musical Arts, where he graduated in 1957. Later studies took him to Moscow with Professor Neugaus and to Bale with Professor Baumgartner. In 1963 he began teaching at the Prague Conservatory. His recordings for Supraphon of the complete piano works of Dvořák, Leoš Janáček, and Bohuslav Martinu have brought him worldwide acclaim and many recital tours across the United States. He and his family presently live in Prague.

"I began studying the piano music of Dvořák back in the early 1960s when I came to Prague. I was twenty-four years old and already performing recitals of all-Czech music. Few pianists at the time were doing such a thing. The Dvořák music, particularly, they dismissed as unimportant. The Smetana repertoire they played, yes; but not the Dvořák. I have been to many of the places where Dvořák lived and worked. I have visited the room where Dvořák was born and played his music there. There is not an excellent piano, but the atmosphere is so marvelous. In Vysoka there is still the Dvořák house and I have played there, too. And the small castle where his great love, Josefina, was living. Also the Dvořák Museum and the small concert hall in Prague where Dvořák played the organ.

"People at Supraphon heard some of my concerts and asked me if I would record the Dvořák music. Of course I said yes, and from 1967–69 I made six records, beginning with the 'American' Suite and the *Humoresques*. At about the same time I did the Janáček recordings, too. Then the records went abroad and there was a sensational response, especially in England. In America Mr. Avery Fisher heard them, and he managed my concert debut in New York. (I think he really liked the sound of my Boesendorfer piano!)

"There is a very special 'sound' to [Dvořák's] piano music. We know that his family was poor and that he had few opportunities to study the piano. His first real piano writing doesn't come until the accompaniments for the eighteen songs called *Cypresses*. They have absolutely marvelous piano parts! They are very Schumannian. And yet they were written by someone who had hardly touched the piano! He didn't write a solo piece until the Opus 35 Dumka and Opus 36 Variations, which he wrote about the same time as his Piano Concerto. You know, I don't think he was looking for something 'new,' and certainly he did not want the virtuosity, the big sound, the clichéd passagework and many notes of a Franz Liszt. He hated unnecessary notes and stripped away anything that was excessive. He made every note so very important. So he wrote things that can be incredibly awkward and difficult but sound fresh and new. He mostly kept to shorter forms and had special ideas and a great sensitivity to color. You can see as early as the Concerto almost a textbook of unusual techniques, discoveries, and sounds. If I could go back and ask him about his scores, I would ask him to change some of these passages that are not playable! Unfortunately, there are some versions of the Concerto that have removed these passages and 'smoothed them out,' I think you would say. They must be restored, as I did in my recording for Supraphon.

"The 'American' Suite and the *Humoresques* are some of his most beautiful and—how do you say it?—condensed works. Yes, I am convinced that they have some 'American' ideas, but to understand them you must also listen to the earlier pieces, especially the *Silhouettes*, Waltzes, Mazurkas, and *Poetic Tone Pictures* [respectively, Opp. 8, 54, 56, and 85]. The *Silhouettes* is like Schumann, perhaps—especially the *Papillons*.* They come from a great love, for Josefa Čermák [Josefina Čermáková (later Kaunitzová), his wife's sister] and are very short, with lots of connections between them. There is this most important melody in Dvořák, which first appeared in the *Cypresses*. It is called 'In the Deepest Forest Glade I Stand,' and he wrote it to a poem by the Czech poet Pfleger. It appears in the first *Silhouette* right away. There are other themes taken from the First and Second Symphony. One example is an arpeggio that appears at the very beginning of Number 1 and later in Numbers 5 and 12—like the Schumann scale that opens and closes the *Papillons*, I think. Other themes from the Scherzo and Finale of the First Symphony show up in the sixth and eleventh pieces. I loved playing the *Silhouettes* as a boy, and I have a very special relation to them. They have such a special fantasy and should be played more.

"The other pieces are also unknown to many listeners. The dance music of the Waltzes and Mazurkas is not like what Smetana did. Smetana's music must be almost fifty percent dances, particularly polkas. Dvořák didn't compose so much dance music, although the Scottish Dances [Opus 41] are wonderful, very Schubertian, and he loved the furiant, which was very significant for him. The furiant is a very active dance that always changes the rhythm from two to three beats. (You can see this sort of thing in the Slavonic Dances, Numbers 1 and 8.) His Mazurkas are not like Chopin at all. They are very Czech.

"The *Poetic Tone Pictures* (*Poetické nálady*) he wrote in Prague and Vysoka in 1889. He gave to them his own titles, and you can see musical pictures, fairy tales, elves, castles, festivals, peasant songs. They are not made in a polyphonic way. No, they concentrate on mood and color. Color is very important. They are on the border of Impressionism. The first one, '*Nočni cestou*' (Twilight Way), has a deeply Impressionistic feeling, although the harmonies are very Romantic. Some of the last pieces, like the 'Burial Scene for a Hero' (*U mohyly*), are very strong—no, very *stark*, like late Grieg. Here we

---

* Editor's note: *Papillons* (Butterflies) was one of Robert Schumann's early keyboard works, Opus 2. Composed in 1829–31, it was the prototype for the many piano cycles he wrote throughout the 1830s such as *Carnaval*, Opus 9, and *Humoreske*, Opus 20. The brief pieces are thematically interrelated and contain many autobiographical references. In both form and character, Schumann's *Papillons* do indeed prefigure Dvořák's *Silhouettes*.

again see the same sort of thing in some of the 'American' works. You know, the piano is a rather poor instrument for just single notes. It is hard to develop anything without the many notes and thick textures that Liszt gives you in his earlier pieces. If you strip away everything to the main notes, you have less to work with, you feel there is something missing. But it is the secret of Dvořák and Janáček that they can evoke fantasy in the listener with just these few notes. But you must be careful and listen with great concentration to see the constant changing he does with these notes. Subtle changes, a slight change as the melody repeats, etc. This is the beginning of a new epoch in piano writing. It is very sophisticated. When you look at the score you see how complicated it really is.

"This is the secret of some of the music in the Suite. It is one of my favorite pieces because it has everything that is significant for Dvořák and some of the things I think are 'American.' There are lots of pentatonic figures and phrases that turn downward and all of that. The slow movement, it is so simple that it repeats and repeats. But it is incredibly difficult to make those subtle changes each time—you must practice it hours every day! I would love to see the country that inspired it, to see Spillville and the countryside. That is always so important in Dvořák—if you don't see Vysoka, for example, how can you understand the Poetic Pictures?

"Everywhere in the *Humoresques* I hear the kinds of things I hear in the other works written in America—especially the chamber works. There are pentatonic scales and these little dotted-note figures—so much like the birdcalls in the Quartet [Opus 96] and the drums in the Quintet [Opus 97]. So many people might think 'Humoresque' means happy, do you know?—to be in good humor. But do you know Schumann's piece called *Humoreske* [Opus 20]? I think Dvořák must have known it and that's why he has this title. It means 'humors,' moods, sometimes to be happy and sad at the same time. The ideas are like little jewels. They are so short and go by so quickly, they change all the time. But that is not the reason to ignore them, as so many pianists do. Beethoven wrote his Bagatelles [Opus 126] near the end of his life, and they are all short. But that does not mean they are not important."

NOTES

1. See the following: Alec Robertson, *Dvořák* (London: J. M. Dent and Sons, Ltd, 1947), 104. He continues, "[h]e rarely knew how to [write for the piano] in the most effective way. He reminds us that no great music for the piano has been composed by only moderate pianists." Gervase Hughes, *Dvořák: His Life and*

Music (London: Cassell & Company, Ltd., 1967), 172; John Clapham, *Antonín Dvořák: Musician and Craftsman* (New York: St. Martin's Press, 1966), 150; Otakar Šourek, *Antonín Dvořák and His Works* (Prague: Artia, 1956), 27; Harriet Cohen, "The Piano Compositions" in *Antonín Dvořák: His Achievement*, ed. Viktor Fischl (London: Lindsay Drummond, 1942).

2. Many biographers reject this notion. In his biography Gervase Hughes writes: "This is a work of little character, which apart from a few 'negro' touches in the finale might have been produced by almost any competent composer, whether hailing from Bohemia, Berlin or either of the two Bostons." (172) In his *Dvořák* Alec Robertson refers to these "American" traits sarcastically: "Dvořák is being consciously American, and this lends distinct interest to the Suite. He evidently thinks the Americans a very sentimental race. . . . Was Dvořák pulling the American leg?" (109)

3. Professor Beckerman presented a paper on the Suite at the Dvořák Sesquicentennial Conference and Festival in New Orleans, 14–20 February 1991.

4. Gerald Abraham, "Dvořák's Musical Personality," in *Antonín Dvořák: His Achievement*, ed. Viktor Fischl, 224.

5. Dvořák's letter from Spillville to Emil Kozanek, 15 September 1893, quoted in *Antonín Dvořák: Letters and Reminiscences*, ed. Otakar Šourek, trans. Roberta Finlayson (Prague: Artia, 1954), 166.

6. John Clapham, *Antonín Dvořák: Musician and Craftsman*, 217.

7. Quoted in Alec Robertson, *Dvořák*, 104.

8. John Clapham, *Antonín Dvořák: Musician and Craftsman*, 217.

9. Author's interview with Maurice Peress, New Orleans, 18 February 1991.

10. Author's interview with Radoslv Kvapil, New Orleans, 17 February 1991.

CHAPTER TWENTY-ONE

Sonatina for Violin and Piano

John C. Tibbetts

*I*n December 1893 Dvořák's fifteen-year-old daughter Otilie wrote to her "dear old godfather," Alois Göbl, in Bohemia: "And now he [Daddy] has written a Sonata [*sic*] for piano and violin in an easy style and dedicated it to me and Tony."[1] A month later Dvořák characterized this new Sonatina, Opus 100, the last of his "American" chamber works, as a work "intended for young people (dedicated to my children) but grown-ups, too, let them get what enjoyment they can out of it"[2] Her name and brother Tony's appear on the first sketch, to be joined later by the other dedicatees, Anna, Mařenka (Magdalena), Otakar, and Zinda (Aloisie).

The intentions and effects of this music recall Schumann, who wrote not only simple sonatinas for his own children but more sophisticated music generally evocative of the fancies of childhood—especially the *Kinderscenen*, Opus 15, and the Opus 132 *Maerchenerzählungen* (Fairy Tale Pieces).[3] It seems rather severe, therefore, when commentators such as Abram Loft and Gervase Hughes complain that the fifty-two-year-old Dvořák should write something so "studiedly naive" and so beneath Schumann's own standard.[4] For his part, Otakar Šourek acknowledges the deeper moments behind the amiable surfaces, admiring its "passages of pensive melancholy and wistfulness."[5]

Dvořák may have begun the work as early as September 1893. One of the happiest anecdotes of his American sojourn describes him pausing before a view of the Minnehaha Falls near St. Paul, Minnesota, to scribble down on his starched shirt cuff a theme later used in the second movement.[6] Back in New York that October, Dvořák began assembling this and other sketches for an intended D minor orchestral suite. Abandoning these plans, he began

Example 21-1. Dvořák, Sonatina, Opus 100, first movement, mm. 1–8.

sketching the present version of the Sonatina between 19 and 22 November, scoring the first movement on 23–24 November, the second and third movements in the next two days, and finishing the fourth on 3 December 1893.

All four movements are simple in form with occasional digressions away from standard thematic handling. The first movement is in G major, Allegro risoluto, and is cast in sonata form. The opening theme over eight bars (Example 21-1) is first given to the violin, then briefly to the piano, its phrases ending with an appoggiatura on the cadential note. The melody actually consists of two parts, a question and an answer—the first forceful and declamatory, the second more tender and resigned. The subordinate theme, in E minor rather than the expected D major, involves the violin and piano in some delicious imitative interplay. Clapham says this melody is similar to the well-known Moravian folk song "*Dolina, dolina, níže nových Zámků*" (The Valley Below Nove Zamky).[7] The exposition grows in power and intensity, with sforzando accents on alternating first and second beats of the bar. There is a striking transition to a development section with unexpected modulations to B-flat major, D-flat major, and several other adventuresome harmonic changes. The concluding measures of the movement display very exotic harmonic colors. The opening material reappears, fading finally against rolled chords in the piano. A lovely cadence substitutes a B minor chord for what would normally be a C major chord, and the movement comes to a hushed and serene close.

The most famous movement of the four is the Larghetto, in G minor. Characteristically, the opening melody—the one Dvořák purportedly composed at the Minnehaha Falls—is repeated frequently with subtle variations (Example 21-2). At first the violin theme is spare, almost stark, and the piano accompaniment is confined to simple, yet piquant harmonic changes. Gradually, the theme grows more expansive, and the piano figures spread out into thrumming patterns and running figures. A modulation to B-flat major

Example 21-2. Dvořák, Sonatina, Opus 100, second movement, mm. 1–4.

lightens the mood and presents, in quick succession, two ravishing, interrelated melodies based on the pentatonic scale (so characteristic of Dvořák's other "American" works). A repeated two-note figure, E-flat and D-natural, span fifteen bars and lead to another modulation, this time to G major, preparing the way for a blissful piano melody against the violin's scrubby sixteenth-notes (or a slow trill on D and E ?). The roles reverse in the restatement. After a moody bridge, there is a return to the opening theme, followed by a haunting passage of chromatic color where the piano's G-natural tremolo figure acts as a pedal point against the violin's drone (an alternating D-octave and E-flat/C-sharp chord). Tom-tom beats from the opening theme are heard again from the piano, and the movement concludes on a hushed, lamenting note as the violin line sinks to the lowest G on the G-string. The dusky-hued colors and drooping, plaintive lines recall the conclusion of the second movement of the F Major Quartet. The publisher, Simrock, issued the movement separately in various instrumental arrangements (without the composer's authorization). Fritz Kreisler popularized this piece in his recitals, dubbing it the "Indian Lament."

The third movement is marked molto vivace and is in the home key of G major. It is a perky little scherzo that encloses a syncopated trio between its outer sections. After some furious C minor bariolages in the violin generate friction against the opening melody, the trio returns to C major with sharp accents on the second beat of the bar. The overall character of the movement again recalls the F major Quartet—this time the scherzo.

The fourth movement is in G major and is a return to sonata form. Somewhat unusually for Dvořák, the music is characterized by an apparent four-bar consistency that, in the opinion of Loft,[8] becomes too predictable for its length of 379 bars. (Actually, that "consistency" is broken four times in the exposition alone.) The principal theme is marked by a descending scale with accents on the first two notes and a syncopated stamp in the third bar. A second theme in E minor swings along in sturdy dotted rhythms with "scotch snaps" at bars 69 and 79 (Šourek calls them "skočná," or tapping rhythms) for extra propulsion. The cadential figure shifts into a magical E major section, marked molto tranquillo, with two stunning eight-bar melodic lines—one rising and one falling—that seem to sum up all of Dvořák's longing for home (Example 21-3). At the repetition there is a tantalizing brief shift into C major. It is an extraordinary passage of great beauty. The coda draws upon the descending scalar figure of the opening theme for a quickening return to good humor. The tempo gradually accelerates, and the movement concludes with unabashed high spirits.

Example 21-3. Dvořák's Sonatina, Opus 100, fourth movement, mm. 106–121.

The Sonatina contains such a wealth of melodic and rhythmic invention, such a diversity of spirits, that it is a wonder it is not better known. Its relative simplicity makes it accessible to amateur violinists, and children can readily negotiate its low positions. But it requires a great degree of poetic insight and professional musicianship to bring it off. For example, a child might want to use the A-string for the opening melody of the second movement, but an artist would prefer to play the entire line on the more difficult but warmer D-string. The beginner might be content to feel the three-beat meter of the opening movement, while the more advanced player will feel it in just one beat per bar. Care must be exercised to differentiate between Dvořák's accent and sforzando markings throughout. If the Sonatina is redolent of the whimsies and capricious moods of childhood, it is nonetheless wrought with an industry and sophistication that utterly effaces itself. "To have a lovely thought is nothing so remarkable," Dvořák said. "A thought comes of itself, and if it is fine and great it is not our merit. *But to carry out a thought well and make something great of it, that is the most difficult thing, that is, in fact—art!*"[9]

NOTES

1. Quoted in John Clapham, *Antonín Dvořák: Musician and Craftsman* (New York: St. Martin's Press, 1966), 209.

2. Quoted in Otakar Šourek, *The Chamber Music of Antonín Dvořák* (Prague, Artia, n.d.), 172.

3. On more than one occasion Dvořák compared his own love for "insignificant" material for amateur performance to Schumann's. (See John Clapham, *Antonín Dvořák: Musician and Craftsman*, 178.) Certainly Schumann's example was well known to him. In a famous passage from a letter from Schumann to his fiancée, Clara Wieck, in 1838, he referred to childlike tendencies in his personality and compositions: "You once wrote saying I sometimes seemed to you like a child [and] I took flight and amused myself with working out thirty droll little pieces, twelve of which I have selected and christened *Kinderszenen*. You will like them, though you will have to forget you are a virtuoso for the time being." See Dr. Karl Storck, *The Letters of Robert Schumann* (London: John Murray, Albemarle Street, W., 1907), 187.

4. Abram Loft, *Violin and Keyboard: The Duo Repertoire* (New York: Grossman, 1973), vol. 2, 186; and Gervase Hughes, *Dvořák: His Life and Music* (London: Cassell, 1967; rprt., Portland, OR: Amadeus Press, 1991), 170.

5. Otakar Šourek, *The Chamber Music of Antonín Dvořák*, 209.

6. The anecdote is repeated without comment in John Clapham, *Antonín Dvořák: Musician and Craftsman*, 209.

7. John Clapham, *Antonín Dvořák: Musician and Craftsman*, 210.

8. Abram Loft, *Violin and Keyboard: The Duo Repertoire*, vol. 2, 184–187.

9. Quoted in Otakar Šourek, *Antonin Dvořák: Letters and Reminiscences*, 195.

CHAPTER TWENTY-TWO

Thoughts of Home
The Cello Concerto in B Minor, Opus 104

Robert Battey

*T*he Cello Concerto in B minor, Opus 104, was Dvořák's only new work completed during his third year in America. He wrote the sketch and the score simultaneously, beginning the first movement on 8 November 1894 and the finale on "New Year's Day, 1895." The full score was completed on 9 February of that year. He made an important emendation in the score after his return to Bohemia the following spring, about which I will have more to say later.

Dvořák did not feel comfortable with the cello as a solo instrument, despite his obvious affinity with its lyrical soul. He had tried in 1865 to compose a cello concerto, but was so dissatisfied that he left the score in short form.[1] His orchestral and chamber music contains many unforgettable passages for the instrument, but he remained daunted by the many problems a cello concerto poses in terms of texture and balance.

Hanuš Wihan[2] was a superb Bohemian cellist and an old friend and colleague of Dvořák's from the Prague Conservatory days. Wihan had pressed Dvořák for years to try another cello concerto, but the composer obliged only with short recital pieces, including *Waldesruhe* (itself an arrangement of an earlier four-hand piano piece) and the Rondo, Opus 94, which were both written in late 1891. These were quite well received, and in 1893 Wihan wrote Dvořák asking for orchestrated versions so that he could use them in full concert dress. Dvořák was happy to comply, and his satisfaction with the results may have been encouraging. Then in March, during Dvořák's second trip to America, Victor Herbert performed his own Cello

Concerto No. 2 in Brooklyn, with Dvořák in attendance.[3] This piece was clearly influenced by the popular Saint-Saëns Cello Concerto No. 1, composed in 1873, in terms of its cyclical form and the arresting early entry of the soloist. In turn, Herbert's concerto made a very favorable impression on Dvořák, who then began to give serious thought to Wihan's long-standing request.

Victor Herbert was a popular American composer and a colleague of Dvořák's at the National Conservatory. His Second Cello Concerto purportedly was a model for Dvořák's own Cello Concerto. Drawing by John C. Tibbetts.

Dvořák completed the first version on 9 February the following year. After returning to Prague in the spring of 1895, he revised the Concerto's ending, and his publisher Simrock brought it out in 1896 as Opus 104, bearing a dedication to Wihan. It was premiered on 19 March of that year in Queen's Hall, London, the composer conducting the London Philharmonic Society with the young English cellist Leo Stern as soloist.[4] The American premiere was in December 1896 in Boston with Alwin Schroeder as soloist.[5] Wihan himself did not perform it until 25 January 1899, but he played it frequently thereafter, including a performance on 20 December in Budapest with Dvořák conducting.

It is somewhat surprising, given Dvořák's prolific output in all the standard instrumental genres of his time, that there are only three mature concerti—one each for piano, violin, and cello. It was certainly a popular form, one which, with committed performers, could rapidly bring recognition and success to a composer. It is significant that passages of dramatic and technical fireworks are not to be found in Opus 104. It is indeed difficult, but even the extroverted "licks" are carefully woven into the overall fabric and spirit of the piece. He used his largest orchestra yet for a concerto, including three trombones, tuba, piccolo, and even a triangle. These were the forces he ranged against the cello, an instrument with little carrying power! But, as Brahms had already done before him, Dvořák solved his problems by approaching the work more as a symphony than a concerto.

Arguably, the work gives little hint that the composer had ever heard of America, let alone lived and worked there; it breathes the pure air of the Bohemian countryside, though it is an atmosphere sometimes charged with menace. Clapham writes, "For the first time in an important work composed in America we find American colouring reduced to a bare minimum."[6] He was palpably homesick and there is a strong sense of nostalgia throughout the work. The woodwind writing, in particular, recalls the serene pastoral character of his middle symphonies; as we shall see, there were extra-musical elements in the Concerto expressing his desire to return home. Although there were no actual folk songs, or even generalized folk dances, two characteristic Bohemian traits can be found throughout the work, namely pentatonic scales and aaB phrase pattern, where a melody begins with a repeated phrase followed by a two-bar "answer."[7]

The first movement's brooding opening recalls Dvořák's monumental D minor Symphony (1884); significantly, the very first sketch of the concerto begins in that key. The low strings and clarinets create a mood of foreboding that duly rises to a thunderous climax (Rehearsal No. 1). After a rather extended transition passage, he reaches the relative major with the justly famous horn melody (Example 22-1)

Example 22-1. Dvořák, Cello Concerto, Opus 104, first movement, mm. 143–148.

This tune cost him great labor, but, as he wrote to a friend, the final results always excited him. It is indeed the quintessential romantic horn solo, and the cellist is hard put to match its luminous beauty. After an ebullient closing theme (never to be heard again), the mood changes swiftly to trembling expectation, and the soloist enters with a "call to arms." This use of the opening motif in the tonic major is a masterstroke that Dvořák had confidently settled on from his earliest sketch. Indeed, it is an arresting moment. This first solo is marked *Quasi improvisando,* and it almost suggests a Bach organ toccata in its spirited "trying out" quality. The passage winds up with a series of trills from the soloist that underline an ardent passage in the woodwinds—a relationship that will continue to develop throughout the work.

A more regular exposition proceeds from here (Reh. No. 4) with the "big tune" being approached through E minor, as it was before. When the cello tries it on for size, it also takes the follow-up passages that the woodwinds had negotiated earlier and leads to a new section (Reh. No. 6). This enchanting writing, featuring very difficult seesaw arpeggios on the cello beneath a yearning choralelike woodwind passage, defines the basic mood of the concerto in its glowing colors and nostalgia. The exposition's impending close is announced at the end of the passage as we arrive at the dominant. This closing material gave the composer a surprising amount of trouble; the Šourek critical edition shows four versions prior to the printed one, each quite different from the others. After a bucolic exchange among the three horns, the soloist closes out the section with appropriate dramatic bluster.

The development begins with a great tempest (Reh. No. 8), after which Dvořák takes us through some ingenious modulations to the remote-sounding key of A-flat minor. This is really some sleight-of-hand, since A-flat is the same as G-sharp, which is the relative minor of B major, which is where everything is heading. In other words, instead of being miles away, we're just down the street. The soloist enters (Reh. No. 10) with a hushed variant of the opening motif that expresses an almost unbearable longing. After a timpani roll on the dominant, the cello intensifies into double-stops. Then, after a dramatic pause, a scale rushes upwards in octaves, announcing Dvořák's second formal masterstroke of the movement.

A recapitulation, almost by definition, requires that the opening theme be stated in the tonic key. Dvořák's idea, derived from his first sketch, was to dispense with the entire first theme group and have the full orchestra blaze forth with the horn melody now in the tonic major. This wonderful torrent is immediately answered by the soloist. The coda is brief and crisp, featuring lighthearted variants of the neglected opening theme. A characteristic little march appears at the very end.

The radiant Adagio ma non troppo opens with another woodwind chorale, this one led by the clarinet. This theme was substantially altered from the first sketches, showing that the composer was working carefully to find exactly the right tone for the movement. The soloist soon enters with the first phrase of the melody, but what then follows is one of the most exquisitely beautiful moments in the entire concerto: over soft chords in the low brass (perhaps suggested by similar orchestration in the slow movement of Herbert's Second Concerto), punctuated by gentle strummed chords from the celli in the orchestra, the soloist and pairs of woodwinds engage in the most celestial dialogue imaginable. This tender exchange (Reh. No. 1) is another longing glance back to Dvořák's homeland. The mood, however, soon turns dark and agitated, and after a "sobbing" passage from the soloist (again in a duet with the flutes), the opening serenity is restored. This is only a brief bridge, however, to one of the cardinal events in the concerto.

In his youth Dvořák was in love with one of his pupils, Josefina Čermáková. Although she rejected his marriage proposal, they always retained affectionate relations; and she later became his sister-in-law. While working on this movement in December, Dvořák received a distressing letter from Josefina indicating that she was seriously ill. "I have been continuously confined to bed," she wrote, ". . . I may never be able to look forward to anything any more."⁹ Clapham states flatly that the letter was a warning to Dvořák that it was unlikely she might survive her illness for more than a few months. "The composer experienced more acute fits of nostalgia during that winter than at any other period while he was in America," continues Clapham, "and we may be certain that, besides the separation from most of his children, he also missed his dear sister-in-law."¹⁰ This could only have increased his eagerness to return to Bohemia; and at this point in the piece the orchestra suddenly roars out in a thunderous rage. Close on the heels of this, Dvořák introduces an altered version of one of his songs, a favorite of Josefina's, "*Lasst mich allein*" (Leave Me Alone), Opus 82, No. 1. He develops it symphonically in rich colors, twice recalling the "sobbing" motif from the first section (Example 22-2).

Example 22-2. Dvořák, Cello Concerto, Op. 104, second movement, mm. 42–46.

The recapitulation radically expands and transforms the opening chorale—first in a noble paragraph for the three horns, then in a glowing quasi-cadenza for the soloist, who later takes turns exchanging playful arabesques with flutes and bassoons. The mood becomes serious again, and the "celestial dialogue" returns once more over a tender heartbeat in the low strings (Reh. No. 7). At this point the composer seems to have some difficulty bringing the movement to a close. Earlier sketches indicated a shorter ending. The final coda is somewhat disjointed and lingering, though it begins with a most clever transformation of the "cry of rage," now in a pastoral setting in the woodwinds accompanied by the cello (Reh. No. 8). After a peaceful climb up to a trill in the top register, the soloist meanders down a pentatonic scale lulled by the flutes and clarinets to a gently radiant conclusion.

The Finale, which is mostly in rondo form, opens with a departure from tradition. Most concerto finales, from Mozart through Prokofiev, begin with the soloist announcing the main material at once. It seems a species of overkill to build up a long introduction in preparation for the soloist's entry, but this concerto's Finale almost suggests an entr'acte to an opera scene. Over a measured drumbeat in the low strings, the horns begin a fairly long orchestral buildup until two dramatic pauses herald the soloist's appearance, which is marked risoluto. The theme contains a hint of E minor, preparing us already for the upcoming extended G major episode. After the orchestra restates the theme once again, the soloist reenters with new material in a brilliant virtuoso vein, including an idea derived from the first movement (Example 22-3).

Example 22-3. Dvořák, Cello Concerto, Op. 104,
third movement, mm. 57–59.

Another long tutti brings in a little rhythmic motif that dominates the next forty bars (Reh. No. 2), including the soloist's reentry (Example 22-4).

Example 22-4. Dvořák, Cello Concerto, Op. 104,
third movement, mm. 95–96.

This section prepares the way for a lovely new duet in D major between cello and clarinet (Example 22-5).

Example 22-5. Dvořák, Cello Concerto, Op. 104,
third movement, mm. 143–146.

The cello line becomes more flowing and decorative and finally breaks forth into the closest thing to a pure display passage in the concerto, though one that exhibits an interesting harmonic coloring. It rushes in a torrent to the final tutti of the first section (Reh. No. 6), which, with a further brief interjection from the soloist, ties all the previous ideas together and sets the stage for the glorious G major episode (Example 22-6).

Example 22-6. Dvořák, Cello Concerto, Opus 104,
third movement, mm. 281–286.

This noble song is scored in rich autumnal colors for cello, bassoons, and clarinets in their low register; and though other instruments soon join in, the cello remains in dialogue with the clarinets until a jaunty new duet begins with the flute. The rather fussy-sounding passage work for the soloist serves to prepare us for some ambitious modulations. In order to reach the tonic major, he creates a mood of hushed expectancy by a circuitous chain of unexpected harmonies, moving through A major (Reh. No. 11), a C-sharp dominant seventh, and a B-flat dominant seventh from which he springs into the brilliant sunshine of B major. This modulating passage again features the soloist in dialogue with pairs of woodwinds, so it is a startling new color when the return to the tonic is highlighted by, of all things, a solo violin. Over an impassioned trill from the soloist, the violin pours out the noble song, and in this setting suggests almost cinematically the rush of joy at catching a glimpse of a long-lost beloved. The movement is clearly drawing to an end, and Dvořák rounds out the section with a new treatment of the Finale's opening theme, featuring some joyous virtuoso display for the cello.

The coda was originally thirty-seven bars long and consisted mainly of murmurings of the main rondo theme (now smoothed out into triplets) in either the cello or woodwinds, followed by a brief crescendo in the full orchestra for a strong finish. Dvořák finished it on 9 February 1895. Here things stood until he returned to Bohemia in the spring of 1895. After the death of his beloved Josefina on 27 May 1895, he set out immediately to revise the coda. He extended it by more than sixty bars, allowing the soloist more gentle rumination, in order to bring back not only the first movement's main theme (making the concerto a cyclical work) but also a hidden reference to Josefina's song from the slow movement.[11] Thus, the concerto becomes something of a shrine, or memorial. The cello's brooding final bars introduce (with the D-natural) a tragic note that the orchestra immediately takes up in a cataclysm of pain. The final eight bars, which burst forth in Dvořák's most ebullient Slavonic Dances style, seem a bit forced, however, as if he wants to thrust away unhappy reminders in the music. The work was completed in its final form on 11 June 1895, two weeks after Josefina's death.

There are no cadenzas in the concerto. Perhaps Dvořák felt that the contemplative and noble character of the instrument was unseemly in a purely display role. Certainly the dedicatee, Hanuš Wihan, felt that a cadenza was needed. When Dvořák gave him the completed score in the summer of 1895, Wihan immediately revised several passages, mainly to add brilliance and difficulty to the solo part. Next he added a solo cadenza near the end of the Finale. When Dvořák played through the piece with Wihan in August, the composer objected to these changes. Possibly he felt they disrupted his intentions to make these final pages a eulogy to Josefina. Nonetheless, there was apparently some arrangement with Simrock whereby Wihan was empowered to edit the concerto for publication; so, in some distress, Dvořák wrote Simrock to enjoin him from adopting Wihan's changes. The letter reveals the vehemence of Dvořák's feelings on the matter:

> I have had some differences of opinion with Friend Wihan on account of a number of places. I do not like some of the passages—and I must insist on my work being printed as I have written it. The passages in question can be printed in two versions, an easier and a more difficult version. I shall only then give you the work if you promise not to allow anybody to make changes—Friend Wihan not excepted—without my knowledge and consent—and also not the Cadenza which Wihan has added to the last movement. . . . I told Wihan straight away when he showed it me that it was impossible to stick such a bit on.[12]

Although the cadenza was eventually taken out, a number of rewritten passages remain in the final version. Today, musicologically inclined cellists are trying to restore Dvořák's original intentions where they can be ascertained.

Dvořák's Opus 104 is among his finest and most deeply moving works. I believe it to be the greatest of all cello concertos—an opinion shared by most cellists. Certainly there have been many magnificent recordings (see John Yoell's discography in Appendix C), among which personal favorites are the Feuermann/Taube from the 1920s and superb readings from Casals/Szell and Starker/Dorati. The oft-repeated quote of Brahms is apposite: when he saw the score, he reportedly said, "Why on earth didn't I know one could write a violoncello concerto like this? If I had only known, I would have written one long ago!"

[Editor's note: In an interview with this writer in October 1991, cellist Lynn Harrell discussed the concerto:

> I have visited the house in New York where he wrote the Cello Concerto. To me it's "American" in that it reflects a Bohemian's immersion in the American experience. He was very happy with the freedom he saw in America, but he was also very homesick and very sad not to be in Bohemia—particularly as he knew his sister-in-law was dying. The music, and those references to her, are a kind of testament to what never was and what might have been. It's homesickness and love but over all tinged with the success and fame he had in America. The emotional utterance is profound and touching. It's a unique piece of music.]

Notes

1. The earlier Concerto in A Major only came to light in the early twentieth century. The autograph, now in the British Museum, is only a piano score (and apparently a sketchy one). The two published realizations, one by Gunter Raphael in 1929, the other by Jarmil Burghauser a year later, differ quite substantially. The latter, incidentally, has been recorded by Milos Sadlo and is available on a Supraphon compact disc.

2. Hanuš Wihan (1855–1920) was one of the great cellists in Europe at the turn of the century. He studied with the great Karl Davidov, played for Liszt and Wagner, and premiered Richard Strauss's Cello Sonata. He founded the Bohemian (later the Czech) String Quartet, which was for forty years one of the greatest ensembles in Europe and which premiered most of Dvořák's mature chamber works. In addition to the works discussed herein, he inspired Dvořák's great Dumky Trio, Opus 90.

3. Victor Herbert (1859–1924) was born in Ireland and became an important cellist/conductor/composer. He was principal cellist of orchestras in Stuttgart and New York, music director of the Pittsburgh Symphony (1898–1904), and composer of over thirty successful operettas.

4. Leo Stern (1862–1904) studied with Piatti and Davidov and had a solid career in England. His performance of the Cello Concerto with Dvořák must have pleased the composer, because he reengaged Stern in introducing the concerto in Prague and Vienna. Stern also gave first performances of the work in New York and Chicago.

5. Alwin Schroeder (1855–1928) studied with his brother Karl and was for many years solo cellist of the Boston Symphony. He purportedly gave Dvořák technical advice during the composition process.

6. John Clapham, *Antonín Dvořák: Musician and Craftsman* (New York: St. Martin's Press, 1966), 103.

7. Pentatonic scales can be found in the first movement at Reh. No. 4, in the second movement at m. 152, and in the Finale at m. 457. The aaB phrasing can be seen in the first movement, again at Reh. No. 4 and in the Finale at Reh. No. 10.

8. Indeed, it almost seems inappropriate to call it a concerto in B minor since the majority of the first movement is in either D major or B major, and the last movement, aside from its extended section in G major, reaches B major well before the long coda starts and remains in that key to the end.

9. Quoted in John Clapham, "Dvořák's Cello Concerto in B Minor: A Masterpiece in the Making," *Music Review*, vol. 40, no. 2 (May 1979), 131–132.

10. John Clapham, "Dvořák's Cello Concerto in B Minor: A Masterpiece in the Making," 131.

11. M. 468. This actually bears little resemblance to the "Lass mich allein" melody; it is merely a descending one-octave scale in a hesitant rhythm. I suspect that if the composer himself had not explicitly mentioned the link in a letter to his publisher Simrock, no one would be pressing the point today.

12. Dvořák to Simrock, 3 October 1895; quoted in *Antonín Dvořák: Letters and Reminiscences*, ed. Otakar Šourek (Prague: Artia, 1954), 184–185.

PART THREE

DVOŘÁK TODAY

Dvořák late in life. (Courtesy Cyril Klimesh Collection.)

CHAPTER TWENTY-THREE

The Reception of Dvořák's Operas in America

A Social, Political, and Aesthetic Odyssey

David Beveridge

*D*uring Dvořák's stay in America, probably the only major genre of his work not represented in any of the celebratory performances was opera. This may not surprise us since we have not tended to think of Dvořák as an operatic composer. But he had composed eight works for the operatic stage by the time of his arrival in New York, and he himself attached great importance to them. In the years following his American visit, he concentrated even more heavily on opera, and in 1904, the last year of his life, he characterized his orientation as follows:

> In the last five years I have written nothing but operas . . . because I consider opera the most suitable form for the nation. . . . I am viewed as a composer of symphonies and yet I proved long years ago that my main bias is towards dramatic creation.[1]

Dvořák neglected to mention here a few small nonoperatic works composed in his last years. And his apparently grudging attitude toward the composition of symphonies must surely be understood to apply *only* to his last period; to minimize the importance of instrumental music in his life's output would be absurd. But his persistent devotion to opera over the span of his career had indeed been remarkable, resulting in eleven major works between 1870 and 1903,[2] and it is instructive to contemplate that the total performance time of his operas probably exceeds that of all his orchestral and chamber works combined. An overview of his operatic works is in Table 23-1.

Title (English)	Title (original)	Dates composed	Type
Alfred	*Alfred*	1870	Serious opera
King and Collier (or *King and Charcoal-Burner*)	*Král a uhlíř*	1871	Comic opera
King and Collier (second setting)	*Král a uhlíř*	1874; revised 1887	Comic opera in the manner of Smetana
The Stubborn Lovers (or *The Pig-headed Peasants*)	*Tvrdé palice*	1874	One-act comedy
Vanda	*Vanda*	1875	Grand opera
The Cunning Peasant (or *The Peasant, a Rogue;* or *The Scheming Farmer*)	*Šelma sedlák*	1877	Comic Opera
Dimitrij	*Dimitrij*	1881–82; revised 1883, 1885, 1894–95	Grand opera
The Jacobin	*Jakobín*	1887–88; revised 1897	Comic/serious
The Devil and Kate (or *Kate and the Devil*)	*Čert a Káča*	1898–99	Comic fairy tale
Rusalka (*The Water Nymph*)	*Rusalka*	1900	Tragic fairy tale
Armida	*Armida*	1902–03	Grand opera

Table 23-1. Dvořák's operas.

Dvořák's "American" period, 1892–95, lies in the middle of what turned out to be the biggest temporal gap in his operatic output. But if events had progressed just a little differently, this might not have been so.

There is no doubt that opera was on Dvořák's mind during his stay in America—his extensive revision of *Dimitrij* was accomplished largely in New York in 1894 as an indirect result of conversations with the director of the New York Philharmonic, Anton Seidl.[3] And opera was also on the mind of Dvořák's employer, Jeannette Thurber, who had created the American

Opera Company in 1886 for the production of operas in English. Though the American Opera Company lasted only through the 1887–88 season,[4] she continued the pursuit of her operatic ambitions with a composition contest in which a distinguished opera would receive the grand prize.[5] One of Dvořák's first tasks following his arrival in America (27 September 1892) was to serve as a judge for this contest, and by the 5th of October we find him already busily engaged in studying the scores.[6]

Unfortunately, no opera was deemed worthy of a prize in the competition, but it was not long before Mrs. Thurber interested Dvořák himself in composing an opera on an American subject. He was much intrigued by *The Song of Hiawatha*, which he already knew from its translation into Czech, and was prepared to write an opera on this subject if a suitable libretto could be found. He even made some sketches—some of which apparently found their way into the "New World" Symphony (see Michael Beckerman's article, Chapter 15)—but unfortunately the libretto never materialized and the project had to be abandoned. How tantalizing it is to contemplate the addition of a *Hiawatha* to Dvořák's operatic catalog—a most remarkable complement not only to that list but to the repertoire of nineteenth-century opera generally![7]

So Dvořák's American opera was not to be, and the story of his operas in the United States must be a story of his European operas. But that is a remarkable story in itself and tells us much about the musical culture of America as well as our culture's background in the Old World.

In contemplating the failure of America to produce any Dvořák opera during his stay here (or even to consider a production, as far as we know), we must remember that the opera *Rusalka*, now usually considered his best, had not yet been composed. Nor had another of his more successful works in this genre, *The Devil and Kate*. Moreover, his two best operas existing at that time had been published only in piano-vocal score (*Dimitrij*) or not at all (*The Jacobin*) and had not been translated into any language from the original Czech. An American performance of a major work in Czech in the 1890s would have been unthinkable; and there was probably not enough time for the task of producing a translation, obtaining the unpublished performing materials, and preparing a performance of an unknown work. Only twenty-nine months expired between Dvořák's definite agreement to accept the position in America (12 December 1891) and his first return to Bohemia (19 May 1894). To be sure, he then came back for an additional academic year in New York starting in fall 1894, but it was not known with certainty that he would do so until 15 May of that same year.

What *is* surprising is not so much the absence of any Dvořák operatic performance during his stay, but a similar absence during the next forty years! That's how long it took before America saw a Dvořák opera for the first time—a performance of *Rusalka* in 1935 (see Table 23-2). Even then, it was heard only in suburban Chicago in a production by a Czech-American civic organization. *Rusalka* cropped up again several times over the next few decades at various locations in the country, but it was usually performed only by amateurs and never by a regular company.[8] The idea of Dvořák as an opera composer still failed to "catch on." While his orchestral works became ubiquitous—a few of them, in fact, being virtually played to death—most music-lovers in America remained not merely unfamiliar with the music of his operas, but unfamiliar with their very existence. It was 1961 before a second Dvořák opera—*The Cunning Peasant*—was performed, again by a group of Czech enthusiasts, the Sokol Opera in Washington, D.C. There were no follow-ups to the production of this work.

As of 1975, it appeared that the judgment of history had been passed and that Dvořák's operas, to which he attached so much importance, would never see the light of day in this country. But then something happened. In that year productions of *Rusalka* were undertaken separately by a highly respectable school, Juilliard, and for the first time by a regular professional company, the San Diego Opera. Then, in 1977 and 1979, two more Dvořák operas—*The Stubborn Lovers* and *The Jacobin*—were given their American premieres by the Sokol Opera in Washington.

In the 1980s the Sokol Opera offered yet another premiere—*The Devil and Kate*—which was then taken up within the decade in a new production by Berkeley Opera (California). A fifth work, *Dimitrij,* was given a concert performance by the Collegiate Chorale in New York. And there was a virtual explosion of performances of *Rusalka,* including separate productions by a number of medium-sized companies.

The 1990s have already (as of January 1992) brought a number of dramatic developments for Dvořák operas. Another concert performance of *Dimitrij* was given by the Oregon Bach Festival, in 1991, under Helmuth Rilling. *The Devil and Kate* was taken up for the first time by a company of some stature—Opera Theatre of St. Louis. A professional semi-staged presentation of large portions of *The Jacobin* was given at the Dvořák Sesquicentennial Festival in America (New Orleans, 1991) along with small excerpts from two more operas not yet heard in America, *King and Collier* and *Armida.* And *Rusalka* finally reached the level of the major companies in a joint production by the Seattle Opera and Houston Grand Opera (1990 and 1991).

Table 23-2. Productions of Dvořák's Operas in the U.S. Through January 1992.

Dates	Title	Place/Organization	Remarks
10 Mar 1935	*Rus.*	Cicero-Berwyn, IL Czechoslovak-American Legion- naires' Society	Czech U.S. Premiere
25 May 1945	*Rus.*	Detroit, MI Detroit Friends of Opera	English
14 Oct 1950	*Rus.*	NYC Lida Brodenová and the Sokol Artists	Czech
11 Mar 1955	*Rus.*	NYC; Town Hall American Choral Foundation	English
11 Mar 1961	*C.P.*	Washington, D.C.; Sokol Opera Czechoslovak Society of Arts and Sciences	Czech U.S. Premiere
30 Apr 1961	*C.P.*	NYC	same as Washington production
7 Dec 1963	*Rus.*	Cambridge, MA Cambridge Workshop	English?
7, 13, 15 Dec 1963	*Rus.*	Los Angeles University of Southern California	English
3 May 1969	*Rus.*	Chicago, IL (Ravinia); ?	English?
Fall 1972	*Rus.*	Washington, D.C. Washington Civic Opera	English
9, 10, 11 Feb 1973	*Rus.*	Ft. Worth, TX Texas Christian University	English
12+? Dec 1975	*Rus.*	San Diego Opera	English
19-23 Dec 1975	*Rus.*	NYC Juilliard American Opera Center	English
30 Oct 1977	*S.L.*	Washington, D.C. Sokol Opera	Czech U.S. Premiere
28 Oct 1979	*Jac.*	Washington, D.C. Sokol Opera	Czech U.S. Premiere

Dates	Title	Place/Organization	Remarks
17–18 Oct 1981	*D.+K.*	Washington, D.C. Sokol Opera	Czech U.S. Premiere
28 Mar 1984	*Dim.*	NYC; Collegiate Chorale	English
13 Apr 1985	*Rus.*	Riverside, CA Riverside Opera Association	
1987	*Rus.*	Carnegie Hall Opera Orchestra of New York	Czech
Apr 1988	*Rus.*	University of Texas, Austin	
22–30 Apr 1988	*Rus.*	Minnesota Opera, St. Paul	
21–28 May 1988	*D.+K.*	Berkeley, CA Berkeley Opera	English
June 1988	*Rus.*	Charleston, SC Spoleto USA	Czech w/titles
18, 20 Nov 1988	*Rus.*	Madison, NJ; Opera at Florham (Fairleigh Dickinson University)	Czech
21, 25 Nov 1988	*Rus.*	Opera Company of Philadelphia	Czech w/titles
14–20 June 1990	*D.+K.*	Opera Theatre of St. Louis	English
27–28 Oct; 31 Oct; 2, 3, 7 Nov 1990	*Rus.*	Seattle Seattle Opera/Houston Grand Opera	Czech w/titles
16 Feb 1991	*arias/ scenes*	New Orleans Dvořák Sesquicentennial Festival in America	English
7 Jul 1991	*Dim.*	Eugene, OR; Oregon Bach Festival	Czech w/titles
18, 20, 24, 26, 30 Oct; 1 Nov 1991	*Rus.*	Houston Seattle Opera/Houston Grand Opera	Czech w/titles
11 Jan 1992	*Rus.*	San Rafael, CA; Marin Opera	

To some extent, the sharp rise in interest in Dvořák's operas reflects a recent general trend toward unearthing little-known works of the past. A survey by the Central Opera Service of all opera performances in America during the 1980s shows an amazing number of American premieres of old works during this period. The large majority of these, however, are from the seventeenth and eighteenth centuries (Cavalli, Handel, and Haydn are especially conspicuous). Among composers of the nineteenth century, there were just nine that received two or more U.S. operatic premieres during the decade. One of these was the Brazilian composer Antonio Gomes. Seven more were composers already well-known for their operas—Donizetti (four premieres), Rossini (four), Offenbach (three, but having only one act each), Mascagni (two), Smetana (two), Verdi (two), and Wagner (two). The remaining one is Dvořák, who with the premieres of *The Devil and Kate* and *Dimitrij* seems to stand out among the group as a composer of stature not previously known for his works in this field.[9] The fact that another Dvořák premiere (*The Jacobin*) occurred just one year earlier than the survey, in 1979, that the two works premiered in the 1980s were then performed elsewhere, and that *Rusalka* meanwhile continued its ascent, all would tend to corroborate the view of Dvořák as an outstanding "discovery" for the repertoire of romantic opera.

Based on examination of forty reviews in American newspapers and magazines published between 1975 and 1991, critical reaction to the Dvořák operas has generally been very favorable. The reviews surveyed are all based on American productions, with the exception of two reports by Andrew Porter in the *New Yorker*—one concerning the English National Opera production of *Rusalka* in 1983, the other commenting on *The Cunning Peasant,* apparently heard in a British production. In all, twenty of the reviews concern primarily *Rusalka;* seven, *Dimitrij;* six, *The Devil and Kate;* five, *The Jacobin;* one, *The Stubborn Lovers;* and one, *The Cunning Peasant.*[10]

All but three of the reviews surveyed at least give the reader the impression that the opera in question is worth performing. (Of the three exceptions, one pertains mainly to *The Jacobin* and the other two to *The Devil and Kate*.[11] For both of these operas, however, the negative reviews are "outvoted" by others that are positive.) The favorable reviews range from modest approval, with some reservations, to wild enthusiasm. As an example of the latter, the Washington *Post* said of *The Jacobin:* "How this and other operas by one of the most celebrated of composers can continue to languish in obscurity is indeed puzzling. There are a number of mainstays of the repertory that, quite simply, pale by comparison."[12] The *Times-Picayune* of New Orleans judged: "More than an hour's worth of *The Jacobin* [in a program of opera scenes] made this romantic comedy seem like an obligation to any company serious about enriching the repertoire."[13] *Dimitrij* was hailed by *Ovation* as "one of those operas which prove immediately winning from the first measure of its first hearing . . . an exciting story with exciting music."[14] And of the twenty reviews surveyed of *Rusalka*, six termed it a "masterpiece," a "truly masterful operatic composition," a "truly great and neglected masterpiece," an "operatic gem," and/or explicitly called for it to be taken up by major opera houses.[15]

The most comprehensive picture of Dvořák's operas painted by any single American critic is that by Andrew Porter, who also happens to be perhaps the most authoritative and influential among his breed in this country. In his column for the *New Yorker*, Mr. Porter has reviewed *Dimitrij* (New York, 1984), *The Devil and Kate* (St. Louis 1990), *Rusalka* twice (one article on both the Juilliard and San Diego productions of 1975, one on the English National Opera's in 1983), and the Dvořák Sesquicentennial Festival and Conference in America (New Orleans, 1991), with its program of opera scenes emphasizing *The Jacobin*. In the *Dimitrij* review he writes, "The Dvořák operas I have seen in the theatre—*The Cunning Peasant, Kate and the Devil, Rusalka* in several productions—hold the stage well."[16] (He also has kind words for *Dimitrij*, which was heard in concert performance.) An advocate of Czech opera in general, he actually prefers Janáček and Smetana to Dvořák, yet has stated more than once that *Rusalka* should be taken up by a major house in New York.[17] And he (unusually) likes *The Devil and Kate* even better than *Rusalka*, saying he's sure it "could be a hit at the City Opera."[18] In reference to the Dvořák Sesquicentennial Festival, he writes, "I left New Orleans eager to hear more of the operas."[19]

If the critics are correct, and if Dvořák's operas are indeed valuable works worthy of repeated performance, we face a challenging investigation into the question of why this discovery had to wait so long. It is an investigation that is very revealing of the patterns by which repertories are established and histories of music written. The obstacles to the dissemination of Dvořák's operas have been varied and complex, often having nothing to do with the inherent quality of the works.

In Europe, Dvořák's operas are performed much more frequently than in America—in fact there may well have been more productions in Great

Britain alone than in the whole United States.[20] As I shall demonstrate, there are certain special conditions of music reception in America that have worked to block the dissemination of Dvořák's operas in this country. However, the current difference between the American and the European reception of Dvořák's operas results partly from the larger overall number of operatic performances in Europe, and partly from the more experimental and innovative attitudes of European houses. One could say that the trend in Europe is "ahead" of that in America, for by 1985 Arthur Jacobs, writing for the British journal *Opera*, could call *Rusalka* "no longer an operatic oddity."[21] This statement, however, correctly implies that it once *was* an operatic oddity, and even now Dvořák's operas are not quite standard repertoire in Europe. In summary, it must be admitted that the neglect of Dvořák's operas is not a uniquely American phenomenon. To understand the patterns in this country we shall have to go back to the Old World.

Is it, then, a question of obstacles to the dissemination of Dvořák's operas outside his own small country? In large part, yes. But the reception of these works even in Bohemia, both today and in Dvořák's lifetime, has not been quite the success story we might imagine. We must start our investigation by going all the way back to the beginning of Dvořák's career in Prague in the 1860s.

First and foremost, Dvořák had a formidable rival in the field of opera—his older contemporary, Bedřich Smetana—and in this rivalry Dvořák always fell short. Let it be stated at the outset that Smetana may well have been (as Andrew Porter believes) a better opera composer than Dvořák. If we imagine, however, that the two were equally skilled in this area, we shall find a number of reasons why Smetana may nevertheless have come out on top. In other words, the relative failure of Dvořák's operas with the Bohemian public and critics does not necessarily prove that his operas are less worthy. But it did set the pattern for their neglect over the next century, extending to contemporary America.

One of Smetana's advantages was chronology. Older than Dvořák by seventeen years, he reached the height of his creative power precisely at the time of the great upswing in Czech national pride. This upswing was represented musically by the establishment in 1862 of a Provisional Theater for the performance of plays and operas in Czech. (Previously, the language of culture had usually been German, imposed by the ruling Hapsburgs from Vienna.) The presentation at this theater in 1866 of Smetana's first opera, *The Brandenburgers in Bohemia*, was hailed as the dawn of a new era in Czech culture.

By far the best opera ever written in the Czech language up to that time, *The Brandenburgers* had the further advantage of having an explicitly nationalistic plot. Its success was great enough to win for Smetana the post of chief conductor at the Provisional Theater, obviously an advantageous position from which to advance his own cause.[22] Already he began to be viewed by many as the father of Czech music—an image he solidified with his next opera, *The Bartered Bride*. Here we have no explicit national-historical associations, but Smetana consciously tried to give the opera a Czech national character, as noted in his diary of 24 April 1853.[23] *Dalibor*, another opera based on Czech history, followed shortly, and by 1869 he was already working on his grandiose *Libuše*, conceived, in John Clapham's words, "as a glowing apotheosis of the greatness of the Czech nation."[24] John Tyrrell, in his book *Czech Opera*, comments extensively on the preference shown by Czech opera audiences of the nineteenth century for nationalistic works, concluding that "an opera without Czech connections seemed at a disadvantage."[25] There can be no doubt that Smetana's position in this matter contributed to his success.

In 1870, when the young Dvořák entered the field of opera composition with his *Alfred*, he would obviously have had difficulty overcoming Smetana's lead regardless of what approach he took. Amazingly, his approach was to set a German libretto about an episode from the history of England! Could he have been consciously trying to avoid comparison with Smetana by steering clear of the nationalist trend? If so, his strategy backfired. In any case, Dvořák never tried to appeal to Czech nationalist sentiment in the same measure as Smetana did. His other serious operas based on history or historical legend—*Vanda, Dimitrij,* and *Armida*—are likewise set in non-Czech locales (Poland, Russia, and Syria, respectively). *King and Collier, The Cunning Peasant,* and *The Jacobin*, it is true, take place in Bohemia and do celebrate Czech culture in passing, though it is certainly not their main topic or in any way essential to their message. *The Devil and Kate*, though based on a Czech fairy tale, specifies no location and makes no explicit references to any nationality. Neither does *Rusalka*, whose fairy-tale background comes mainly from Western Europe.[26]

Besides having the advantages of a chronological "head start," an orientation toward nationalism, and a position of influence at the Theater, Smetana may also have been helped in his operatic career by the perception that he was a specialist in this particular genre of music—that it was his personal métier. In the end, he completed fewer operas than Dvořák—eight, to Dvořák's eleven. But in proportion to his total output, Smetana's operas occupy a much more prominent position than do Dvořák's, for he did not engage himself in other genres—especially the genres of chamber and orchestral music—to nearly the extent that Dvořák did. (Altogether, he was a less prolific and diverse composer than Dvořák.)

Because of Smetana's emphasis on opera as well as his popular programmatic works for orchestra (especially the cycle *My Fatherland*), he was labeled a "progressive" composer, representing a Czech counterpart to the "New German" school of Liszt and Wagner. This orientation toward the "Music of the Future" came to be viewed by leading Czech critics and musical academics as the proper path of Czech music. But in this light Dvořák had to be seen as something of a reactionary because of his many instrumental works in the old-fashioned genres of "absolute" music—symphony, concerto, and string quartet. Corroboration for this image, conditioned by the machinations of musical politics, came from the world of *real* politics, in that two of Dvořák's opera librettos were written by the daughter of a leading conservative statesman, František Ladislav Rieger.[27]

Meanwhile, Smetana suffered the personal tragedy of deafness and eventual insanity, arousing sympathy from his supporters (and perhaps a little jealousy of Dvořák's rapid and smooth ascent, achieved largely in foreign countries with his instrumental works). In the twentieth century a strident battle arose between advocates of Smetana and Dvořák, with the musicological community (led by Zdeněk Nejedlý) on the side of Smetana. As Marta Ottlová put it in her revealing study of this phenomenon, "The reverence for Smetana explained the vehemence of the anti-Dvořák drive, motivated in the Nejedlý camp by the fear that Dvořák's international success could overshadow Smetana's legacy."[28] The dispute has continued almost to the present day.

Despite these obstacles, several of Dvořák's operas did have a modest success in Bohemia, and it is worth noting that his popularity among Czech opera composers during his lifetime ranked second only to that of Smetana, surpassing a number of lesser contenders. But it was a rather distant second.

What, then, of Dvořák's image in foreign lands? Here we must speak first and foremost of the German-speaking regions where Dvořák had his first international success and where his chief publisher, Fritz Simrock, resided.

In the German-speaking lands, the strife between adherents of absolute music on the one hand and programmatic or operatic music on the other was on its home turf, and it influenced the reception of musical works perhaps even more decisively than in Bohemia. The German scholar Karin Stöckl-Steinebrunner has shown recently how Germanic critics resisted the idea that Dvořák could "straddle the fence" in this dispute.[29] His alignment had been established in their eyes by the mode of his initial entry into the German musical world. This entry had come, naturally enough, by way of Vienna—the capital of the Hapsburg Empire. But Vienna was not only a political capital. In music it represented the headquarters of the absolutists, and it was through the absolutist camp—especially through the composer Johannes Brahms, the critic Eduard Hanslick, and the conductor Hans Richter—that Dvořák found his way to fame.

Ms. Stöckl's study, which focuses on the reception of Dvořák's late symphonic poems, finds that Germanic critics, especially in Vienna, rejected these works but used convoluted and inconsistent arguments. Their criticisms tell us more, she says, about their underlying attitudes than about the pieces themselves: those who had been in the habit of supporting Dvořák the absolutist could not stomach his abandonment of their cause. No doubt the absolutists had a similar prejudice against Dvořák's operas. And this prejudice would probably have been shared by Simrock, for he was himself associated with the absolutist camp, claiming Brahms as his most famous client. Nevertheless, Simrock did publish *The Stubborn Lovers* and *The Cunning Peasant*, complete with German translations, and the latter was then performed in Dresden and Hamburg with some success. But when the work came to Vienna in 1885, the result was a fiasco. Neither Simrock nor any other German publisher ventured further with Dvořák's operas.

Even to this day, the trappings of the absolutist image have clung to Dvořák's name. These trappings include the notions of naiveté and spontaneous, unreflective inspiration, associated by philosophers like Schopenhauer with pure instrumental music as an idealized expression of the Will. According to this aesthetic, music should be created without conscious mental deliberation and without reference to the distortions of the real world outside itself. Dvořák's obituary notice published in the Vienna newspaper *Die Zeit* extols these qualities as his special strength: he was a "great artist in the field of absolute music, 'naive' . . . in the highest and purest sense," for music came to him "naturally, spontaneously and self-evidently. . . . Music is with him only music, nothing more and nothing less. . . . The personality seems here only an executant and vehicle for the work, who bows before the loftiness of his mission with a childlike and calm devotion, indeed perhaps isn't even aware of his true greatness."[30]

But this image of Dvořák, while glorifying his genius, clearly placed limits on it as well, and these perceived limits had a powerful effect when it came to an evaluation of his operatic efforts. This effect was made explicit by the German musicologist Alfred Einstein in his book *Music of the Romantic Era*: "That a musician who created so easily and richly should have tried his hand at opera is not to be wondered at; but likewise little to be wondered at is the fact that a musician so naive, so little 'intellectual' could not become a genuine dramatist."[31]

Did Dvořák's "naiveté" mean that music came to him "spontaneously"? This has been shown to be completely false by numerous studies of Dvořák's sketches, where the working and reworking at every structural level betray an extensive and obviously conscious process of thought.[32] In any case, the image of the naive Dvořák is always coupled with the erroneous assumption that he preferred absolute instrumental music—an assumption apparently made in ignorance of the real proportional distribution of his works among the instrumental and vocal genres. Certainly Einstein's statement that he merely "tried his hand" at opera is misleading; nowhere does Einstein say how many operas Dvořák wrote or mention even one of them by name.

Einstein's book, published forty years after the obituary in *Die Zeit*, represents well the longevity of the conventional image of Dvořák, and also its successful transplantation to America. Einstein and a number of his German compatriots brought their preconceptions with them when they immigrated to this country and found fertile ground for them among impressionable American minds. *Music in the Romantic Era* was the first, and for a long time the only, book on its subject published in this country.

In the tradition of Einstein, misleading or even false information about Dvořák's operatic works is still being propagated in America today. For example, Prentice-Hall's recent book *Music and Society: The Late Romantic Era* cites *Dimitrij* as Dvořák's first opera, apparently unaware of the six operas that in fact came before.[33] Even Leon Plantinga, who affords Dvořák the most complete and accurate coverage in any American general reference work, gets mixed up in his discussion of *Rusalka*, speaking of an Act II love duet between the Prince and Rusalka that does not exist.[34]

The widely circulated view that opera was a sideline for Dvořák, together with his portrayal as "so naive, so little intellectual" (Einstein), doubtless lurks in the back of reviewers' minds when they attempt an assessment of his dramatic works. As John Rockwell has said, "People in this country are desperately unsure of their aesthetic judgment. They are fearful of looking ridiculous if some 'authority' proclaims them 'wrong.'"[35] Thus, it should not be surprising that, in our survey of forty American reviews, the conventional wisdom about Dvořák is to some extent regurgitated. The music itself is almost invariably praised, but many critics—even those favorably disposed toward the work in question—express reservations about Dvořák's thinking in instrumental rather than vocal terms (four reviews), his faulty handling of the drama (five) and/or his poor choice of libretto (twelve).

Rusalka receives proportionately the largest number of criticisms of the libretto. What can you expect, after all, from a libretto that, according to *Opera News*, had been "rejected by several other composers before Dvořák accepted it."[36] The implication here that Dvořák had a very low level of literary discrimination is certainly consistent with his conventional image, but the anecdote turns out to be false. It represents only a slight distortion of the librettist's own testimony, according to which he had shown his work to several composers without really offering it to them; being occupied with other things, they responded with only friendly interest. But the librettist's testimony has recently been exposed as something of a distortion itself: at least one of the composers had in fact responded enthusiastically to the libretto but suggested that the only proper composer for it was Dvořák.[37] Here we can see how distorted views tend to perpetuate themselves, and invent their own justification.

Another legacy of the German critical and historiographical tradition is a peculiar attitude toward nationalism. As already pointed out, Dvořák's operas are *not* especially nationalistic. But in the first histories of nineteenth-century music (which were written by Germans) any composer not living or working in Germany, Austria, France, or Italy was automatically categorized as a nationalist. And Alfred Einstein made explicit the value judgments that lay hidden in this attitude by distinguishing between "nationalism" on the one hand and "universalism" on the other. No composers from "outlying" countries were placed under the "universal" heading.[38]

German ethnocentrism affected Dvořák directly even during his lifetime. In 1885 he asked his publisher Simrock not to print the German form *Anton* for his first name, but rather to use the abbreviation *Ant.*, which would serve both for the German and for the Czech *Antonín*. Simrock's response has unfortunately been lost, but apparently it was negative. Dvořák's next letter begins, "Don't make fun of my Czech brothers. . . . If you cannot fulfill my wish . . . I have the right to consider it an offense on your part which I have not experienced with either English or French publishers."[39]

Racial tension between Germans and Czechs affected Dvořák's operatic ambitions very concretely. Twice in the 1880s he was asked to compose an opera in German for the Vienna Court Opera and urged by some of his Viennese friends to accept the commission. In part, it was a simple matter of practicality—the potential audience for opera in German was inarguably larger than for the Czech equivalent, and it was better that it be composed originally in German rather than relying on often-faulty translations. But the issue of language also symbolized something deeper. In 1882, while conveying one of the requests for a German opera, Hanslick suggested that Dvořák *move to Vienna* for a year or two, for "after such great initial successes your art requires a wider horizon, a German environment, a bigger, non-Czech public." Much later, in 1896, Brahms made the same suggestion and even offered to help Dvořák financially with the move (according to the recollection of Dvořák's son-in-law, Josef Suk). These men knew it would behoove Dvořák to deemphasize his Czech heritage.[40]

All of these invitations and suggestions Dvořák refused, no doubt to the detriment of his operatic career. To the Czechs, as previously mentioned, his nationalism was insufficient, but to the Germans it was excessive.

As though to punish Dvořák for his recalcitrance, the performance in German translation of *The Cunning Peasant* at Vienna in 1885 failed miserably. Besides Dvořák's uncomfortable position vis-à-vis the disputes between absolutists and the New Germans, this failure was certainly influenced by the anti-Czech sentiment in Vienna, which just at that time precipitated student riots. In his sketch for the first part of the oratorio *St. Ludmila*, on which he was working at the time, Dvořák wrote, "Finished during the time when *The Cunning Peasant* was murdered in Vienna."[41] It was to be the last production of any of his operas by a foreign company during his lifetime.

As already stated, German ethnocentric attitudes have surfaced in twentieth-century historiography and criticism through the insidious distinction between "national" and "universal" music. Interestingly, this distinction is rarely made in Great Britain, where Dvořák and other Slavic composers have always fared especially well in the press. But in America, where the discipline of musicology was established largely by German immigrants and where culture seems still to be dependent on its European models, the Germanic viewpoint has taken firm root. If Dvořák's operas are mentioned at all in American reference works, it is invariably under the heading of nationalism, with an implication that their value lies chiefly in the evocation of local color.

Occasionally in the American reviews the supposed nationalism of Dvořák's operas is explicitly blamed for their failure outside his homeland. Hans W. Heinsheimer's pronouncement in *Opera News* is typical:

> Only a few [of Dvořák's operas] made the perilous voyage across the frontier, and never with any lasting luck. Their stories were unappealing if not incomprehensible to audiences not familiar or in natural sympathy with their background, their characters, their spirit and language. . . . Dvořák's operas resist transplanting.[42]

One small symptom, no doubt, of the prevalence of old-line German views in America today is the persistence—one hundred years after Dvořák's dispute with Simrock—of the first name *Anton*. It can even be seen in print among the reviews in our survey, both in *Opera News* and in the *New York Times*.

Ironically, a cursory glance through recent reviews in Germany finds consistent adherence to the Czech form *Antonín*. Indeed, American music critics now seem to be more German than the Germans. Something truly momentous has occurred: the nationalist-universalist dichotomy, along with the procedure of assuming all "outlying" countries to be nationalistic, has now been rejected by the compatriots of its original perpetrators. Carl Dahlhaus, the most respected German musicologist of recent years, has even specifically criticized American music historiography for clinging to this outmoded point of view.[43] His advice on Dvořák's operas would probably be that we should listen to them more as music and less as "Czech" music.

Some few Americans, at least, have begun to suspect that Czech music might have just as broad an appeal as the music of any other country. How refreshing, for example, to find Michael Beckerman's illuminating comment in his program notes for *The Devil and Kate* in St. Louis:

> Some might find it odd that the plot of Dvořák's opera is almost identical to that of the famous old Appalachian folk song . . . "The Farmer's Cursed Wife." Yet this kinship reminds us that it was the universal quality of folklore which appealed to the composer as much as the local color.[44]

Having examined some of the more thorny issues in the reception of Dvořák's operas, issues that took us back in time over a century, let us now proceed to those that are relatively straightforward and more readily evident in our own time.

The most obvious of these issues is the language. A number of the American reviews have gone so far as to speculate that the Czech language is the *only* obstacle to the success of Dvořák's operas.[45] His very first opera, *Alfred*, has a libretto in German, but the composer himself never tried to have it performed or published. All his other operas are in Czech.

Many have taken the view that translation is the appropriate solution. Andrew Porter apparently is of this opinion, attributing the success of *Rusalka* at the English National Opera in part to the use of English.[46] Already the practice of translation has become a virtual cottage industry: *Rusalka* and *The Devil and Kate* have each been given in America in two different English versions. Meanwhile, in 1960, a vocal score of *Rusalka* with yet a third English translation by Daphne Rusbridge was published in Prague by Artia. Still unused in this country, as far as can be traced, are the translations by Arthur Lief for *The Devil and Kate, The Cunning Peasant, Rusalka,* and *The Stubborn Lovers.*[47] Whereas the availability of translations was perhaps a hindrance in the past, it is surely no longer a factor, although the quality of the translations may be another question.

But there seems to be no consensus as to whether English is preferable over the original language. *Rusalka, The Devil and Kate, The Jacobin,* and *Dimitrij* have all been done in America both ways.

The late Lida Brodenová, director of the Sokol Opera in Washington, which gave so many of the American premieres, is one who has attributed the obscurity of Dvořák's operas chiefly to the difficulties of singing in Czech, and yet insisted that they *must* be sung in the original language—that their Czech spirit must be maintained down to the smallest detail.[48]

With this purist approach, one obvious problem is that the audience cannot understand the words. But Paul Horsley, reviewing the Houston *Rusalka*, rightly objects that "American opera-goers don't understand much Italian or German, either, and operas of Verdi and Mozart still form the cornerstones of our repertory."[49] Nevertheless, the use of foreign languages in general may favor inertia in the repertoire once it is set, discouraging the introduction of new works. If it is difficult to become familiar with the stage action, then the audience will favor the works it already knows (Mozart and Verdi). Dvořák's operas missed their chance to enter the repertoire when the works were new (for whatever reasons), and thereafter had a handicap. Recently—but *only* recently—this problem has been ameliorated by the advent of supertitles, used in all the Dvořák performances sung in Czech during the last few years. George Heymont, again reviewing *Rusalka*, put it well: "Today, thanks to the use of supertitles, audiences are ready, willing, and eager to experience anything new."[50]

But there is also the problem of the singers. While most opera stars are familiar with Italian, German, and French, Czech is obviously a rarity and requires special training. Here it may be objected that the Czech lan-

guage did not prevent Janáček's operas from becoming popular—well before
the current interest in Dvořák and still to a much greater degree (at least in
the major houses). But the fact that Janáček overcame this obstacle does not
negate its existence. (As with Smetana, Janáček may indeed have been a better composer than Dvořák, but again there have been factors other than
inherent worth that favored the dissemination of his works—see below.)
Perhaps, to an extent, Dvořák will come in "on Janáček's coat tails," as more
singers become comfortable with the idea of singing in Czech.

Another factor in the neglect of Dvořák's operas has been the Iron
Curtain—now, happily, a part of history. The "Velvet Revolution" of 1989
in Czechoslovakia may actually have contributed in a small way to a positive
interest in things Czech. But for long decades the Iron Curtain most certainly did present an obstacle, involving the internal inefficiencies of the
Communist system as well as barriers to trade and communication. For most
of the last forty years, the dissemination of scores, performing materials, and
recordings of Dvořák's operas has been at the mercy of bureaucratic quag-
mires in Czechoslovakia.

All commercial recordings of Dvořák's operas have originated in
Czechoslovakia, and while a number of them are very fine, their availability
in the West has been spotty at best. Supraphon decided some years ago to
stop selling LPs in the West and has not yet reissued any Dvořák operas on
compact disc with the notable exception of *Rusalka* (see John Yoell's discography in Appendix C.)

Even more serious than the problem of recordings has been the matter
of publication. As mentioned earlier, *The Stubborn Lovers* and *The Cunning
Peasant* were published in Germany during Dvořák's lifetime by Simrock, a
firm that still exists and even has a regular American agent. But neither of
these works is among Dvořák's best efforts, and his other operas have been
published only in Czechoslovakia, meaning that since the advent of the
Communist system they have been difficult to access. Three of them—
Alfred, King and Collier (first setting), and *Vanda*—remain unpublished to
this day. They, of course, were to be included in the Complete Critical Edition of Dvořák's works, begun by the Czechs with high aspiration in the
1950s; but that edition has become bogged down in bureaucratic and financial difficulties and remains unfinished.[51] (On the other hand, we may note
as signal achievements that this edition has indeed published full scores of
Rusalka in 1960, *The Jacobin* in 1966, and *The Devil and Kate* in 1972.)

Regarding publication, Dvořák stands in stark contrast to Janáček,
most of whose operas were published by Universal Edition in Vienna during

his lifetime[52]—and also to Smetana, whose *Bartered Bride* was published in 1893 by Bote and Bock in Berlin. It is not a problem to obtain a score and performing materials for these works. But when the Iron Curtain fell, Dvořák's operas were buried.

The reception of Dvořák's operas in America seems to be in a period of transition. At this time, the words of Peter Berqquist in his program notes for the Oregon *Dimitrij* represent an eminently sane point of view:

> Antonín Dvořák, like Joseph Haydn, set great store by his operas, though neither man's operas are usually considered his finest achievement. Now that Haydn's operas have been more frequently performed, this judgment is increasingly called into question, and perhaps Dvořák's stage works will also be revalued when they have been performed and studied more widely. Since several of them remain unpublished a century after their composition, a final judgment is highly premature.[53]

Given all the obstacles to the dissemination and appreciation of Dvořák's operas, it is perhaps surprising how far they have come in recent years. Now, with the advent of supertitles, the waning of the old musical polemics in Czechoslovakia, the demise of the Iron Curtain, and the abandonment of old Germanistic attitudes in Europe as well (one hopes) as in America, the outlook is more propitious than ever before. If the recent reviews are correct—if Dvořák's operas are valuable art works and deserving of greater attention—then we may expect their progress toward regular repertory status to continue.

NOTES

1. Interview for the Vienna newspaper *Die Reichswehr*, 1 Mar 1904 (author's translation). See *Antonín Dvořák: Letters and Reminiscences*, ed. Otakar Šourek, trans. Roberta Finlayson Samsour (Prague: Artia, 1954), 223. The complete interview in the original German may be found in Klaus Döge, *Dvořák: Leben, Werke, Dokumente* (Mainz: B. Schott's Söhne, 1991), 348–352.

2. Counting as two operas the two completely different settings he made of *King and Collier*.

3. John Clapham, *Dvořák* (New York and London: W. W. Norton, 1979), 135; and also his *Antonín Dvořák: Musician and Craftsman* (New York: St. Martin's Press, 1966), 276.

4. "Opera" in *The New Grove Dictionary of American Music* 3:412–424.

5. John Clapham, *Dvořák*, 116. Clapham refers to the National Conservatory prospectus for 1892.

6. Letter to Jindřich Geisler of 5–6 October 1892. See *Korespondence a dokumenty,* vol. 3, 1890–95, ed. Milan Kuna et al. (Prague: Edition Supraphon, 1989), 149–150.

7. There was also a rumor that Dvořák was working on an opera based on *Uncle Tom's Cabin,* but it was apparently unfounded. See John Clapham, *Antonín Dvořák: Musician and Craftsman,* 282.

8. For information on Dvořák opera performances in the United States before 1960, I depend almost entirely on an invaluable study by Barbara A. Renton, "Dvořák's Operas in the United States: A Preliminary Survey of Performances and Their Reception," in *Musical Dramatic Works by Antonín Dvořák: Papers from an International Musicological Conference,* Prague, 19–21 May 1983, ed. Markéta Hallová et al. (Prague: Česká hudební společnost, 1989), 152.

   For the performances through 1982 I have made no systematic attempt to augment Dr. Renton's data but have added the performance of *The Cunning Peasant,* which came to my attention through correspondence with the late Lida Brodenová of the Sokol Opera. (Details on all Sokol productions were kindly provided by Ms. Brodenová's friend, Judith Fiehler.)

   The status of the 1935 *Rusalka* as the American premiere is well documented by Dr. Renton (147, note 1) and is corroborated by Andrew Porter in the *New Yorker* of 22 December 1975 ("Strange Encounter," 81). My knowledge of productions after 1982 is based on bibliographic searches for reviews, cursory scannings of *Opera News,* and "the grapevine"; there can of course be no guarantee of completeness.

9. *Central Opera Service Directory,* vol. 30, nos. 2–4 (Summer 1990): *Directory of Contemporary Operas & Music Theater Works & North American Premieres 1980–89* (New York: Metropolitan Opera), 261–277. The number of premieres given for Dvořák is actually three, but one of these—the supposed performance of *King and Collier* by Sokol Opera—is a mistake; only one scene from this opera was performed (according to information from Judith Fiehler and Dagmar White).

10. Andrew Porter's New Orleans report ("Czech Masters," the *New Yorker,* 18 March 1991, 98–99) is counted in the survey as two reviews: one of *The Jacobin,* of which large excerpts were performed in New Orleans, and one of *The Cunning Peasant* based on his incidental comments. Otherwise *The Cunning Peasant* would not be represented in the survey, because its only American performance (1961) seems to have been reviewed only in the Czech-American press, *Sokol americký, New Yorské listy,* where the opinions expressed are not suitable for comparison. The Washington *Post,* 9 March 1961, D6, did give a short advance article but made no comments on the merits of the work.

    This survey of reviews is certainly not comprehensive, but it does represent most or all reviews in national magazines or major newspapers, together with a substantial smattering of reports from smaller local papers. Many reviews were provided by the producing organizations, and their selective process (if any) could conceivably reflect a bias in favor of the positive reviews; however, based on comparison of the reviews they provided with those obtained independently, I do not believe this to be the case. I wish to thank the staffs of the Collegiate Chorale (New York), Opera Theatre of St. Louis, Seattle Opera, Houston Grand Opera, and especially, for reviews and general information on the Sokol Opera, Judith Fiehler.

11. Christina Vella, "Review: The Dvořák Festival," the *St. Bernard Voice*, 22 February 1991, 7: "It was clear from the presentation [of opera scenes, in which *The Jacobin* accounted for half the program] that Dvořák's center of gravity was instrumental, not vocal . . . that Dvořák squandered his talent on worthless librettos, just as his critics complained, and that he had a serious problem balancing comic and tragic moods in the same opera." John von Rhein, in "Opera Matters," the Chicago *Tribune*, 1 July 1990, Section 13:18, condemns *The Devil and Kate*, saying it "has heretofore defeated all attempts to export it to opera houses outside its native Bohemia; the St. Louis production showed us why. The music . . . has its charming moments but is insufficient to redeem a libretto that is an ungainly muddle of folkish farce and lofty social idealism." And *The Devil and Kate* is called by Bernard Holland, in the *New York Times*, "a muddled folk opera that testified, against its will, to a composer's single-minded affinity for the orchestra." ("In St. Louis, Small Is Swell, So, Too, Is the Bel Canto," 19 June 1980)

12. 29 October 1979, B11: Lon Tuck, regarding the Sokol Opera performance.

13. 19 February 1991, C-5: Frank Gagnard, "New Orleans Singers Give Voice to Rich Appreciation of Dvořák."

14. Bill Zakariasen, vol. 5, no. 5 (June 1984).

15. Gary Baker, "*Rusalka* by Dvořák—Bring on the Neglected Masterpieces," *Gay News* (Seattle), 16 Nov 1990; Maria Coldwell, "Magic Mermaid," *Seattle Weekly*, 30 October 1990; Steven Smith, "Seattle Opera Creates the Perfect *Rusalka*," University of Washington Daily; Carl Cunningham, "HGO Presents Breathtaking Tale of *Rusalka*," the Houston *Post*, 21 October 1991; Heidi Waleson, "The Sound of the Cutting Edge at Spoleto," the *Wall Street Journal*, 31 May 1988, 20 (W), 22 (F); Andrew Porter, "Strange Encounter," the *New Yorker*, 22 December 1975, 84.

16. The *New Yorker*, 16 April 1984, 150.

17. 22 December 1975, 84; 18 March 1991, 99.

18. 22 December 1975, 84; 16 April 1984.

19. 18 March 1991, 99.

20. See John Clapham, "Dvořák's Operas in Britain," in *Musical Dramatic Works by Antonín Dvořák*, ed. Markéta Hallová et al.

21. Review of the English National Opera production, in *Opera*, January 1985, 106.

22. Smetana was in fact accused by his adversaries of failing to promote Czech operas other than his own. See John Clapham, "The Smetana-Pivoda Controversy," *Music and Letters* 3 (1971), 353–364. However, the present study does not mean to imply that Smetana himself tried to suppress the career of the

young Dvořák. He accepted *King and Collier* (first setting) for a production, though the singers had such difficulty with the work that it had to be withdrawn before the performance. In 1872 he programmed and conducted the overture to this work at an orchestral concert, marking the first time a substantial work of Dvořák had been performed in public, and he followed this up in 1874 with two further landmarks in the young composer's career—the performances of his Third Symphony and the Scherzo from the Fourth Symphony. See John Clapham, *Dvořák*, 26, 32.

23. John Clapham, *Smetana* (London: J. M. Dent & Sons, 1982), 94.

24. John Clapham, *Smetana*, 99.

25. John Tyrrell, *Czech Opera*, Cambridge University Press, 1988, 122–123.

26. Perhaps sensitive to his country's preference for things Czech, *Rusalka's* librettist, Jaroslav Kvapil, argued in his preface to the work that he had imparted a Czech character to the story. (See John Tyrrell, *Czech Opera*, 150.) He admitted, however, that its underlying plot comes not from any Czech source but rather from *Undine* by the German novelist Friedrich de la Motte-Fouqué, and *The Little Mermaid* by Hans Christian Andersen. Another influence, not acknowledged, was Gerhart Hauptmann's *Die Versunkene Glocke*.

27. Marie Červinková-Riegrová, who wrote the librettos for *Dimitrij* and *The Jacobin*.

28. Marta Ottlová, paper delivered at the Dvořák Sesquicentennial Conference in America (New Orleans, 1991). Forthcoming in *Rethinking Dvořák: Views from Seven Countries on the Sesquicentennial of the Composer's Birth*, ed. David Beveridge.

29. Paper read at the Dvořák Symposium of the Saarland Musik Festival, June 1991. Forthcoming in English translation as "The 'Uncomfortable' Dvořák: Critical Reactions to the First Performances of his Symphonic Poems in German-Speaking Lands," in *Rethinking Dvořák: Views from Seven Countries on the Sesquicentennial of the Composer's Birth*, ed. David Beveridge.

30. "Der Fall Dvořák," *Die Zeit*, no. 503 (21 May 1904), 93ff., as quoted by Karin Stöckl-Steinebrunner, ibid.

31. Alfred Einstein, *Music in the Romantic Era* (New York: W. W. Norton Company, 1947), 302.

32. The frequently heard emphasis on Dvořák's melodic gift as his chief asset seems to be a corollary to his portrayal as naive and unthinking. One writer in Seattle attacked this view, quoting page 43 of Erich Leinsdorf's autobiography, *The Composer's Advocate*, where the conductor couples Dvořák with Tchaikovsky. They both "had not only the gift of melodic invention but also their own brand of intellect—a kind that, unfortunately, goes unnoticed by those who declare that polyphony is of foremost importance." See Lois Elliott Hartzell, "Looking Back," *I Virtuosi del Canto* (Newsletter of the Seattle Opera), vol. 3, no. 6 (Jan–Feb 1991), 3.

33. Jim Samson, "East Central Europe: The Struggle for National Identity," in *Music and Society: The Late Romantic Era* (Englewood Cliffs, New Jersey: Prentice-Hall, 1991), 229–230.

34. Leon Plantinga, *Romantic Music: A History of Musical Style in Nineteenth-Century Europe* (New York: W. W. Norton, 1984), 352. Plantinga most likely means the duet between the Prince and the Foreign Princess.

35. *All-American Music: Composition in the Late Twentieth Century* (New York: Alfred A. Knopf, 1983), 80. As quoted in Renton (op. cit., note 8), 146.

36. Yveta Synek Graff, "Water Nymph," *Opera News* vol. 51, no. 12 (28 February 1987), 32.

37. "Rusalka and Its Librettist, Jaroslav Kvapil: Some New Discoveries." Paper read at the Dvořák Sesquicentennial Conference in America (New Orleans, 1991). Forthcoming in *Rethinking Dvořák: Views from Seven Countries on the Sesquicentennial of the Composer's Birth*, ed. David Beveridge.

38. Alfred Einstein, *Music in the Romantic Era*.

39. Letters of 8 August and 22 August 1885. *Antonín Dvořák: Korespondence a dokumenty* 2:75, 87

40. John Clapham, "Dvořák's Relations with Brahms and Hanslick," the *Musical Quarterly*, April 1971, 249–250, 253–254.

41. John Clapham, *Dvořák*, 79.

42. Hans W. Heinsheimer, "In Nature's Realm," *Opera News*, vol. 40, no. 6 (6 December 1975), 34ff.

43. Review of Leon Plantinga's *Romantic Music* in *19th-Century Music*, vol. 9 (1987–88), 195.

44. Michael Beckerman, "Themes and Contexts in Dvořák's *The Devil and Kate*," Opera Theatre of St. Louis Program Book, 1990, 38.

45. Maria Coldwell, "Magic Mermaid," in *Seattle Weekly*, 30 October 1991; and Bill Zakariasen in the *Daily News* (New York), 30 March 1984.

46. Andrew Porter in the *New Yorker*, 25 April 1983, 135–137.

47. Advertisement by Arthur Lief, the *Opera Journal*, vol. 21, no. 4 (1988). I thank Dane Evans for bringing this advertisement to my attention.

48. Lon Tuck, "Washington's Intrepid Impresario," the Washington *Post*, 28 October 1979, G3.

49. Paul Horsley, "Raison d'Opera," Houston *Press*, 31 October 1991.

50. George Heymont, "Risky Repertoire," *Bay Area Reporter*, 7 March 1991.

51. A vocal score of the first version of *Dimitrij* appeared in 1886. *King and Collier* (2nd setting), *The Jacobin* (1st version), *The Devil and Kate*, and *Rusalka* were all published posthumously in Prague between 1905 and 1915. And in 1941, vocal scores of *Armida* and the second version of *The Jacobin* came out in Prague.

52. Mainly in the 1920s (i.e., after the demise of the Hapsburg Empire).

53. Program Notes: *Dimitrij* (program book for the Oregon Bach Festival, Eugene Oregon, 23 June–7 July 1991, 109).

CHAPTER TWENTY-FOUR

How I Wrote "Dvořák in Love"

Josef Škvorecký

$\mathcal{E}$ditor's note: In reviewing Josef Škvorecký's novel *Dvořák in Love* (1987), the *New York Times Book Review* noted that it treated events in the life of the composer "in a highly unorthodox and inventive fashion." It viewed Dvořák, in effect, "through a medley of stories, anecdotes, slices of musical history and tidbits of little-known Americana that is dizzying in its diversity." Compared with the somberness of his previous novels, many of which had music as part of their subject matter, especially jazz— *The Cowards* (1970), *The Bass Saxophone* (1977), and *The Engineer of Human Souls* (1979)—the new novel, translated into English by Paul Wilson, was a benign and tender fable, "a kind of caprice." (Indeed, the Czech title, *Scherzo Capriccioso*, was taken from one of Dvořák's liveliest compositions.) In its shifting moods, to borrow a description offered by one of the characters about blues music, "[It was] great and ordinary. Happy, yet terribly sad." Like music in general, the reviewer concluded, the book intertwined many narrative threads in a sort of counterpoint, compressing and stretching our sense of felt time.[1]

It takes on what Graham Greene described as "the most difficult of all subjects, the life of an artist."[2] In spirit and effect it ranks with a select company of recent novelizations about real composers, such as James Hamilton-Paterson's novel about Edward Elgar, *Gerontius* (1991), and with Ken Russell's flamboyant movie biographies, including *The Debussy Film* (1965), *Mahler* (1974), and *Song of Summer* (about Frederick Delius, 1968). However, unlike Russell, who once boasted he told his stories "in a totally unreal way" in order to "make them more real than ever,"[3] Škvorecký has steeped himself in Dvořák and limited his fantasies to the realms of the probable.

Thus, his novel tantalizes us so cleverly with its deft mixture of fact and speculation, of historical and fictional characters, that even expert Dvořák authorities might have difficulty differentiating among them. Could Dvořák—
irreverently called "Old Borax" by his friends—really have met Will Marion
Cook in Bohemia, as the book reported? Did he hear Scott Joplin's ragtime
music in Chicago at the World's Fair, shake hands with the American theater
visionary, Steele MacKaye, and go barhopping with the music critic and educator, James Huneker? While in Spillville did he serve as foreman in a jury
trial of local bootleggers and assist in disposing of the evidence (an incrimi-
nating barrel of beer)? Was Dvořák's daughter having an affair with her
father's secretary, J. J. Kovařík—and did she almost marry him in a ram-
shackle little Spillville church? Who was "Josephine Harper" (a young black
woman who, in one of the more charming subplots, is befriended by the
aging, gallant Harry Burleigh)? These scenes, moreover, are vividly etched—
the boisterous and boozy nights in New York's Lower East Side saloons, the
summer gardens at Vysoká on a Sunday afternoon, the glittering premiere at
Carnegie Hall of the "New World" Symphony, and that luminous Iowa
night along the Turkey River where, in the book's most spectacular scene,
Dvořák witnesses a vision that inspires his opera *Rusalka*. . . . Moreover,
Dvořák in Love has its own *sound*. Music seeps from the pages, a blend of nasal
saxophones, groaning cellos, thumping sousaphones, and ragtime pianos.

Almost half of *Dvořák in Love* depicts Dvořák's three years in America. Images, vignettes, sketches, letters, and dream sequences flutter by in a
quick succession of changing patterns that create an effect not at all unlike
the experience of listening to the motific repetitions, transformations, and
episodic constructions of Dvořák's late tone poems, or his piano cycle *Silhouettes*. They are narrated through the personae of Dvořák's wife and his friends
and colleagues: Huneker, Burleigh, J. J. Kovařík, Jeannette and Francis
Thurber, several Spillville residents, and a number of incidental characters.

In all, the book is a dazzling performance, and it may have sent more
readers scrambling to find out about Dvořák and his music than anything—
academic or popular—that has been written before or since. It even led Mr.
Škvorecký to his next book. While researching *Dvořák in Love*, he came
across the stories of a number of Czech soldiers who served in Sherman's
Army during the Civil War. In a subsequent novel, *Bride from Texas*, the
author presented a poetic account of how those soldiers took part in the
march through Georgia to the sea on their way to participate in the last big
battle of the war at Bentonville, North Carolina.

In *Dvořák in Love*, the composer emerges as one of those celebrities who, in the words of Leo Braudy in *The Frenzy of Renown*, present a kind of *elasticity* that allows him to signify different things to different generations. "The ability to reinterpret [such figures]," concludes Mr. Braudy, "fills them with constantly renewed meaning, even though that meaning might be very different from what they meant a hundred years before. Such people are vehicles of cultural memory and cohesion."[4] Škvorecký's agenda, clearly, is to view Dvořák as a crucial pivot in American music between Old World traditions and the birth of jazz.

In a paper presented at a symposium in Texas on Czech music, Mr. Škvorecký spoke about *Dvořák in Love* and how he came to write it. The following remarks, based on that address, have been revised by him especially for this volume.[5]

I had never been much interested in what is called "serious" music until I married my wife, who has had a lifelong love affair with Antonín Dvořák. She plays Dvořák's opera *Rusalka* on her stereo at least once a month. From her I got infected with Dvořák's music; or better, she stirred an old memory, half forgotten, which now came back in the full force of beauty, such as most of us can perceive only in our youth.

As a youngster I was deeply in love (platonically, as was not unusual in those days) with a girl in my native town of Náchod by the name of Marie Dyntarová. She was a peach of a girl—golden-haired, with a big red mouth and blue eyes, like an illustration by Rockwell Kent. The town had a Symphony Society which, from time to time, invited famous singers from the National Theatre Opera to perform with the local symphony orchestra. So it happened, one day, that I was watching the stage in the town's fin de siècle theater, U Beránka, sitting in the darkened auditorium. The local mixed choir was rehearsing the great aria of the Waterman character from *Rusalka*, "The Wedding Song," with the National Theater's distinguished basso Eduard Haken. It is an incredibly beautiful melody—for Dvořák was one of the great masters of melodies—and out of the darkness of the stage the spotlight lit up, miraculously, it seemed to me, Marie's face. She was singing with the altos. Her mouth really looked like a sweet strawberry, her blue eyes seemed to have an inner light, and the melody just carried me straight to heaven.

Listening to my wife's *Rusalka* record brought all this back to me. My wife did not mind when I told her. It was so long ago, so innocent, in another country, and besides, the wench was married and had put on a lot of weight.

In 1969, on our way from California where I had a temporary job to Toronto where a steady job awaited me, we decided to visit Spillville, a little village in Iowa, for I knew that Dvořák had spent his first American summer there. We had about a month to reach Toronto, and so we zigzagged across the States to see as much of the "Krásná Amerika" as possible. And so we drove through the Iowa fields and were reminded of the shape of the country in central Bohemia, and when we arrived at the village, we were both charmed. It is still purely Czech: most people manage to speak the language to some extent, and the Czech past is indelibly written across the face of the village. St. Wenceslas Church, according to the local people, was designed by an architect in Prague and modeled on the St. Barbara Cathedral in Kutná Hora. I failed to see the likeness, but it is a sweet, simple Czech church, surrounded by a cemetery the likes of which I had seen nowhere in America. In Dvořák's time, a local blacksmith—who was really an artist—made cast-iron crosses of baroque design for the graves and painted them in silver, so that in moonlight the cemetery is luminescent; and under the full moon it sparkles with an eerie and beautiful sheen. I thought of Dvořák, who played the organ in St. Wenceslas and took walks among the radiating graves in the cemetery, and then and there I decided that one day I would write something about the Maestro. Something. Originally, I was thinking about a film script because everything was so visual in Spillville, but the experience of the years that followed convinced me that I should stick to my proper trade, writing novels. Trying to sell a script—unless you have really good connections in Hollywood—is hopeless. If I managed to write a decent novel and publish it in the States, chances are somebody would eventually film it.

By the early 1980s I felt I was capable of trying the Dvořák novel. Why I felt that is one of the mysteries of fiction. You carry a story in your mind, sometimes for years, knowing you are not yet ready. Then one day you feel that now is the time. And so I took a year of unpaid leave from the University of Toronto, and with the $10,000 from my Neustadt International Prize for Literature, and with a Guggenheim Fellowship, I set out on a journey of research.

You know that in the novel I show that many Americans have a hard time pronouncing Dvořák's name. Actually, that was a real problem. Dvořák was touchy about the pronunciation of his name and tried to teach it to his American friends. The háček (ˇ) above the *r* gives it essentially the same sound as the American *r* in words like *trip* or *pretty,* but more stressed. The

acute accent (ˊ) is used over the vowel to indicate that it should be pronounced long. Meanwhile, the accent goes on the first syllable (all Czech
nouns, verbs, and adjectives are accented on the first syllable). So, "Dvořák"
is pronounced with that first accent, a stressed *r*, and a long vowel. His secretary, J. J. Kovařík spelled his name so that it should be pronounced
"kovarzeek," again with the accent on the first syllable. My own name is pronounced "Shquoretskee," also with the accent on the first syllable.

Enough on Czech phonetics. First, I revisited Spillville and interviewed two old ladies—they were both one hundred years old that
summer—who, when they were twelve-year-old girls, had known Dvořák.
To them, naturally, he looked like an old man, reeking of cigars, though he
was only fifty-two at that time. The girls were not interested in him, but his
children became their playmates, and they kept up correspondence with
some of them for many years afterwards. So I learned quite a few good little
things about life in Spillville in those days.

Second, I walked through the areas in New York City where Dvořák
lived and worked. There is a flavor of myth connected with such places—
that is, if you deeply care about the great man and his lovely daughter, about
Harry Burleigh and Mrs. Thurber, and the others who trod those pavements.

Two more interesting interviews also stimulated my imagination. The
first was in Detroit with Mrs. Josephine Love who, as a young girl, was a
friend of Harry Burleigh, the favorite black colleague of Dvořák from whom
the Master heard, for the first time, Negro spirituals. Burleigh did not really
study with Dvořák, for he studied singing, which Dvořák did not teach. But
he played the timpani in the school orchestra that Dvořák conducted, and
because of his singing he became a friend of Dvořák's family. Among other
things he actually claimed that Dvořák decided to give the great solo in the
second movement (Largo) of the "New World" Symphony to the English
horn, not to the clarinet as he had originally intended, after realizing that
Burleigh's voice had the timbre of the English horn. Whether this is true or
just Burleigh's fantasy, I don't know. But the novel is largely a thing of the
imagination, so I liked the story. From Mrs. Love I learned quite a few interesting things about Burleigh that are not to be found in books, because piti-
fully little has been written about Burleigh—an academic study, a few short
articles, and an obituary (see Dr. Jean Snyder's essay, Chapter 9, on Burleigh.)

Anyway, an interesting thing happened at a party given for me by
Mrs. Love, to which she invited several of her friends. I was the only white
person at the party, and so I did not want to ask one particular question.
There is a portrait of Dvořák in which he does look rather like a Negro. I did
not know how these ladies would take it from me; I thought they might say,

"Oh, you see a Negro in everybody, because you have always been fascinated by Negro music and, according to your own confession, as a student at Charles University you were deeply in love with an African American girl because you discovered that she had pink palms. You are crazy, everybody knows that!" But when the party was at its best, Mrs. Love suddenly turned to me and said, "Don't you think that Dvořák had Negroid features?" I replied, "Thank you for asking me," then borrowed this exchange to use in the book.

My second interview was with Prof. Mercer Cook, the son of Will Marion Cook, who was Dvořák's student for just one semester but became one of the crucial figures to support my secret thesis in the novel, namely, that Dvořák had some influence on the acceptance of jazz in America.

It may sound farfetched, and of course many people will accuse me of seeing jazz in everything because I am simply an aficionado, a buff, and I write about it a lot. For example, some characters in my book *The Cowards* form a jazz band in defiance of the Nazis; and in my *The Bass Saxophone* I touch on the strange life American jazz has had in Czechoslovakia during the forties and fifties. Jazz music is for me a very political thing, a great passion, and an important symbol. It stands for everything Hitler and Brezhnev hated. The Nazis called jazz "Judeo-Negroid music." In my essay "Red Music," I wrote about the swing bands that played in the ghetto at Terezin and in Buchenwald. [Russell Davies, writing in the *Times Literary Supplement*, declared that Škvorecký often employs jazz "in its familiar historical and international role as a symbol (and a breeding-ground) of anti-authoritarian attitudes," Ed.]

Dvořák was a musical genius, but he was not a formally educated man, an intellectual. It is said about him that he was a very lousy teacher of mediocre or bad students, for he was unable to explain things to them. He would look at their homework and then sit down and rewrite it for them. And when one student asked, "But Master, why did you change this to this?" Dvořák would angrily retort, "Don't ask me! This is how it should be — *a basta!*" But he was a great teacher of very talented students. He was simply an inspirational force, but only talented people can be inspired.

So he had a rather simple theory about how great music should be written—a theory inherited from the German Romantic scholars. A composer must first immerse himself in the folk music of his nation. When he is full of that music, he should compose in the spirit of those tunes and melodies and harmonies. He should not *quote*, just write *in the spirit* of that music.

I wonder what must have been going on in the minds of his Negro students (and there were many Negroes at the National Conservatory then) when, at the end of his first year, he conducted the school orchestra, which was all black except for the pianist. In those days many blacks were not interested in discovering their roots. They wanted to forget about them. They wanted to prove that anything the white man could do, they could do equally well; and that included music. Will Marion Cook is a good example. The Negro community of Washington collected money so that he could go to Berlin to study the violin under Josef Joachim, the greatest violin pedagogue of the time, a personal friend of Dvořák. Will went and became a sensation, partly because of the amount of money he had at his disposal (which he quickly squandered but which, for a short time, made him one of the wealthiest students at the school); and partly because he was a very handsome young man—at the time the only *black* man in Berlin. So he became a sensation among the Fräuleins of Berlin, as he writes in his unfinished autobiography. Under Joachim he became an accomplished virtuoso in the classical European style. Then he returned to America, and after one semester under Dvořák something happened to him. Mind you—I do not want to create the impression that it was just because of Dvořák that Will Marion Cook became what he became—there were his friends, among them Paul Laurence Dunbar, who formed the nucleus of what later became the Harlem Renaissance. Things were in the air. But still, if you remember Dvořák's simple theory and think of the fact that the classically schooled violinist turned from the violin to composing Negro musicals, you might just agree that Dvořák's influence had a wee bit to do with it. What might Dvořák have written had he stayed here and lived to see the age of the saxophone? Anyway, Cook composed the very first Negro musical show to be produced on Broadway, *Clorindy; or, The Origin of the Cake Walk*, and his mother's reaction to this piece of musical creation is characteristic of the thinking of the blacks of those times. When the poor lady witnessed her son's first success, she said, "Oh! Will! I send you all around the world so that you become a great musician, and you return such a Nigger!"

Later, Cook conducted his own band, the Southern Syncopated Orchestra, with which he toured Europe in 1919. It was the first non-military black band to tour Europe. Among his sidemen was also one Sidney Bechet who, on this tour, discovered in a London music shop what he first believed was a metal clarinet and what, in fact, was the soprano saxophone. On the repertoire of the orchestra there was also Dvořák's *Humoresque* in Cook's arrangement. It was not a jazz band, just a proto–jazz band. But still. . . .

Then, don't forget, some of Dvořák's students of composition became professors at the National Conservatory, and among their students were people like Aaron Copland and George Gershwin. *Porgy and Bess,* for example, seems to have been composed according to Dvořák's recipe, in the spirit, without quotes. After Cook had lost most of his orchestra he became, among other things, a tutor of Duke Ellington. The Duke talks about him in several interviews and even says that everything he learned about arranging he learned from Cook. They were very good friends indeed. Ellington named his son *Mercer* after Will Marion Cook's middle name. (Cook had replaced it with *Marion* since the man after whom he had been named did not behave, in the opinion of Will, as a proud black should behave.)

My first problem was determining what approach I should take to writing about Dvořák himself. I decided right at the beginning that I would not attempt to enter the Master's mind. I don't like to enter anybody's mind; therefore I usually use the first person singular narrative mode, or—if I use the third person—then there is usually one center of consciousness. And to enter Dvořák's mind . . . he was a musical genius, a nineteenth century man. . . . It would be preposterous. Moreover, he was in the States in the 1890s, which was an extremely interesting decade, the decade of transition between two life-styles, the decade of the big inventions that changed life so much, the decade of the great Columbian Exhibition, the time when the blacks first tried to find a voice of their own among the many voices of the continent.

So I decided two things: I should look at Dvořák through the eyes of several people, tell his story through the voices of both Czechs and Americans, men and women, intellectuals and simple people, blacks and whites. Secondly, I should try to paint not only Dvořák but also the society, the lives, the times, the America of his days. At least as much as I would be able to.

So I read many books—not just the books that have been written about Dvořák in Czech, English, and German but also many books on the 1890s in America. And I had to decide which of the real people around him would become my narrative "voices" and which I would create myself. Then I had to deal with the blending of fictional events and characters with factual history. I don't know if I have a method, but I do have one rule: invented events that could have happened, and which do not conflict with the known characters of persons involved, are permitted in historical fiction. I suppose that's a rule that everybody respects.

I was attracted to Mrs. Jeannette M. Thurber as one of my narrators, "voices," for example, because she was a truly great lady of the past century (she died in 1946 in her mid nineties), the founder of the American Opera Company, which was based on the typical patriotic-democratic idea that the American people were entitled to the great operas in their own language. (In the nineteenth century, operas in America were usually sung in their original languages.) Another idea of Mrs. Thurber's was that only the best was good enough for the simple American theatergoer, and so she spent so much money on her Opera Company that the company went bankrupt after two seasons. Then she founded the National Conservatory, basing it on an ingenious scheme. Poor pupils, which included blacks, were to be admitted. They would pay no tuition fee, but after graduation, for the next five years, they would pay a certain percentage of their professional income back to the school. The trouble was that the majority of the students were girls, and in the nineteenth century the first career for every woman was marriage, which ended all possibilities of another career. So most graduates never had any professional careers, and therefore they had no professional incomes of which to pay a percentage. But Mrs. Thurber persisted, and the Conservatory remained a living institution for many years.

Another voice was Mrs. Thurber's husband. He was also an interesting character, a typical self-made man of the nineteenth century with schemes that sound like "people's capitalism." He sold shares of his vast enterprises to his employees, and he was one of the leaders in the antimonopolist movement. Eventually he lost his fortune (the cause of some financial misunderstandings between Dvořák and Mrs. Thurber), went into law, and soon made another fortune.

Many other characters begged me to let them speak out. There was Theodore Thomas, the first serious American conductor, the man who introduced Dvořák's music to America in many instances, also a self-made man. There was Adele Margulies, the Viennese pianist whom Mrs. Thurber sent to Dvořák as her emissary. Some readers think I made her up. No, I found out about her in a German music dictionary. She apparently toured America at the turn of the century with her own piano trio. She died in Vienna shortly before Hitler's Anschluss.

I also decided to look at Dvořák through the eyes of a simple but lively Czech servant girl named Rosie. She was the creation of a Czech-American journalist. I found out about her in the old nineteenth-century Czech humorous weekly, *Šotek*, published in Chicago. She wrote frequent letters about America to her sister Márinka in Skrčená Lhota. The letters are in very radical American Czech so that Miss Rosie's family in Skrčená Lhota cannot understand them now, and even the local priest is unable to decipher the mysterious messages. I could not resist her. I later edited and published her letters with my company, the Sixty-Eight Publishers in Toronto.

Which incidents in *Dvořák in Love* are fictional and which can I fully document? Well, I cannot prove that Will Marion Cook ever visited Bohemia, which is how my book begins, but he was in Berlin at the time of Miss Margulies's recruiting visit. She knew him and he was indeed something of a dandy, so I felt entitled to send him to Bohemia to meet Dvořák. There are incidents in the book where Dvořák goes barhopping with James Huneker. Well, they *did* go barhopping—Huneker wrote about it! I based the character of Jessie—the young lady who meets the aging Harry Burleigh—on Josephine Love. I mentioned interviewing her. She is still very much alive, and I met her in the fall of 1991 at a Dvořák commemorative concert in Washington. I had first heard about her from a librarian in Chicago who told me about her friendship with Burleigh. She graciously agreed to write the Introduction to my recent publication of the manuscript score of Dvořák's "Old Folks at Home" (see Dr. Root's essay on that work, Chapter 18).

Elsewhere in the book I included scenes where Dvořák meets Scott Joplin at the Chicago 1893 World's Fair and where he shakes hands with the great American theater entrepreneur Steele MacKaye in New York. Well, it is practically certain that Dvořák did hear some early prototypes of ragtime in the States, and it is not unlikely that he met Scott Joplin. Joplin was at the Columbian Exhibition when Dvořák was there. And there is, of course, the testimony of James Huneker, Dvořák's colleague from the Conservatory and one of the few men who did not like the "New World" Symphony. He was probably envious. A man of many talents, none of them perhaps really great, he wrote the first American novel in which Dvořák appears, *The Painted Veils*. More important, he wrote an obituary when Dvořák died in which he says that Dvořák's influence on young American composers was thoroughly detrimental because it is owing to him and others like him that these young composers now listen to ragtime and think it is music!

As for Steele MacKaye, he too was active at the World's Fair and a prominent part of the New York theater world. In the book I quoted an article from *Harper's Monthly* that he met Dvořák. There is no such article! I based my suppositions on the biography of MacKay, *The Life of Steele MacKaye*, written in 1927 by his son, Percy, and I copied its pompous and

exaggerated tone when I fabricated the *Harper's* article. The biography, by
the way, mentions that Dvořák at one time was going to write music for a
production MacKaye was planning for the World's Fair.

Elsewhere, I tried to solve an old puzzle that no one else, to my
knowledge, had yet unraveled. I may be mistaken here, but anyway. . . I
speculated that while in Spillville Dvořák's daughter had fallen in love with
his secretary, J. J. Kovařík, and that they had tried to elope. I thought this
might have been the reason the Dvořák family left rather suddenly to return
to New York. There has always been a persistent rumor in Prague that while
in Spillville Dvořák's oldest daughter, Otilka, fell in love with an Indian and
tried to elope with him. They were caught in time and Dvořák cut the
sojourn in Spillville unexpectedly short (although, according to the testimony of his letters, he enjoyed himself in Spillville immensely). You can find
echoes of this rumor even in some less scholarly articles on Dvořák's American years. Now, I never quite believed it. First, there were no Indians in
Spillville in the 1890s—they had been moved elsewhere years before. Indian
musicians and dance groups visited the village from time to time, performed,
collected the pitiful money the villagers gave them, and moved on. One such
group did actually perform in the village while Dvořák was there. But these
Indians were poor, destitute, probably dirty, mostly probably alcoholic
unfortunates. That a girl from one of the best Prague families could fall in
love with such a creature who certainly was nothing like the idealized noble
savages of James Fenimore Cooper—that seemed to me impossible. Nevertheless, I asked Mrs. Mary Klimesh, one of the old ladies still living in
Spillville, "Is it true, Mrs. Klimesh, that Otilka tried to elope with an
Indian?" The lady's reaction was quite strong. "No!" she cried. "Not with an
Indian!" The formulation of the sentence and the stress told me, of course,
that while the seducer of innocence was not of the Indian race, there *was* a
seducer of innocence. So I harped on the identity of the villain, until Mrs.
Klimesh said hesitantly, "Well . . . there was some talk about her and the son
of Mr. Kovářík (her pronunciation), the headmaster." And I was home. The
headmaster's son was J. J. Kovařík, whom Dvořák hired to teach him English
in Prague, where the young man was studying the violin. He returned home
to America with Dvořák's family, became Dvořák's American secretary, and
persuaded the Maestro that he should not go back to Bohemia for his first
summer vacation but to Spillville to see how American Czechs were living.
Even books as chaste as Šourek's biography of Dvořák mention the fact of J.
J. Kovařík's tender feelings for Otilka. The less Victorian biographies write
about that attachment quite freely. And Dvořák had a nickname for the love-

lorn youngster who later became a very successful musician in New York and married another lovely Czech girl. The Maestro called his daughter's suitor "Ty indiáne!" or "Indian!" So I decided to include a scene in my book where Kovařík attempts to elope with Otilka and marry her in a small church outside of Spillville. I think such an event is quite possible. Such things cannot be proven—not until the Dvořák family in Prague releases family letters that are known to exist but have never been seen by researchers. For now, at least, I think it quite legitimate to include that scene.

Finally, some readers have questioned me about the episode in the book where Dvořák, during one of his nightly walks along the Turkey River in Spillville, is inspired to compose the "Song of the Moon" aria, which later appeared in the opera, *Rusalka.* Yes, I do think the first sketch for that aria was in Dvořák's American notebooks. Obviously, this haunting melody was written in America. The episode itself, of course, is fiction.

Well, I'll stop here. I know this is a rambling account, but I am still so full of the Dvořák adventure that I find it difficult to sort out and organize my thoughts. . . .

NOTES

1. Eva Hoffman, "A Soft Spot for Sousaphones," the *New York Times Book Review,* 22 November 1987, 11.

2. Graham Greene's remarks on "artist biographies" as a genre occur in his review of Alexander Korda's film, *Rembrandt* (1936). See *Graham Greene on Film,* ed. John Russell Taylor (New York: Simon and Schuster, 1972), 117.

3. John Baxter, *An Appalling Talent: The Films of Ken Russell* (London: Joseph, 1973), 138. This volume consists of a series of interviews with the filmmaker. For more detailed discussions of Russell's composer biographies, see Ken Hanke, *Ken Russell's Films* (Metuchen NJ: Scarecrow Press, 1984). For a more general discussion of such films by Russell and other filmmakers, see John C. Tibbetts, "The Lyre of Light: Composers on Film, *Film Comment,* vol. 27, no. 6 (January–February 1992).

4. Leo Braudy, *The Frenzy of Renown* (New York: Oxford University Press, 1986), 15.

5. Josef Škvorecký's "How I Wrote Dvořák in Love" originally appeared in a different form in *Papers from Czech Music in Texas: A Sesquicentennial Symposium,* ed. Clinton Machann (College Station TX: Komensky Press, 1987), 159–169. Reprinted by permission. Revision courtesy of Josef Škvorecký.

CHAPTER TWENTY-FIVE

New Soundings

The Dvořák Sesquicentennial Conference and Festival in America (New Orleans, 1991)

John C. Tibbetts

*M*ardi Gras stayed late in New Orleans this year. Several days after Fat Tuesday, exotic apparitions crowded the stage of Le Petit Théâtre du Vieux Carré in the French Quarter. Three Wood Nymphs clad in leaf-green tatters fled from the advances of a savage-looking Gnome wearing a great headdress made of sea-weeds. Presiding over the revels was a beautiful Mermaid, slim and tall in her aqua-green sheath.

This was not a Carnival ritual, but a scene from Antonín Dvořák's fairy-tale opera, *Rusalka*. Participants and guests of the "Dvořák Sesquicentennial Festival and Conference in America," held February 14–20, 1991 in New Orleans in honor of the composer's 150th birthday year, had gathered this evening for a program of excerpts from seven of Dvořák's rarely produced operas—including *Rusalka, King and Collier* (Second Setting), *Dimitrij,* and *The Jacobin.* Some of these scenes were receiving their North American premiere—thanks to the stalwart efforts of performers from the University of New Orleans, Tulane University, the New Orleans Opera, and Loyola University.

A cross-stitch of exotic tints, half-lights, smells, and sounds continued throughout the week-long meetings and concerts in the French Quarter and other parts of the city. The step-rhythms of Czech Obkročák and Sousedská dances mingled with the driving riffs of Dixieland jazz. Czech folk costumes moved among stiff business suits. Pungent aromas of Cajun spices and craw-fish blended with Czech dishes like *Pivní Polévka* and *Ryba Na Černo*—beer

The Hotel St. Marie in the Latin Quarter of New Orleans was the site for the conferences of the Dvořák Sesquicentennial event. (Courtesy of John C. Tibbetts.)

soup and fish in black sauce. (By the way, I must here go on record and declare I am *not* a fan of beer soup!) A mix of languages created an international "music" of its own—Russian, Czech, German, and English peppered with Slavic consonants, Southern drawls, and London slang. Native Czechs discoursed on American music; Americans authoritatively talked about Czech music; and a Texan named Danny Jann spoke of his great-great-grandfather—Antonín Dvořák.

"Bringing together so many scholars, musicians, and enthusiasts from so many different countries is the thing I'm most proud of," said conference and festival director David Beveridge, an associate research professor of music at the University of New Orleans. Working with Dr. Alan Houtchens, the conference coordinator, and assisted by Emily Corbello and Lucinda Houtchens, he was the busiest man in town this week. He coordinated the transportation, punched the tickets, manned the phones, introduced the guests, guided the tours, and lost a lot of sleep. "After more than ten years of Czech-related conferences all around the United States—from San Diego to St. Louis—we can at last have Dvořák here in New Orleans. And we can keep most of the events within walking distance of the French Quarter!"

The conference's scholarly presentations, most of which were held in the Hotel St. Marie, just a block from Bourbon Street, were grouped into six major categories: (1) Dvořák in historical perspective; (2) Dvořák as a Czech nationalist; (3) Dvořák as a European composer; (4) Dvořák's impact upon America; (5) America's impact upon Dvořák; and (6) Dvořák's relatively unknown vocal and instrumental works. Impressive indeed was the fact that all the Czech guests conversed and delivered their papers in English.

Dr. Jarmil Burghauser of Prague, an eminent Dvořák and Janáček scholar and president of the Dvořák Society in Czechoslovakia, opened the conference sessions with a general portrait of the composer. "Some saw him as both a progressive and a conservative; to others he was a primitive, a simpleton—a kind of 'popular' Brahms, incapable of deeper artistic reflection. Some Germans distrusted his personal, 'Czech' style, while the English loved him for it." (Later, speaker Alan Rich of the Los Angeles *Daily News* quoted Sir Donald Tovey's description of the composer as "naive," his music possessing "the solemnity of a cat chasing its tail.") Dr. Burghauser continued, "Now we are in a position to better assess Dvořák's importance as an international artist and citizen. He was a *second* generation Czech composer," he said. "While Smetana was of that first generation to proclaim Czech nationalism, Dvořák opened a window not only to get Czech music out to the rest of the world but to let European music *in.*"

Papers delivered by Professors Klaus Döge, Jarmila Gabrielová of Prague, Malcolm Hamrick Brown of Indiana University, Miroslav K. Černý of Prague, Leon Plantinga of Yale, Conrad Donakowski of Michigan State, and Dr. Graham Melville-Mason of the British Dvořák Society all dealt in one way or another with the paradox of Dvořák's Czech roots and international citizenship—that he could synthesize Bohemia's national idioms with European and American traditions. Dr. Donakowski compared Dvořák to the character of the Schoolmaster Benda in *The Jacobin* (scenes from which had been performed during the previous evening's opera concert). Benda had used music to mediate the disputes between Old and New, represented by the characters of a conservative Count and his son, accused of being a "radical" Jacobin. "Like Benda, Dvořák managed to be both tribal and cosmopolitan," Dr. Donakowski said. "On the one hand, he knew the outside 'avant-garde music' of Wagner; the world was his town. But on the other, he was also a village craftsman, a man of his own soil." In more purely musical terms, Dr. Miroslav Černý of Prague and Dr. Rey Longyear of the University of Kentucky assessed Dvořák's musical accomplishment as essentially a progressive extension of traditional form: "He used the technique of developing variation to loosen up the stiff forms of the early nineteenth century," concluded Dr. Černý.

By way of a rather whimsical contrast to all this, Dr. Melville-Mason recounted some of the perplexities Europeans and Americans have always had with Dvořák: "When the young Edward Elgar first heard Dvořák's music in 1883, for example, Elgar said, 'I cannot describe it—it must be heard.' On the whole, an astute observation! Anticipating the problems encountered later by the Americans, Elgar spelled out Dvořák's name with linguistic markings over *every* letter—just to make sure he would get *something* right!" Most of the papers were insightful and thought-provoking. A few—notably Dr. Brett Cooke's excursion into the "mermaid themes" of *Rusalka*—were delightfully comic, almost ribald, while a few others almost drowned in their own academic, rather humorless sauce. In the latter instance, for example, in his zeal to link Dvořák with the European musical establishment, one scholar exceeded his time limitation by more than a half hour, citing dozens of musical parallels, exhaustively piling thematic and harmonic illustrations one on top of the other until the whole stack (and the conference audience) threatened to collapse. Howls of protest arose. "This is nothing more than shooting fish in a barrel," muttered a disgruntled Maurice Peress, former assistant conductor of the New York Philharmonic.

If Peress occasionally adopted the role of iconoclast, Professor Gary Cohen of the University of Oklahoma maintained a more cool, objective stance. A specialist in Czech-Austrian history in the late nineteenth century, he called for a closer study of Dvořák's specific social and cultural contexts. Who were Dvořák's friends? Whom did he read? What were his politics, his civic functions, his intellectual interests? "Too much Western scholarship here is narrow," he explained to me later. "Too often music scholars in the West have too little access to the collateral fields of general history and intellectual history in these countries. Plus, it is difficult for us to master the Czech language. And all this is compounded by a rather limited access to the scholarship in monographs and journals not readily available to the West. So you see narrowness and gaps in much of the work by Western scholars. As a result, other scholars see this as a second- or third-rank area of research and leave it as a kind of 'backwater.' Improving the situation is what this conference is all about."

A particularly important topic of the conference sessions was Dvořák's three-year sojourn in America. According to Dr. Milan Kuna, of Prague, Dvořák decided to come to the United States because he was curious about the musical traits of the African Americans and the Native Americans. "He was the only composer in Europe capable of understanding America's native musical idioms," he explained. Dr. Mark Germer of the University of the

Arts in Philadelphia reminded us rather dryly that another prime motivation was the large salary offered him. Maurice Peress, who is currently preparing New York concerts of the music of Dvořák's Conservatory pupils, delivered one of the more enthusiastically acclaimed presentations on these topics. He sensed an éminence grise, a shaping power, behind Dvořák's controversial New York *Herald* articles championing native music. Peress argued they were heavily influenced by music critic Henry Krehbiel, who had his own agenda in promoting the music of African Americans.

Yet, argued Dr. Charles Hamm of Dartmouth in an important address, there is no mistaking Dvořák's genuine interest and prescient vision regarding American music. Dr. Hamm claimed that Dvořák never said a "native" American music should be based on a particular ethnic group, such as Native American or African American idioms. There was actually no such thing as just one single "American" race, since the country was made up of the commingling of many different nationalities. American music inevitably must be a mixture of the musics of the various groups cohabiting the country. To be sure, Dvořák's statements antagonized a New England establishment more preoccupied with linking American identity with Anglo-Saxon roots rather than with "alien" groups like Jews, Indians, and blacks. "For example," said Hamm, "Dvořák knew that the songs of Stephen Foster and others were not the folk songs of Southern blacks but the contemporary products of white, professional songwriters. The future of American music, he predicted, would bring similar songs derived from other ethnic groups, reflecting the complex multicultural contemporary life of the United States. This new 'classical music' would *grow out of,* not be based upon, these specific ethnic groups. This would in fact become the Anglophile's worst nightmare—music by immigrant, urban, Jewish composers with names like Berlin, Gershwin, Copland, drawing on elements of black, Jewish, Irish, Italian, and Anglo-American styles." In conclusion, Dr. Hamm suggested that Dvořák's most important contribution to American music was "his vision, his foresight and audacity in suggesting that contemporary, commercially produced, popular music could be the national song of the United States at a time when his American peers were blinded by their ethnocentricity."

And what of the supposedly "American" character in Dvořák's music? David Beveridge reiterated at one point that he remains convinced there are indeed distinctive American qualities in the "New World" Symphony and the "American" Quartet and Quintet, and it is merely a question of time and work to locate and identify them. A song recital by Cynthia Haymon allowed us to compare some of Dvořák's American songs (the *Biblical Songs*) with spirituals arranged by his friend and associate, the black composer Harry T. Burleigh—the man who first acquainted Dvořák with the spirituals that purportedly inspired the "New World" Symphony. Thomas Riis of the University of Georgia traced the connections between Dvořák's pupils and later composers Duke Ellington and Aaron Copland. In what was to me one of the more memorable presentations of the conference, Michael Beckerman discussed the piano Suite, Opus 98, a work written just after Dvořák's Spillville summer. It is a major work, Beckerman declared, not the unimportant trifle dismissed by many critics. Its "American" qualities do not reside so much in its use of "Indian" pentatonic scales, but in its evocation of a distinctively American landscape. Indeed, it is a new kind of "pastoral." Quoting passages from Dvořák's letters, Beckerman claimed that the composer was overwhelmed by the vast spaces of the American prairie. The static forms and melodies in the Suite successfully reflect this new sensibility. It was a singularly moving moment when, after Beckerman's paper, the man who first recorded the Suite, Radoslav Kvapil, came forward to perform an excerpt for us.

Edward "Duke" Ellington credits Will Marion Cook as an important influence on his musical career. Drawing by John C. Tibbetts.

There were also many insights into Dvořák's other, non-American musical works—many of them relatively unknown. The Emerson String Quartet played and discussed passages from the rarely heard Terzetto and the C Major String Quartet. They isolated instrumental textures and daring harmonic experiments, showing us how Dvořák's music occasionally foreshadowed the advanced harmonies of Schoenberg. "There are passages," admitted first violinist Philip Setzer, "where you have to be careful about balancing the instruments, but on the whole the writing is better than you see in Brahms." Each of the players had questions for the Czech editors in our midst who had prepared the very editions they were playing. It was a stimulating give-and-take conversation. "Rarely can we perform before such a unique, informed group," cellist David Finckel and his wife, pianist Wu Han later told me. (She celebrated her birthday during the Festival week.) "We can learn a lot. Besides, we want to perform more of this repertoire in the future."

Czech pianist Radoslav Kvapil shared with us his lifelong devotion to the underrated Dvořák piano music. In the suite called *Silhouettes*, for example, he demonstrated Dvořák's unique piano sound. "It has not the big shape of Liszt," he told us, isolating and repeating certain passages for analysis. "It is something new, simpler, with a beauty of *details* and tones that changes constantly with every repetition." As for the Piano Concerto, which he had performed at the Festival's opening concert, he explained how Dvořák's original conceptions for the work had been altered later by other editors. "In the version most of you know, they changed his sound, they 'watered it down,' as you say, making it more like a German music," he explained, comparing original and altered passages. It was clear how in each instance, the original conception was more fresh and distinctive than the smoother, more conventional later revisions. "That is why I play the original version," he concluded, "although many pianists don't like it because it's so difficult in ways that don't show them off."

Some of the works examined were so obscure they were virtually unknown to all but the most learned scholars. Choral conductor Nick Strimple, of the Choral Society of Southern California, introduced us to the massive *St. Ludmilla* oratorio. He had revived it for a 1985 performance in Los Angeles—the first American performance in this century. "This is a major discovery," he said after playing some excerpts. "I have seen audiences stunned by this music. Absolutely stunned." Professors Klaus Döge of Freiburg, Dan Jacobson of the University of North Dakota, and Bruce Gbur of the University of Georgia respectively tantalized us with, presentations on the rarely heard *Cypresses* song cycle, the Gypsy Songs, and works for male chorus. Another highlight was the full-scale performance at a Sunday evening concert in St. Louis Cathedral of Dvořák's Mass in D Major. The Louisiana State University A Cappella Choir and the University of New Orleans Chamber Singers, from their positions along the flag-bedecked galleries, filled the golden dome with the sounds of Dvořák's assured and serene faith.

☙❧

Inevitably I found myself wondering, perhaps not inappropriately, how it might have been had Dvořák himself come to New Orleans. "If he had, he'd have put more syncopation into his famous *Humoresque*," quipped Dr. Michael Beckerman of Washington University in St. Louis. It was near the end of the week and we were sitting in the courtyard adjoining the conference rooms of the Hotel St. Marie. A chill, gray morning had brightened by noontime. Beckerman was quick to credit the various funding agencies for their invaluable support of Czech music conferences over the last ten years—especially the National Endowment for the Humanities and the International Research and Exchanges Board (IREX). "Without IREX, particularly, this small but invigorating field of Czech musical studies would not exist as it does today," he said. "You know, the amount of ignorance today about Eastern Europe, even from the viewpoint of academics and intellectuals, is astonishing. People have no idea where the countries are and what other countries they border. But we happen to think Czech music is simply quite a marvelous place from which to look at the musical landscape. It's of the mainstream but not in it. We all came from the German tradition and yet we have this other bailiwick from which we can look back and forth and see how the traditions interact."

The sun was out now, and the splashing sounds of a fountain drifted across the courtyard. "I guess in a way we've been able to mount a real attack on the primarily German-bound approach to music history," Beckerman continued. "Here in America the idea about what was good in music came from German articles of faith toward music. This dominated the field of musicology, and I was told in my student years that Dvořák was 'watered-down Brahms,' for example. Part of our job is to gently but forcefully suggest that there are other ways of writing music history. But we mustn't forget not to get carried away with our advocacy. In a scholarly context, too much advocacy can smack of a kind of nepotism—an intellectual nepotism where we may seem so predisposed to like something by a particular composer or group of composers that a real spirit of inquiry is abandoned. We must be prepared to find problems with the music we study. We study Czech music because we love it but we're trying to find a more even-handed view of music in general. We even perhaps wish to rewrite the musical maps, suggesting that how we listen to music has been conditioned by the way we have been preconditioned to hear it. These conferences are exchanges in a real sense.

"It is now the turn of the Czechs to propose a series of initiatives on their own. Some things being talked about in the near future include conferences about nationalism in music—be it Czech or Iranian or whatever; and the role of Prague in the musical life of several centuries."

As I reflect back on this incredibly rich and stimulating week of conferences and concerts, I cannot escape the image of Dr. Jarmil Burghauser, always smiling, always impeccably dressed, always present to contribute to every session. In many ways he was the soul of this festival and conference. Twenty years ago political repression hampered his researches in Prague. "I was not allowed to go abroad," he told me. "During Dubcek's time I was 'on ice,' how you say. My writings about Dvořák were published without my name." Now, at seventy, Burghauser enjoys newly regained freedoms. He has been to America three times, and during this last trip he and his Czech colleagues were designated Honorary Citizens of New Orleans by Mayor Barthelemy. In turn, he has played hospitable host and counselor to the young American scholars who now visit him regularly in Prague. He divides his time between working as the "Chief Scout" of the Boy Scouts of Bohemia and Moravia and completing the long-awaited Critical Edition of Dvořák's works, begun since the copyrights lapsed in the mid-1950s. He is also revising his Dvořák Thematic Catalogue. One of his most cherished hopes is that he can help stimulate a new generation of scholars and enthusiasts in their own Czech studies.

But there is another hope, as yet unfulfilled.

"One thing we do not yet have in Prague," he mused rather sadly, "is a statue or monument to Dvořák! Do you know that to this day there is *not one statue* to honor Dvořák?" After a pause he smiles broadly again, a speculative light in his eyes.

I think I know what's on his mind.

CHAPTER TWENTY-SIX

The Melody Lingers On

John C. Tibbetts, Mark Rose, and Steven Richman

*D*vořák left New York with his wife and son Otakar for the last time on 16 April 1895, missing the American premiere of *The American Flag* on 4 May by less than three weeks. They sailed on the SS *Saale*, the same ship that had brought the composer to the New World nearly three years before. There had been financial complications between him and Mrs. Thurber and, as he had written her earlier, "I love the American people very much and it has been my desire to help Art in the United States, but the necessities of life go hand in hand with Art, and t[h]ough I care very little for worldly things, I cannot see my wife and children in trouble."[1]

Although the financial complications were resolved in part, the composer nonetheless missed his family very much, and he was heard to complain that Conservatory duties were restricting his composing time. "If I could work as free from cares as at Vysoka," he wrote a friend in Prague, "but here it is not possible—on Monday I have work at school—on Tuesday I am free—the other days are more or less taken up—in short I cannot give so much time to my work, and if I could, again I am not always in the mood etc. . . . . Oh, if only I were [at Vysoka] again!"[2] He decided, therefore, not to extend his teaching contract, and he wrote his letter of resignation to Mrs. Thurber from Bohemia on 17 August. It was a ticklish situation: for his part Dvořák still was under some obligations to her; but she still owed him money. Presumably, under the circumstances, notes Clapham, Thurber accepted his resignation with good grace.[3]

He had arrived almost three years before, full of anticipations. Now he left brimming with memories. Crowding his mind's eye were the strange localities and the unfamiliar faces he had seen. It was still a mystery what he would remember and what he would forget. How odd—and how wonderful, in a way—that we must find a place only to lose it again. . . .

He brought back to Bohemia what other travelers bring back to their native lands after their journeys—a greater sense not so much of where he had been, perhaps, but of what he was returning to. Travel had narrowed his mind in the sense that he had whittled down his fanciful dreams of the New World and replaced them with more specific images, sounds, and places. As a result, his homeland and the joys of family and hearth had been thrown into high relief, and he loved them now all the more keenly. He had wandered around the world, in other words, solely in order to come home again.

Nine years were left to him—nine years that saw the death of his beloved sister-in-law Josefina Kaunitzová and his great friend Johannes Brahms; on a happier note there were the wedding of his daughter Otilka to Josef Suk, his assumption of the directorship of the Prague Conservatory, and the composition of some of his greatest works, including the G Major and A-flat Major Quartets, the five symphonic poems, and the operas *Kate and the Devil, Rusalka,* and *Armida.* While the "New World" Symphony was being played everywhere (including a performance at La Scala in Milan by the young conductor, Arturo Toscanini), Dvořák restricted his composing in his last four years to opera. Perhaps as a result of his contact with the "American push" of the New York streets, he was more convinced than ever that operas, more than any other form of music, were "listened to by the broad masses."[4]

Ominous symptoms of a pain in his side appeared in the spring of 1904. There were signs of kidney disease. Then, at midday on 1 May, he finished a light lunch and said, "I feel kind of giddy; I think I had better go and lie down." The rest of the story was recounted by the Czech magazine, *Dalibor.*

> These were the Master's last words, for on the instant he turned pale and then dark red and fell back in his chair. He wanted to say something but only unintelligible sounds came from his throat. His pulse was still to be felt and then was very weak and finally stopped altogether, and the doctor, who had been sent for in haste, could only certify the Master's death.[5]

Although the precise nature of his fatal illness is unknown, it is fairly certain that vascular problems and cerebral anoxia contributed to his demise. Four days later he was buried in Vysehrad Cemetery beside the Vltava River.

∽❧∾

The America he left behind was quickly changing. After the Panic of 1893, worldwide depression was growing. As the cities tumbled up, so to speak, there was a resulting loss of community. Evolutionary theory was assisting in the dismantling of systems of absolutes in science, in religion, and in the arts. Great monopolies were taking over industry, and they seemed immune to governmental controls.

As has been suggested, imperialist expansion seemed a way out of the many quickening national anxieties: "The conquest of 'primitive' peoples might offer such perplexed Americans a basis for rebuilding their morale by resuscitating their faith in their power to shape the world," wrote historians Peter Gay and John A. Garraty. "And if one kind of response to fear is to become a bully, an imperialist policy could restore the courage of millions."[6] Thus, after almost a half century when America had not been involved in a foreign war, President McKinley marshaled the "New Navy" and declared war on Spain in 1898. As a result, the nation emerged an imperial power and acquired the Philippines and the islands of Guam and Puerto Rico.

New forces were unleashed upon the world. Henry Adams in 1900 proclaimed that the new century would worship electricity as its new god. It would be an age where man would break his neck genuflecting before great machines, "watching them run as noiselessly and as smoothly as the planets," wondering all that time "where in Hell they are going." Philosopher William James enthused that this would bring man the challenge and adventure of a dynamic universe. Adams retorted pessimistically that the new age will be "one of compression, concentration, and consequent development of terrific energy, represented not by souls, but by coal and iron and steam."[7] The millennium was coming, he concluded. He gave the world another fifty years.

On a less cosmic level, meanwhile, the brave vision of the Columbian Exposition of 1893—"a grand opportunity to proclaim America's greatness before the world"—had quickly faded. One of its guiding forces, Chicago's mayor, Carter Harrison, was assassinated. The architectural marvels of the White City crumbled to powder. (The building materials used a substance called "staff," a mixture of cement and fibers with plaster. It was a cheap expedient and proved to be impermanent.) Meanwhile, the fifty-cent admission fee was prohibitive to most of the minority groups that were supposedly being celebrated at the Fair. In general, the Fair itself, in the words of historian R. Reid Badger, "expressed . . . the confusions and contradictions at the core of the society, between what was believed, desired, and desperately hoped for, and what was becoming inescapably more real and actual."[8]

⌘

And what of Dvořák's family and contemporaries—his friends, colleagues, and students? Tragically, just one year after the composer's death, his daughter Otilka died at age twenty-seven. Her husband, Josef Suk, purportedly never really recovered from the tragedy. He died thirty years later. His grandson Josef became a celebrated violinist, founded the Josef Suk Trio, and lives today in Prague. Dvořák's widow, Anna, lived long enough to see Bohemia freed from the Hapsburg domination. She died in 1931 at the age of seventy-seven.

After the completion of his education in Bohemia, Josef Jan Kovařík, Dvořák's secretary, joined the New York Philharmonic where he remained for forty-two years, serving as principal cellist for part of that time.

Following his tenure on the faculty of the National Conservatory, Victor Herbert went on to compose more than forty operettas, including the phenomenally popular *Babes in Toyland* (1903), *The Red Mill* (1906), and *Naughty Marietta* (1910). In 1914 he was one of the founders of ASCAP. He died in New York City in May 1924 of a heart attack.

James Gibbons Huneker, Dvořák's colleague and friend, was music critic for a number of New York papers from 1891 to 1921 and wrote many novels (*Painted Veils*, 1920; *Steeplejack*, 1925) and music studies. He died in 1921.

Mrs. Jeannette Thurber, Dvořák's patroness, continued to work in behalf of a "National Conservatory" concept for the rest of her long life (see Emanuel Rubin's article, Chapter 6). She died in 1946 at the age of 95. Her dream has not yet been realized. Indeed, today, federal support of the arts is under increasing fire.

Harry T. Burleigh, one of Dvořák's closest American friends, became baritone soloist for St. George's Church in 1894 and held the position until 1946. He remained active most of that time, performing, composing, and sitting on the Board of Directors of ASCAP (the first African American to hold such a position). He died in Stamford, Connecticut, in 1949.

Among Dvořák's students, Will Marion Cook left the National Conservatory in 1898 to pursue a career on Broadway. Shows like his *Clorindy; or, The Origin of the Cakewalk* were among the first nonminstrel music-theater shows by African American composers. His wife, soprano Abbie Mitchell, introduced "Summertime" in Gershwin's *Porgy and Bess* (1935). Cook was a great influence on songwriter Harold Arlen and composer Duke Ellington (who referred to Cook as his "Conservatory"). He died in New York City in 1944. Rubin Goldmark taught at the National Conservatory until 1894. In 1924 he became director of the Department of Composition at the Juilliard School of Music. Among his pupils were Aaron Copland and George Gershwin.

And what of the Dvořák legacy in America today? Before the "Velvet Revolution," Americans had few opportunities to belong to the various Dvořák Societies and related organizations in Czechoslovakia; similarly, many Czech citizens, for a variety of reasons, were reluctant to join international organizations. But, as Michael Beckerman wrote prophetically in the *Bulletin of the Czechoslovak Music Society* in the spring of 1990:

> We are living in exciting times and we have seen the world change dramatically in the space of a few months. Not long ago it seemed that the place we non-Czechoslovaks traveled to for our work was a dusty backwater, of not much interest to anyone. Indeed, we may have seemed exotic simply for going there. Now all the signs are that Czechoslovakia will become a very important place. . . . Let us hope that the music of this region will make an even bigger impact on the world in the years to come, and let us play a leading role in that process.[9]

Accordingly, events like the Dvořák Sesquicentennial Festival and Conference in America (see John C. Tibbetts's article, Chapter 25) have brought together citizens and scholars hitherto divided by politics and geography. Numerous organizations claim international memberships and produce conferences, festivals and publications—the Dvořák Society in England, the A.M.A.T. in France, the Janáček Society in Switzerland, the Friends of Czech Music and the Czechoslovak Music Society in America, and of course the Dvořák Society in Czechoslovakia. With the establishment of a "Dvořák Databank" in 1990 at the Dvořák Museum in Prague, an international data collecting agency is now in operation.

In America Dvořák is rapidly becoming a cultural icon, a celebrity of the concert hall, books, and movies. The "New World" Symphony was performed by the New York Philharmonic for the 210th time in October 1991; and it was transmitted to the moon while astronaut Neil Armstrong hoisted the American flag. Novelist Josef Škvorecký wrote a quasi-fictional account of Dvořák's life in his popular *Dvořák in Love* (see Chapter 24 for Mr. Škvorecký's account of this book). More dubiously, perhaps, we have heard the popular *Humoresque* No. 7 in every possible circumstance and arrangement. Most memorably, perhaps, it was sung in counterpoint to "Old Folks at Home" in Frank Capra's *Mr. Deeds Goes to Town* (1936); and recently there was that startling moment in Bruce Beresford's *Driving Miss Daisy*

(1990) when the "To the Moon" aria from *Rusalka* was heard on the sound track during Miss Daisy's visit to the cemetery. Speaking of the movies, Dvořák's famous Largo tune has appeared in many films. To cite just two examples, it is the ongoing theme music of the Danny Kaye picture, *A Song is Born* (1948); and in its popular version, "Goin' Home," it is sung by Deanna Durbin in *It Started with Eve* (1941). At this writing, a major Hollywood motion picture about Dvořák is in the planning stages. Actor Kevin Kline, who is a graduate of Juilliard and has an extensive musical background, is considering portraying the composer. "It's something that I've been considering for a while," he told this writer on 31 October 1992. "It might happen. I've always wanted to play a musician or composer in a movie. A recent movie like *Impromptu* is the sort of direction I'd like to go with it. It didn't exalt or mythologize the artists. Instead of being portentous, it was a lot of fun. That's the way to do it for today's audiences. Not like all those movies in the 1940s that put them on pedestals—you know, Cornel Wilde as Chopin [*A Song to Remember,* 1945] and Katharine Hepburn as Clara Schumann [*A Song of Love,* 1947]. I've read the script, and if we do Dvořák, we would reveal his humor and that earthy personal quality he had. And probably go into the special love he had for his sister-in-law, Josefina."

Pilgrims by the thousands still travel annually to Spillville, Iowa. For millions of television viewers it became an "official" landmark when Charles Kuralt's CBS Sunday Morning visited there. Happily, as was reported earlier in these pages, most of the relevant buildings and locations are still intact. The Centennial Festival in observance of Dvořák's visit, to be held 6–9 August 1993, will be an international event and will doubtless generate a fresh interest in the region. Two other Dvořák Centennial events planned for the summer of 1993 are also worth noting. Preceding the Spillville event is the Iowa Dvořák Centennial Symposium, 4–7 August, on the campus of the nearby University of Iowa. Just a week later convenes Dvořák and His World, a music festival at Bard College in upstate New York at Annandale-on-Hudson. This prestigious annual two-week event—which selects a particular composer each year for intensive scrutiny—will bring together musicians, scholars, and enthusiasts from all over the world to discuss Dvořák and his music. In the planning stages at this writing are several more Dvořák events in observance of his visit to America, including a series of concerts at the Brooklyn Academy of Music in the spring of 1994.

In New York these days it is still possible to take some of the same walks Dvořák did a hundred years ago and visit some of the same places. You can begin at the site of the Dvořák House at 327 East Seventeenth Street and

The area in the Stuyvesant District where Dvořák lived was designated "Dvořák Place" in February 1992. Scheffel's Tavern was probably one of the places where Dvořák would gather with friends. (Courtesy John C. Tibbetts.)

within a minute's walk reach St. George's Church, facing Stuyvesant Park West. The interior is much as it was when Burleigh sang there. Below in the catacombs, located in what is now a secondhand-clothing shop, stands a pillar upon which Burleigh's name has been inscribed. Farther west on Seventeenth Street, near the corner of Irving Place, is a multistory structure presently on the site of what was once the National Conservatory (no trace of the Conservatory itself survives). Across the street at No. 49 Irving Place is the house of Washington Irving and, later, of Elsie De Wolf; No. 47 was once occupied for a time by Oscar Wilde. One street over, at 129 East Eighteenth, is Pete's Tavern (Dvořák knew it as Healy's), where at the turn of the century O. Henry purportedly wrote some of his stories. And between Seventeenth and Eighteenth at Third Avenue still stands Scheffel Hall (now called Tuesday's). Built in 1894, it is almost certain that Dvořák met friends for food and drink in its dark, high-ceilinged interior.

The fate of the Dvořák House, sadly, is another matter. In 1941 on the one-hundredth anniversary of Dvořák's birth, Mayor Fiorello La Guardia, along with the Minister of Foreign Affairs for the Czechoslovak government-in-exile, Jan Masaryk, placed a plaque on the four-story brick row house proclaiming it "The Dvořák House." Pianist Rudolf Firkušný, who was present at the ceremony, remembered that La Guardia had promised to seek landmark status for the house. But, as is often the case with such matters in New York, this was delayed and finally abandoned.[10]

The Dvořák House in New York City, 327 East Seventeenth Street, as it looked before the 1991 demolition. (Courtesy Adrienne Fried Block.)

Closer view of the Dvořák House and the plaque that was installed at the 1941 dedication ceremonies. (Courtesy Adrienne Fried Block.)

In 1975 the Stuyvesant Square Historic District was established, although the house itself was excluded from protection. A few years later efforts were made to redraw the area to include the Dvořák House, but this also was not to be. In 1989, when Beth Israel Medical Center purchased the property and announced its intention to tear down the house, preservationists redoubled their efforts. As a result, on 26 February 1991, the New York City Landmarks Preservation Commission (LPC), supported by the Historic Districts Council, the Stuyvesant Park Neighborhood Association, and many concerned citizens from the Czechoslovak-American community, finally moved to confer landmark status on the structure. But after a contentious and divisive battle, the designation was overturned by the City Council on 20 June 1991 in a twenty-to-fourteen vote, clearing the way for the destruction of the house.[11] Reporting the event, the *Times* noted that it was the first time the Council had used its power to block landmark status. Mayor Dinkins refused to exercise his veto power to overturn the decision.

The debate had been heated. In a controversial editorial in the *New York Times* entitled "Dvořák Doesn't Live Here Anymore," it was argued that

New York should not turn every site "of sentimental interest" into a landmark. The landmark designation of February 1991 had been misguided in the first place: "The Landmarks Commission weakens its own authority when it makes frivolous decisions."[12] Two other New York newspapers also published editorials urging the city to overturn the house's landmark protection.

Response from the other side of the aisle was immediate and heated. In a "Letter to the Editor" in the *New York Times*, the eminent *New Yorker* critic Brendan Gill wrote:

> Dvořák doesn't live here anymore! Mozart doesn't live in Salzburg anymore: should the house in which he lived be torn down? Should we tear down the Jumel mansion in Manhattan because Washington doesn't live in it anymore? You pretend to fear the city will be "dotted with shrines because a celebrity passed through." Is Dvořák to you merely a celebrity? Is three years passing through?[13]

Complicating the issue was the fact that the Dvořák House was landmarked by the LPC for *cultural*, not architectural reasons. A few buildings in New York have attained such designation—Louis Armstrong's house in Queens, Langston Hughes's Harlem abode, Giuseppe Garibaldi's residence in Staten Island, and the Edgar Allan Poe Cottage in The Bronx. The *Times* editorial (already cited) explained that the Dvořák House had been substantially altered since his time: the original stoop was gone, the front door was now a kitchen window, and rooms had been partitioned and repartitioned. The Beth Israel authorities described it as a "totally nondescript and lackluster building."[14] It was claimed that to locate, purchase, and develop another site—or even to retain the facade of the house—would have taken too much time and money.

A writing campaign was organized by the preservationists. Supporting letters arrived from notables and concerned citizens around the world, including Czech movie director Milos Forman, theater producer Joseph Papp, Czech President Vaclav Havel, the Archbishop of Prague, pianist Rudolf Firkušný, violinist Josef Suk, conductor Rafael Kubelik, cellist Yo-Yo Ma, and many others. "The greatest cello concerto was composed by Antonín Dvořák at 327 E. 17th St.," wrote Maestro Maurice Peress, former assistant conductor of the New York Philharmonic, added, "The Dvořák years in New York were a golden age of American music. Dvořák did remarkable things when he was here. He had eleven students at the National Conservatory, three were black and one was a woman, unheard of in those days. His students went on to teach Aaron Copland, Duke Ellington and

The Dvořák House was razed in in late August 1991, just a few days short of the composer's 150th birthday. (Courtesy Todd Maisel.)

George Gershwin. He was a great booster of American music. He was absolutely unique. That house was a locus for great talent and great things happened there."[16] Perhaps most poignant, Josef Suk wrote Mayor Dinkins: "I dare ask you, dear Mr. Mayor, to save this house for next generations [*sic*], for the glory of music. You can recommend the granting of Landmark Designation to the Dvořák House, for which I and all the Czechoslovak people would be very gratefull [*sic*] to you."[17]

"Dvořák tours" of the area were conducted and concerts were presented. On 19 May 1991, for example, a rally and songfest were held on the steps of the house; and baritone William Warfield, assisted by pianist Dick Hyman, performed in a Dvořák program at St. George's Episcopal Church. Present at the ceremonies was Jarmila Novotná, a Metropolitan Opera soprano and Czechoslovak by birth, who had been present at the 1941 La Guardia ceremony.

However, the fate of the house was sealed, and in the end Beth Israel Medical Center demolished it in August 1991 to make way for a twenty-eight-bed AIDS facility. "We still feel that this is our best plan," said Peter

Stuyvesant Park, the central area of "Dvořák Place" along East Seventeenth Street. It is hoped that a statue of the composer will soon be located here. (Courtesy John C. Tibbetts.)

Kelly, the Medical Center's Executive Vice President.[18] He added that the new facility, far from representing a cultural loss, would give Czechoslovak-Americans an increased sense of pride. On the other hand, writing in *District Lines*, the quarterly newsletter of the coalition of New York City's historic neighborhoods, chairman Anthony C. Wood charged that the whole affair had been "a real-estate ploy." Further, "with the destruction of this landmark, the real-estate interests have tasted blood, and their victory at the City Council only ensures that they will be back for more." He concluded that preservationists in the nineties would have to become more politically astute: "Preservationists must get politically sensitized and acquire political power. We need to make sure that candidates for the City Council are pro-preservation. If not, we must find candidates who are."[19]

Meanwhile, in what was described in *Town & Village* as a "consolation prize,"[20] Mayor Dinkins signed into law the establishment of a "Dvořák Place" on 28 November 1991. This area, officially dedicated in a ceremony on 27 February 1992, encompasses Seventeenth Street between First and Second avenues. Street signs in the area now bear a double inscription— "17th Street" and "Dvořák Place." Plans are also afoot, according to Jack Taylor, coordinator for the Dvořák American Heritage Association, to estab-

This is all that remains at this writing of the Dvořák House. Plans are to convert the site into an AIDS hospice. (Courtesy John C. Tibbetts.)

lish a Dvořák Museum in a turn-of-the-century building on East Seventy-Third Street, headquarters of the Bohemian Benevolent & Literary Association, long known as Bohemian National Hall. "Some of the items rescued from the Dvořák House will be on display, including the marble mantelpiece from the parlor and a piano of the same kind that Dvořák received as a gift from William Steinway Sons," explains Mr. Taylor.[21]

And then there's the strange story of the recent discovery of the "Dvořák Statue." Taylor continues, "It's been located on the roof of Avery Fisher Hall, 'hidden' there for more than twenty-seven years! It was originally presented to the New York Philharmonic by the Czechoslovak National Council of America in 1963. At the presentation was Dr. Alice Masaryk, daughter of Czechoslovakia's first president, Thomas Masaryk. She had also attended the 1941 Dvořák House ceremony. The statue was created by the well-known Yugoslav-American sculptor Ivan Mestrovic. Then, for some reason, it was hidden away on the roof of Avery Fisher Hall. Now we've found it and there's an effort underway to move it to Stuyvesant Square Park—just across the street from the site formerly occupied by the Dvořák House."

Nonetheless the Dvořák House itself is gone. Irretrievably. At this writing, all that remains is a great, gaping hole. It is a sobering discord among the many other, happier events that celebrated the composer's Sesquicentennial anniversary in 1991 (see John C. Tibbetts's article, Chapter 25, about the Dvořák Sesquicentennial Festival and Conference in America). As Maestro Peress has pointed out, there is tragic irony also in the fact that while the Czech nation is honoring American institutions in their country, America has, in effect, turned its back on the Czech hero who was "Czechoslovakia's deepest connection to the democracy they emulate."[22]

The proud inscription on the tablet affixed to the Dvořák House in 1941 has a special poignancy now:

> In memory of [Dvořák's] 100th birthday and for future generations of free Czecho-Slovakia the grateful government caused this inscription to be erected on Dec. 13, 1941. Longing for his Czech home, yet happily inspired by the freedom of the American life, he wrote here among other works the New World Symphony, Biblical Songs, the 'Cello Concerto. The famous Czech composer, Antonín Dvořák, 1841–1904, lived in this house from 1892 until 1895.

In attendance that day were Dvořák's good companions, including J. J. Kovařík, Harry Rowe Shelley, and Harry T. Burleigh. The house had been decked with the flags of America and Czechoslovakia. Jan Masaryk proudly declared to Mayor La Guardia that, in honoring the house, free Czechs were helping "to compose the real new-world symphony of free people."[23]

The house is gone and the plaque has been presented to the Honorable Eduard Kukan, Ambassador of the Czech and Slovak Federal Republican Mission to the United Nations, who is expected to turn it over to the proposed Dvořák Museum in the restored Bohemian National Hall. In this way, at least, that spirit of a "new world," like a gentle melody, may linger on.

NOTES

1. Quoted in John Clapham, *Dvořák* (New York: W. W. Norton & Company, 1979), 134.

2. Dvořák to Josef Boleska, 15 January 1895; in *Antonín Dvořák: Letters and Reminiscences*, ed. Otakar Šourek (Prague: Artia, 1954), 182.

3. John Clapham, *Dvořák*, 141.

4. From an interview with Dvořák for the Vienna daily *Die Reichswehr*, quoted in *Antonín Dvořák: Letters and Reminiscences*, ed. Otakar Šourek (Artia: Prague, 1954), 223.

5. Quoted in Otakar Šourek, ed., *Antonín Dvořák: Letters and Reminiscences*, 228–229.

6. John A. Garraty and Peter Gay, eds., *The Columbia History of the World* (New York: Harper & Row, 1972), 935–936.

7. This debate, which involved William James and Henry Adams is discussed at length in Paul F. Boller, Jr., *American Thought in Transition: The Impact of Evolutionary Naturalism, 1865–1900* (New York: Texas Christian University, 1981), 227–249.

8. R. Reid Badger, *The Great American Fair: The World's Columbian Exposition and American Culture* (Chicago: Nelson Hall, 1979), *xiii.*

9. Michael Beckerman, "Towards a Truly International Music Society," *Bulletin of the Czechoslovak Music Society,* Spring 1990, 1–2.

10. Mark Rose, "Lust for Land: The Real Story Behind the Destruction of the Landmarked Dvořák House," New York *Press,* vol. 4, no. 45 (6–12 November 1991), 1, 6.

11. "Dvořák House Is Gone; Dvořák Place Is Here," *Town & Village,* vol. 44, no. 49 (28 November 1991), n.p.

12. "Dvořák Doesn't Live Here Anymore" (editorial), the *New York Times,* 7 March 1991, n.p.

13. Brendan Gill, "The Great Lost Spirits," (letter of 8 March 1991), the *New York Times,* 19 March 1991, n.p.

14. Quoted in Mark Rose, "Lust for Land," 6. See also Steven Richman, "The Dvořák Debacle—How Antonín Dvořák's Historic New York House Was Razed," *High Performance Review,* Summer 1992, 6–7, 14.

15. Letter from Yo-Yo E. Ma to the Honorable David F. M. Todd, 8 March 1990 (provided to the author by Jack Taylor).

16. Quoted in Mark Rose, "Lust for Land," 6.

17. Letter from Prof. Josef Suk to the Honorable David N. Dinkins, 6 June 1990 (provided to the author by Jack Taylor).

18. Quoted in Joanne Furio, "A Preservation Effort, Set to Music," New York *Newsday,* 24 May 1991, n.p.

19. Anthony C. Wood, "The Dvořák Defeat: Will It Hurt Future Designations?" *District Lines,* vol. 6, no. 2 (Autumn 1991), 3.

20. "Dvořák House Is Gone; Dvořák Place Is Here," *Town & Village,* n.p.

21. Author's interview with Jack Taylor in New York, 13 February 1992.

22. Quoted in Mark Rose, "Lust for Land," 6.

23. "Plaque Dedicated at Dvořák House," the New York *Sun,* 15 December 1941.

Newspaper and Magazine Articles

Editor's Note: Writings by and about Dvořák concerning his American sojourn are frequently quoted piecemeal and out of their original contexts. Most of the following texts are reprinted complete (with only a few cuts in some irrelevant material—indicated by ellipses) and in chronological order.

THE REAL VALUE OF NEGRO MELODIES
NEW YORK HERALD, 21 MAY 1893

It was Rubinstein who bitterly said that the world would make no more progress in music until the controlling influence of Wagner, Berlioz, and Liszt had passed away. Right on the heels of this anathema Dr. Antonín Dvořák, the foremost figure among living composers, came to America the acknowledged leader of the dramatic school and the obvious target for the arrows of the lyric school.

The great Bohemian composer had just ended his first season of musical exploration in New York and his opinion ought to stir the heart of every American who loves music.

"I am now satisfied," he said to me, "that the future music of this country must be founded upon what are called the negro melodies. This must be the real foundation of any serious and original school of composition to be developed in the United States. When I first came here last year I was impressed with this idea and it has developed into a settled conviction. These beautiful and varied themes are the product of the soil. They are American. I would like to trace out the traditional authorship of the negro melodies, for it would throw a great deal of light upon the question I am most deeply interested in at present.

"These are the folk songs of America and your composers must turn to them. All of the great musicians have borrowed from the songs of the common people. Beethoven's most charming scherzo is based upon what might now be considered a skilfully handled negro melody. I myself have gone to the simple, half forgotten tunes of the Bohemian peasants for hints in my most serious work. Only in this way can a musician express the true sentiment of his people. He gets into touch with the common humanity of his country.

POSSIBILITIES OF NEGRO MELODY

"In the negro melodies of America I discover all that is needed for a great and noble school of music. They are pathetic, tender, passionate, melancholy, solemn, religious, bold, merry, gay or what you will. It is music that suits itself to any mood or any purpose. There is nothing in the whole range of composition that cannot be supplied with themes from this source. The American musician understands these tunes and they move sentiment in him. They appeal to his imagination because of their associations.

"When I was in England one of the ablest musical critics in London complained to me that there was no distinctively English school music, nothing that appealed particularly to the British mind and heart. I replied to him that the composers of England had turned their backs upon the fine melodies of Ireland and Scotland instead of making them the essence of an English school. It is a great pity that English musicians have not profited out of this rich store. Somehow the old Irish and Scotch ballads have not seized upon or appealed to them.

"I hope it will not be so in this country, and I intend to do all in my power to call attention to the splendid treasure of melody which you have.

"Among my pupils in the National Conservatory of Music I have discovered strong talents. There is one young man [Maurice Arnold] upon whom I am building strong expectations. His compositions are based upon negro melodies, and I have encouraged him in this direction. The other members of the composition class seem to think that it is not in good taste to get ideas from the old plantation songs, but they are wrong, and I have tried to impress upon their minds the fact that the greatest composers have not considered it beneath their dignity to go to the humble folk song motifs.

"I did not come to America to interpret Beethoven or Wagner for the public. This is not my work and I would not waste any time on it. I came to discover what young Americans had in them and to help them to express it. When the negro minstrels are here again I intend to take my young composers with me and have them comment on the melodies."

And saying so Dvořák sat down at his piano and ran his fingers lightly over the keys. It was his favorite pupil's adaptation of a Southern melody.

Here, then, is a programme of musical growth, laid down by the most competent mind that has yet studied the American mold—a plan made without hesitation or reservation. It is the result of an almost microscopic examination and comes from a man who is always in earnest.

ELEMENTS TO CULTIVATE

The scheme outlined by Dr. Dvořák is in its very nature an utterance of the dramatic school. The land is full of melody. The countryside school echoes the songs of the working people. Take those simple themes and weave them into splendid and harmonious forms. Glorify them: give them breadth. So the Dutch painter talks to his pupils. Do not try to imagine the angel in heaven, but try to paint that wrinkled peasant woman at your side, that the angel in her may be seen by ordinary eyes. It is not what you paint that counts, but how you paint it. Dr. Dvořák takes a similar position. He cannot teach, nor can any one, a system of melody-creation. Bacon asks:

> Who taught the raven in a drought to throw pebbles into a hollow tree so that the water might rise so that she might come to it? Who taught the bee to sail . . .

Dr. Dvořák cannot cause melodies to bubble up in the minds of his pupils, but he can show them how to utter what is in them. And if it be granted that America teems with original songs, that the common people are tuneful, that their heads are properly formed by nature, that the creative faculty lies in them, is not method and style the most important thing in the formative period of a national school?

Rubinstein told me that Wagner was a poor musician because he lacked the power of musical invention, and yet with a theme borrowed from the soil, as it were, Wagner accomplished more than the Russian master divinely endowed with the lyric quality.

Many of the negro melodies—most of them, I believe—are the creations of negroes born and reared in America. That is the peculiar aspect of the problem. The negro does not produce music of that kind elsewhere. I have heard black singers in Hayti [*sic*] for hours and, as a rule, their songs are not unlike the monotonous and crude chantings of the Sioux tribes. It is so also in Africa. But the negro in America utters a new note, full of sweetness and as characteristic as any music of any country.

To Admit Colored Students

This leads to an important announcement that the HERALD is authorized to make today, which is that the National Conservatory of Music, over which Dr. Dvořák presides, is to be thrown open free of charge to the negro race. Here is Mrs. Thurber's official announcement:

The National Conservatory of Music of America
126 and 128 East Seventeenth Streets

New York, May 16, 1893

The National Conservatory of Music of America proposes to enlarge its sphere of usefulness by adding to its departments a branch for the instruction in music of colored pupils of talent, largely with the view of forming colored professors of merit. The aptitude of the colored race for music, vocal and instrumental, has long been recognized, but no definite steps have hitherto been taken to develop it, and it is believed that the decision of the conservatory to move in this new direction will meet with general approval and be productive of prompt and encouraging results. Several of our trustees have shown special interest in the matter. Prominent among these is Mrs. Colus P. Huntington. Tuition will be furnished to students of exceptional talent free of charge. Two young but efficient colored pupils have already been engaged as teachers, and others will be secured as circumstances may require.

Application for admission to the Conservatory classes is invited, and the assignment of pupils will be made to such instructors as may be deemed judicious.

Dr. Antonín Dvořák, director of the Conservatory, expresses great pleasure at the decision of the trustees and will assist its fruition by sympathetic and active cooperation.

May I ask you to place these facts before your readers and in favoring a worthy cause once again oblige yours truly, very truly,

Jeannette M. Thurber, President

The importance of this step can only be appreciated in the light of Dr. Dvořák's declaration that negro melody furnishes the only sure base for an American school of music. It is a bold innovation but those who have heard the Black Patti sing or "Blind" Tom play must have wondered why it was that no serious attempt was made to organize, train and refine the musical talent of the negro race in the United States.

This institution has determined to add to the 800 white students as many negroes of positive talent as may apply. There will be absolutely no limit. I have the authority of Mrs. Thurber herself for that.

After the expenditure of thousands of dollars the National Conservatory of Music is now beginning to see light. There is little hope that the government will ever endow it, and Mrs. Thurber long ago gave that idea up. Dr. Dvořák, of course, cannot understand why the national authorities should not support such a broad educational enterprise out of the public Treasury. He looks back at the eighty years work done by the famous conservatory at Prague and recalls the long line of noble names that fostered it in conjunction with the government until all the arts were grouped together virtually under one roof. But in America the wealthy citizens must do the work done by foreign governments. . . .

[DVOŘÁK'S] LETTER TO THE EDITOR
NEW YORK HERALD, 28 MAY 1893

To the Editor of the *Herald*:

I was deeply interested in the article in last Sunday's Herald, for the writer struck a note that should be sounded throughout America. It is my opinion that I find a sure foundation in the Negro melodies for a new national school of music, and my observations have already convinced me that the young musicians of this country need only intelligent directions, serious application and a reasonable amount of public support and applause to create a new musical school in America. This is not a sudden discovery on my part. The light has gradually dawned on me.

The new American school of music must strike its roots deeply into its own soil. There is no longer any reason why young Americans who have talent should go to Europe for their education. It is a waste of money and puts off the coming day when the Western world will be in music, as in many others, independent of other lands. In the National Conservatory of music, founded and presided over by Mrs. Jeannette M. Thurber, is provided as good a school as can be found elsewhere. The masters are competent in the highest sense and the spirit of the institution is absolutely catholic. A fresh proof of the breadth of purpose involved in this conservatory is the fact that it has been opened without limit or reservation to the Negro race.

I find good talent here, and I am convinced that when the youth of the country realizes that it is better now to stay at home than to go abroad we shall discover genius, for many who have talent but cannot undertake a foreign residence will be encouraged to pursue their studies here. It is to the poor that I turn for musical greatness. The poor work hard; they study seriously. Rich people are apt to apply themselves lightly to music, and to abandon the painful toil to which every strong musician must submit without complaint and without rest. Poverty is no barrier to one endowed by nature with musical talent. It is a spur. It keeps the mind loyal to the end. It stimulates the student to great efforts.

If in my own career I have achieved a measure of success and reward it is to some extent due to the fact I was the son of poor parents and was reared in an atmosphere of struggle and endeavour. Broadly speaking the Bohemians are a nation of peasants. My first musical education I got from my schoolmaster, a man of good ability and much earnestness. He taught me to play the violin. Afterward I travelled with him and we made our living together. Then I spent two years at the organ school in Prague. From that time on I had to study for myself. It is impossible for me to speak without emotion of the strains and sorrows that came upon me in the long and bitter years that followed. Looking back at that time, I can hardly understand how I endured the privations and labour of my youth.

Could I have had in my earlier days the advantages, freely offered in such a school as the National Conservatory of Music, I might have been spared many of my hardest trials and have accomplished much more. Not that I was unable to produce music, but that I had not technique enough to express all that was in me. I had ideas but I could not utter them perfectly.

There is a great opportunity for musicians in America and it will increase when grand opera sung in English is more firmly established, with public or private assistance. At the present time this country needs also the materials for orchestral work. The death of good native performers on reeds and brass instruments is marked. Every one wants to sing or play the piano, violin or violoncello. Nobody seems to realize the importance of good cornetists, trombonists, clarinetists, oboists, flutists, trumpeters and the like. In Bohemia applicants for admission to the Conservatory are assigned to instruments according to the necessities of the time. Of course nearly every young musician wants to play the violin, but to encourage that tendency would be to undermine the orchestral system and leave composers without the means of properly presenting their works.

I do not agree with those who say that the air here is not good for vocalists. The American voice has a character of its own. It is quite different from the European voice, just as the English voice is different from the German and Italian. Singers like Lloyd and M'Guckin have an entirely different vocal quality from that of German singers and members of the Latin race. The American voice is unlike anything else, quite unlike the English voice. I do not speak of method or style, but of the natural quality, the timbre of the voice. I have noticed this difference ever since I have been in New York. The American voice is good; it pleases me very much.

Those who think that music is not latent in the American will discover their error before long. I only complain that the American musician is not serious enough in applying himself to the work he must do before he is qualified to enter upon a public career. I have always to remind my most promising pupils of the necessity of work. Work! work! work! to the very end.

The country is full of melody, original, sympathetic and varying in mood, colour and character to suit every phase of composition. It is a rich field. America can have great and noble music of her own, growing out of the very soil and partaking of its nature—the natural voice of a free and vigorous race.

This proves to me that there is such a thing as nationality in music in the sense that it may take on the character of its locality. It now rests with the young musicians of this country and with the patrons of music to say how soon the American school of music is to be developed. A good beginning has been made in New York. Honour to those who will help to increase and broaden the work.

Antonín Dvořák
New York. 25 May 1893

FOR NATIONAL MUSIC
CHICAGO TRIBUNE, 13 AUGUST 1893

Every nation has its music. There is Italian, German, French, Bohemian, Russian; why not American music? The truth of this music depends upon its characteristics, its colour. I do not mean to take these melodies, plantation, Creole or Southern, and work them out as themes; that is not my plan. But I study certain melodies until I become thoroughly imbued with their characteristics and am enabled to make a musical picture in keeping with and partaking of those characteristics. The symphony is the least desirable of vehicles for the display of this work, in that the form will allow only of a suggestion of the colour of that nationalism to be given. Liberty in this line is never allowable. Opera is by far the best mode of expression for the undertaking, allowing as it does of freedom of treatment. My plan of work in this line is simple, but the attainment is subtle and difficult because of the minute and conscientious study demanded and the necessity to grasp the essence and vitality of the subject. I have just completed a quintet for string instruments, written lately at Spielville [*sic*], Ia. The quintet will be played in New York during the winter. In this work I think there will be found the American colour with which I have endeavoured to infuse it. My new symphony is also on the same lines—namely: an endeavor to portray characteristics, such as are distinctly American. At present I have studying with me in New York seven pupils; next year I shall have a much larger number. I take only those far advanced in composition; that is, understanding thorough bass, form, and instrumentation. The most promising and gifted of these pupils is a young Westerner [Maurice Arnold] Strathotte by name, a native of St. Louis. A suite of "Creole Dances" [also entitled "Plantation Dances"] written by him, and which contain material that he has created in a style that accords with my ideas, will be given in New York during the winter. [Louis Moreau] Gottschalk also recognized and worked upon this plan.

DVOŘÁK ON HIS NEW WORK
NEW YORK HERALD, 15 DECEMBER 1893

Dr. Antonín Dvořák, the Bohemian composer and director of the National Conservatory of Music, has been in this country a little over a year. America has strongly affected his sensitive imagination. He has made a serious study of the national music of this continent as exemplified in the native melodies of the negro and Indian races. What the effect of this study has been the New York public will have the opportunity of hearing this afternoon. Then will be played at Carnegie Music Hall the first fruits of his musical genius in this country. It is a long symphony for full orchestra, is called "From the New World" and will receive its first performance in public at the Philharmonic concert to-day.

Chattily at his residence, No. 327 East Nineteenth [*sic*] Street, last evening Dr. Dvořák gave a few details regarding this his latest composition. "Since I have been in this country I have been deeply interested in the national music of the Negroes and the Indians. The character, the very nature of a race is contained in its national music. For that reason my attention was at once turned in the direction of these native melodies. I found that the music of the two races bore a remarkable similarity to the music of Scotland. In both there is a peculiar scale, caused by the absence of the fourth and seventh, or leading tone. In both the minor scale has the seventh invariably a minor seventh, the fourth is included and the sixth omitted.

THE SCOTCH SCALE

"Now the Scotch scale, if I may so call it, has been used to impart a certain color to musical composition. I need only instance Mendelssohn's "Hebrides" Overture. The device is a common one. In fact the scale in question is only a certain form of the ancient ecclesiastical modes. These modes have been employed time and time again. For example Felicien David in his symphonic ode "Le Desert," Verdi in "Aida." I have myself used one of them in my D minor Symphony.

"Now, I found that the music of the Negroes and of the Indians was practically identical. I therefore carefully studied a certain number of Indian melodies which a friend gave me, and became thoroughly imbued with their characteristics—with their spirit, in fact.

"It is this spirit which I have tried to reproduce in my new Symphony ["The New World"]. I have not actually used any of the melodies. I have simply written original themes embodying the peculiarities of the Indian music, and, using these themes as subjects, have developed them with all the resources of modern rhythms, harmony, counterpoint and orchestral color.

"The Symphony is in E minor. It is written upon the classical models and is in four movements. It opens with a short introduction, an Adagio of about thirty bars in length. This leads directly into the allegro, which embodies the principles which I have already worked out in my Slavonic Dances; that is, to preserve, to translate into music, the spirit of a race as distinct in its national melodies or folk songs.

"The second movement is an Adagio. But it is different to the classic works in this form. It is in reality a study or sketch for a longer work, either a cantata or opera which I propose writing, and which will be based upon Longfellow's "Hiawatha." I have long had the idea of someday utilizing that poem. I first became acquainted with it about thirty years ago through the medium of a Bohemian translation. It appealed very strongly to my imagination at the time, and the impression has only been strengthened by my residence here.

"The Scherzo of the Symphony was suggested by the scene at the feast in "Hiawatha" where the Indians dance, and is also an essay which I made in the direction of imparting the local color of Indian character to music.

The Final Movement

"The last movement is an Allegro con feroce. All the previous themes reappear and are treated in a variety of ways. The instruments are only those of what we call the "Beethoven orchestra," consisting of strings, four horns, three trombones, two trumpets, two flutes, two oboes, two clarinets, two bassoons and tympani. There is no harp and I did not find it necessary to add any novel instrument in order to get the effect I wanted.

"I have indeed been busy since I came to this country. I have finished a couple of compositions in chamber music, which will be played by the Kneisel String Quartet, of Boston, next January, in the Music Hall [later renamed Carnegie Hall]. They are both written upon the same lines as this Symphony and both breathe the same Indian spirit. One is a String Quartet in F major, and the other a Quintet in E-flat for two violins, two violas and violoncello."

How Dr. Dvořák Gives a Lesson
New York Herald, 14 January 1894

If you write well by accident once, you will be just as likely to write badly ten times. Have a reason for everything you do. Examine your reason from every point of view. Make up your mind as to the merit of a musical theme, its treatment or its accompaniment, only after careful thorough consideration. Then, having come to a decided opinion on the matter, set to work and write it out. You may find many things to change upon further reflection, you may modify the work in many ways, but if your reasoning has been thorough you will find that the foundation, the kernel, of your work remains just the same. I have no patience with the people who write down the first thing that comes into their head, who accompany it with the harmonies that happen to suggest themselves at the moment, who then score it for any instrument, or combination of instruments, that catches their fancy without any regard to effect! There would not be so much nonsense written if people thought more.

You must not imitate. Model your style upon all that is best, all that is noble and elevated in the literature of music, but remain yourself. Do not become the copyist of anyone, for you will invariably copy your model's defects, while his merits will be so subtle that they will escape you.

Mozart! Ah, Mozart is the greatest of them all. Beethoven is grand. His works are always sublime in conception and sublime in working out. But it is awe that he inspires, while Mozart touches my heart. His melodies are so loveable, are so inspired and so inspiring, that only to hear them is the greatest enjoyment that exists in the world for me. Schubert also has somewhat of Mozart's qualities so far as impressing me is concerned.

HEAR THE "OLD FOLKS AT HOME"
NEW YORK HERALD, 23 JANUARY 1894

The fifth week of the HERALD Clothing Fund opened yesterday with a good stock of clothing on hand, except in the women's department, and with a continuance of the unusual weather that has been such a boon to the poor. . . . [particulars on the donations]

After weeks of preparation and faithful rehearsal the grand concert projected by Mrs. Jeannette Thurber for the benefit of the HERALD fund will take place this evening at eight o'clock in the concert hall of the Madison Square Garden.

The full orchestra and chorus of the National Conservatory of Music will take part, together with some volunteers of celebrity. Dvořák, who will conduct, has worked with great enthusiasm and sympathy to make this concert one of the most notable ever given in New York—notable from the fact that in the programme he has involved many of his interesting theories concerning the negro melodies of the United States, and notable because he has arranged that famous old song "Old Folks at Home" for solo, orchestra and chorus.

The full programme of the concert is as follows:

1. OVERTURE "Midsummer Night's Dream" . . . . Mendelssohn
   Conservatory Orchestra. Dr. Antonín Dvořák, conductor.
2. STABAT MATER "Inflammatus" . . . . Rossini
   Mme. Sissieretta Jones and members of St. Philip's choir
   Conductor Mr. Edward B. Kinney (pupil of Dr. Dvořák)
3. HUNGARIAN FANTASIE. . . . . Liszt
   Miss Bertha Visanska
4. SERENADE FOR STRING ORCHESTRA (two movements). . Volkmann
5. AMERICAN PLANTATION DANCES . . . . Maurice Arnold
   Conducted by the composer (pupil of Dr. Dvořák)
6. "OLD FOLKS AT HOME". . . . . Arranged by Antonín Dvořák
   For solo, chorus and orchestra
   Mme. Jones, soprano; Mr. Harry E. Burleigh, barytone [*sic*]
   Conservatory Orchestra and colored chorus

The principal number of the programme, "Old Folks at Home," will be sung entirely by negroes. Of the song itself Dvořák says:

TREAT FOR MUSIC LOVERS

It is a folk song and a very beautiful one, too. The only difference it has from what usually comes under that head is that we know the composer's name. And that is only because he happened to write it at a period when the art of preserving music by writing it down existed, whereas most folk songs have been handed down from mouth to mouth until in later years they were copied in manuscript by some musician. But by that time the composer's name had been forgotten. American music is music that lives in the heart of the people, and therefore this air has every right to be regarded as purely national."

Here is, indeed, a treat for all lovers of music, as well as for those who take interest in the development of our national schools of music and in the negro race.

Of course, this concert has created the greatest interest among the immediate friends of the National Conservatory of Music, but Mrs. Richard Irwin, Mrs. William Jay, Mrs. John Lowery, Mrs. William P. Douglas, Mrs. Alfred Loomis and other patronesses of the fund who have been selling tickets for the concert report that society, with its usual discrimination and goodness of heart, will be largely represented at the performance this evening.

DVOŘÁK LEADS FOR THE FUND
THE NEW YORK HERALD, 24 JANUARY 1894

Honor to Mrs. Jeannette M. Thurber, to Dr. Antonín Dvořák and to the students of the National Conservatory of Music!

Thanks to their generous assistance, the Herald's Free Clothing Fund has been augmented by a donation of $1,047. This sum represents the net proceeds of the concert given last evening in Madison Square Garden Concert Hall by the pupils of the conservatory, under the conductorship of Dr. Dvořák, the director of that institution.

Success of the most pronounced kind crowned the concert from every point of view. Long before the hour fixed for the opening the hall was filled with an immense throng of people. At eight o'clock there was hardly standing room, only the aisles being kept free, and as the concert proceeded the ranks of anxious listeners standing at the back became more and more closely serried until they overflowed into the passageways.

It was a unique programme. Each soloist, with one exception, belonged to the colored race. This idea was due to Mrs. Thurber. She threw open the doors of her excellently equipped musical educational establishment to pupils of ability, no matter what their race, color or creed. Emancipation, in her idea, had not gone far enough. Bodies had been liberated, but the gates of the artistic world were still locked.

Her efforts in this direction were ably seconded by Dr. Dvořák. The famous Bohemian studied the race, their songs, their folklore. He saw that in their intellectual make-up there lay, ignored or unknown, the germs of an original musical organization, the foundation of a truly national school of music.

UNIQUE COLORED CHOIR

When the audience entered the hall last night the first thing which attracted attention was the gallery at the back of the stage, a gallery fitted with a chorus composed entirely of colored pupils. It was an interesting sight, and one not without its pathetic side, for there was a look of earnestness upon the faces of the members so intense as to cause a feeling of sadness.

And how they sang when the time came! Their very lives might have depended upon it. As the shrill voices of the boys of St. Philip's colored choir rose in Rossini's "Inflammatus," voices with the curious tonal color which is one of the characteristics of the colored race, you were compelled to admit that had the National Conservatory of Music done nothing more than to open wider to them music's unlimited resources of enjoyment it would have achieved a noble work.

There was one little fellow who attracted everybody's attention. He had no music sheet, but he apparently needed none, singing with an evident enjoyment that showed how deeply he was interested in the work. He never took his eyes from the conductor's baton, and at every attack he made a funny little convulsive start as though he said, "Now for it!"

His ardor was shared by every individual in the choir. Their attention was riveted upon the affair in hand. The proof of this was found in the fact that every attack was as unanimous as though it were sang by one huge voice.

The sopranos and altos were all dressed in pure white, pink or blue, while the tenors and basses all wore the conventional dress suit. In all there were about one hundred and thirty members in the choir, which is made up of pupils in the conservatory.

An Evening of Surprises

Not often have so many novel surprises been given at a pupils' concert. The most striking came with the entry of a slim young white girl upon the platform. This child, Bertha Visanska, walked quietly up to the piano, bowed timidly to the audience, settled herself before the instrument and then gave a grand bow to Dr. Dvořák, which said as plainly as words, "I am quite ready."

Dr. Dvořák then plunged into the work of directing the orchestral accompaniment to Liszt's "Hungarian Fantasie," and the audience settled down with a resigned air, evidently prepared to listen to the usual style of school girl solo. In a few minutes the general expression had changed from one of indifference to one of surprise. Was it possible that such a child, twelve or thirteen years old at the most, could be the brilliant pianist who was playing the difficult passages of Liszt's opus 25 with such breadth, with such distinct, clear technique, even with authority!

Miss Visanska is really what the French call "une nature." Already she plays artistically. Her finger technique is admirable. Her touch is very musical. She plays with power, with delicacy, with charm. Her instruction has been manifestly so thorough that to the child's teacher must every praise be given, and if she was not proud of her young pupil's success then Miss Margulies must indeed be very difficult to please.

There is a stringent rule at all the Conservatory pupils' concerts—a law that is almost as inflexible as those of the Medes and Persians—that no performer shall be allowed to accord an encore. Last night Dr. Dvořák had for once to relax this regulation in favor of Miss Visanska, so great was the enthusiasm her playing aroused. It only remains for her to study as assiduously in the future as she has so evidently done in the past for her name to be a well known one in the world of music.

The Black Patti Success

Mme. Sissieretta Jones, the "Black Patti," the only soloist not a pupil at the Conservatory, sang the soprano solo in the "Inflammatus" from Rossini's "Stabat Mater," the chorus being sung by the colored male choir of St. Philip's Church, under the direction of Mr. Edward B. Kinney, the organist and choirmaster of the church and a pupil in Dr. Dvořák's composition class. Mme. Jones was an enormous success with the audience. To those who heard her for the first time she came in the light of revelation, singing high C's with as little apparent effort as her namesake, the white Patti. It was impossible to refuse the demand for an encore, so Mme. Jones responded with the "Robert, toi que j'aime," in which she was accompanied by her pianiste, Miss Wilson.

Mendelssohn's overture to the "Midsummer Night's Dream," played by the Conservatory orchestra, opened the concert. This orchestra, numbering about fifty members, is composed entirely of pupils in the various classes at that institution. It is a young, untried organization, but the orchestral numbers rendered last evening were quite sufficient to demonstrate the excellence of the instruction given at the Conservatory. Notably was this shown in the strings. The players produced an admirable tone. They played steadily, accurately and in tune. The Mendelssohn overture is not the easiest composition in the literature of orchestral music, but it received a most commendable performance last evening. The light, tripping passages were given with considerable delicacy. The attacks in the woodwinds were a little lacking in unanimity, but the general effect was remarkable for a pupils' performance.

Perhaps the strings showed the greatest advantage in a couple of movements from Volkmann's serenade for string orchestra. The valse in particular was very good, the violas making quite an effect.

Those "Plantation Dances"

One of the pupils in Dr. Dvořák's composition class, Mr. Maurice Arnold, produced a novelty in the shape of a series of four "American Plantation Dances," for full orchestra. These dances were written upon the lines laid down by Dr. Dvořák as being essential for the foundation of a national school of music. In other words, the characteristic features of negro music have been closely studied and adapted for use in serious composition. Rhythms, harmonies, melodic forms, in these dances, all originate in the folk music of the negroes. This spirit Mr. Arnold has conveyed into his composition with some degree of success. The themes are all original, but they have about them a flavor of a music which we have been accustomed to associate with the negro race. The orchestration is praiseworthy, particularly in the second, though the third is bound to be the most popular.

These dances can claim to be looked upon as national and would be found admirable for performance at patriotic gatherings. There is such a gay swing about the last that nearly every boy in the choir marked time with his head, and I am pretty sure that under cover of that friendly gallery front they were all patting "juba." Under Mr. Arnold's vigorous leadership the dances received a very spirited performance from the orchestra.

Gold Mounted Baton for Dr. Dvořák

When Dr. Dvořák came upon the stage to conduct the last number upon the programme he was astonished to see one of the first violinists, Mr. Friedlander, leave his post and walk toward him. The kindly Doctor was just waving him back to his seat when Mr. Friedlander held out a gold mounted ebony baton, and in a short address presented it as a token of loving esteem from the orchestra to their distinguished director.

Dr. Dvořák was too much overcome by his feelings to reply. He thanked the orchestra by gestures that were more eloquent of his appreciation of their kindness than any words could have been, and then taking up the beautiful present he commenced to conduct. Appropriately enough, seeing that Dr. Dvořák is the apostle of national music, the first number he directed with the baton was his own arrangement of America's most popular folk song, "The Old Folks at Home," which he scored specially for this concert in aid of the HERALD's Clothing Fund.

Mr. Harry Jones [Harry T. Burleigh], baritone, a pupil at the conservatory, and Mme. Jones sang the solos, the chorus being given by the colored choir. It is a very effective arrangement, quite desolate character being imparted to it by the air being allotted to the flute in the prelude, with a very quiet and simple accompaniment. . . .

MUSIC IN AMERICA
HARPER'S NEW MONTHLY MAGAZINE, FEBRUARY 1895
ANTONÍN DVOŘÁK

It is a difficult task at best for a foreigner to give a correct verdict of the affairs of another country. With the United States of America this is more than usually difficult, because they cover such a vast area of land that it would take many years to become properly acquainted with the various localities, separated by great distances, that would have to be considered when rendering a judgment concerning them all. It would ill become me, therefore, to express my views on so general and all-embracing a subject as music in America, were I not pressed to do so, for I have neither travelled extensively, nor have I been here long enough to gain an intimate knowledge of American affairs. I can only judge of it from what I have observed during my limited experience as a musician and teacher in America, and from what those whom I know here tell about their own country. Many of my impressions therefore are those of a foreigner who has not been here long enough to overcome the feeling of strangeness and bewildered astonishment which must fill all European visitors upon their first arrival.

The two American traits which most impress the foreign observer, I find, are the unbounded patriotism and capacity for enthusiasm of most Americans. Unlike the more diffident inhabitants of other countries, who do not "wear their hearts upon their sleeves," the citizens of America are always patriotic, and no occasion seems to be too serious or too slight for them to give expression to this feeling. Thus nothing better pleases the average American, especially the American youth, than to be able to say that this or that building, this or that new patent appliance, is the finest or the grandest in the world. This, of course, is due to that other trait—enthusiasm. The enthusiasm of most Americans for all things new is apparently without limit. It is the essence of what is called "push"—American push. Every day I meet with this quality in my pupils. They are unwilling to stop at anything. In the matters relating to their art they are inquisitive to a degree that they want to go to the bottom of all things at once. It is as if a boy wished to dive before he could swim.

At first, when my American pupils were new to me, this trait annoyed me, and I wished them to give more attention to the one matter in hand rather than to everything at once. But now I like it, for I have come to the conclusion that this youthful enthusiasm and eagerness to take up everything is the best promise for music in America. The same opinion, I remember, was expressed by the director of the conservatory in Berlin [probably Joseph Joachim, director of the Hochschule für Musik], who, from his experience with American students of music, predicted that America within twenty or thirty years would become the first musical country.

Only when the people in general, however, begin to take as lively an interest in music and art as they now take in more material matters will the arts come into their own. Let the enthusiasm of the people once be excited, and patriotic gifts and bequests must surely follow.

It is a matter of surprise to me that all this has not come long ago. When I see how much is done in every other field by public-spirited men in America—how schools, universities, libraries, museums, hospitals, and parks spring up out of the ground and are maintained by generous gifts—I can only marvel that so little has been done for music. After two hundred years of almost unbroken prosperity and expansion, the net results for music are a number of public concert halls of most recent growth, several musical societies with orchestras of noted excellence, such as the Philharmonic Society in New York, the orchestras of Mr. Thomas [Conductor of the Chicago Orchestra since its inception in 1891] and Mr. Seidl [Conductor of the New

York Philharmonic Society since 1891], and the superb orchestra supported by a public-spirited citizen of Boston; one opera company, which only the upper classes can hear or understand, and a national conservatory which owes its existence to the generous forethought of one indefatigable woman [Jeannette Thurber].

It is true that music is the youngest of the arts, and must therefore be expected to be treated as Cinderella, but is it not time that she were lifted from the ashes and given a seat among the equally youthful sister arts in this land of youth until the coming of the fairy godmother and the prince of the crystal slipper?

Art, of course, must always go a-begging, but why should this country alone, which is so justly famed for the generosity and public spirit of its citizens, close its door to the poor beggar? In the Old World this is not so. Since the days of Palestrina . . . princes and prelates have vied with each other in extending a generous hand to music. Since the days of Pope Gregory the Church has made music one of her own chosen arts. In Germany and Austria, princes like Esterhazy, Lobkowitz, and Harrach, who supported Haydn and Beethoven, or the king of Bavaria, who did so much for Wagner, with many others, have helped create a demand for good music, which has since become universal, while in France all governments, be they monarchies, empires or republics, have done their best to carry on the noble work that was begun by Louis XIV. Even the little republic of Switzerland annually sets aside a budget for the furtherance of literature, music and the arts.

A few months ago only we saw how such a question of art as whether the operas sung in Hungary's capital would be of a national or foreign character could provoke a ministerial crisis. Such is the interest in music and art taken by the governments and people of other countries.

The great American republic alone, in its national government as well as in the several governments of the States, suffers art and music to go without encouragement. Trades and commerce are protected, funds are voted away for the unemployed, schools and colleges are endowed, but music must go unaided, and be content if she can get the support of a few private individuals like Mrs. Jeannette M. Thurber and Mr. H. L. Higginson [*sic*— Dvořák may have been referring to Col. T. W. Higginson].

Not long ago a young man came to me and showed me his compositions. His talent seemed so promising that I at once offered him a scholarship in our school, but he sorrowfully confessed that he could not afford to become my pupil because he had to earn his living by keeping books in Brooklyn. Even if he came just two afternoons in the week, or on Saturday afternoon only, he said, he would lose his employment, on which he and others had to depend. I urged him to arrange the matter with his employer, but he only received the answer: "If you want to play, you can't keep books. You will have to drop one or the other." He dropped his music.

In any other country, the State would have made some provision for such a deserving scholar, so that he could have pursued his natural calling without having to starve. With us in Bohemia, the Diet each year votes a special sum of money for just such purposes, and the imperial government in Vienna on occasion furnishes other funds for talented artists. Had it not been for such support I should not have been able to pursue my studies when I was a young man. Owing to the fact that, upon the kind recommendation of such men as Brahms, Hanslick and Herbeck, the Minister of Public Education in Vienna on five successive years sent me sums ranging from four to six hundred florins, I could pursue my work and get my compositions published, so that at the end of that time I was able to stand on my own feet. This has filled me with lasting gratitude towards my country.

Such an attitude of the State towards deserving artists is not only kind but wise. For it cannot be emphasized too strongly that art, as such does not "pay," to use an American expression—at least, not in the beginning—and that the art that has to pay its own way is apt to become vitiated and cheap.

It is one of the anomalies of this country that the principle of protection is upheld for all enterprises but art. By protection I do not mean the exclusion of foreign art. That, of course, is absurd. But just as the State here provides for its poor, industrial scholars and university students, so should it help the would-be students of music and art. As it is now, the poor musician not only cannot get his necessary instruction in the first place, but if by any chance he has acquired it, he has small prospects of making his chosen calling support him in the end. Why is this? Simply because the orchestras in which first-class players could find a place in this country can be counted on one hand; while of opera companies where native singers can be heard, and where the English tongue is sung, there is none at all. Another thing which discourages the student of music is the unwillingness of publishers to take anything but light and trashy music. European publishers are bad enough in that respect, but the American publishers are worse. Thus, when one of my pupils last year produced a very creditable work, and a thoroughly American composition at that, he could not get it published in America, but had to send it to Germany, where it was at once accepted. The same is true of my own compositions on American subjects, each of which has had to be published abroad.

No wonder American composers and musicians grow discouraged, and regard the more promising conditions of music in other countries with envy! Such a state of affairs should be a source of mortification to all truly patriotic Americans. Yet it can be easily remedied. What was the situation in England but a short while ago? Then they had to procure all their players from abroad, while their own musicians went to the Continent to study. Now that they have two standard academies of music in London, like those of Berlin, Paris, and other cities, the national feeling for music seems to have been awakened, and the majority of orchestras are composed of native Englishmen, who play as well as the others did before. A single institution can make such a change, just as a single genius can bestow an art upon his country that before was lying in unheeded slumber.

Our musical conservatory in Prague was founded but three generations ago, when a few nobles and patrons of music subscribed five thousand florins which was then the annual cost of maintaining the school. Yet that little school flourished and grew, so that now more than sixfold that amount is annually expended. Only lately a school for organ music has been added to the conservatory, so that the organists of our churches can learn to play their instruments at home, without having to go to other cities. Thus a school benefits the community in which it is. The citizens of Prague in return have shown their appreciation of the fact by building the "Rudolfinum" as a magnificent home for the arts. It is jointly occupied by the conservatory and the Academy of Arts and besides that contains large and small concert halls and rooms for picture-galleries. In the proper maintenance of this building the whole community takes an interest. It is supported, as it was founded, by the stockholders of the Bohemian Bank of Deposit, and yearly gifts and bequests are made to the institution by private citizens.

If a school of art can grow so in a country of but six million inhabitants, what much brighter prospects should it not have in a land of seventy millions? The important thing is to make a beginning, and in this the State should set an example.

They tell me that this cannot be done. I ask, why can't it be done? If the old commonwealths of Greece and Italy, and the modern republics of France and Switzerland, have been able to do this, why cannot America follow their example? The money certainly is not lacking. Constantly we see great sums of money spent for the material pleasures of the few, which, if devoted to the purposes of art, might give pleasure to thousands. If schools, art museums and libraries can be maintained at the public expense, why should not musical conservatories and playhouses? The function of the drama, with or without music, is not only to amuse, but to elevate and instruct while giving pleasure. Is it not in the interest of the State that this should be done in the most approved manner, so as to benefit all of the citizens? Let the owners of private playhouses give their performances for diversion only, let those who may, import singers who sing in foreign tongues, but let there be at least one intelligent power that will see to it that the people can hear and see what is best, and what can be understood by them, no matter how small the demand.

That such a system of performing classic plays and operas pleases the people was shown by the attitude of the populace in Prague. There the people collected money and raised subscriptions for over fifty years to build a national playhouse. In 1880 they at last had a sufficient amount and the "National Theatre" was accordingly built. It had scarcely been built when it was burned to the ground. But the people were not to be discouraged. Everybody helped, and before a fortnight was over more than a million had been collected, and the house was at once built up again, more magnificent than it was before.

In answer to such arguments I am told that there is no popular demand for good music in America. That is not so. Every concert in New York, Boston, Philadelphia, Chicago or Washington, and most other cities, no doubt, disproves such a statement. American concert halls are as well filled as those of Europe, and, as a rule, the listeners—to judge them by their attentive conduct and subsequent expression of pleasure—are not a whit less appreciative. How it would be with opera I cannot judge, since American opera audiences, as the opera is conducted at present, are in no sense representative of the people at large. I have no doubt, however, that if the Americans had a chance to hear grand opera sung in their own language they would enjoy it as well and appreciate it as highly as the opera-goers of Vienna, Paris, or Munich enjoy theirs. The change from Italian and French to English will scarcely have an injurious effect on the present good voices of the singers, while it may have the effect of improving the voices of American singer, bringing out more clearly the beauty and strength of the timbre, while giving an intelligent conception of the work that enables singers to use pure diction, which cannot be obtained in a foreign tongue.

The American voice, so far as I can judge, is a good one. When I first arrived in this country, I was startled by the strength and the depth of the voices in the boys who sell papers on the street, and I am still constantly amazed at its penetrating quality.

In a sense, of course, it is true that there is less of a demand for music in America than in certain other countries. Our common folk in Bohemia know this. When they come here, they leave their fiddles and other instruments at home, and none of the itinerant musicians with whom our country abounds would ever think of trying their luck over here. Occasionally, when I have met one of my countrymen whom I knew to be musical in this city of New York or in the West, and have asked him why he did not become a professional musician, I have usually received the answer, "Oh, music is not wanted in this land." This I can scarcely believe. Music is wanted wherever good people are, as the German poet has sung. It only rests with the leaders of the people to make a right beginning.

When this beginning is made, and when those who have musical talent find it worth their while to stay in America and to study and exercise their art as the business of their life, the music of America will soon become more national in its character. This my conviction, I know, is not shared by many who can justly claim to know this country better than I do. Because the population of the United States is composed of many different races, in which the Teutonic element predominates, and because, owing to the improved method of transmission of the present day, the music of all the world is quickly absorbed in this country, they argue that nothing specially original or national can come forth. According to that view, all other countries which are but the results of a conglomeration of peoples and races, as, for instance, Italy, could not have produced a national literature or a national music.

A while ago I suggested that inspiration for truly national music might be derived from the Negro melodies or Indian chants. I was led to take this view partly by the fact that the so-called plantation songs are indeed the most striking and appealing melodies that have yet been found on this side of the water, but largely by the observation that this seems to be recognized, though often unconsciously, by most Americans. All races have their distinctively national songs, which they at once recognize as their own, even if they have never head them before. When a Tcech [*sic*], a Pole, or a Magyar in this country suddenly hears one of his folk-songs or dances, no matter if it is for the first time in his life, his eyes light up at once, and his heart within him responds, and claims that music as his own. So it is with those of Teutonic or Celtic blood, or any other men, indeed, whose first lullaby mayhap was a song wrung from the heart of the people.

It is a proper question to ask, what songs, then, belong to the American and appeal more strongly to him than any others? What melody could stop him on the street if he were in a strange land and make the home feeling well up within him, no matter how hardened he might be or how wretchedly the tune were played? Their number, to be sure, seems to be limited. The most potent as well as the most beautiful among them, according to my estimation, are certain of the so-called plantation melodies and slave songs, all of which are distinguished by unusual and subtle harmonies, the like of which I have found in no other songs but those of old Scotland and Ireland. The point has been urged that many of these touching songs, like those of Foster, have not been composed by the Negroes themselves, but are the work of white men, while others did not originate on the plantations, but were imported from Africa. It seems to me that this matters but little. One might as well condemn the Hungarian Rhapsody because Liszt could not speak Hungarian. The important thing is that the inspiration for such music should come from the right source, and that the music itself should be a true expression of the people's real feelings. To read the right meaning the composer need not necessarily be of the same blood, though that, of course, makes it easier for him. Schubert was a thorough German, but when he wrote Hungarian music, as in the second movement of the C-Major Symphony, or in some of his piano pieces, like the Hungarian Divertissement, he struck the true Magyar note, to which all Magyar hearts, and with them our own, must forever respond. This is not a *tour de force*, but only an instance of how music can be comprehended by a sympathetic genius. The white composers who wrote the touching Negro songs which dimmed Thackeray's spectacles so that he exclaimed, "Behold, a vagabond with a corked face and banjo sings a little song, strikes a wild note, which sets the whole heart thrilling with happy pity!" had a similarly sympathetic comprehension of the deep pathos of slave life. If, as I have been informed they were, these songs were adopted by the Negroes on the plantations, they thus became true Negro songs. Whether the original songs which must have inspired the composers came from Africa or originated on the plantations matters as little as whether Shakespeare invented his own plots or borrowed them from others. The thing to rejoice over is that such lovely songs exist and are sung at the present day. I, for one, am delighted by them. Just so it matters little whether the inspiration for the coming folk songs of America is derived from the Negro melodies, the songs of the creoles, the red man's chant, or the plaintive ditties of the homesick German or Norwegian. Undoubtedly the germs for the best in music lie hidden among all the races that are commingled in this great country. The music of the people is like a rare and lovely flower growing amidst encroaching weeds. Thousands pass it, while others trample it under foot, and thus the chances are that it will perish before it is seen by the one discriminating spirit who will prize it above all else. The fact that no one has as yet arisen to make the most of it does not prove that nothing is there.

Not so many years ago Slavic music was not known to the men of other races. A few men like Chopin, Glinka, Moniuszko, Smetana, Rubinstein, and Tchaikovsky, with a few others, were able to create a Slavic school of music. Chopin alone caused the music of Poland to be known and prized by all lovers of music. Smetana did the same for us Bohemians. Such national music, I repeat, is not created out of nothing. It is discovered and clothed in new beauty, just as the myths and the legends of a people are brought to light and crystallized in undying verse by the master poets. All that is needed is a delicate ear, a retentive memory, and the power to weld the fragments of former ages together in one harmonious whole. Only the other day I read in a newspaper that Brahms himself admitted that he had taken existing folk-songs for the themes of his new book of songs, and had arranged them for piano music. I have not heard nor seen the songs, and do not know if this be so; but if it were, it would in no wise reflect discredit upon the composer. Liszt in his rhapsodies and Berlioz in his *Faust* did the same thing with existing Hungarian strains, as for instance the Racokzy March; and Schumann and Wagner made a similar use of the Marseillaise for their songs of the "Two Grenadiers." Thus, also, Balfe, the Irishman, used one of our most national airs, a Hussite song, in his opera, *Bohemian Girl,* though how he came by it nobody has as yet explained. So the music of the people, sooner or later, will command attention and creep into the books of composers.

An American reporter once told me that the most valuable talent a journalist could possess was a "nose for news." Just so the musician must prick his ear for music. Nothing must be too low or too insignificant for the musician. When he walks he should listen to every whistling boy, every street singer or blind organ-grinder. I myself am often so fascinated by these people that I can scarcely tear myself away, for every now and then I catch a strain or hear the fragments of a recurring melodic theme that sound like the voice of the people. These things are worth preserving, and no one should be above making a lavish use of all such suggestions. It is a sign of barrenness, indeed, when such characteristic bits of music exist and are not heeded by the learned musicians of the age.

I know that it is still an open question whether the inspiration derived from a few scattered melodies and folk songs can be sufficient to give a national character to higher forms of music, just as it is an open question whether national music, as such, is preferable. I myself, as I have always declared, believe firmly that the music that is most characteristic of the nation whence it springs is entitled to the highest consideration. The part of Beethoven's Ninth Symphony that appeals most strongly to all is the melody of the last movement, and that is also the most German. Weber's best opera, according to the popular estimate, is *Der Freischütz*. Why? Because it is the most German. His inspiration there clearly came from the thoroughly German sounds and situations of the story, and hence his music assumed that distinctly national character which has endeared it to the German nation as a whole. Yet he himself spent far more pains on his opera *Euryanthe*, and persisted to the end in regarding it as his best work. But the people, we see, claim their own; and after all, it is for the people that we strive.

An interesting essay could be written on the subject how much the external frame-work of an opera—that is, the words, the characters of the personages and the general *mise en scene*—contributes towards the inspiration of the composer. If Weber was inspired to produce his masterpiece by so congenial a theme as the story of *Der Freischütz*, Rossini was undoubtedly similarly inspired by the Swiss surroundings of William Tell. Thus one might almost suspect that some of the charming melodies of that opera are more the product and property of Switzerland than of the Italian composer. It is to be noticed that all of Wagner's operas, with the exception of his earliest work, *Rienzi*, are inspired by German subjects. The most German of them all is that of *Die Meistersinger*, that opera of operas, which should be an example to all who distrust the potency of their own national topics.

Of course, as I have indicated before, it is possible for certain composers to project their spirit into that of another race and country. Verdi partially succeeded in striking Oriental chords in his *Aida*, while Bizet was able to produce so thoroughly Spanish strains and measures as those of *Carmen*. Thus inspiration can be drawn from the depths as well as from the heights, although that is not my conception of the true mission of music. Our mission should be to give pure pleasure, and to uphold the ideals of our race. Our mission as teachers is to show the right way to those who come after us.

My own duty as a teacher, I conceive, is not so much to interpret Beethoven, Wagner, or other masters of the past, but to give what encouragement I can to the young musicians of America. I must give full expression to my firm conviction, and to the hope that just as this nation has already surpassed so many others in marvellous inventions and feats of engineering and commerce, and has made an honourable place for itself in literature in one short century, so it must assert itself in the other arts, and especially in the art of music. Already there are enough public-spirited lovers of music striving for the advancement of this their chosen art to give rise to the hope that the United States of America will soon emulate the older countries in smoothing the thorny path of the artist and musician. When that beginning has been made, when no large city is without its public opera house and concert hall, and without its school of music and endowed orchestra, where native musicians can be heard and judged, then those who hitherto have had no opportunity to reveal their talent will come forth and compete with one another, till a real genius emerges from their number, who will be as thoroughly representative of his country as Wagner and Weber are of Germany, or Chopin of Poland.

To bring about this result we must trust to the ever youthful enthusiasm and patriotism of this country. When it is accomplished, and when music has been established as one of the reigning arts of the land, another wreath of fame and glory will be added to this country which earned its name, the "Land of Freedom," by unshackling her slaves at the price of her own blood.

DVOŘÁK AS I KNEW HIM
THE ETUDE, NOVEMBER 1919, 693–694
JEANNETTE THURBER

In the year 1891 I was so fortunate as to secure Bohemia's foremost composer, Antonín Dvořák, as artistic director of the National Conservatory. In his letter of acceptance, dated December 12, 1891, there is a sentence so characteristic of his modesty and naiveté (he was as free from vanity as his idol, Schubert) that I cannot refrain from citing it: "Mme. Dvořák and my eldest daughter, Otilka, are very anxious to see Amerika, but I am a little afraid that I shall not be able to please you in everything in my new position. As a teacher and conductor I feel myself quite sure, but there (are) many other *trifles* which will make me much sorrow and grieve—but I rely on your kindness and indulgence and be sure I shall do all to please you."

He kept his promise. From the start he devoted himself to his new duties with the utmost zeal, and the influence he exerted on his many pupils in both the vocal and instrumental departments is felt to this day, and all over the country. Many of our most gifted young men eagerly seized the opportunity of studying with him. Among these young students were Harvey Worthington Loomis, Rubin Goldmark, Harry Rowe Shelley, William Arms Fisher, Harry T. Burleigh and Will Marion Cook, who now rank with our best composers.

His greatest achievement in America, it is needless to say, was the composition of the *New World Symphony*, one of the most inspired symphonic works ever created. When he wrote this work he attempted to reproduce in it, here and there, the spirit (though not the exact notes) of negro songs. I helped him to the best of my ability in securing the material, and so did Harry T. Burleigh, his pupil, now the foremost composer of his race.

In looking back over my thirty-five years of activity as President of the National Conservatory of Music of America there is nothing I am so proud of as having been able to bring Dr. Dvořák to America, thus being privileged to open the way for one of the world's symphonic masterpieces, as well as some chamber works which are admittedly even better than the chamber music he wrote in Europe. Well do I remember how the Kneisel Quartet came to the Conservatory to try over this music in the composer's presence! A gala day in New York's concert life was the first performance of the *New World Symphony* by the Philharmonic Orchestra under Anton Seidl. It was the most important event in the long history of the Philharmonic.

On the whole, Dvořák seemed to be happy in his new surroundings, although he suffered much from homesickness, being intensely patriotic. He passed two [*sic*] of his summers in Spillville, because of the number of Bohemians living there. Anton Seidl was probably right in declaring that the intense pathos of the slow movement of the *New World Symphony* was inspired by nostalgia—by longing for home. It was at my suggestion that he composed this symphony. He used to be particularly homesick on steamer days when he read the shipping news in the *Herald*. Thoughts of home often moved him to tears. On one of these day I suggested that he write a symphony embodying his experiences and feelings in America—a suggestion which he promptly adopted.

Some have held that the slow movement of his American symphony was inspired by Longfellow's *Hiawatha*, but that was one of his operatic projects. In one of his letters to me he says, "As you know, I am a great admirer of Longfellow's *Hiawatha*, and I get so attached to it that I cannot resist the attempt to write an opera on this subject, which would be very good fitted for that purpose." I secured the permission of the publishers and of Miss Alice M. Longfellow for him to use the poem, but Dvořák did not live to carry out this plan. One may doubt whether he would have succeeded so well as he did with his symphony, for, outside of Bohemia, his operas have not obtained a foothold, though there is much beautiful music in them. He was deeply interested in his project for a *New World* opera. One day he wrote me: "But I am longing for the libretto of *Hiawatha*. Where is it? If I cannot have it very soon—much is lost."

We discussed the possible librettists, and I took him to see Buffalo Bill's Indians dance as a suggestion for the ballet. It is really to be regretted that his operatic project came to naught. *Hiawatha* would have been sung in English. When I first met Dr. Dvořák, in London, he told me that he had wanted to meet me, as he considered I "had made music a possibility in America by having opera sung in the vernacular."

On June 25, 1892, he wrote me from Vysoka, Bohemia: "Just now I got a letter from Littleton, of New York, from which I see that you have the splendid idea I should write a Columbus Cantata (or something like) which ought to be given at my first appearance in New York." He subsequently did write a cantata, "America's [*sic*] Flag," which is listed as his Opus 102. It was given, but did not meet with much success. The date of his first public appearance in New York was October 21, 1892.

Dvořák was not only one of the most original composers of his time, but one of the most emotional. This was partly due to the depth of his religious feeling. He was a most conscientious church-goer, and often spent hours on his knees in prayer. He had a passion for Schubert. On Schubert he wrote, in collaboration with Henry T. Finck (who has been connected with the National Conservatory for three decades), an article for the *Century Magazine*, concerning which Sir George Grove wrote to him that he considered it the best essay on that composer ever printed.

While Dvořák was not of a markedly social disposition, he established intimate friendship with some of the eminent musicians associated with the National Conservatory, among them Rafael Joseffy and Anton Seidl, with whom he spent many of his evenings.

Nothing could have given me greater pleasure than to continue Dr. Dvořák's directorship indefinitely, but after three years with us and a promised renewal of his contract for the fourth year, he found his home ties strongest, and in a long letter to me, gave numerous family reasons for wishing to be released from his agreement, closing with these lines: "Mrs. Thurber, you know well how much I value your friendship, how much I admire your love for music, for its development you have done so much, and, therefore, I may hope that you will agree with me and that you will kindly recognize and acknowledge all the above-mentioned reasons."

DVOŘÁK AS I KNEW HIM
THE ETUDE, NOVEMBER 1919, 694
HARRY ROWE SHELLEY

Dvořák was a child of nature in the class room, where his decision in the greatness of matters musical was absolute; once his mind was made up nothing could alter his views. To be a successful student under the direction of this man, a thorough knowledge of preliminaries was necessary—upon these no time was ever spent by him. His mission lay in telling the musical aspirant the good or bad points of the subject material brought for development; natural key relationship for contrasting themes; orchestral color best suited to the inception of the content of the subject; not setting music haphazard to a certain instrument, but knowing the appropriate instrument for the music's demands for expression. He was insistent upon continuous work, and constant new material from his students, demanding three new portions of a composition (of large form) each week, saying "when you cannot do that, then are you no composer."

He stipulated the right of command either to teach a pupil or to dismiss him because of the lack of talent in composition, saying "this heartache is only one: it will save you many, bye-and-bye."

Charlatanism was to Dvořák especially provocative of disgust. An encroachment by a pupil upon the field of another composer; an inadvertent borrowing of another's successful musical thoughts; even a thematic treatment overtly resembling the recognized music of some master brought down vials of vituperation from the master, and the indignant remark: "yes, maybe—but it is not yours!"

He found the student in America somewhat different in his attitude toward study from those of his native land; also lacking in respect toward the general art of music, which he held in the highest esteem: he abhorred the popular lilt of the so-called "Viennese swing," which he termed "Coffee House."

He quoted the opinion of Hanslich [*sic*] regarding the published critique of the three Slavic Dances, which called the first one the most musicianly; the second, the most national; the third, the most beautiful; saying "the critic is right."

He played the theme of the largo of the *New World Symphony* twenty minutes after he had written it, singing the immortal theme with great passion and fervor, his eyes bulging out; his blood purple red in the neck veins (years later he died of Bright's disease from red meat eating), his whole body vibrating as he played this music to his first listener; saying: "Is it not beautiful music? It is for my symphony; but—it is not symphonic music." Seidl was responsible for this movement being marked Largo, which Dvořák had marked Larghetto; Seidl was extremely fond of conducting this symphony which was upon the last program he conducted, and he often spoke of it, saying: "It is not a good name: *New World Symphony,* it is homesickness—home-longing!"

Dvořák spent whole afternoons at the Vienna Cafe with one or two friends talking music, drinking coffee, an occasional glass of beer, with always a clear vision of the music under discussion. He produced a letter from Zimrock [*sic*] written to him (Dvořák), in which the former said that Brahm's [*sic*] had just told him how much he admired the music of Dvořák, and that he wished that he (Brahms) "could write with the same sunshiny-ness (sonnenshine [*sic*])."

Dvořák kept one pupil at work for forty weeks upon the thematic development (Durch fuehrung) of an overture, three lessons weekly, during which period the pupil wrote thousands of measures, before the master expressed himself; saying "Now is it right; now you know the durch fue-hrung treatment from Haydn to me, and if you imitate any composer, you are a bad musician. Now go your own way."

Dvořák would sometimes be asked by pupils why he had discrimi-nated against certain portions of their compositions, of which they were per-sonally very proud and fond: the answer would be: "I don't know; only—no!" Therein his judgment was faultless: his decision had been for the pupil's future good and development; he had neither time, desire nor academic equipment to go into the mathematics of music.

He disliked fugues, saying, "Yes that is a good theme, but why bore your listeners by telling them the same thing over and over again; they should feel insulted!"

He advised writing fifteen minutes in the morning, for themes and material to be worked out later, saying, "If you should be allowed to com-pose, then will your ideas be the best and freshest."

He was a great man and rose from being a street player upon the vio-lin, to the Bohemian Parliament, of which he was a member at the time of his death, and better still, he became one of that group of immortal compos-ers whose music is the divine inheritance of the world.

Letters and Memoirs of Dvořák

Editor's Note: This selection of translated letters and other documents pertaining to Dvořák's American sojourn are taken from Otakar Šourek, *Antonín Dvořák: Letters and Reminiscences*, trans. Roberta Finlayson Samsour (Prague: Artia, 1954). The arrangement and framing remarks are my own.

Dvořák to A. Göbl at Sychrov in Bohemia, 20 June 1891. He speaks about his invitation to come to America.

Dear Friend,

Yesterday, after 40 hours of travelling, we arrived home safely. Everything turned out splendidly—as I already informed you in my letter from Cambridge. It will remain an unforgettable memory for the rest of my life. It would take me a long, long time to tell you about it. Perhaps you will read of it in the papers. . . . *I am to go to America for 2 years*. The directorship of the Conservatoire and to conduct 10 concerts (of my own compositions) for 8 months and 4 months vacation, for a yearly salary of 15,000 dollars or over 30,000 gold francs. Should I take it? Or should I not? Write me a word or two. I am waiting for *Dr. Tragy* before I make a decision. Write to me at Vysoka which I am leaving for *tomorrow*, Monday, with my family.

With affectionate greetings to Yourself and kind regards to all at Sychrov,

Yours,

A. Dvořák

Dvořák to A. Göbl at Sychrov in Bohemia, 1 August 1891. He considers accepting Mrs. Thurber's offer to come to America.

Dear friend,

. . . And now something about America. Yesterday I got a copy of the contract. It is very long but I don't know yet whether I shall accept it. It seems that I should have 3 hours a day teaching composition and instrumentation and, in addition, prepare in 8 months 4 concerts with the pupils of the Conservatory and give 6 concerts in American towns at which the main works to be performed would be Stabat, The Spectre's Bride, Ludmilla, Requiem, Symphonies and Overture etc. For that I should get 15,000 dollars, or, in Czech money, 35,000 gulden. Before I leave they will deposit half the remuneration in Prague and the other half I should get by the month in advance. There is only one little hitch. I want the 7,500 dollars to be paid up by the end of *May* 1893 so that I could have holidays in June, July, August and the first half of September—which I should prefer to spend in Bohemia. If they meet this condition I shall probably accept. What people say of America is very mixed. As always in this world some are for and some against. Whether I shall get to see you or not I cannot say. . . . Then we shall have a lot to talk about. Especially about the Requiem and how it turned out in Birmingham. Very soon I shall be getting the arrangement for piano and I shall send you a copy at once.

    Your

    A. Dvořák

Dvořák to Aug. Bohdanecky at Cimelice in Bohemia, 24 October 1891. Dvořák anticipates his arrival in America.

Dear Friend,

    Thank you first of all for having sent what I asked for my pigeons. They will have a fine feed!

    You will probably have read that I am safely back from England and that the Requiem was a tremendous success.

    . . . Yesterday I sent the contract, revised for the third time, to London, and if they agree to all my changes—I shall sign. In America they write a great deal about my coming and have great expectations of my artistic activity.

    Well, there will be a fine to-do when I get there! And then the

Czechoslovaks—how they are looking forward, as I hear, to my arrival!

Once more my warmest thanks,

Your affectionate friend,

Antonín Dvořák

From Josef Jan Kovařík's *Reminiscences*. Dvořák's trip to New York.

. . . I made Master Dvořák's acquaintance during my studies at the Prague Conservatoire to which I came from my native town of Spillville and where I finished in 1892. . . .

When, on taking my final examinations at the Conservatoire, I mentioned that I would be leaving as soon as possible for America, the Master said quite simply: "You know what—we shall do it like this: you will wait till September and then we shall go nicely together." On my asking what I should do in Bohemia for two whole months, the Master said: "You will come for the holidays to our place at Vysoka and then we shall set out together for America!" And that was what happened.

At Vysoka life ran in the channels cut out by the Master during his previous visits. The Master himself was very diligent this summer. First of all he finished the "Te Deum" which was to be given its first performance at his first appearance in New York and then, when an English poem reached him from Mrs. Jeanette [*sic*] Thurber, the founder of the National Conservatory in New York, he started work on the cantata "The American Flag," the sketch for which he had completed before his departure for America. Otherwise the quiet tenor of life at Vysoka was considerably enlivened by the arrival on a visit of Oskar Nedbal and Josef Suk who were to work out the piano arrangement of some of the Master's works. Especially Nedbal was up to all sorts of pranks which sometimes made the Master really angry. . . .

In the middle of September 1892, the Master, with his wife, his daughter Otilie and his son Antonín, set out on the journey to America. We left Prague at 3 o'clock in the afternoon—on a Thursday—: at the station a lot of the Master's friends had come to see him off, and the last word the Master addressed to them was "au revoir in summer!" On Friday we were in Bremen and on Saturday we boarded the SS *Saale*, which was to convey us across the ocean. The ship weighed anchor at about 1 p.m., and at 5 p.m. on Sunday we reached Southampton in England from where the Master sent a telegram to the children who had remained behind in Prague that "everything is all right, all well."

The voyage lasted nine days and was very pleasant on the whole, except for three days when it was quite stormy and all the passengers, with the exception of the Master, kept to their cabins. The Master proved an excellent sailor; the whole day, it might be as stormy as you like, he walked up and down the deck. Several times it happened that he was the only one to put in an appearance in the dining-room, and when Capt. Rinck saw him so alone, he invited him to his table. When they had breakfasted or dined at their ease, they lit their cigars and chatted.

On Monday, the 26th of September, if I am not mistaken, after 6 o'clock in the evening, the ship docked in New York harbour. Here the Master was met by Mr. Stanton, then Secretary to the National Conservatory who, after the usual customs examination, took us to the Clarendon Hotel where a room had been reserved for the Master—complete with concert grand. The Master did not, however, find it quiet enough there and longed for a private lodging. This was found, at last, in no. 327 East 17th Street, opposite the Stuyvesant Park—with a Mrs. Drew—and as the Conservatory was in the same street [126–128 East Seventeenth Street], the Master had not far to go.

Dvořák to Dr. Emil Kozdnek at Kromeriz in Moravia, 7 a.m., 12 October 1892. His first impressions of America.

Dear Friend,

I promised to write to you and am doing so now and very gladly because when I write to the old country (as they say here) or, what is the same, to a very good friend,—being thus engaged with him—it seems to me as if I saw him here before me. And so it is today. I see you, as on a fine autumn morning, walking through the Kromeriz Park and looking sadly at the trees from which the leaves are falling one by one. But what help is there? Nature, too, needs her *diminuendo* and *morendo* so that she may come to life again and gather herself up for a great crescendo, achieving then her full strength and height in a mighty *ff*.—Where have I got to?—what am I telling you? I should be writing to you about our journey—about our crossing to America and perhaps about things concerning me personally?

Well, listen!

Our journey was lovely except for one day when everybody on board was sick except me—and so after only a short period of quarantine, we arrived safely in the promised land. The view from "Sandy Hook" (harbour town)—of New York with the magnificent Statue of Liberty (in whose head alone there is room for 60 persons and where banquets etc. are often held)—

is most impressive! And then the amount of shipping from all parts of the world?! As I say amazing. On Tuesday the 27th we reached the town (Hoboken) where all ships dock, and there we were awaited by the Secretary to the National Conservatory, Mr. Santon—and what gave me special pleasure—by a Czech deputation. We exchanged greetings and a few words and then—a carriage was waiting for us and in a short time we were in New York, and are still in the same hotel. The city itself is magnificent, lovely buildings and beautiful streets and then, everywhere, the greatest cleanliness. It is dear here. Our gulden is like a dollar. At the hotel we pay 55 dollars a week for three rooms, of course in the most central part of the city, "Union Square." That does not matter, however, for we shall not spend more than 5000 and so, I am thankful to say, we shall be able to leave the rest untouched. On Sunday the 9th, there was a big Czech concert in my honour. There were 3000 people present in the hall—and there was no end to the cheering and clapping. There were speeches in Czech and English and I, poor creature, had to make a speech of thanks from the platform, holding a silver wreath in my hands. You can guess how I felt! Besides you will learn about it later from the newspapers. What the American papers write about me is simply terrible—they see in me, they say, the saviour of music and I don't know what else besides! All the scientific and political papers have been writing and are still writing about me.

I must finish as I have no more room. A hundred thousand, affectionate greetings from

A. Dvořák

1st concert at the "Music Hall," 21st October. Te Deum, Three Overtures. Please address your letter: A. D. National Conservatory of Music 126–128. 17th Street New York, North America.

Dvořák to Mr. and Mrs. Hlavka in Prague, 27 December 1892. Dvořák describes his life and work in America.

Parker House, Boston (Hotel)

Dear Sir, Esteemed Madam,

I have been wanting to write to you for a long time but have always put it off, waiting for a more suitable moment when I could tell you something of particular interest about America and especially about the musical conditions here. There is so much to tell and all so new and interesting that I cannot put it all down on paper and so I shall limit myself to the most important things.

The first and chief thing is that, thanks be to God, we are all well and liking it here very much. And why shouldn't we when it is so lovely and free here and one can live so much more peacefully—and that is what I need. I do not worry about anything and do my duty and it is all right. There are things here which one must admire and others which I would rather not see, but what can you do, everywhere there is something—in general, however, it is altogether different here, and, if America goes on like this, she will surpass all the others.

Just imagine how the Americans work in the interests of art and for the people! So, for instance, yesterday I came to Boston to conduct my obligatory concert (every thing connected with it being arranged by the highly esteemed President of our Conservatory, the tireless Mrs. Jeanette [*sic*] M. Thurber) at which the Requiem will be given with several hundred performers. The concert on December 1st will be for only the *wealthy and the intelligentsia*, but the preceding day my work will also be performed for poor workers who earn 18 dollars a week, the purpose being to give the poor and uneducated people the opportunity to hear the musical works of all times and all nations!! That's something, isn't it? I am looking forward to it like a child.

Today, Sunday, I have a rehearsal at three o'clock in the afternoon and wonder how it will come off. The orchestra here, which I heard in Brooklyn, is excellent, 100 musicians, mostly German as is also the conductor. His name is Nikisch and he comes from somewhere in Hungary. The orchestra was founded by a local millionaire, Colonel Higginson, who gave a big speech at my first concert (a thing unheard of here), spoke of my coming to America and the purpose to be served by my stay here. The Americans expect great things of me and the main thing is, so they say, to show them to the promised land and kingdom of a new and independent art, in short, to create a national music. If the small Czech nation can have such musicians, they say, why could not they, too, when their country and people is so immense.

Forgive me for lacking a little in modesty, but I am only telling you what the American papers are constantly writing.—It is certainly both a great and splendid task for me and I hope that with God's help I shall accomplish it. There is more than enough material here and plenty of talent. I have pupils from as far away as San Francisco. They are mostly poor people, but at our Institute teaching is free of charge—anybody who is really talented pays no fees! I have only 8 pupils, but some of them are very promising.

And then not less so are the entries for the competition for prizes offered by Mrs. Thurber. 1000 dollars for an opera, 1000 for an oratory, 1000 for a libretto, 500 for a symphony, and, for a cantata, a piano or a violin concerto, 300 dollars each.

A great deal of music has come in from all over America and I must go through it all. It does not take much work. I look at the first page and can tell straight away whether it is the work of a dilettante or an artist.

As regards operas, they are very poor and I don't know whether any will be awarded a prize. Besides myself there are other gentlemen on the jury—for each kind of composition five of us. The other kinds of composition such as symphonies, concertos, suites, serenades etc. interest me very much.—The composers are all much the same as at home—brought up in the German School, but here and there another spirit, other thoughts, another colouring flashes forth, in short, something Indian (something a la Bret Harte). I am very curious how things will develop. As regards my own work, this is my programme: On Mondays, Wednesdays and Fridays, from 9–11, I have composition; twice a week orchestra practice from 4–6 and the rest of my time is my own. You see that it is not a great deal and Mrs. Thurber is very "considerate" as she wrote to me in Europe that she would be.

She looks after the administration side herself—has a secretary—also a founding member of the co-operative (very wealthy), a Mr. Stanton, an intimate friend of Mr. Cleveland, whereas Mrs. Thurber is a Republican—, but in matters of ar they get on very well together and work for the good of our young and not yet fully developed institute. And so it is all right. The second secretary is Mrs. MacDowel [sic] and she is mainly in charge of the correspondence.

And now something about our own domestic affairs. We live in 17th street East, 327 (only 4 mins. from the school) and are very satisfied with the flat. Mr. Steinway sent me a piano immediately—a lovely one and, of course, free of charge, so that we have one nice piece of furniture in our sitting-room. Besides this we have 3 other rooms and a small room (furnished) and pay 80 dollars a month. A lot for us but the normal price here.

We have breakfast and supper at home and go to a boarding-house for dinner.

I must stop. My kind regards to yourself and your wife,

I remain, Gratefully Yours,

Antonín Dvořák

My wife, who is with me, asks to be remembered to you.

~

From Josef Jan Kovařík's *Reminiscences*. City life in New York.

. . . The Master lived in New York very quietly and, I believe, more free from care than in Prague. The first year, however, when he left his children behind in Prague (Anna, Magda, Otakar and Aloisie) and then the last (third) year when he came to America with only his wife and son, Otakar, he often longed for his children. But the second year, when he had his whole family round him, was, I am firmly convinced, the happiest year of his life.

The Master in general did not go out anywhere. He regularly attended the concerts of the New York Philharmonic (beside which he was only twice at the Metropolitan Opera during his whole stay in New York), twice in succession he went to hear the Kneisel Quartet and twice he was at a concert of the Boston Philharmonic which now as then comes to New York five times in the season and gives ten concerts.

The Master did not go out into society and, if he happened to be invited somewhere, he usually declined the invitation. In America, too, social life is not the same as in Europe. The American, engaged all day in business, likes to spend the evenings at home with his family.

What the Master missed in America were his pigeons and locomotives. He felt the want of these two "hobbies" very much, but here, too, he at length found a modest substitute. One day we went with the Master to the Central Park where there is a small Zoological Garden and buildings with different kinds of birds. And then we came to a huge aviary with about two hundred pigeons. It was a real surprise for the Master and his pleasure at seeing the pigeons was great and even though none of these pigeons could compare with his "pouters" and "fantails," we made the trip to Central Park at least once and often twice a week.

With locomotives it was a more difficult matter. In New York at the time, there was only one station—the others were across the river (the city of New York is situated on the island of Manhattan). At the main station they did not allow anybody on to the platform except the passengers and it was in vain that we begged the porter to let us look at the "American locomotive." We travelled by overhead tram to 155th Street, a good hour from the Master's house, and there, on a bank, waited for the Chicago or Boston express to go by. Only it took up a lot of time, nearly the whole afternoon, as we always waited for a number of trains so that it would be worth the journey—and then the Master found a new hobby in steamships. For one thing the harbour was much nearer and then, on the day of departure, the public was allowed on board, an opportunity which the Master made full use of.

There was soon not a boat that we had not inspected from stem to stern. The Master always started a conversation with the ship's captain or with his assistants, and so, in a short time, we knew all the captains and mates by name. And when a ship was due to sail we went there and watched it from the shore till it was out of sight. If it happened that the Master remained a little longer than usual at the Conservatory or was engrossed in his work at home and so forgot about the departure of the boat and there was no longer time to go to the harbour, we went by overhead tram to Battery Park (the most southerly tip of the City) and from there followed the ship in her outward journey for as long as she remained in sight.

In the evening then, after a game of "darda," we discussed with the Master how many knots the ship had probably made, where she might be etc. In the morning, the Master's first work was to take the "Herald" and read the "shipping news."

Dvořák to Dr. Emil Kozanek in Moravia, 7 a.m., 12 April 1893. Dvořák talks about the New York newspaper gossip and discloses plans about the upcoming trip to Spillville, Iowa.

My dear Friend Doctor Kozanek,

In order to satisfy you straight I shall tell you at once that I am as fit as a fiddle and in good heart and (except for some trifles) very well off. Boys in the street and the policemen—and drunken Irish women in the street, these are the things that annoy me, but one gets accustomed and *disaccustomed* to everything. But don't think that the "dis" refers to my friends at home (God bless them!) I think of you every day—but I say so only because it is an old saying, that is, only for the sake of saying something. It's true that with many people it often is so, but I shall not get used to the "dis" and as to the accustomed "to" I have a good disposition and am not afraid of anything, not even of the bad, spiteful critics in Vienna and here, too.

I have not met with opposition but the papers here are terribly fond of gossip which not even Cleveland escapes—and so they wrote a variety of things about me and it was all what they call: *sensational gossip*, nothing more. Have you read, perhaps, in Narodni Listy the tattle about Stabat Mater? It was given in Brooklyn and here in New York. I was to conduct it there but I did not as our president (an excellent woman and my staunch supporter), did not wish me to conduct when Madam Juch was singing—there had been some disagreement between them which, however turned out unfavourably for Madam Juch, and this was the reason for the rage of some of the papers. The local Czech newspapers copied it and then the Narodni Listy from them. That is what you may have read, but Mrs. Thurber is in the right. I am to go to Chicago, too, but I do not know what arrangements will be made. On the 15th and 16th April they are going to give a grand performance of the "Requiem," I was to conduct but shall not be able to do so. Last week, on the 6th April, they gave "The Spectre's Bride" here, and previous to that I conducted the "Hussite."

A small but good choir, the soloists good, with one exception, the orchestra weak for such a big hall—the "Carnegie Hall," and so the full effect was not always achieved. In autumn, however, we hall have a big concert and I shall be conducting and it will be different. Here, too, some of the critics are against me but the others are all good friends and write fairly and sometimes enthusiastically. I should like to have still more enemies than I have in Vienna, with the great exception of Dr. Hanslick. I have a good disposition, I can stand a lot and still be quite ready to forgive them. As far as this is concerned, you may be quite at rest. I sit firmly in the saddle and I like it here, except, as I say, for some trifles.

My wish to return to Bohemia will not be realized this year, we have decided otherwise.

The children and my sister-in-law, Mrs. Koutecká [Terezie Koutecká was the children's aunt], are coming here and will leave Prague on the 23rd May, on board the "Havel" from Bremen, so that, God grant, on the 31st May I shall look upon the faces of my dear and long-missed children. Then we shall go straight to Chicago, have a look at the Exhibition, and then set out straight for *our summer Vysoka* in the State of Iowa, for the Czech village of Spillville where the teacher and the parish priest and everything is Czech and so I shall be among my own folks and am looking forward to it very much.

The teacher, Mr. Kovařík (from Pisek and here 26 years), and the priest, Mr. Bilý, a very lively fellow, so they say (from Budejovice in Bohemia), will be the people with whom I shall be in closest contact. I shall have *pigeons* there and maybe we shall even play "darda"? How grand it will be. The priest has two pairs of ponies and we shall ride to Protivin, a little town near Spillville. Here in America there are *names of towns and villages of all nations under the sun!!*

The State of Iowa to which we are going is 1300 miles from New York but here such a distance is nothing. Thirty-six hours by express and we are there. It is father than from where you are to London. Very soon we are going to see Buffalo, a town near *Niagara* and so we shall see the gigantic waterfalls. How I am looking forward to it. And now, what shall I write to you about?

I have not much work at school so that I have enough time for my own work and am now just finishing my E Minor Symphony. I take great pleasure in it and it will differ very considerably from my others. Well, the *influence* of America must be felt by everyone who has any "nose" at all. Now I am negotiating with Novello (he has also his firm and agents here) and so my most recent compositions will be published at last.

They are: 1. Overture in F major, 2. Overture in A major, 3. Overture in F sharp major, 4. Dumky . . . , 5. Rondo for 'cello, 6. Te Deum, 7. The American Flag for choir and orchestra, 8. Symphony in E minor.

I have no room left again. More another time.

With affectionate greetings to You and to All,

Ant. Dvořák

Write soon!

Tomorrow the Hamburg boat "*Columbia*" is sailing so I hope you will get this letter sooner.

From Josef Jan Kovařík's *Reminiscences.* Dvořák's trip from New York to Spillville.

On Saturday, June 3rd 1893—the third day after the children's arrival, we set out for Spillville in Iowa—for our holidays.

Our "caravan" or squad numbered ten persons—the Master with his wife, Mrs. Koutecka, six children, a maid (brought by Mrs. Koutecka from Bohemia) and myself. The journey from New York to Spillville (about 1320 English miles or 2112 km) took us by way of Philadelphia, Harrisburg, the Allegheny Mountains to Pittsburgh and from there via Chicago to Spillville. The Master took an immense interest in everything on the journey. I had constantly to explain what country we were passing through etc. The journey passed pleasantly, everything went smoothly, the train was up to time and the Master's interest kept growing.

On Sunday at 11 o'clock, we reached Chicago where my brother met us. There we made a ten-hour stop, in the afternoon we drove through the town and at 9 o'clock in the evening we set out again for Spillville. On Monday at 8. a.m. we were in McGregor (Iowa) where the train stopped for an hour, had breakfast, watched the sweeping currents of the Mississippi—and left again at 9 for our destination. The Master, after a good breakfast, was in excellent spirits, everything interested him greatly and he was specially glad that in two hours he would at last leave the train and be at our journey's end—in the country and before we realized it, we had reached Calmar— our last station (the railway does not go to Spillville). In Calmar we were met by my father, the Rev. Tomas Bilý, parish priest in Spillville and a native of Luznice by Trebon and the Rev. František Vrba, parish priest in American Protivin (Iowa)—I do not remember what part of Bohemia he comes from. After a short exchange of greetings, the Master and his family got into the carriage and we set out on the last stage of our journey to Spillville—about 8 km.

When the Master decided to spend his holiday in Spillville, I wrote to my Father to ask him whether there was not a little house to let. There was not, however, and so Father secured a lodging with a Mr. Schmidt (a German) consisting of eight rooms, and Father also saw to having it furnished so that on our arrival everything was in readiness—except a piano.

In our family, Mother was always the early bird and when, on the following morning, she caught sight of the Master at 5 o'clock in the morning walking up and down in front of the school, she got a great fright as she thought something unpleasant must have happened to them in the house. She ran out and began asking the Master what had happened (she did not know that the Master was also an early riser) whereupon the Master replied: "Nothing happened—and yet a great deal. Imagine, I was walking there in the wood along by the stream and after eight months I heard again the singing of birds! And here the birds are different from ours, they have much brighter colours and they sing differently, too. And now I am going to have breakfast and after breakfast I shall come again."

He went off but was soon back—we, lazy ones, were only getting up—and asked at what time was mass, that he would like to play the organ. Mass was at seven. Meantime the other members of the Master's family had appeared and we went to church. The Master at the organ began "God before Thy majesty"—and we started singing, but the old women looked up in surprise to the choir to see what was happening. They were not accustomed to be disturbed at "silent mass" by the organ and singing. And so the Master sat at the organ every day except the days he spent in Chicago, Omaha and St. Paul. The old women got used to the Master's "disturbing" them and began to sing too, which pleased the Master very much; things progressed so far, indeed, that after mass some granny or grandad ventured to address him: "Mr. Dvořák, the singing was fine today," and "What will you be playing us tomorrow?"

The Master's day in Spillville was more or less as follows: He got up about four o'clock and went for a walk—to the stream or the river—and returned at five. After his walk he worked, at seven he was sitting at the organ in church, then he chatted a little, went home, worked again (in Spillville Dvořák wrote the F major string quartet and the E flat major string quintet) and then went for a walk. He usually went alone—here he had none of the nerve storms which he sometimes suffered from in Prague—and often nobody knew where he had gone. Almost every afternoon he spent in the company of some of the older settlers. He got them to tell him about their bitter and difficult beginnings in America: the old men told him how they went to help with the building of the railway—40 miles from Spillville— and how they went the long distance to work on foot, while their wives with the children toiled on the farms.

In Spillville the Master scarcely ever talked about music and I think that was one of the reasons he liked being there and why he felt so happy there.

Dvořák to A. Rus in Bohemia, 17 August 1893. After his return to Spillville from Chicago, Dvořák talks about the Chicago Columbian Exhibition and describes some new works.

Dear Friend,

We have just come back from Chicago where, as you probably know, the 12th August was "Czech Day" at the Exhibition and I hasten to write and tell you something about this great day.

On this day there was a great procession of all American Czechs at the Exhibition where a big concert was held and a big Sokol display. There were about 30,000 Czechs in the procession and the concert was in the big Festival Hall (orchestra 114 performers) and I conducted my own compositions and Mr. Hlavac from Russia conducted the other works by Czech composers. The orchestra, as also the rendering, was splendid and the enthusiasm general. All the papers wrote enthusiastically as you will probably learn from your papers. The Exhibition itself is gigantic and to write of it would be a vain undertaking. It must be seen and seen very often, and still you do not really know anything, there is so much and everything so big truly "made in America." In spite of everything there will be a big deficit and many people here at the Exhibition are complaining and especially in Chicago business is suffering badly.

In September, about the 17th, we are leaving here for New York and will stop for a day or two again in Chicago, and on the 25th September I must be back at school. So if you write, write straight to New York, for it will be the first days of September before you get this letter and I am afraid your letter would no longer find us in Spillville. Except for the great heat, we have spent a very nice and pleasant holiday among the Czechs and the children are already saying that they will miss it here.

That I have written a new E minor Symphony and that I have a new quartet for strings you probably already know, and I hope that during the coming season all my compositions will come out. At last Simrock has eaten humble pie and says that he will take all my works. I knew that he must come first to me and not I to him. So I have punished him after all with my waiting. It will be a whole pile of things when it is published. Three Overtures, Dumky, Rondo, "Silent Woods," Symphony, Quartet and Quintet, besides which I still [*sic*] the "Te Deum" and "The American Flag" for choir and orchestra which Mr. Novello is interested in. But I do not know whether or when we shall come to terms.

With affectionate greetings to All,

Entirely yours,

Antonín Dvořák

Dvořák to Dr. Kozanek in Kromeriz, 15 September 1893. During his last days in Spillville, Dvořák describes his life there.

Dear Friend,

Your last letter dated the 26th August arrived safely and I was very happy to get it. Thank you. You wish to have a letter, too, from Spillville—and it's now or never as we are going tomorrow, Saturday, by way of Chicago and Niagara Falls, and then straight on to New York where I am to start work on the 21st September. The three months spent here in Spillville will remain a happy memory for the rest of our lives. We enjoyed being here and were very happy though we found the three months of heat rather trying. It was made up to us, however, by being among our own people, our Czech countrymen, and that gave us great joy. If it had not been for that, we should not have come here at all.

Spillville is a purely Czech settlement, founded by a certain "Bavarian," "German," "Spielmann," who christened the place Spillville. He died four years ago, and in the morning when I went to church, my way took me past his grave and strange thoughts always fill my mind at the sight of it as of the graves of many other Czech countrymen who sleep their last sleep here. These people came to this place about 40 years ago, mostly from the neighbourhood of Pisek, Tabor and Budejovice. All the poorest of the poor, and after great hardships and struggle they are very well off here. I liked to go among the people and they, too, were all fond of me, and especially the grandmas and grandads were pleased when I played to them in church "God before Thy Majesty" and "A Thousand Times We greet Thee."

I became very good friends with Father Bilý, as were also our children—and often we went to visit Czech farmers 4–5 miles away. It is very strange here. Few people and a great deal of empty space. A farmer's nearest neighbour is often 4 miles off, especially in the *prairies* (I call them the Sahara) there are only endless acres of field and meadow and that is all you see. You don't meet a soul (here they only ride on horseback) and you are glad to see in the woods and meadows the huge herds of cattle which, summer and winter, are out at pasture in the broad fields. Men go to the woods and meadows where the cows graze to milk them. And so it is very "wild" here and sometimes very sad—sad to despair. But habit is everything. I should have to go on and on telling you things and you would hear many curious things about this America. And now about something else. Not long ago we went on a trip to the State of Nebraska, to the town of Omaha, where there are also many Czechs. I went to visit Mr. Rosewater (Czech from Bukovany). He is a personal friend of [President] Harrison's and [President] Cleveland's and of many outstanding politicians. He has grown rich here and his magazine, the Omaha "Bee," is the most influential in the West and, in general, he is highly esteemed and respected. We stayed with him the three days of our stay there. In the evening Czechs came to play me a "standerl" and when we were leaving, an American band came, too, and played a few pieces. As you can imagine, a banquet was not wanting and we were very jolly and the Czechs were tremendously happy and so was I. Omaha is 400 miles from our place and then we went to visit—guess who?—Father Rynd whom I met on Czech Day in Chicago—and do you know where? in the state of Minnesotta [*sic*]—in the town of St. Paul, 400 miles from Nebraska—where there are also many Czechs. He is a Moravian from Kojetin and so maybe we shall travel together. I hope very much that I shall be able to pay a visit home to Bohemia, if my contract is prolonged—or if it isn't—I must see Bohemia, no matter what. I hear the papers at home are writing as if I wished to stay here in America for good! Oh no, never! I am very well off here, God be praised, I am in good health and am working well and I know that, as for my new Symphony, the F major String Quartet and the Quintet (composed here in Spillville)—I should never have written these works "just so" if I hadn't seen America. You will hear later, after their performance in New York. Simrock wrote and bought *everything I have* and so I hope that by Spring you will have some news of them. The "Dumky," Overtures, Symphony, Quartet, Quintet, Rondo etc., while the "Te Deum" and "The American Flag" for choir and orchestra will probably be published *by Novello.*

　　With affectionate greetings,
　　Yours,

　　Antonín Dvořák

From Josef Jan Kovařík's *Reminiscences.* Dvořák's "New World" Symphony.

　　One day at the cafe, [Anton] Seidl said that he had heard that the Master has a new symphony and asked him for permission to perform it at one of the next concerts of the New York Philharmonic. The Master thought it over—but on taking leave he promised to give Seidl the Symphony to perform. That was in the middle of November 1893. The following day Seidl informed the Master that the symphony would be given at the concert to be held about the 15th December and that he should send him the score as soon as possible. The same evening, before I set out with the score, the Master wrote at the last minute on the title-page, "Z Noveho sveta" ("From the New World"). Till then there was only E minor Symphony no. 8 [*sic*]. The title "From the New World" caused then and still causes today, at least here in America, much confusion and division of opinion. There were and are many people who thought and think that the title is to be understood as meaning the "American" symphony, i.e. a symphony with American music. Quite a wrong idea! This title means nothing more than "Impressions and Greetings from the New World"—as the Master himself more than once explained. And so when at length it was performed and when the Master read all sorts of views on it whether he had or had not created an "American" music, he smiled and said, "It seems that I have got them all confused" and added: "at home they will understand at once what I meant." I do not know, however, if he was not in part mistaken about those "at home." . . .

　　At the first performance of the symphony—on the 15th December 1893, in the Carnegie Hall—at the Friday afternoon concert which, in distinction from the evening concert, was called a "public rehearsal," Dvořák was not present. I went alone—the Master and his family heard the symphony at the Saturday evening concert.

Dvořák to Adolf Heyduk, 29 October 1894. After a summer vacation in Vysoka, Bohemia, Dvořák describes his second voyage back to America (accompanied this time by his wife and younger son, Otakar).

Dear Friend,

I know that you have always been a dear and rare friend and so I wish to write to you knowing that it will give you a little pleasure.

Now I shall tell you first of all that we got safely to this country of America and that our journey was quite agreeable except for about two days—when it was so stormy that only very few were not affected by seasickness—and I was among the lucky few, so that we may thank God that it fell out so fortunately.

We travelled on the *Bismarck* from Hamburg. She is a fine ship and crossed the immense ocean, 3100 miles (not including the 450 miles from Hamburg to Southampton), in 6 days, 10 hours and some minutes, so that we anchored before New York on Thursday, the 25th October at 8 o'clock in the evening.

We have been here only 3 days and so I have not really any news for you—I shall leave it for next time. In the meanwhile accept my kind regards to yourself and your wife,

Yours affectionately,

Antonín Dvořák

Dvořák to A. Rus in Pisek, Bohemia, 18 December 1894. Reflections upon returning to America for the second time.

Dear Friend,

It is quite a long time since I wrote to you—and as I have not had any word from you, I think you must not have got my first letter from New York.

We are well, God be praised, but this time we do not feel so at ease as last year. We were used to the children and now we haven't them and are sad at having to be without them. Otherwise everything would be all right.

... The children write to us twice a week and we always await the ships coming from Europe expectantly in the hope that they have brought us something. And when a letter does come from the children, you can imagine with what impatience we seize it and read it.

They write that they are well and getting on nicely—only Otla always writes how glad she would be to see us again in Prague. I believe her—and we the same.

In the musical world there is plenty going on here. The New York Philharmonic presented me with an honorary diploma as an honorary member and played my new Symphony not long ago. In January again they will play all three Overtures. The Symphony has been given in Chicago and many other towns and everywhere it was a success.

The "Luzany Mass" [Mass in D major, Opus 86] which I composed at the request of Mr. Hlavka—in the year 1887 (if I am not mistaken)—this mass will be given at Christmas here in New York at the Catholic Church of St. Stephen, and then in other towns such as Saint Paul, where we were last year, in Minneapolis, in New Orleans etc. And now I have still to tell you that I am working at a concerto for violoncello. But I must not forget the chief thing: A New Year is coming round again and greetings. I wish you from my heart every good thing and especially health and contentment and God grant that we shall see each other in the coming year and that we shall be as good friends as we have always been, which is the heartfelt wish of

Your devoted friend,

Antonín Dvořák

Dvořák to Josef Boleska in Prague, 15 January 1895. Thoughts on finishing the Cello Concerto.

Dear Friend,

. . . Now I am finishing the Finale of the Violoncello Concerto.

If I could work as free from care as at Vysoka, it would have been finished long ago. But here it is not possible—on Monday I have work at school—on Tuesday I am free—the other days are more less taken up—in short I cannot give so much time to my work, and when I could, again I am not always in the mood etc.

In short, the best thing is to sit at Vysoka—there I have the best recreation, the best refreshment—and am happy. Oh if only I were there again!

The Boston Kneisel Quartet has already given its 50th performance of the F major Quartet. Not bad, is it? . . .

With kindest regards,
Your

Antonín Dvořák

∽

From Josef Jan Kovařík's *Reminiscences.* Dvořák's working practices.

. . . The Master, who was a tireless worker, at once fell into a bad mood if he was without employment. He was more or less irritable, bad-tempered, distraught, there was, so to speak, no making anything of him sometimes. The most trifling question put him in a fury. . . . And so it was, always, when his mind was taken up and his thoughts concentrated on a new work.

No sooner, however, was the future work decided upon, his thoughts collected and work started than the Master was quite a different creature. . . . He took no heed whether the earth turned from east to west or the other way about, worked calmly and contentedly, was glad when his work went forward satisfactorily, and if, as he was in the habit of saying, "he brought something off," then he was in a particularly good mood; a truly delightful person, always smiling and joking; and if it happened that anybody came to the Master at such a time with some request, no matter what,—none went away unheard and if it was a matter of financial support—the Master emptied his pocket to the last heller—a proceeding to which I was often a witness.

APPENDIX C

Dvořák in America
A Discography

John H. Yoell

*T*he long-play revolution of the early
1950s marked the greening of Dvořák on records. While the symphonic core
of his works had begun to emerge during the 78 rpm era, the LP brought the
adventurous listener into contact with Dvořák's operas, large-scale choral
pieces, and seldom-heard chamber music. The compact disc and minicas-
sette continue to revive the recorded past as well as provide new discoveries.
Unless stated otherwise, all items listed here are on the compact disc format.

TE DEUM
OPUS 103 (B. 176), 1892
This stunning, vigorous Te Deum served as Dvořák's calling card when he
stepped ashore in New York in 1892, just in time to help celebrate the 400th
anniversary of Columbus's voyages. The raw power generated in this work
seems to foreshadow the *Glagolitic Mass* by Leoš Janáček (a logical coupling
carried out in Robert Shaw's Teldec recording). The advanced opus number
refers to the date of its publication in 1896 rather than to the strict chronological order of composition.

> Supraphon C37-7230; Gabriela Beňačková (soprano) and Jaroslav
> Souček (baritone), with the Prague Philharmonic Chorus and the
> Czech Philharmonic Orchestra conducted by Václav Neumann
> (+ *Hymnus*, Psalm 149).

> Teldec CD-80287; Soloists, with the Atlanta Symphony Orchestra
> and Chorus conducted by Robert Shaw (+ Janáček).

Supraphon MS 0981/2, LP; Maria Helenita Olivares (soprano) and Gianni Maffeo (baritone), with the Czech Philharmonic Chorus and the Prague Symphony Orchestra conducted by Václav Smetáček (+ Mass in D, Psalm 149, *Biblical Songs*).

THE AMERICAN FLAG CANTATA
OPUS 102 (B. 177), 1893

The text for this outlandish cantata, its bellicose doggerel lying somewhere between "The Star Spangled Banner" and the Nazi "Horst Wessel Song," belongs to a bygone era. It was chosen for Dvořák by his patroness, Mrs. Jeannette Thurber.

The Czech master dutifully fulfilled his commission, pocketed a handsome fee from the house of Schirmer and, significantly, failed to linger in New York to catch the premiere. Yet there are points of musical interest: passages for solo harp, for example, and a rather jolly march bearing a striking resemblance to the famous "Rakoczy March" from Hungary. In any event, in writing this curiosity Dvořák displayed more professional competence than genius. As if to stress this disparity, Dvořák began work on the "New World" Symphony two days later.

Columbia M 34513, LP; Joseph Evans (tenor) and Barry McDaniel (baritone), with St. Hedwig's Cathedral Choir, the RIAS Chamber Choir, and the Berlin Radio Symphony Orchestra conducted by Michael Tilson Thomas (+ "American" Suite).

SYMPHONY NO. 9 IN E MINOR ("FROM THE NEW WORLD")
OPUS 95 (B. 178), 1893

A continual deluge of recordings testifies to the sustained popularity, durability, and marketability of Dvořák's last symphony. The creative wellsprings for this work may derive as much from his acute sensitivity to environmental sound as from ethnomusicological probing predating Bartók and Janáček. It may be a concert hall war-horse, but after a century it still flies the flag of a remarkable achievement. Long known as the Symphony No. 5, it was the first of the symphonies to be recorded: Hamilton Harty conducted the Hallé Orchestra for Columbia in 1924.[*] The work came home to American gramophiles in 1927 with Leopold Stokowski and the Philadelphia Orchestra in their landmark album Victor M-1 (LP reissue RCA CRL2-0334). Very few major conductors have failed to add this enormously vital work to their discographies.

---

[*] An apparently abridged version with Landon Ronald conducting the Royal Albert Hall Orchestra (H.M.V.) may have been issued previously.

Recordings of American Origin

RCA/Gold Seal 60279-2RG (vol. 24 of "The Toscanini Collection"); NBC Symphony Orchestra conducted by Arturo Toscanini (+ Kodály, Smetana).

RCA 5606-2RC; Chicago Symphony Orchestra conducted by Fritz Reiner (+ *Carnival*, Smetana, Weinberger).

RCA/Papillon 6530-2RG; Boston Symphony Orchestra conducted by Arthur Fiedler (+ *Carnival, Humoresque/*Swanee River).

RCA RCD1-4552; Chicago Symphony Orchestra conducted by James Levine.

RCA/Silver Seal 60537-2RV; Philadelphia Orchestra conducted by Eugene Ormandy (+ *Carnival, Scherzo capriccioso*).

CBS MK 42417; Cleveland Orchestra conducted by George Szell (+ *Carnival*, Slavonic Dances Nos. 1, 8).

CBS MK 42039; Columbia Symphony Orchestra conducted by Bruno Walter.

Angel CDC 49114; Philadelphia Orchestra conducted by Wolfgang Sawallisch (+ *Scherzo capriccioso*).

Deutsche Grammophon 423 882-2; Chicago Symphony Orchestra conducted by Carlo Maria Giulini (+ Schubert).

London 414 421-2 LH; Cleveland Orchestra conducted by Christoph von Dohnányi.

Philips/Concert Classics 426073; San Francisco Symphony Orchestra conducted by Seiji Ozawa (+ *Carnival*).

London 410 116-2 LH; Chicago Symphony Orchestra conducted by Sir Georg Solti.

Philips 412 542-2, 2 CDs; Minnesota Orchestra conducted by Sir Neville Marriner (+ Symphonies 7, 8).

Telarc CD-80238; Los Angeles Philharmonic conducted by André Previn (+ *Carnival*).

Virgin Classics VC 7 91476-2; the Houston Symphony conducted by Christoph Eschenbach (+ Tchaikovsky).

Recordings of Czechoslovak Origin

Supraphon C37-7702; Czech Philharmonic conducted by Václav Neumann.

Naxos/Enigma Classics 7 746700-2; CSR Symphony Orchestra of Bratislava conducted by Ondrej Lenárd (+ Slavonic Dances).

LaserLite 15517; Prague Festival Orchestra conducted by Urbanek (+ *Romance, Carnival*).

Opus 9150 0282; Slovak Philharmonic conducted by Zdeněk Košler.

Supraphon/Collection 11 0290-2; Czech Philharmonic conducted by Václav Talich (+ Serenade, Opus 22); recorded 1949–50.

Sonata CD 91018; Slovak Philharmonic conducted by Libor Pešek.

RECORDINGS OF AUSTRO-GERMAN ORIGIN

Angel CDD 63900; Berlin Philharmonic conducted by Klaus Tennstedt (+ Kodály).

Deutsche Grammophon 423 129-2, 6 CDs; Berlin Philharmonic conducted by Raphael Kubelik (+ complete symphonies).

London 400047-2; Vienna Philharmonic conducted by Kiril Kondrashin.

Deutsche Grammophon 427805-2; Vienna Philharmonic conducted by Lorin Maazel (+ *Carnival*).

Deutsche Grammophon 415 509-2; Vienna Philharmonic conducted by Herbert von Karajan (+ Smetana).

Teldec 43359; Bamberg Symphony Orchestra conducted by Joseph Keilberth (+ *Carnival*).

Angel/Studio Series CDM 69005; Berlin Philharmonic conducted by Herbert von Karajan (+ Smetana).

Deutsche Grammophon 423 384-2; Berlin Philharmonic conducted by Ferenc Fricsay (+ Liszt, Smetana).

Allegretto ACD 8008; Bamberg Symphony Orchestra conducted by Heinrich Hollreiser.

London/Weekend 417 678-2; Vienna Philharmonic conducted by István Kertész (+ Smetana).

AS Disc AS-111; Berlin Philharmonic conducted by Wilhelm Furtwängler (+ Symphony No. 9/Toscanini).[†]

---

† This performance attributed to Furtwängler, dated 1941, is held to be spurious.

Recordings of British Origin

Angel/Laser Series CDZ 7 62514-2; Philharmonia Orchestra conducted by Carlo Maria Giulini (+ *Carnival, Scherzo capriccioso*).

Virgin Classics VC 7 90723-2; Royal Liverpool Symphony Orchestra conducted by Libor Pešek (+ "American" Suite).

Angel CDB 62006; London Philharmonic conducted by Zdenek Macal (+ Symphonic Variations).

Teldec 2292-46468-2; Philharmonia Orchestra conducted by Eliahyu Inbal (+ *Wild Dove*).

London/Jubilee 417724-2; London Symphony Orchestra conducted by István Kertész (+ *Carnival, Scherzo capriccioso*).

Chandos CHAN 8510; Scottish National Orchestra conducted by Neeme Järvi (+ *My Home*).

Chesky Records CD 31; Royal Philharmonic conducted by Jascha Horenstein (+ Wagner).

Angel CDM 63774; Hallé Orchestra conducted by John Barbirolli (+ Symphony No. 7).

Collins Classics 1002-2; London Philharmonic conducted by James Loughran.

Menuet 160014-2; Royal Philharmonic conducted by Rudolf Kempe (+ R. Strauss).

Sony Classical SBT 46331; London Symphony Orchestra conducted by Eugene Ormandy (+ Serenade, Opus 22).

Odyssey MB2K 45618. 2 CDs; Pilharmonia Orchestra conducted by Andrew Davis (+ *Carnival*, Symphonies 7, 8).

Recordings of Diverse Origin

Teldec 243 731-2; Concertgebouw Orchestra conducted by Willem Mengelberg.

White Label HRC 064; Hungarian State Orchestra conducted by Giuseppe Patané (+ Smetana).

Philips 420 349-2; Concertgebouw Orchestra conducted by Colin Davis (+ Symphonic Variations).

Stradivari SCD 6030; Slovenian Philharmonic Orchestra conducted by Milan Horvat (+ *Carnival*, Glinka).

Hunt Productions CD 526; Turin Symphony Orchestra of RIA conducted by Sergiu Celebidace (+ Borodin, Bartók).

Deutsche Grammophon 427 346-2; Israel Philharmonic conducted by Leonard Bernstein (+ Slavonic Dances Nos. 1, 3, 8).

London 421 106; Concertgebouw Orchestra conducted by Riccardo Chailly (+ *Carnival*).

AS Disc AS 321; Danish Radio Symphony Orchestra conducted by Fritz Busch (+ *Carnival*).

Price-Less D 16530; Zurich Tonhalle Orchestra conducted by Josef Krips.

Erato/Success ECD 40005; Orchestre Philharmonie de Strasbourg conducted by Alain Lombard.

Black Pearl BPCD 2019; Radio Luxembourg Symphony Orchestra conducted by Louis de Froment.

RCA/Red Seal 7929-2-RC; Kazuhito Yamashita (guitar transcription) (+ Stravinsky).

STRING QUARTET IN F MAJOR ("AMERICAN")
OPUS 96 (B. 179), 1893

Dubbed the "Nigger" in a more insensitive era, and today wearing the label "American," the F major Quartet could be just as easily renamed "Spillville" because that is where it was sketched and composed during the summer of 1893. Perhaps no other work by Dvořák so deeply and vividly mirrors his responses to the American landscape.

Unfortunately, the Kneisel Quartet of Boston, which had premiered the work, made no recordings before disbanding in 1917. The group made a few tests, but came away with a distrust of what then was a relatively primitive medium.

On the other hand, the Bohemian Quartet forged ahead with two recordings of Opus 96 before its demise in 1933; these vintage Vox and Polydor pressings may eventually resurface on CD. The celebrated Flonzaley Quartet failed to document Dvořák's complete work, but a 1926 version by the Budapest Quartet again has become available (Novello NVCLD 903).

RECORDINGS OF AMERICAN ORIGIN

Philips 420 803-2; Guarneri Quartet (+ Smetana).

RCA 6263-2; Guarneri Quartet (+ Piano Quintet, Opus 81).

Newport Classic NC-60033; Manhattan String Quartet (+ Barber and others).

Arabesque Z-6558; Portland String Quartet (+ Quintet, Opus 97).

ProArte CDD-237; Cleveland Quartet (+ *Cypresses*).

Book-of-the-Month Club BOMR 21-7526 ("Great Romantic Quartets"), 4 CDs; Emerson Quartet (+ Borodin and others).

Deutsche Grammophon 429 723-2; Emerson Quartet (+ Smetana).

Gasparo GS-223; Fine Arts Quartet (+ Shostakovich, Turina).

RECORDINGS OF CZECHOSLOVAK ORIGIN

Denon C37-7338; Smetana Quartet (+ Piano Quintet, Opus 81).

Denon CO-72540; Smetana Quartet (+ Sextet).

Denon C37 7234; Kocian Quartet (+ Quartet No. 13).

Calliope CAL 9617; Talich Quartet (+ Quartet No. 11).

Supraphon 11 0581-2; Panocha Quartet (+ Quartet No. 10).

Supraphon C37-7565; Panocha Quartet (+ Quartet No. 14).

Cadenza CAC C-8728; Stamitz Quartet (+ Quartet No. 13).

Bellaphon 690-91-918; Doležal Quartet (+ Quartet No. 14).

Naxos 8.550251; Moyzes Quartet (+ Quartet No. 14).

London/Jubilee 425 537-2; Janáček Quartet (+ Quintet, Opus 97).

Deutsche Grammophon 429 193-2, 9 CDs; Prague Quartet (+ complete works for string quartet).

Supraphon/Treasury DC-8048; Prague Quartet (+ Schubert).

Opus 9351 2049; Travniček Quartet (+ Quartet No. 10).

RECORDINGS OF DIVERSE ORIGINS

CBS MK-44920-2; Tokyo String Quartet (+ Piano Quintet, Opus 81).

Deutsche Grammophon 419 601-2; Hagen Quartet (+ *Cypresses*, Kodály).

Philips 420 396-2; Orlando Quartet (+ Mendelssohn).

Ottavo OTR C69028; Orlando Quartet (+ Smetana).

Virgin Classics VC 7 90807-2; Endellion Quartet (+ Smetana).

Forlane UCD 16538; Enesco Quartet (+ Enesco, Janáček).

MCA Classics MCAD 25214; Delme Quartet (+ Brahms).

White Label HRC-122; Bartók Quartet (+ Ravel, Debussy).

Teldec 44145; Vermeer Quartet (+ Mendelssohn).

Chandos CHAN 8919; Chilingirian Quartet (+ Quartet No. 14).

London 430 077-2LH; Takacs Quartet (+ Quartet No. 14).

DiscoCenter Sas 007 061; Zagreb Quartet (+ Smetana).

International Music Service (IMS) BNL 112 727; Maragues Quintet (arrangement for wind quintet by D. Walker) (+ Grieg, Mendelssohn).

STRING QUINTET IN E-FLAT MAJOR
OPUS 97 (B. 180), 1893

Another product of the Spillville idyll, the robust, extroverted Quintet is perhaps the most strongly accented of all Dvořák's American works. As with the Quartet, the world premiere performance took place in Boston on New Year's Day, 1894, with the Kneisel Quartet (augmented); the Bohemian Quartet took care of the Prague premiere several months later. Yet, for various reasons the appealing Opus 97 seems to have lagged behind its Spillville sibling in frequency of performance and recordings.

Supraphon 11 1424-2 131; Smetana Quartet (Josef Suk, viola) (+ Sextet).

Denon CO-72507; Smetana Quartet (Josef Suk, viola) (+ Quintet No. 1).

London 425 537-2; Members of the Vienna Octet (+ String Quartet No. 12).

Hyperion CDA 66308; Raphael Ensemble (+ Sextet).

SONATINA IN G MAJOR FOR VIOLIN AND PIANO
OPUS 100 (B. 183), 1893

The famous anecdote about Dvořák's visit to the Minnehaha Falls where he scribbled on his shirt cuff the theme for the Larghetto movement has been recounted elsewhere in this volume. The entire work has great charm (it was dedicated to his children) and abounds with dance characteristics.[‡]

[‡] The Larghetto movement has been subject to unauthorized versions, including the famous "Indian Lament" by Fritz Kreisler (see Pavilion GEMM CD 9324, Fritz Kreisler and Carl Lamson; includes works by Kreisler and others). Other Kreisler/Dvořák dabblings are revived on Biddulph Recordings LAB 040 and LAB 019/020.

Supraphon/Josef Suk Treasury 11 0703-2; Josef Suk and Alfred Holeček (+ Sonata in F, *Romantic Pieces*).

Angel CDC 47399; Itzhak Perlman and Samuel Sanders (+ *Romantic Pieces*, Smetana).

RCA 7802-2 RC; James Galway and Phillip Noll in a version for flute and piano (+ Martinů, Feld).

Campion Records RRCD 1301; Camerata Nova (+ *Miniatures*, "Song to the Moon"). Arranged for string orchestra.

SUITE IN A MAJOR ("AMERICAN"), 1894
OPUS 98 (ORIGINAL PIANO VERSION, B. 184)
OPUS 98B (DVOŘÁK'S ORCHESTRATION, B. 190)

To many listeners the Ninth Symphony serves as the standard by which to judge Dvořák's management of perceived Americana. Yet his undervalued, even maligned, "American" Suite offers an alternate, equally valid glimpse into the composer's New World experiences. If less dramatic and forceful than the symphony, the suite evokes the prairie vastness and pastoral tranquillity of the American heartland. A comparison between it and Delius's *Florida Suite*, begun a decade earlier, makes for an enlightening experience.

Dvořák's orchestral version was not performed until after his death. Only one recording of this version has come so far from an American conductor leading an American orchestra.

London 411 735-2, 2 CDs; Royal Philharmonic Orchestra conducted by Antal Dorati (+ Slavonic Dances).

Virgin Classics VC 7 90723-2; Royal Liverpool Philharmonic conducted by Libor Pešek (+ Symphony No. 9).

Elektra/Nonesuch 79078-2; Rochester Philharmonic conducted by David Zinman (+ *Festival March*, Janáček).

CBS M-34513, LP; Berlin Radio Symphony Orchestra conducted by Michael Tilson Thomas (+ *The American Flag*).

Supraphon 1 11 0865 (also Genesis 1025) LP; piano version by Radoslav Kvapil (+ *Humoresques*).

CELLO CONCERTO IN B MINOR
OPUS 104 (B. 191), 1895

Although nourished more by personal feelings than a response to actual locale, the B Minor Concerto belongs to the last winter in New York. Certainly a major stimulus was the first performance of Victor Herbert's Cello

Concerto No. 2. Revisions occupied Dvořák upon his return to Bohemia, precipitated by the death of his beloved sister-in-law Josefina Kaunitzová, whose memory is enshrined here.

Nearly every important member of the international cellist's community has brought this "king" of the cello concertos to recordings. A few like Rostropovich and Starker offer a number of modern performances. The reading by Pablo Casals in Prague in 1937 has achieved legendary status.

RCA/ Papillon 6531-2RG; Lynn Harrell and the London Symphony Orchestra conducted by James Levine (+ Schubert).

Chandos CHAN 8662; Raphael Wallfisch and the London Symphony Orchestra conducted by Sir Charles Mackerras (+ Dohnányi).

CBS MK-42206; Yo-Yo Ma and the Berlin Philharmonic conducted by Lorin Maazel (+ Rondo, *Silent Woods*).

Deutsche Grammophon 413 819-2; Mstislav Rostropovich and the Berlin Philharmonic conducted by Herbert von Karajan (+ Tchaikovsky).

Angel CDC 49306; Mstislav Rostropovich and the London Philharmonic conducted by Carlo Maria Giulini (+ Saint-Saëns).

Erato ECD 88224; Mstislav Rostropovich and the Boston Symphony Orchestra conducted by Seiji Ozawa (+ Tchaikovsky).

Angel CDC 47614; Jacqueline du Pré and the Chicago Symphony Orchestra conducted by Daniel Barenboim (+ Haydn).

Deutsche Grammophon/ Galleria 423 881-2; Pierre Fournier and the Berlin Philharmonic conducted by George Szell (+ Elgar).

RCA Red Seal 60717-2RC; Janos Starker and the St. Louis Symphony Orchestra conducted by Leonard Slatkin (+ Bartók).

Mercury 432 001-2; János Starker and the London Symphony Orchestra conducted by Antal Dorati (+ Bruch, Tchaikovsky).

Supraphon CO-1152; Angela May and the Czech Philharmonic conducted by Václav Neumann (+ Martinů).

Supraphon/ Crystal Collection 11 0631-2; Miloš Sádlo and the Czech Philharmonic conducted by Václav Neumann (+ Cello Concerto No. 1).

Philips 422 387-2; Julian Lloyd Webber and the Czech Philharmonic conducted by Václav Neumann (+ *Rusalka Polonaise, Carnival*).

Panton CD 81 076 2031; Michaela Fukačová and the Prague Symphony Orchestra conducted by Jiří Bělohlávek.

Historic Reissues

Angel CDH 63498; Pablo Casals and the Czech Philharmonic conducted by George Szell (+ Elgar, Bruch).

Philips/ Legendary Classics 420 776-2; Emanuel Feuermann and the National Orchestral Association conducted by Leon Barzin (+ Rondo, *Silent Woods*, Bloch).

Movimento Musica 011 006; Antonio Janigro and the Cologne Radio Symphony Orchestra conducted by Erich Kleiber (+ Violin Concerto).

Chanterelle HS 2001; Emanuel Feuermann and the Berlin State Opera Orchestra conducted by Michael Taube.

Supraphon 11 1327-2; Mstislav Rostropovich and the Czech Philharmonic conducted by Václav Talich (+ *Othello, Noonday Witch*).

Eight Humoresques
Opus 101 (B. 187), 1894

These fanciful pieces belong to the summer of 1894, after Dvořák had returned to Bohemia while on leave from the New York Conservatory. Much of the incorporated material came from his American sketchbooks, including ideas considered for a never-realized opera about Hiawatha. A second projected set was never completed.

Complete Set

Vox Prima MWCD 7114; Rudolf Firkušný (+ Piano Concerto).

Candide CE 31070, LP; Rudolf Firkušný (+ Mazurkas).

Supraphonet 11 1113-2; Radoslav Kvapil (+ Concerto).

Note: in the *Humoresques* the discophile encounters one of Dvořák's "greatest hits," the *Humoresque* No. 7. Separately, it has been recorded by the following:

CBS MLK 45628 (vol. 2 of "Greatest Hits for Piano"); Philippe Entremont (piano) (+ Chopin and others).

Naxos/ Enigma Classics 7 74611-2 (vol. 1 of "Romantic Piano Favorites"); Balazs Skokolay (piano) (+ Bartók and others).

London/ Weekend Classics 417 884-2 ("Liebestraum"); Joseph Cooper (piano) (+ Liszt and others).

Kingdom KCLCD 2002 ("Pictures and Pleasures"); Christopher Headington (piano).

LaserLite 15 603; Jeno Jando (piano).

EMI/Laser CDZ 762523; Moura Lympany (piano).

AVM Classics AMVCD 1005 (vol. 1 of "Music in Miniature"); Richard Pilling (piano) (+ Chopin and others).

Pearl 132 250/51, 2 CDs; Fritz Kreisler (violin adaptation).

Philips 420-818-2 ("Magic of the Violin"); Arthur Grumiaux (violin adaptation) and István Hajdu (piano).

Deutsche Grammophon/ Musikfest 413 249-2; Christian Ferras (violin adaptation) and Jean-Claude Amrosini (piano).

White Label HPC 091 ("Altweiner Tanzweisen und Fritz Kreisler"); Péter Csaba (violin adaptation) and Zoltán Kocis (piano).

It was the ingenious idea of Richard Hayman to combine the *Humoresque* No. 7 contrapuntally with the Stephen Foster melody "Old Folks at Home." Arthur Fiedler recorded this happy pairing in an RCA Victor album "Holiday for Strings" (LSC-2855) in the 1960s, and this version has been reissued on compact disc as a filler for the Ninth Symphony (RCA/Papillon 6530-2RG).

     A number of songs have been based on the *Humoresque* No. 7. Perhaps the most notable is "Christina's Lament," to words by Creyke. Both Maggie Teyte and Geraldine Farrar made recordings in the 78 rpm days. Another song version was "Eine kleine Frühlingsweise" (words by Lengsfelder), recorded by Richard Tauber, among others.

BIBLICAL SONGS
OPUS 99 (B. 185), 1894

Apart from the Gypsy Songs, the *Biblical Songs* rank as Dvořák's best-sustained contribution to the repertoire of the solo singer. Each of these ten settings of the Psalms of David expresses Dvořák's need for faith, hope, and consolation during a time of middle age and homesickness. His texts came from the vernacular Bible of Kralice (16th Century), one of the core documents of Czech Protestantism.

     The first five songs were arranged for solo voice and orchestra by Dvořák; Nos. 6–10 by Vilém Zemánek.

Chandos CHAN 8608; Brian Raynor Cook (baritone, singing in Czech), with the Scottish National Orchestra conducted by Neeme Järvi (+ Symphony No. 4).

Capriccio 10053; Peter Schreier (tenor, singing in German) and Márian Lapšanský (piano).

Big Ben 861 006; Birgit Finnilä (alto, singing in German), with the Malmö Symphony Orchestra conducted by Vernon Handley (+ Fernström).

"OLD FOLKS AT HOME"
ARRANGEMENT OF A STEPHEN FOSTER SONG
FOR SOLO VOICES, CHORUS, AND FULL ORCHESTRA

This curiosity was conducted by Dvořák at a Benefit Fund concert sponsored by the New York *Herald* in 1894. Harry T. Burleigh and Sissieretta Jones sang the solo parts. It was not published and subsequently not publicly performed again for almost a hundred years. In April 1990 it was presented in concert in Pittsburgh PA. The manuscript full score and some of the parts were published in facsimile for the first time by Sixty-Eight Publishers in August 1991 with both Czech and English text. Accompanying the booklet is a cassette tape of both language versions. The English version is conducted by Leslie B. Dunnard with the Detroit Civic Orchestra; the Czech version features Bohumil Kulinsky conducting the Prague Philharmonic Players. A commercial recording of the piece is not known to this compiler.

DIMITRIJ (HISTORIC OPERA IN FOUR ACTS)
OPUS 64 (B. 127; 186), 1882; REVISED 1885, 1895

Dvořák's seventh opera had already been performed and revised by 1894, when conversations in New York between the composer and the conductor Anton Seidl again focused attention on further revision—more or less in Wagnerian directions. Material relative to the final revision takes up much space in Dvořák's American sketchbooks. The time and effort expended may help account for Dvořák's failure to fulfill Mrs. Thurber's desire to coax a "great American opera" from him.

Supraphon 11 1259-2 (complete opera); sung by Vodička, Drobková, Hajóssyová, Aghová, Kusnjer, Mikuláš, and Vele, with the Prague Radio Chorus and the Czech Philharmonic Chorus and Orchestra conducted by Gerd Albrecht.

Marco Polo 8.223272 (overture only); ČSSR State Philharmonic (Košice) conducted by Robert Stankovsky (+ opera overtures and preludes).

STRING QUARTET NO. 14 IN A-FLAT MAJOR
OPUS 105 (B. 193), 1895

Before leaving New York for the last time Dvořák had composed substantial portions of what was to be his farewell to chamber music in the United States. This quartet was completed in Bohemia, following the interposed G Major Quartet, which carries the Opus number 106. "Americanisms" are largely absent from this smoothly articulated, genial Czech work that celebrates the composer's grateful return to his homeland.

Denon C37-7235; Kocian Quartet (+ Quartet No. 10).

Supraphon C37-7565; Panocha Quartet (+ Quartet No. 12).

Bayer BR 100 142; Stamitz Quartet (+ Quartet No. 10).

Bellaphon 690 01 018; Doležal Quartet (+ Quartet No. 10).

London 430077-2LH; Takács Quartet (+ Quartet No. 12; Bagatelles).

Telarc CD 80283; Cleveland Quartet (+ Quartet No. 12).

Bibliography

BOOKS AND MAGAZINES

Aborn, M. R. *The Influence on American Musical Culture of Dvořák's Sojourn in America*. Ann Arbor, 1966. University Microfilms, Inc.

Abraham, Gerald, ed. *Antonín Dvořák: His Achievement*. London: Lindsay Drummond, 1942.

Allen, Oliver E. *New York New York*. New York: Atheneum, 1990.

Arvey, Verna, "Antonín Dvořák and American Music." *Common Ground*, Winter 1942: 84–88.

Austin, William W. *"Susanna," "Jeanie," and "The Old Folks at Home": The Songs of Stephen Foster from His Time to Ours*. New York: Macmillan Publishing Co., 1975.

Badger, R. Reid. *The Great American Fair: The World's Columbian Exposition and American Culture*. Chicago: Nelson Hall, 1979.

Beckerman, Michael. "Towards a Truly International Music Society," *Bulletin of the Czechoslovak Music Society*, Spring 1990: 1–2.

Berlin, Edward A. *Ragtime: A Musical and Cultural History*. Berkeley: University of California Press, 1980.

Beveridge, David, "Sophisticated Primitivism: The Significance of Pentatonicism in Dvořák's American Quartet." *Current Musicology*, no. 24 (1977): 25–36.

Blesh, Rudi, and Harriet Janis. *They All Played Ragtime*. New York: Alfred A. Knopf, 1950. Rev. ed., 1959, 1966, 1971.

Block, Adrienne Fried, "Boston Talks Back to Dvořák." *I.S.A.M. Newsletter* 18, no. 2 (May 1989).

———. "Dvořák, Beach and American Music." In *A Celebration of American Music: Words and Music in Honor of H. Wiley Hitchcock*, ed. Richard Crawford, R. Allen Lott, and Carol J. Oja, 256–280. Ann Arbor: University of Michigan Press, 1990.

Boller, Paul F. *American Thought in Transition: The Impact of Evolutionary Naturalism, 1865–1900.* New York: University Press of America, 1981.

Bradley, Kenneth. "National Conservatory." *Musical Courier*, 10 February 1925: 56.

Burleigh, Harry T. "The Negro and His Song." In *Music on the Air*, ed. Hazel Gertrude Kinscella. New York: The Viking Press, 1934.

Butcher, Margaret Just. *The Negro in American Culture.* 2d ed. New York: Alfred A. Knopf, 1972.

Butterworth, Neil. *Dvořák: His Life and Times.* Tunbridge Wells, Kent: Midas Books, 1980.

Cadman, Charles Wakefield. "The Idealization of Indian Music." *Musical Quarterly* 1, no. 3 (July 1915): 387–396.

Chase, Gilbert. *America's Music, from the Pilgrims to the Present.* New York: McGraw-Hill, 1955. 2d rev. ed., 1966.

Chiffriller, Joe. "The Life and Local Times of Antonín Dvořák." *Town & Village*, 15 December 1983: 16.

Clapham, John. "Dvořák and the Impact of America." *The Music Review* 15, no. 3 (1954).

———. "Dvořák and Folk Song." *Monthly Musical Record* 86, no. 24 (1956).

———. "The Evolution of Dvořák's Symphony 'From the New World.'" *The Musical Quarterly*, 44 (1958): 167–183.

———. "Dvořák and the Philharmonic Society." *Music & Letters* 39 (1958): 123–134.

———. "The National Origins of Dvořák's Art." *Proceedings of the Royal Musical Association 89th Session* (May 1963): 75–88.

———. "Dvořák and the American Indian." *Musical Times* 107, no. 1484 (1966): 863–867.

———. *Antonín Dvořák: Musician and Craftsman.* New York: St. Martin's Press, 1966.

———. "Dvořák's Musical Directorship in New York." *Music & Letters*, 47 (1967): 40–51.

———. "Dvořák's Relations with Brahms and Hanslick." *The Musical Quarterly*, April 1971: 250, 253–254.

————. "The Smetana-Pivoda Controversy," *Music and Letters* 3 (1971): 353–364.

————. "Dvořák's Musical Directorship in New York: A Postscript." *Music & Letters* 59 (1978): 19–27.

————. "Dvořák's Cello Concerto in B Minor: A Masterpiece in the Making." *Music Review* 40, no. 3 (1979): 123–140.

————. *Dvořák.* New York and London: W. W. Norton and Co., 1979.

————. "Antonín Dvořák." Article in the *New Grove: Late Romantic Masters.* New York: W. W. Norton and Company, 1980.

————. "Dvořák on the American Scene." *Nineteenth Century Music* 5, no. 1 (Summer 1981): 16–21.

Clark, J. Bunker. *The Dawning of American Keyboard Music.* Westport, CT: Greenwood Press, 1988.

Colles, H. C. "Antonín Dvořák in the New World." *The Musical Times* 82, no. 1180 (1941).

Cook, Will Marion. "Clorindy; or, The Origin of the Cakewalk." In *Readings in Black American Music*, ed. Eileen Southern. New York: Norton, 1971.

Cron, Theodore O., and Burt Goldblatt. *Portrait of Carnegie Hall.* New York: The Macmillan Company, 1966.

Culbertson, Evelyn Davis. "Arthur Farwell's Early Efforts on Behalf of American Music," *American Music* 5, no. 2 (Summer 1987): 167.

Davis, Elizabeth A. *Index to the New World Recorded Anthology of American Music.* New York and London: W. W. Norton and Company, 1981.

Davis, L. and K. Carley. "When Minnehaha Falls Inspired Dvořák." *Minnesota History* 41, no. 3 (Fall 1968).

DeLarma, Dominique René. *Will Marion Cook, Antonín Dvořák and the Earlier Afro-American Musical Theater.* Baltimore: Music Dept., Morgan State University, 1979.

DeLong, Kenneth. "The Dvořák Sesquicentennial Festival and Conference in America." *Bulletin of the Czechoslovak Music Society*, Summer 1991: 1, 4–6.

Dostal, W. A. "Dvořák's Visit to Spillville." *Iowa Catholic Historical Review.* n.d.

"Dr. Dvořák's Proposed School: How It Is Viewed." *The Keynote*, 10 June 1893: 26–27.

"The Dvořák Defeat: Will It Hurt Future Designations?" *District Lines* 6, no. 2 (Autumn 1991): 6.

Dvořák, Antonín. "Music in America." *Harper's New Monthly Magazine* 90, no. 537 (February 1895): 428–434. [Authorial assistance by Edwin E. Emerson, Jr.]

Edmiston, Susan, and Linda D. Cirino. *Literary New York: A History and Guide.* Boston: Houghton Mifflin Company, 1976.

Ellington, Edward Kennedy. *Music Is My Mistress.* Garden City: Doubleday, 1973.

Epstein, Dena. "Jeannette Meyers Thurber." In *Notable American Women 1607–1950*, ed. Edward T. James. Cambridge MA: Belknap Press of the Harvard University Press, 1971.

Erenberg, Lewis A. *New York Nightlife and the Transformation of American Culture, 1890–1930.* Westport, CT: Greenwood Press, 1981.

Evans, R. "Dvořák at Spillville." *The Palimpsest* 2, no. 3 (March 1930): 113–118.

Feder, Stuart. "The Nostalgia of Charles Ives: An Essay in Affects and Music." *The Annual of Psychoanalysis* 10 (June 1981): 301–332.

––––––. *Charles Ives, "My Father's Song": A Psychoanalytic Biography.* New Haven and London: Yale University Press, 1992.

Finck, Henry T. *My Adventures in the Golden Age of Music.* New York: Funk and Wagnalls, 1926.

Fischl, V., ed. *Antonín Dvořák: His Achievement.* London: 1943.

Flack, Frank M., "Dvořák and American Opera," *Opera News* 19, no. 12 (24 January 1955): 8–9, 29–30.

Floyd, Samuel A., Jr., and Marsha J. Reisser. *Black Music in the United States: An Annotated Bibliography of Selected Reference and Research Materials.* Millwood, NY, London, and Schaan, Lichtenstein: Kraus International Publications, 1983.

Graff, Yveta Synek, "Water Nymph." *Opera News* 51, no. 12 (28 February 1987).

Grunfeld, F. "Antonín Dvořák in the New World." *HiFi-Stereo Review* 15, no. 6 (December 1965).

Hallova, Ed., *Musical Dramatic Works by Antonín Dvořák: Papers from an International Musicological Conference, Prague, 19–21 May 1983.* Prague: Ceska hudebni spolecnost, 1989.

Hamm, Charles. *Yesterdays: Popular Song in America.* New York: W. W. Norton and Company, 1979.

––––––. *Music in the New World.* New York: W. W. Norton and Company, 1983.

––––––. "Way Down Upon the Yangtze River; or, American Music in the People's Republic of China." *Newsletter: Institute for Studies in American Music* 18, no. 2 (May 1989): 1–2, 7.

Hempl, Patricia. *Spillville.* Minneapolis: Milkweed Editions, 1987.

Hitchcock, Wiley. *Music in the United States: A Historical Introduction.* Englewood Cliffs, NJ: Prentice-Hall, 1969. 2d ed., 1974.

Hodges, Fletcher, Jr. "The Research Work of the Foster Hall Collection." Reprint from *Pennsylvania History* 15, no. 3 (July 1948).

Hoffman, Eva. "A Soft Spot for Sousaphones." *The New York Times Book Review*, 22 November 1987: 11.

Hopkins, H. P. "Student Days with Dvořák." *The Etude* 30, no. 5 (May 1912): 327–328.

———. "How Dvořák Taught Composition." *The Etude* 49, no. 2 (1931): 97–98.

Howard, John Tasker. *Stephen Foster: America's Troubador.* New York: Thomas Crowell, 1953.

Hughes, Gervase. *Dvořák: His Life and Music.* London: Cassell, 1967.

Hughes, Rupert, "A Eulogy of Ragtime." *Musical Record,* no. 447 (1 April 1899): 157–159.

Huneker, James. *Painted Veils.* New York: 1920.

Jahoda, Gloria. *The Road to Samarkand: Frederick Delius and His Music.* New York: Charles Scribner's Sons, 1969.

James, Henry. *The American Scene.* 1905. Reprint. Bloomington: Indiana University Press, 1968.

Johnson, J. Rosamond. "Why They Call American Music Ragtime." *New York Age,* 24 December 1908.

Jones, Sissieretta. "Negro Folk Song." *New York Age,* 24 December 1908.

Karras, John. "Spillville's Czech Treat." *The Iowan* 39, no. 1 (Fall 1990).

King, Moses. *New York: The American Cosmopolis, the Foremost City in the World.* Boston: Moses King, 1893.

Kinscella, H. G. "Dvořák and Spillville Forty Years After." *Musical America,* 53 (25 May 1933): 4, 49.

Klimesh, Cyril M. *They Came to This Place: A History of Spillville, Iowa and Its Czech Settlers.* Sebastopol, CA: Methodius Press, 1983.

Kramer, A. Walter. "H. T. Burleigh: Composer by Divine Right and the American Coleridge-Taylor," *Musical America* 23, no. 26 (29 April 1916): 25.

Krehbiel, Henry E. "Antonín Dvořák," *Century Illustrated Monthly Magazine* 44, no. 5 (September 1892): 657–660.

———. *Afro-American Folksongs: A Study in Racial and National Music.* New York: Frederick Ungar, 4th printing, 1975; a reprint. of the 1914 edition.

Larkin, Oliver W. *Art and Life in America.* New York: Rinehart, 1949.

Lawrence, Vera Brodsky, ed. *Strong on Music: The New York Music Scene in the Days of George Templeton Strong, 1836–1875.* New York: Oxford University Press, 1988.

Leighton, Jennie. "Pen Pictures of Dvořák." *The Etude* 37, no. 11 (November 1919): 702.

Levine, Lawrence W. *Highbrow Lowbrow: The Emergence of Cultural Hierarchy in America.* Cambridge, MA: Harvard University Press, 1988.

Lichtenwanger, William. "Matilda Sissieretta Joyner Jones." In *Notable American Women 1607–1950,* ed. Edward T. James. Cambridge, MA: Belknap Press of the Harvard University Press, 1971.

Love, Josephine Harreld. "Antonín Dvořák in America." In "Old Folks at Home." Sixty-Eight Publishers Corp.: 8–23.

Lowenbach, Jan. "Czechoslovakian Composers and Musicians in America." *Musical Quarterly,* August 1943: 155.

Mellers, Wilfrid. *Music in a New Found Land.* New York: Alfred A. Knopf, 1964.

Moore, MacDonald Smith. *Yankee Blues: Musical Culture and American Identity.* Bloomington: Indiana University Press, 1985.

Murray, C. W. "The Story of Harry T. Burleigh." *The Hymn* 17, no. 4 (October 1966).

"National Conservatory of Music of America." *Harper's Weekly,* 13 December 1890.

"Negro Music." *The Crisis* 1, no. 4 (February 1911): 12.

Nugent, Walter. "Dvořák: An American Interlude." *Timeline,* October–November 1986: 2–13.

Offenbach, Jacques. *Orpheus in America: Offenbach's Diary of His Journey to the New World,* ed. Lander MacClintock. Bloomington: Indiana University Press, 1957.

O'Connor, Richard. *Hell's Kitchen.* Philadelphia and New York: J. D. Lippincott Company, 1958.

Overmyer, G. "Dvořák in the New World." *Musical America* 61, no. 4 (September 1941).

Owen, M. W. "Negro Spirituals: Their Origin, Development and Place in American Folk Songs." *The Musical Observer* 19, no. 12 (December 1920).

Pleasants, Henry. *Death of a Music? The Decline of the European Tradition and the Rise of Jazz.* London: Gollancz, 1961.

Porter, Andrew. "Czech Master." *The New Yorker,* 18 March 1991: 84, 98–99.

Pratt, Waldo Selden, ed. "National Conservatory." In *Grove's Dictionary of Music and Musicians,* 3d ed. (1920, American Supplement): 6, 306.

Rathbun, F. G. "The Negro Music of the South." *The Black Perspective in Music* 4, no. 2 (July 1976).

Renton, Barbara, "Dvořák's Operas in the United States: A Preliminary Survey of Performances and Their Reception." In *Musical Dramatic Works by Antonín Dvořák: Papers from an International Musicological Conference, Prague, 19–21 May 1983*, ed. Marketa Hallova. (Prague: Ceska hudebni spolecnost, 1989).

Richman, Steven. "The Dvořák Debacle—How Antonín Dvořák's Historic New York House Was Razed." *High Performance Review,* Summer 1992, 6–7, 14.

Riis, Thomas L. *Just Before Jazz: Black Musical Theater in New York, 1890–1915.* Washington: Smithsonian Institution Press, 1989.

Robertson, Alec. *Dvořák.* London: J. M. Dent and Sons, Ltd., 1947.

Root, Deane L. "Myth and Stephen Foster." *Carnegie Magazine,* January–February 1987: 10.

———. "The Myth and History of Stephen Foster; or, Why His True Story Remains Untold." *American Music Research Center Journal* 1 (1991): 20–36. Transcript of a lecture for the American Music Research Center, University of Colorado, Boulder (March 1990).

Rossiter, Frank R. *Charles Ives & His America.* New York: Liveright, 1974.

Rubin, Emanuel. "Jeannette Thurber and the National Conservatory of Music." *American Music* 8, no. 4 (Fall 1990): 294–325.

Sampson, Henry T. *Blacks in Blackface: A Source Book on Early Black Musical Shows.* Metuchen, NJ: The Scarecrow Press, 1980.

Schindler, K. "Will Marion Cook." *Schirmer's Bulletin on New Music* (15 October 1912).

Seagle, Oscar. "Utilizing the 'Negro Spirituals' for the Concert Platform." *Musical America,* 14 April 1917: 33.

Shelley, H. R. "Dvořák As I Knew Him." *The Etude* 37, no. 2 (November 1919): 541–542.

Simpson, Anne Key. *Hard Trials: The Life and Music of Harry T. Burleigh.* Methuen, NJ: Scarecrow Press, 1990.

Skilton, Charles Sanford. "Realism in Indian Music." *Proceedings of the Music Teachers' National Association: Studies in Musical Education, History, and Aesthetics,* 13th series (Hartford, CT: MTNA 1919).

Skowronski, Jo Ann. *Black Music in America: A Bibliography.* Metuchen, NJ: The Scarecrow Press, 1981.

Skvorecky, Josef. *Dvořák in Love.* New York: Alfred A. Knopf, 1987.

Smith, Fanny Morris. "Peculiarities of the Growth of American Music." *The Etude* 6, no. 4 (April 1888): 68.

Šourek, Otakar, ed. *Antonín Dvořák: Letters and Reminiscences.* Trans. Roberta Finlayson Samsour. Prague: Artia, 1954.

————. *Antonín Dvořák.* Prague: Artia, 1956.

————. *The Orchestral Works of Antonín Dvořák.* Trans. Roberta Finlayson Samsour. Prague: Artia, 1956.

Stefan-Gruenfeldt, Paul. "Why Dvořák Would Not Return to America." *Musical America* 58 (25 Feb 1938): 34.

————. *Antonín Dvořák.* Trans. Y. W. Vance. New York: The Greystone Press, 1941.

Stransky, Josef. "Echoes of Musical Czecho-Slovakia." *The Etude* 37, no. 11 (November 1919): 687–688.

Taylor, Jack. "Dvořák's Banished Statue: Out of Sight, out of Mind?" *The Artists' Proof* 5, no. 1 (Autumn 1991).

Thurber, Jeannette M. "Personal Recollections of a Great Master: Dvořák As I Knew Him." *The Etude* 37, no. 11 (Nov 1919): 693–694.

Tibbetts, John C. "Dvořák in the New World: A Spillville Adventure." *Classical* 3, no. 2 (February 1991): 32–36.

————. "In Search of Stephen Foster." *The World and I* 6, no. 7 (July 1991): 252–259.

————. "Dvořák Conference in New Orleans." *The Sonneck Society Bulletin for American Music* 17, no. 3 (Fall 1991): 100–102.

Tyrrell, John. Czech Opera, Cambridge University Press, 1988.

Visman, H. M. "Dvořák—Cook—Ellington." *Doctor Jazz*, no. 37 (Aug 1969).

————. "Will Marion Cook." *Doctor Jazz*, no. 34 (Feb 1969).

Upton, William Treat. *Anthony Philip Heinrich: A Nineteenth-Century Composer in America.* New York: Columbia University Press, 1939.

Vella, Christina. "Review: The Dvořák Festival." *The St. Bernard Voice*, 22 February 1991: 7.

W., H. M. "Henry T. Burleigh's Contribution to the Discussion of the True Meaning of 'The New World Symphony.'" The Philadelphia Orchestra Program, 24, 25 February 1911.

Waters, Edward N. *Victor Herbert, A Life in Music.* New York: Macmillan, 1955.

White, Clarence Cameron. "The Musical Genius of the American Negro." *The Etude* 42, no. 5 (May 1924): 305.

Witmark, Isadore, and Isaac Goldberg. *From Ragtime to Swingtime.* 1939. Reprint. New York: Da Capo Press, 1976.

Yellin, Victor. "Chadwick, American Musical Realist." *Musical Quarterly* 61, no. 1 (January 1975): 96.

Yoell, John H. "Lacunae in the Dvořák Discography: Fact or Fancy." *Fanfare* 13, no. 2 (November–December 1989): 561–564.

———. *Antonín Dvořák on Records.* New York: Greenwood Press, 1991.

Zeckwer, Camille W. "Dvořák As I Knew Him." *The Etude* 37, no. 11 (Nov 1919): 694.

NEWSPAPERS

"American Music: Dvořák Thinks Little Has been Done Here." *Boston Daily Traveller,* 10 December 1892: 13.

"American Music: Dr. Antonín Dvořák Expresses Some Radical Opinions." Boston *Herald,* 28 May 1893: 23.

Downes, Olin. "A Dvořák Reminiscence: Man and Musician Recalled in Memories of American Pupil." *New York Times,* 12 August 1934, Music Section: 4–5.

"Dr. Dvořák's American Music." New York *Tribune,* 13 January 1894.

"Dr. Dvořák's Great Symphony." New York *Herald,* 16 December 1893.

"Dvořák Doesn't Live Here Anymore." *New York Times,* 7 March 1991.

"Dvořák Hears His Symphony." New York *Herald,* 17 December 1893.

"Dvořák House Declared a Manhattan Landmark." *New York Times,* 27 February 1991.

"Dvořák Leads at the Music Hall." New York *Herald,* 22 October 1892.

"Dvořák Leads for the Fund. New York *Herald,* 24 January 1894.

"Dvořák on His New Work." New York *Herald,* 15 December 1893.

"For National Music: Dvořák, the Great Bohemian Composer." Chicago *Tribune,* 13 August 1893.

Furio, Joanne. "A Preservation Effort, Set to Music." New York *Newsday,* 24 May 1991, Section 2.

Hale, P. "The Kneisel Quartet Plays Dvořák's New Quartette [*sic*]," Boston *Journal,* 2 January 1894.

Hale, P. "The Symphony of a Homesick Genius," Boston *Herald,* 30 June 1907.

"Harry T. Burleigh, Composer, 82, Dies." *New York Times,* 12 September 1949.

"Hear 'The Old Folks at Home.'" New York *Herald,* 23 January 1894.

Horowitz, Joe. "Beach, Chadwick: New World Symphonists." *New York Times,* 27 October 1991, Arts and Leisure: 25, 28.

Huneker, James (?). "The Second Philharmonic Concert. Dvořák's New Symphony." *The Musical Courier,* 20 December 1893.

Krehbiel, Henry E. "Dr. Dvořák's American Symphony." New York *Daily Tribune,* 15 December 1893.

———. "Dr. Dvořák's Symphony." New York *Daily Tribune* (17 December 1893).

———. "Dvořák's American Compositions in Boston." New York *Daily Tribune* (1 January 1894).

———. "Dvořák's American Compositions." New York *Daily Tribune* (7 January 1894).

———. "Some Words on Negro Music." New York *Tribune,* 24 April 1899.

———. "Songs of the American Indians," 1. New York *Tribune,* 24 September 1899.

———. "Songs of the American Indians," 2. New York *Tribune,* 1 October 1899.

———. "Songs of the American Indians," 3. New York *Tribune,* 8 October 1899.

"The Letter Box." *New York Times Supplement,* 25 November 1928. [Four letters to the editor regarding alleged black influences on the "New World" Symphony.]

Lynch, Colum. "In New York, a Clash of Art and Life." Boston *Globe,* 20 June 1991.

"Mrs. Thurber's Plan for Maintaining Her Conservatory." Washington *Post,* 20 April 1890.

"Mrs. Thurber Talks: Gives Plans for Future." Boston *Daily Globe,* 11 January 1887.

"National Conservatory Concert." [New York] *Evening Post,* 22 February 1899.

"Plaque Dedicated at Dvořák House." New York *Sun,* 15 December 1941.

Prial, Frank J. "Dvořák House Declared a Manhattan Landmark." *New York Times,* 27 February 1991.

"Real Value of Negro Melodies," New York *Herald,* 21 May 1893.

Redell, Holly. "A Fight to Save the Dvořák House." New York *Newsday,* 13 June 1990.

Rose, Mark. "Lust for Land: How Beth Israel Trampled the Memory of Antonín Dvořák." New York *Press,* 6–12 November 1991: 1, 6–7.

"'Sweet Chariot' Inspired Anton Dvořák to Immortalize Negro Spirituals." New York *World Telegram,* 12 September 1941.

"Women Can't Help. Dvořák Says They Have not Creative Talent: Interview with the Great Composer." Boston *Post,* 30 November 1892.

Index

Numbers in italic refer to illustrations in the text.

S

Index of
Dvořák Compositions Cited

Contributors

John C. Tibbetts

$\mathcal{R}$obert Battey is currently associate professor of cello and chamber music at the University of Missouri-Kansas City. He holds degrees from the Cleveland Institute of Music and the State University of New York and has done doctoral work at Indiana University. He has appeared as orchestra soloist or in recital throughout America and in Canada and Mexico with organizations like the Kennedy Center Opera House orchestra, the National Symphony, the New College Quartet in Florida, and the Volker Quartet in Missouri. He has performed at the Phillips Collection in Washington and Carnegie Recital Hall, and he has given highly praised cycles of the complete cello works of Bach, Beethoven, and Brahms. His teachers include Bernard Greenhouse and Janos Starker. His articles, reviews, and program notes have appeared in *Strings* magazine.

$\mathcal{M}$ichael Beckerman is an associate professor of music at Washington University in St. Louis, where he is president and (co-founder) of the Czechoslovak Music Society of America. He is the general editor of a series of books on Czech music for the Pendragon Press in New York. In 1988 and 1990, he organized and hosted in St. Louis international conferences on Leoš Janáček and Bohuslav Martinu, respectively. His efforts on behalf of Czech composers have won him medals from the Janáček, Martinu, and Dvořák Societies. His many articles and reviews have appeared in *Nineteenth Century Music, Notes,* and *Musical Quarterly*. Currently he is at work on a book, *Janáček the Theorist* (forthcoming from Pendragon Press).

*D*avid R. Beveridge is an associate research professor at the University of New Orleans, where he was one of the principal organizers of the Dvořák Sesquicentennial Festival and Conference, February 1991 (the basis for a forthcoming volume of Dvořák studies). His many Dvořák-related writings have appeared in *Musical America, Current Musicology, Chamber Music Quarterly*, as well as many publications in Czechoslovakia. He is a member of the The Czechoslovak Music Society and the Dvořák Society of Great Britain. His dissertation, "Romantic Ideas in a Classical Frame: The Sonata Forms of Dvořák," University of California at Berkeley, 1980, will be published by Pendragon Press.

*A*drienne Fried Block has been a senior fellow and visiting professor at the Institute for Studies in American Music, Brooklyn College, CUNY; and she currently is codirector of the Project for the Study of Women in Music, CUNY. An authority on American composer Amy Beach, she has written and lectured extensively on the subject, and her biography of Mrs. Beach is forthcoming from Oxford University Press. Other publications include articles on women composers for *A History of Women in Music* (forthcoming from Indiana University Press), the *New Grove Dictionary of American Music* (1986), *The Musical Woman* (1987), and numerous periodicals and recordings. She lives in New York City.

*J*armil Burghauser has had an extraordinarily varied career as a music historian, composer, musicologist, and editor (he has compiled the Dvořák thematic catalogue and critical editions of Dvořák, Fibich, and Janáček). A champion of Czech music in general, he survived decades of political repression under the Dubcek regime (he was "on ice," as he puts it); now he plays generous host for a new generation of scholars and enthusiasts who visit him frequently in Prague. As Alan Houtchens says in his monograph about him, "It is impossible to overestimate how much we have profited from Burghauser's own scholarship and from his professional commitment to help and encourage others in their research of Czech music." He was born in Pisek and studied composition and conducting through the 1930s and 1940s at the Prague Conservatory. Until 1970 he was a member of the Czech State Film Organization and has written many film scores, including that for *Labakan* (1956). Other musical works include a ballet, *Honza a cert* (Honza and the Devil); an orchestral work, *7 reliefu* (Seven Reliefs); and numerous song cycles, choral cycles, and cantatas. Among his many books are a pedagogical manual, *The Reading and Playing of Full Scores* (1960), and studies on the acoustical properties of musical instruments. Yet it is revealing about the warm heart of this man that, in the face of these and many more achievements, he is most proud of his work as a "Chief Scout" for the Boy Scouts of Bohemia.

*J*ohn Clapham, during his lifetime, was in the forefront of non-Czech Dvořák scholars. His numerous articles and his two books, *Dvořák: Musician and Craftsman* (1966) and *Dvořák* (1979), have inspired the work of a new generation of scholars and remain the indispensable works on the composer in English. He has been lecturer at the University College of Wales and senior lecturer and reader at Edinburgh University. Among his many honors are recognition by the Dvořák Society of Prague and the Silver Medal and Diploma of the Society for International Relations of the Czechoslovak Republic. Shortly before his death in November 1992, Prof. Clapham graciously accepted the Dedication of this book.

J. Bunker Clark is currently professor of music history at the University of Kansas. He holds a doctorate from the University of Michigan and has been instructor of organ and theory at Stephens College in Columbia, Missouri and a lecturer in music at the University of California, Santa Barbara. An authority on the history of keyboard music, he has edited the *Anthology of Early American Keyboard Music, 1787–1830* (1977) and *American Keyboard Music through 1865* (1990). He is the author of *The Dawning of American Keyboard Music* (1988) and has been a series editor of *Bibliographies in American Music* (1975–1984) and of *Detroit Studies in Music Bibliography* (1985–). Among the publications for which he has written are *American Organist, Music & Letters, Musica Disciplina, Journal of the American Musicological Society,* and *American Music.* His many honors include a Fulbright scholarship to the UK (1962–1963) and a National Endowment for the Humanities grant (1972–1973.).

*S*tuart Feder, M.D., is a practicing psychoanalyst and a faculty member of the New York Psychoanalytic Institute and the Department of Psychiatry at the Mount Sinai School of Medicine. He holds an advanced degree in music from Harvard University. Dr. Feder is the author of many articles in psychoanalysis and applied psychoanalysis. He is coeditor of *Psychoanalytic Explorations in Music* (Madison CT: International Universities Press, 1989) and the author of a biography, *Charles Ives: "My Father's Song"* (New York and London: Yale University Press, 1992).

*R*udolf Firkušný has been acclaimed as one of the premier keyboard artists of our time. He studied in his native Czechoslovakia with Leoš Janáček and at the Prague Academy of Music with Josef Suk (son-in-law of Antonín Dvořák). After advanced keyboard studies with Alfred Cortot and Artur Schnabel, he came to America in 1941 and made his highly successful New York debut at Town Hall. Although he became an American citizen, his international tours, numerous awards, and teaching positions truly have established him as a citizen of the world. In addition to championing the work of Czech composers Smetana, Dvořák, Janáček, and Martinu, he performs an extraordinary range of classical, romantic, and modern repertoire. In May 1990 he acknowledged the return of democracy to Czechoslovakia by giving his first concert there after an absence of forty-four years. In October 1991 Mr. Firkušný was awarded the Order of Tomas G. Masaryk, First Class, by Czechoslovak President Vaclav Havel. It is the highest civilian honor bestowed by the Czech Government and is named after the man who sponsored Mr. Firkušný's first trips abroad in the 1930s. Mr. Firkušný lives in New York City.

*C*harles Hamm is currently professor emeritus of music history at Dartmouth College and the author of one of the standard histories of American music, *Music in the New World* (1983). He took degrees in composition and musicology at Princeton University and has also taught at the Cincinnati Conservatory of Music, the University of Illinois, and Tulane University. His publications reveal his widely ranging interests—the Renaissance (his dissertation on Guillaume Dufay was published by Princeton University Press), the opera stage (*Opera*, 1964), the American avant-garde (articles about John Cage), and the American popular song (*Yesterdays*, 1979). *Contemporary Music and Music Cultures* (co-written with Bruno Nettl and Ron Byrnside) was a pioneering study of multicultural music expression. His abiding interest in popular music led to his organization in 1983 of the American branch of the International Association for the Study of Popular Music. Among his many awards are a Guggenheim Fellowship, Fulbright Senior Research Award, and the Sonneck Society Irving Lowens Award for *Music in the New World*. Forthcoming projects include two Irving Berlin books: a biography and a volume tentatively entitled *The Early Songs of Irving Berlin, 1907-1914* (part of a series of books from the American Music Society (MUSA). He lives in Norwich, Vermont.

*A*lan Houtchens is an assistant professor of music at Texas A&M University. He holds degrees in musicology and performance from the University of California, Santa Barbara. He has published articles dealing mainly with Czech music and other nineteenth-century topics in many journals and periodicals, including *Czech Music* and *Opera Journal*. An accomplished horn player, he has performed in many orchestras. For the Dvořák Sesquicentennial Festival and Conference in New Orleans, 14–20 February 1991, he coordinated the conference activities. Currently, he is the treasurer of the Czechoslovak Music Society and is preparing the critical edition of Dvořák's opera *Vanda*.

*D*aniel Jacobson currently teaches graduate and undergraduate courses in music history, music theory, guitar, and music technology at the University of North Dakota. He completed Ph.D. programs in musicology and music theory at the University of California at Santa Barbara, holds a master's degree in music history from the California State University at Long Beach, and has a bachelor's degree in voice from Westminster College. He has served as an editorial assistant for the Journal of the American Musicological Society and was planning coordinator of the International Lotte Lehmann Centennial Festival, 1988. Recently he completed archival studies in Vienna on Schubert's Tenth Symphony sketches. As an educator he has authored textbooks on music appreciation and guitar pedagogy, and he has designed and implemented CD-ROM/hypercard and MIDI-based education materials. His published papers and conference presentations include subjects ranging from Thomas Morley's madrigal style to Dvořák's song cycles and Anton von Webern's vocal works.

$\mathcal{G}$raham Melville-Mason became involved with the music of Czechoslovakia during his twenty years associated with the University of Edinburgh, during which time he was also music consultant to the Edinburgh International Festival. For the next ten years he continued this interest while at the British Broadcasting Company, and he has been a regular visitor to Czechoslovakia since 1975. Since the revolution of 1989 he has been spending about five months of each year in that country, where he is a visiting professor at Charles University and president of the advisory board or the Prague Spring Festival. He is currently chairman of the Dvořák Society of Great Britain and the founder and vice-president of the British Czech and Slovak Association.

$\mathcal{D}$eane L. Root wears many hats. He is the curator of the Stephen Foster Memorial and the Foster Hall Collection in Pittsburgh, Pennsylvania, an adjunct assistant professor of music at the University of Pittsburgh, and since 1989, president of the Sonneck Society for American Music. Among his many publications concerning American music in general and Stephen Foster in particular are *The Music of Stephen C. Foster: A Critical Edition* (Smithsonian Institution Press, 1990), *American Popular Stage Music* (1981), and *The New Grove Dictionary of American Music* (1986), for which he wrote thirty-eight articles. Whenever his busy schedule permits, he performs as a tenor vocalist with the Dear Friends, a vocal music ensemble from the University of Pittsburgh specializing in American music.

$\mathcal{M}$ark Rose is a native New Yorker and has worked for five years as a columnist for the New York press. He has written for many newspapers, including the *New York Times*, the *Village Voice*, and the *Los Angeles Times*. His "beat" is neighborhood news—the art, politics, and personalities of the city. He readily admits he is neither a music scholar nor a Dvořák enthusiast; rather, he was attracted to the Dvořák story because of its connections with New York politics and neighborhood development.

$\mathcal{E}$manuel Rubin is professor of music history and literature at the University of Massachusetts, Amherst. He has also been a visiting professor at the University of Haifa in Israel. His publications in *World Literature Today, American Music, Performance Practice Review,* and *Symposium* reflect his varied interests in aviation (he is a licensed pilot), composing, the tradition of the English glee, American music, and computer technology. He is the author of *The Warren Collection,* a four-volume collection of eighteenth-century English glees (Mellifont Press, 1971) and the forthcoming *The Glee in Georgian England.* One of his favorite research topics is Mrs. Jeannette Thurber, and his biographical article on her appears in the anthology *Women Activists in American Music* (1992).

$\mathcal{S}$teven Richman is the conductor of the Harmonie Ensemble/New York, which has performed wind ensemble, chamber orchestra, and orchestra concerts and broadcasts throughout the United States. The group's highly acclaimed compact discs on the Music & Arts label are "Salute to France," (CD-649), and "Dvořák and Friends" (CD-691). He is a founding member of the Dvořák American Heritage Association.

$\mathcal{J}$osef V. Škvorecký was born in Nachod, Czechoslovakia, and emigrated to Toronto, Canada, in 1968, where he now makes his home. He received his Ph.D. at Charles University in Prague, 1951, served in the Czechoslovak Army in 1951–53, and worked as a free-lance writer and educator in Prague. His many distinguished novels and nonfiction works include *The Coward* (1970), *The Tank Corps* (1971), *All the Bright Young Men and Women: A Personal History of the Czech Cinema* (1971), *An Engineer of Human Souls* (1977), *The Bass Saxophone* (1979), and *Scherzo Capriccioso* (American title: *Dvořák in Love,* 1987). An avid detective story enthusiast, he has also written several volumes of stories about the inimitable Lieutenant Boruvka. His many literary awards include the 1980 Neustadt International Prize for Literature and the 1984 Governor General's Award for Fiction in Canada. He is the founder and editor-in-chief of Sixty-Eight Publishers Corp. in Toronto.

$\mathcal{J}$an Smaczny has been a lecturer in music at the University of Birmingham, Great Britain, since 1983. Stimulated by postgraduate work undertaken in Prague in the late 1970s and early

1980s, his main area of interest has been in Czech opera, most particularly the operas of Antonín Dvořák. As a lecturer, he specializes in nineteenth-century music and baroque performance practice. As a performer, he has given concerts with artists such as Emma Kirkby, and he presented Marco da Gagliano's *La Dafne* at the first Moravian Festival of Baroque Opera. His articles on Dvořák and related subjects have appeared in *Zprava*, the *New Oxford Companion to Music, Opera,* and the *Journal of the Royal Music Association*. Prof. Smaczny currently also writes for the British national newspaper, *The Independent* and broadcasts frequently on the BBC.

*J*ean E. Snyder recently received her Ph.D. in ethnomusicology at the University of Pittsburgh, and she holds a master's degree in English from the University of Notre Dame. In addition to a career teaching secondary-school English and vocal music, she has taught English and music in Kenya and Zambia. In the summer of 1985 she spent three months working as a research volunteer for the Jamaica Memory Bank program, assisting in oral history and music research. Her doctoral dissertation is about the life and music of African American composer and performer, Harry T. Burleigh.

*N*ick Strimple is the music director of the Choral Society of Southern California and the music director of the Beverly Hills Presbyterian Church. He holds an M.M. and a D.M.A. from the University of Southern California in Church and Choral Music, and his articles and reviews have appeared in *Choral Journal* and *The Music Library Association Notes*. He is a specialist in Czech music and conducted the first American performance in this century of Dvořák's *St. Ludmila* (Los Angeles, 1985) as well as American premieres of Anton Reicha's *Te Deum*, Jan Hanus's *Glagolitic Mass*, Opus 106, and works by Pavel Haas and Gideon Klein. He has been a guest conductor of the Philharmonia Orchestra of London and the Nuremberg Symphony. He also works in popular music and has been an arranger/choral director for Air Supply, Melissa Manchester, Rod Stewart, and Frank Sinatra. Currently he is researching and performing the music from the Theresienstadt Concentration Camp in Czechoslovakia. He lectured on the subject at the Simon Wiesenthal Center in Los Angeles.

$\mathcal{J}$ohn C. Tibbetts is a journalist, broadcaster, and educator in the arts. He holds a Ph.D. in Theater and Film at the University of Kansas, where he currently is an associate professor. He has written on a wide range of arts subjects for many publications, including the *Christian Science Monitor, Opera News, Classical,* the *Bulletin of the Sonneck Society,* and *Film Comment.* His books include *The American Theatrical Film* (1985), *Introduction to the Photoplay* (1977), and *His Majesty the American: The Films of Douglas Fairbanks, Sr.* (co-written with James M. Welsh, 1977). Recently he was one of four senior editors for the *Encyclopedia of the 20th Century* (Facts on File, 1991). Currently he is preparing a radio series, "Schumann and the Age of Romanticism" for Public Radio. He is also a portrait painter and illustrator; some of his drawings and paintings can be seen in this book.

$\mathcal{J}$ohn Yoell is a Los Angeles physician with an avocation for music. A member of the American-Scandinavian Foundation, he is a past vice-president of the Los Angeles Chapter. His book, *The Nordic Sound* (1974) is a "phonograph-based listener's guide to the art music of Denmark, Norway, and Sweden." Since 1989 he has been editor-in-chief of the *Bulletin of the Czechoslovak Music Society* and currently is president of the Los Angeles chapter of the Association of Recorded Sound Collections (ARSC). His newest book is *Antonín Dvořák on Records* (Greenwood Press, 1991)